Automated Enterprise Systems for Maximizing Business Performance

Petraq Papajorgji
Canadian Institute of Technology, Albania

François Pinet
National Research Institute of Science and Technology for Environment and Agriculture, France

Alaine Margarete Guimarães
State University of Ponta Grossa, Brazil

Jason Papathanasiou
University of Macedonia, Greece

A volume in the Advances in Business Information Systems and Analytics (ABISA) Book Series

An Imprint of IGI Global

Managing Director:	Lindsay Johnston
Managing Editor:	Keith Greenberg
Director of Intellectual Property & Contracts:	Jan Travers
Acquisitions Editor:	Kayla Wolfe
Production Editor:	Christina Henning
Development Editor:	Courtney Tychinski
Cover Design:	Jason Mull

Published in the United States of America by
Business Science Reference (an imprint of IGI Global)
701 E. Chocolate Avenue
Hershey PA, USA 17033
Tel: 717-533-8845
Fax: 717-533-8661
E-mail: cust@igi-global.com
Web site: http://www.igi-global.com

Library of Congress Cataloging-in-Publication Data

Automated enterprise systems for maximizing business performance / Petraq Papajorgji, Francois Pinet, Alaine Margarete Guimaraes, and Jason Papathanasiou, editors.
    pages cm
Includes bibliographical references and index.
Summary: "This book is a reference source for the latest scholarly research on the modeling and application of automated business systems, featuring extensive coverage on a variety of topics relating to the design, implementation, and current developments of such system"-- Provided by publisher.
ISBN 978-1-4666-8841-4 (hbk. : alk. paper) -- ISBN 978-1-4666-8842-1 (ebk.) 1. Information technology--Management. 2. Android (Electronic resource) 3. Automation. I. Papajorgji, Petraq J., editor. II. Pinet, Francois, 1973- editor. III. Guimaraes, Alaine Margarete, 1969-

HD30.2.A9365 2016
658.4'013011--dc23

——— 2015022575

This book is published in the IGI Global book series Advances in Business Information Systems and Analytics (ABISA) (ISSN: 2327-3275; eISSN: 2327-3283)

British Cataloguing in Publication Data
A Cataloguing in Publication record for this book is available from the British Library.

All work contributed to this book is new, previously-unpublished material. The views expressed in this book are those of the authors, but not necessarily of the publisher.

For electronic access to this publication, please contact: eresources@igi-global.com.

Advances in Business Information Systems and Analytics (ABISA) Book Series

Madjid Tavana
La Salle University, USA

ISSN: 2327-3275
EISSN: 2327-3283

MISSION

The successful development and management of information systems and business analytics is crucial to the success of an organization. New technological developments and methods for data analysis have allowed organizations to not only improve their processes and allow for greater productivity, but have also provided businesses with a venue through which to cut costs, plan for the future, and maintain competitive advantage in the information age.

The **Advances in Business Information Systems and Analytics (ABISA) Book Series** aims to present diverse and timely research in the development, deployment, and management of business information systems and business analytics for continued organizational development and improved business value.

COVERAGE

- Data Strategy
- Forecasting
- Big Data
- Algorithms
- Data Analytics
- Business Decision Making
- Management information systems
- Geo-BIS
- Business Systems Engineering
- Information Logistics

IGI Global is currently accepting manuscripts for publication within this series. To submit a proposal for a volume in this series, please contact our Acquisition Editors at Acquisitions@igi-global.com or visit: http://www.igi-global.com/publish/.

Titles in this Series

For a list of additional titles in this series, please visit: www.igi-global.com

Improving Organizational Effectiveness with Enterprise Information Systems
João Eduardo Varajão (University of Minho, Portugal) Maria Manuela Cruz-Cunha (Polytechnic Institute of Cávado and Ave, Portugal) and Ricardo Martinho (Polytechnic Institute of Leiria, Portugal)
Business Science Reference • copyright 2015 • 319pp • H/C (ISBN: 9781466683686) • US $195.00 (our price)

Strategic Utilization of Information Systems in Small Business
M. Gordon Hunter (The University of Lethbridge, Canada)
Business Science Reference • copyright 2015 • 306pp • H/C (ISBN: 9781466687080) • US $195.00 (our price)

Enterprise Management Strategies in the Era of Cloud Computing
N. Raghavendra Rao (FINAIT Consultancy Services, India)
Business Science Reference • copyright 2015 • 359pp • H/C (ISBN: 9781466683396) • US $210.00 (our price)

Handbook of Research on Organizational Transformations through Big Data Analytics
Madjid Tavana (La Salle University, USA) and Kartikeya Puranam (La Salle University, USA)
Business Science Reference • copyright 2015 • 561pp • H/C (ISBN: 9781466672727) • US $245.00 (our price)

Business Technologies in Contemporary Organizations Adoption, Assimilation, and Institutionalization
Abrar Haider (University of South Australia, Australia)
Business Science Reference • copyright 2015 • 337pp • H/C (ISBN: 9781466666238) • US $205.00 (our price)

Business Transformation and Sustainability through Cloud System Implementation
Fawzy Soliman (University of Technology, Sydney, Australia)
Business Science Reference • copyright 2015 • 300pp • H/C (ISBN: 9781466664456) • US $200.00 (our price)

Effects of IT on Enterprise Architecture, Governance, and Growth
José Carlos Cavalcanti (Federal University of Pernambuco, Brazil)
Business Science Reference • copyright 2015 • 307pp • H/C (ISBN: 9781466664692) • US $195.00 (our price)

Technology, Innovation, and Enterprise Transformation
Manish Wadhwa (Salem State University, USA) and Alan Harper (South University, USA)
Business Science Reference • copyright 2015 • 378pp • H/C (ISBN: 9781466664739) • US $195.00 (our price)

Analytical Approaches to Strategic Decision-Making Interdisciplinary Considerations
Madjid Tavana (La Salle University, USA)
Business Science Reference • copyright 2014 • 417pp • H/C (ISBN: 9781466659582) • US $225.00 (our price)

701 E. Chocolate Ave., Hershey, PA 17033
Order online at www.igi-global.com or call 717-533-8845 x100
To place a standing order for titles released in this series, contact: cust@igi-global.com
Mon-Fri 8:00 am - 5:00 pm (est) or fax 24 hours a day 717-533-8661

Table of Contents

Detailed Table of Contents

Chapter 1
> *Lediona Nishani, University of New York in Tirana, Albania*

Security nowadays is not a "nice to have," but a must-have. Cybercriminals have started a new way of encouraging their activities by selling their services on the deep dark web. They are becoming day by day more persistent and smarter than ever. Therefore, the companies have to be smarter in order to face the diversity of new threats every day. The increase of botnets is responsible for an emerging ransomware attacks through cryptolocker. Another modern malware are APT (Advanced persistent threats, sophisticated threats that undertake missions in cyber space). This chapter is about a summary of the most prominent attacks on security threats regarding android mobile devices. In this review chapter we will disclose and analyze chronicles of attack, which cover researching period from 2004 when was discovered the first mobile malware, until 2014. Our research will narrow down just in the two last years because of tremendous surge of android malware that has emerged just in this short period. We have chosen this small research sample in order to provide insights and give significant evidence that in a short period we have to investigate and analyze so many miscellaneous malware and vulnerabilities techniques. In subsequent proceedings, this chapter points out the main threats category we have thought to be more notable or significant to be investigated in this review chapter. Later on, it discusses future trends and some strong recommendation on facing and dealing with the internet technology based area.

Chapter 2
> *Fahmi Ncibi, National High School of Engineering of Tunisia, Tunisia*
> *Habib Hamam, Moncton University, Canada*
> *Ezzedine Ben Braiek, National High School of Engineering of Tunisia, Tunisia*

In this chapter, various aspects pertaining to the open operating system Android OS such as its history, architecture, features, and utility for business purposes will be introduced, following which the role of Android in enterprise management will be explained. The chapter will be concluded by a detailed report of the BYOD approach that uses Android for industrial control and automation. Since mobile devices have become progressively more powerful and accessible, mobile computing has greatly changed our daily lives. As one of the most popular mobile operating systems, Android provides the tools and API for Android developers to develop Android applications. Android is an open source operating system for mobile devices. Today its primary use is lodged in the mobile phone industry. During the recent past years, many projects have been created, with the objective to elevate Android to other platforms, such as sub-notebooks or embedded systems.

Chapter 3

Myoung-Ah Kang, Université Blaise Pascal, France
François Pinet, Irstea – Clermont Ferrand, France
Sandro Bimonte, Irstea – Clermont Ferrand, France
Gil De Sousa, Irstea – Clermont Ferrand, France
Jean-Pierre Chanet, Irstea – Clermont Ferrand, France

More and more data are collected via sensors. Wireless networks can be implemented to facilitate the collection of sensors data and to reduce the cost of their acquisition. In this chapter, we present a general architecture combining Wireless Sensor Network (WSN) and Spatial Data Warehouse (SDW) technologies. This innovative solution is used to collect automatically sensor's information and to facilitate the analysis of these data. The WSN used in this application has been deployed by Irstea and tested during several years in vineyards in South of France. The novel contribution presented in this chapter is related to the use of a SDW to manage data produced by geo-referenced sensor nodes. SDW is one of the most appropriate modern technologies for analyzing large data sets at different temporal and spatial scales. This type of databases is a specific category of information system used to integrate, accumulate and analyze information from various sources. These data are usually organized according to a multidimensional schema to facilitate the calculation of indicators. In this chapter, we introduce the development of a SDW storing the data collected by this WSN. The implemented data warehouse can allow users to aggregate and explore interactively data produced by sensors. With this system, it is possible to visualize on a map the results of these aggregations.

Chapter 4

François Pinet, Irstea – Clermont-Ferrand, France
Nadia Carluer, Irstea – Lyon, France
Claire Lauvernet, Irstea – Lyon, France
Bruno Cheviron, Irstea – Montpellier, France
Sandro Bimonte, Irstea – Clermont-Ferrand, France
André Miralles, Irstea – Montpellier, France

DBMS is a traditional technology for the storage of business application data. In this chapter, we show that this technology can be of interest in scientific fields. We present a survey of the emergence of the concept of simulation result database. Scientific simulation models become more complex, use more data and produce more outputs. Stochastic models can also be simulated. In this case, numerous simulations are run in order to discover a general trend in results. The replications of simulation increase again the amount of produced data, which makes exploration and analysis difficult. It is also often useful to compare the results obtained in using different model versions, scenarios or assumptions (for example different weather forecasts). In this chapter, we provide several examples of projects of simulation result databases. We show that the database technology can help to manage the large volumes of simulation outputs. We also illustrate this type of projects on environmental databases storing pesticide transfer simulation results. We conclude in highlighting some trends and future works.

This chapter reports on research investigating the benefits and barriers of e-Enabling Technologies such as e-Sourcing and e-Purchasing in the healthcare sector. The research is based on a case study conducted at the KAT General Hospital (KGH) in Athens, Greece, and examines aspects regarding the implementation of specific e-Sourcing and e- Purchasing tools, such as e-RFx and e-Auctions, focusing on the resulting benefits and the existing barriers of adoption. Findings suggest that although quantifiable benefits were identified, e-Sourcing and e- Purchasing are still at an early stage of maturity in the Greek Healthcare Sector. The chapter entails a literature review, a description of the research methodology used, the findings based on the case study and the final conclusions.

Chapter 6

ERP systems, supporting and integrating all business processes across functions and offering real time information necessary for taking actions and making decisions, have prevailed in most enterprises worldwide. The costs involved in ERP implementations may be huge and must be justified by the outcomes. However, extant research has reported mixed and in some cases controversial results. In this chapter, certain important dimensions of ERP systems and of business performance are discussed. The chapter has an educational focus and aims at providing an exploration of ERP system's impact on certain business performance dimensions, informing thus scholars, practitioners and students of the issues involved and the areas they should pay attention when considering ERP implementations. Following an extensive literature review, a classification of diverse studies according to their research focus is provided, which reveals the range of business performance dimensions and can help researchers in their future projects.

Chapter 7

Although it has been more than a decade since the emergence of the concept of business processes, there is still a lack of common ground and agreement about their nature and context, their contribution and benefits to the contemporary business environment. This chapter 'rediscovers' business processes in the sense that provides a critical review of the multiple definitions by different authors and constructs a schema with the main structural elements that constitute a business process. It also reviews the main modelling approaches and classifies them into three primary groups according to their diagrammatic, formal and execution capabilities. Lastly, the main business process patterns are identified and the main business process modelling techniques are compared based on their pattern support capabilities. The work presented rediscovers business processes by providing a holistic understanding that will lead to their standardisation and further development.

In this recent technological world, it is necessary that we get accustomed to all types of advanced technological techniques. In the process, we are becoming more aware about database and information system. But what is database system information? The Database Management System which works through the storing of data can be used any time. The importance of database and information Systems in modern business is inevitable. In this chapter, we define Information Systems by its categories of Information System, type and the usefulness for efficient Information System. Then, we will proceed to explaining the management of information systems by taking a short look at its history and list some of its domains of application. After that, we define the relation between Information Systems and database. Finally, we will explore the problem of storage and some issues related to information systems and databases.

The chapter proposes a general methodology on how to use data mining techniques to support total quality management especially related to the quality tools. The effectiveness of the proposed general methodology is demonstrated through their application. The goal of this chapter is to build the 7 new quality tools based on the rules that are "hidden" in the raw data of a database and to propose solutions and actions that will lead the organization under study to improve its business processes by evaluating the results. Four popular data-mining approaches (rough sets, association rules, classification rules and Bayesian networks) were applied on a set of 12.477 case records concerning vehicles damages. The set of rules and patterns that was produced by each algorithm was used as input in order to dynamically form each of the quality tools. This would enable the creation of the quality tools starting from the raw data and passing through the stage of data mining, using automatic software was employed.

The Web service composition refers to the aggregation of Web services to meet customers' needs in the construction of complex applications. The selection among a large number of Web services that provide the desired functionalities for the composition is generally driven by QoS (Quality of Service) attributes, and formulated as a constrained multi-objective optimization problem. However, many equally important QoS attributes exist and in this situation the performance of the multi-objective algorithms can be degraded. To deal properly with this problem we investigate in this chapter a solution based in many-objective optimization algorithms. We conduct an empirical analysis to measure the performance of the proposed solution with the following preference relations: Controlling the Dominance Area of Solutions, Maximum Ranking and Average Ranking. These preference relations are implemented with NSGA-II using five objectives. A set of performance measures is used to investigate how these techniques affect convergence and diversity of the search in the WSC context.

Chapter 11

  Maria Gianni, University of Macedonia, Greece
  Katerina Gotzamani, University of Macedonia, Greece

Information systems collect and disseminate information within organizations based on information technology, while management systems formalize business processes following the standards requirements. Since management standards proliferate, their integrated adoption into a holistic overarching system has emerged as an effective and efficient approach. In this context, this chapter aims to explore the potential synergies among information management and integration. Firstly, a focused literature review is conducted and survey data on the relevant standards evolution are processed in order to provide the information and management practitioners with a clear and oriented depiction of the available norms and their adoption possibilities. Furthermore, a framework is proposed consolidating management sub-systems into an integrated structure including information management and supported by information systems. Finally, the concept of internalization of management systems standards is understood in association with information and knowledge diffusion within an integrated management system.

Chapter 12

  Aristeidis Chatzipoulidis, University of Macedonia, Greece
  Dimitrios Michalopoulos, University of Macedonia, Greece
  Ioannis Mavridis, University of Macedonia, Greece

Information systems of modern enterprises are quite complex entities. This fact has influenced the overall information technology (IT) risk profile of the enterprise and it has become all the more critical now to have sound information systems that can maximize business performance of an enterprise. At this point, the practical challenge for enterprises is how to manage enterprise IT risks for persistent protection of business and security goals. This chapter covers different aspects of managing enterprise IT risks, providing solutions in terms of risk management methods, automated security metrics and vulnerability scoring methods. The purpose is to introduce an in-depth study on enterprise IT risks and add value to enterprise sustainability through an extensive analysis of methods and automated security specifications.

In this chapter, we define Information Security (IS) and elaborate on the different methods and technology used. We proceed to explain some of the IS tools and risks found in private and confidential data. We detail the latest algorithms and systems of security and discuss how to implement those systems in business to upgrade performances and increase profits.

Foreword

Nowadays, it becomes very hard to ensure the performance of a company. There exist external and internal reasons. With the opening of markets, the external environment can quickly evolve all the time with, for example, the emergence of new competitions, the scarcity of certain resources, the setting of new regulations. The internal environment can be also submitted to more or less rough variations. It is thus necessary that any company can acquire a good flexibility to adapt itself quickly to any change and find the best performance.

Methodologies and technologies of information and communication constitute an effective way for adaptation and performance. The interest of this book is precisely to propose adequate descriptions of the main approaches and the main tools of the domain.

First, the book includes several chapters which deal with data organization and data management within an information system: architecture of information systems and implementation within databases, approaches for the integration of information systems, composition of Web services, definitions and concepts to ensure the security of an information system. Also, two chapters deal with data analysis approaches: a generic architecture to combine sensors' networks and data warehouse techniques, a solution to store simulation results in a database in order to facilitate their analysis. It is important to recall that data analysis is now a very useful mean to extract hidden information from data.

A welcome focus is proposed on mobile systems with a presentation of the Android system and a state of the art on the various approaches to ensure the security of this system.

Others important subjects are those related with the modelling and the reengineering of business processes. These subjects are explained in three chapters: general presentation of the concepts and the models, improvement of processes by using techniques of data mining, in-depth focus on the e-sourcing and e-purchasing process with illustrations in the Healthcare sector.

Another chapter reviews the various techniques of the artificial intelligence with pertinent applications to industrial cases. All the functions of a company are concerned and very significant gains of performance can be obtained.

The information and communication techniques induce more or less some risks. So a chapter deals with the evaluation of these risks and operational approaches to minimize them. This is a very hot topic because companies are now the target of frequent cyber attacks.

All the chapters are written in an academic style and are very easy to read. Each includes prerequisites and definitions useful for its presentation. This book is thus accessible to a large public.

Foreword

This book will be very useful for all the actors of the performance of a company: managers, developers, researchers. Managers will find principles and ideas to improve the functioning of their company. For developers, this book will be the opportunity to consolidate their vision and to select new features for incorporating it in their products. For researchers, the reading will help to establish a preliminary state of the art before starting a research action.

Michel Schneider
Blaise Pascal University, France

Preface

The present volume entitled "Automated Enterprise Systems for Maximizing Business Performance" is the collective effort of different authors coming from several countries. The main focus of this publication is the compilation of issues relevant to automated enterprise systems aiming to maximizing business performance. The contributors have presented their work to shed light on several topics directly relevant to enterprise systems. The editors have tried to provide prospective readers with a multifaceted view of the enterprise systems issues related to the efficient and long term improvement of enterprise performance.

One of these issues that is increasingly becoming more important and needs to be addressed seriously is the enterprise security. Cybercriminals are constantly founding new ways to cause great harm to businesses. Designing and implementing solid strategies for protecting precious enterprise data is a real challenge. New threats on Android mobiles arise day by day because cybercriminals are becoming smarter and more persistent than ever. They are relying on the darknet, a close area of Internet, which is designed to resist surveillance and government espionage. As the use of Android in enterprise applications is growing so are Android malwares growing in complexity and maturity. Therefore, there is need to explore not only the evolution malware diversity and threats on mobile but also we develop a forecast on some new malicious, which we have not dealt with yet. Thus, the chapter "Review on Security Threats" is dedicated to the presentation of security threats and corresponding countermeasures. In the same chapter future trends are discussed and the appropriate recommendations are presented.

One of the new technologies that has found wide spread use in enterprise systems is the Android technology. Nowadays, mobile devices have a multiuse purpose, not only for making phone calls. As mobile devices are getting more and more complex, so is their use for every day enterprise functionalities. Businesses have spent great amounts of efforts to make their enterprise functionalities available through mobile devices with the goal of getting closer to fulfilling the demands of their clients. The request for access to corporate information and applications through mobile devices such as devices running Android, Apple's iPhone and iPad, Windows 7 Mobile or Blackberry, are surging as consumers' preferences and behaviour become a top priority for the company's workforce. The rapid rate of adoption of these technologies around the world has left many business managers wondering how to effectively position their firms to benefit from the dominant trends. The drive for mobility is part of the business technology agenda for most companies today. The chapter "Android for Enterprise Automated Systems" is elaborating about the benefits that Android technology has to offer as regards to its use in enterprise systems.

The use of information technology in the field of agriculture and environment is becoming more and more common, and therefore the amount of data collected through the use of sensors is constantly increasing. Even more commonly, data are transferred using wireless networks, thus reducing the cost of data acquisition. Storing great amount of geo-referenced data requires using spatial data warehouses. The collection and the storage of of geo-referenced data require a general architecture combining Wireless Sensor Network (WSN) and Spatial Data Warehouse (SDW) technologies. This is an innovative solution that is used to collect and store automatically sensor's information and to facilitate the analysis of these data. SDW is one of the most appropriate modern technologies for analyzing large data sets at different temporal and spatial scales. This type of databases is a specific category of information system used to integrate, accumulate and analyze information from various sources. The data are usually organized according to a multidimensional schema to facilitate the calculation of indicators. A particular chapter titled "Use of Sensor Data Warehouse for Soil Moisture Analysis" describes an architecture combining wireless sensor networks and spatial data warehouses to facilitate the acquisition and the treatment of massive geo-referenced data.

In order to improve enterprise performance, it is often that simulation techniques are used to study different aspects of enterprise activities. Simulation process is used to assess and analyze phenomena, for example related to the behavior and the change of our environment. Usually, a model of the problem domain needs to be designed for the simulation to take place. The goal of the modelling is to understand, formalize or reproduce phenomena at a simpler scale. Simulation models can be used to predict their future evolutions or assess non-measurable values. The development of models is usually a multi-disciplinary task and thus, requires a multidisciplinary team. The obtained data should be conserved as they may be used in the future for similar purposes. Simulation results can have different formats. Different simulation runs can produce multiple text files, shape files, Excel files, images, etc. The format heterogeneity and the volume of produced files make it difficult the storage, analysis and the tractability of results. For example, text-based storage makes it difficult to explore, select, and visualize the data. Spreadsheet tools (for example, OpenOffice, MS Excel) can help to display and extract the simulation results, but they are not suitable for large volumes of information. Thus, a special chapter dedicated to "Storage of Simulation Result Data - A Database Perspective" describes different strategies for designing and implementing databases for storing and extracting data obtained through running simulations. Authors demonstrate that combining OLAP (On-Line Analytical Processing) based tools with data warehouses can help generating graphs, charts and cartographic maps used to interpret results of various enterprise activities.

The advent of Internet changed the way many sectors of activities present and offer their services or products. It should be noted that the use of technology in various enterprise activities has matured in parallel but following different paths in many countries. Healthcare industry is one of the industries that has been keen of adapting ICT technologies. The global Healthcare industry is one of the world's largest and fastest growing industries, comprising various sectors: medical equipment and supplies, pharmaceutical, healthcare services, biotechnology and alternative medicine sectors. Healthcare is facing an increasingly complex regulatory and legislative environment as well as a variety of economic and business challenges, such as the policy level that may restrict product selection possibilities, the service delivery point that may face frequent stock outs due to poor forecasting, unavailability of transport and a variety of other issues. Thus, it is imperative for corporations addressing these issues sooner rather than later. According to a survey among healthcare executives, investing in new technologies was identified as the top strategy to improve competitiveness and increase efficiency of healthcare services. As the significance of ICT-based approaches in improving healthcare supply chains has been proved, many healthcare organizations have already started several related projects. The healthcare industry is suffering from inconsistent and inaccurate product information, which negatively impacts the rest of the supply chain including the quality of care delivery for patients. This is true even in developed countries such as the US. A case study presenting benefits and barriers of e-sourcing and e-purchasing in the health-care sector in Greece points out issues and lessons learnt as the authors have experienced them; sound recommendations for the future are presented as well. To that end, the chapter "Benefits and barriers of e-Sourcing and e-Purchasing in the Healthcare Sector: A Case Study" is included in this publication.

Enterprise systems as a scientific discipline are the field that has enjoyed most probably the most rapid level of technology applications. Each time a new information technology comes to light there are immediate efforts to apply this technology to better management of enterprise systems. Nowadays there is a general effort to use Information Technology to every aspect of enterprise management. These efforts have given birth to ERP (Enterprise Resource Planning) systems, with the goal of supporting and integrating all business processes horizontally and vertically and offering real time information necessary for taking actions and making proper decisions. The costs involved in ERP implementations may be considerable and must be fully justified by the perceived outcomes. Thus, there is a demand to inform the interested decision makers about what to expect when they plan to implement such an integrated solution to their enterprise management. Chapter "The Evaluation of Business Performance in ERP Environments" is aiming to guide decision makers, to discuss certain important dimensions of ERP systems and to fine-tuning business performance. Many practitioners involved in enterprise management might find in this chapter valuable experiences regarding ERP solutions; experiences gained during hard efforts to address enterprise problems using an ERP system.

Currently, corporations face a daunting problem regarding the design and implementation of business information systems. On the one hand, the systems they need to develop are more and more complex and paradoxically, they have to be delivered in shorter times. The development mantra is "do more with less". On the other hand, there is a plethora of implementation technologies, operating systems, design techniques and development processes. Any one of these technologies could stand on its own, thus making the selection process difficult. Basically, each enterprise chooses the development platform based on its own experience and expertise. The diversity of computing platforms used has the immediate consequence of creating a large number of isolated systems with many difficulties to communicate with each other. To make the problem more difficult, every 5 to 7 years there is a new technology appearing and thus, making existing technologies obsolete. Therefore, it is important to use an approach to design and implement information systems that is resilient to change. Such an approach that has taken relevant consideration in the software industry is the Model Driven Development (MDD) approach. The Model Driven Development approach has taken its deserved place in the world of information systems design and development. Based on meta-models, this approach is expanding its use not only in traditional software systems but even in the area of business processes. Entire information systems can be designed and developed based on business process models. Thus, there is a need to better present what business processes are, the activities they are based on, the actors that will use these business processes and the corresponding resources. A chapter "Rediscovering Business Processes: Definitions, Patterns, and Modeling Approaches" is focusing to these fundamental issues, providing much useful input to stakeholders concerned with the design and implementation of business processes based information systems.

Information systems are naturally heavily based on databases to record transactions. Although databases are well known for some time, it is of value to managers and enterprise supervisors to have a detailed description of database classifications, data dictionaries, database schemas and other related information. Especially, legal concepts related to the 'Freedom of Information Act' are necessary to be studied and be part of the working knowledge management related employees in order to avoid legalities caused by mishandling data. A chapter "Enterprise Databases and Information Systems" dealing with these issues is included in this publication.

The amount of data stored in enterprises nowadays is constantly increasing. This information could be of great benefit to different segments of enterprise managers as it can provide tangible and concrete information about customer's purchasing patterns and enterprise processes effectiveness. The size of data could easily become an obstacle for efficiently using this asset. Data mining techniques could be successfully used to analyze this vast amount of data. Data mining is a relatively young discipline in the field of data analysis, with the aim of providing tools and techniques to assist in the discovery of hidden patterns and relationships in these data sets and in the integration of disparate data sets. Chapter "Business Process Improvement through Data Mining Techniques: An Experimental Approach" provides insights on how to use data mining techniques to improve enterprise business processes. This chapter covers a large number of topics, startin with an initial overview of the field of data mining and its fundamental concepts, to more complex concepts such as data preparation, data warehousing, pattern discovery and data classification. Finally, this chapter describes the current state of data mining research and active research areas. The use of data mining techniques for enterprise improvement could be considered as a rather new and emerging phenomenon.

Usually businesses nowadays offer their produce through web services as well. Web services are software programs that operate independently to offer services over the Internet to other programs, including web applications and other web services. They are developed to allow interoperability among technologies, as well as, protocols, platforms and operating systems. They constitute a key concept of the Service Oriented Architecture (SOA), which conceptually defines a structured data exchanging model, providing applications the ability to be loosely coupled with limited knowledge of each other implementations. The selection among a large number of web services that provide the desired functionalities for the composition is generally driven by QoS (Quality of Service) attributes, and formulated as a constrained multi-objective optimization problem. However, many equally important QoS attributes exist and in this situation the performance of the multi-objective algorithms can be degraded. To deal properly with this problem a chapter "Applying Evolutionary Many-Objective Optimization Algorithms to the Quality-Driven Web Service Composition Problem" is included in this publication to address a solution based in many-objective optimization algorithms.

In order to carry out successfully their multiple tasks, enterprises need integrated management systems as well as information systems. However, a clear distinction has to be made between integrated information systems and integrated management systems. On the one hand, the information systems are consolidated on a technological basis whilst, on the other hand, management systems are amalgamated following certain management principles. Furthermore, information flows along the entire firm and is integrated within the operational structure of an organization using programming languages, software and hardware. Conversely, the integration of management systems needs to be primarily approached in an abstract yet well founded manner at the strategic, tactical and operational levels of the management fabric; chapter "Integrated Management Systems and Information Management Systems: Common Threads" is addressing those issues.

Information Technology (IT) related risks are ambiguous and modern enterprise environments are no exception. Historically, the field of IT risk management has been dominated by theoretical discussions, practical misfits and indecipherable algorithms, all of them usually adding to complexity and sometimes little in essence. Recent corporate failures, which caused severe consequences, including economic turndown and an extended systemic risk in every sector or industry, reveal the failure to identify and manage risk at an enterprise level. Fact is that enterprise IT risk management has evolved but the question remains as to the extent. Concerns about the possibility of compromise or business disruption, have reached critical levels in many enterprises. Therefore, the success of an enterprise is now determined by its ability to maximize business performance through the management of the diversity of enterprise IT risks. Automated security metrics, such as vulnerability scoring methods and standardized specifications, provide a new basis for enterprise IT risk management. At this point of time, the competitive advantage belongs to the enterprises which will use automated tools to maximize business performance, setting new boundaries for standardization and sustainability. In order to address the above issues in this publication chapter "Managing Enterprise IT Risks through Automated Security Metrics" tries to express a position on how to solve the before mentioned problems.

Scientists' efforts and quest to solve the riddle of the human brain's intelligence have been documented throughout history. After the birth of computers, a serious effort started not only to understand how the human brain works but also, how to design, implement and use computer systems that would perform intelligent tasks, thus helping humans to live better. This marked the beginning of a new interesting and challenging scientific field: Artificial Intelligence (AI). According to the Oxford dictionary, AI may be defined as the theory and development of computer systems able to perform tasks that normally require human intelligence, such as decision-making, visual speech recognition, translation between languages and perception. AI is also defined as "the branch of computer science that is concerned with the automation of intelligent behavior". Although AI is a relatively new scientific direction, its list of application is impressive. The list contains directions such as data mining, distributed AI, expert systems, reasoning, neural networks, programming, belief revision, genetic algorithms, knowledge representation, natural language understanding artificial life, machine learning, theory of computation theorem proving, and constraint satisfaction. It must be noticed that not all AI directions had the same success in enterprise applications. One of the early AI developments was the field of expert systems. An expert system, which in artificial intelligence is a computer system that imitates the decision-making ability of a human expert, was first created in the 1970s. Initially it was a huge enthusiasm about expert systems in the scientific community but very soon it was realized that the area of application must be rather small and very well determined; all potential scenarios must be known in advance and the cost of development were prohibitive. This was a serious limitation and later this direction of AI declined consistently. Other fields of AI were more successful and to give to readers a wide perspective of AI and its applications, a chapter titled "Artificial Intelligence: Application in Business to Maximize the Performances of Automated Enterprise Systems" is included in this publication.

The security of private and confidential data and the security the transmission network handling these data are among the most prominent problems encountered in the field of enterprise data processing and communication. Protecting data from the legal point of view was a process that it took some time to create the necessary legal framework. As such a number of legal acts were implemented to protect enterprise data from theft. Such acts were Data Protection Act 1998, Freedom of Information Act 2000, Human Rights Act 1998, Statistics and Registration Services Act 2007, and Environmental Information Regulations Act 2004. A chapter titled "Information Security: Application in Business to Maximize the Security and Protect Confidential and Private Data" is included in this publication to shed light on protection and confidentiality of enterprise data.

We hope that the present compilation of chapters will be of use to a number of enterprise managers, supervisors and decision makers. We tried to bring together the experience of several authors of different backgrounds, origins and disciplines and present in one volume an answer to a number of issues dealing with improvement of business performance. We hope readers will appreciate our effort and wish to sincerely thank the publisher, the reviewers and the authors for their patience, confidence and vision to the successful outcome of this endeavor.

Petraq Papajorgji
Canadian Institute of Technology, Albania

Francois Pinet
National Research Institute of Science and Technology for Environment and Agriculture, France

Alaine Margarete Guimarães
State University of Ponta Grossa, Brazil

Jason Papathanasiou
University of Macedonia, Greece

Chapter 1
Review on Security Threats for Mobile Devices and Significant Countermeasures on Securing Android Mobiles

Lediona Nishani
University of New York in Tirana, Albania

ABSTRACT

Security nowadays is not a "nice to have," but a must-have. Cybercriminals have started a new way of encouraging their activities by selling their services on the deep dark web. They are becoming day by day more persistent and smarter than ever. Therefore, the companies have to be smarter in order to face the diversity of new threats every day. The increase of botnets is responsible for an emerging ransomware attacks through cryptolocker. Another modern malware are APT (Advanced persistent threats, sophisticated threats that undertake missions in cyber space). This chapter is about a summary of the most prominent attacks on security threats regarding android mobile devices. In this review chapter we will disclose and analyze chronicles of attack, which cover researching period from 2004 when was discovered the first mobile malware, until 2014. Our research will narrow down just in the two last years because of tremendous surge of android malware that has emerged just in this short period. We have chosen this small research sample in order to provide insights and give significant evidence that in a short period we have to investigate and analyze so many miscellaneous malware and vulnerabilities techniques. In subsequent proceedings, this chapter points out the main threats category we have thought to be more notable or significant to be investigated in this review chapter. Later on, it discusses future trends and some strong recommendation on facing and dealing with the internet technology based area.

1. INTRODUCTION

Android has become one of the most vulnerable operating system on mobile devices. This is mostly contributed to the fact that Android unlike other operating systems, is an open source system, therefore is more open to different malware and miscellaneous threats induced by cybercriminals.

DOI: 10.4018/978-1-4666-8841-4.ch001

New threats on Android mobiles arise day by day because cybercriminals are becoming smarter and more persistent than ever. They are relying on the darknet, a close area of Internet, which is designed to resist surveillance and government espionage. Android malwares (Friedmana & Hoffmanba, 2008) are growing in complexity and maturity. In this chapter, we explore not only the evolution malware diversity and threats on mobile, but also we develop a forecast on some new malicious, which we have not dealt with yet.

Another trend to investigate is ransomwares coming to Android (ransomware is a kind of malware, which uses very strong encryption in order to make users' files inaccessible, the next step is to blackmail the user and extort cash from them.) The first version of ransomware has been detected 25 years ago (Shih, Lin, Chiang and Shih, 2008).

Other threats combine various techniques of masquerading and misleading by using Smartphone device as the last point of the circle to be completed. Botnets are heading to android devices, too. Recently researchers have pointed out that large-scale botnets are controlling Android devices as much as botnets have controlled PCs. The preoccupying issue to be solved is the speed of malware spreading in shorter time comparing to PC and computer networks. Serious measures have been taken from Google recently in order to stop this exponential and booming of malware in android devices. Google has investigated several apps and ad framework behaviors, which will not be allowed to download malware-attacking Android. The research sample retrieved from security sources narrows down from 2012 until 2014 because it is believed that in these two years we have witnessed a dramatic surge of malware exploiting mobile devices. This work is viewed in two different approaches and perspectives. The first approach based on kinds of malware and the second based on preferred channels and scenarios chosen from cybercriminals to conduct fraudulent behaviors on mobile devices. Subsequently, this review chapter is conceived as follows:

- Section 2 is about chronological framework of malware in general and mobile malware,
- Section 3 involves mobile malwares and their classification and sorting out malwares,
- Section 4 is a collection of mobile vulnerabilities.
- Section 5 comes up with significant countermeasures provided from security community.
- Section 6 comprises the evolvement and trends of malware in the future landscape.
- Section 7 is dedicated to conclusions and analysis been derived from all data gathered. In addition, in this review chapter emerge gaps of malware technology and future work.

2. CHRONOLOGICAL BACKGROUND

In 1986 (Shih, Lin, Chiang and Shih, 2008) was discovered the first computer virus. In our days are counted almost 60,000 viruses and they have been transformed from an entanglement into a significant menace. Companies are losing billion of money regarding to the study of ICSA Labs Virus Prevalence Survey 2004 (Shih, Lin, Chiang and Shih, 2008), which shows that the financial cost of virus infection measured in cost per incident, was listed at over $130 million. The latest virus disaster alone costed them over $40,000 and took 31 person days to fully recovering after a virus disaster. Mobile devices are the fastest growing consumer technology, security researchers have identified an unprecedented growth with worldwide unit sales expected to increase from 300 million in 2010, to 650 million in 2012 (Kumar, 2012).

In addition, in the mobile domain the numbers of malwares, which attack mobile devices, have increased dramatically more than 200. The rate of growth if we compare it with the computer viruses is exponential and if paralleled to the years after the first PC virus was discovered, in the mobile landscape it took only two years to spread malwares, thing that computer waited 20 years. Today, there are more than 300 (Kumar, 2012) kinds of malware including worms, Trojan horses, spyware malware, adware, ransomware, botnets, keyloggers that have been released and other novel threats that we don't know yet how they will look like.

Mobile malware (malicious software) is defined from security researcher's community as software, which intends to damage, or disable computer or mobile system. A mobile virus, scientifically speaking, is an electronic virus, meaning mobile malicious software that attacks mobile phones or PDA (Personal Digital Assistant). The first computer virus, which has targeted a mobile phone for the first time is recalled to VBS. Timofonica, which was released in May 2000 (Shih, Lin, Chiang and Shih, 2008).

In 2004 security researchers came up with a proof of concept on a mobile virus called Cabir (Shih, Lin, Chiang and Shih, 2008), which through Bluetooth it was sending over the airwaves to users who did not suspect for any threat. Cabir ran on Symbian operating system. However, the first virus to infect more than handheld using Windows Mobile operating system was discovered in July 17, 2004 dubbed as Ojam (Shih, Lin, Chiang and Shih, 2008) and had developed an anti-piracy Trojan virus in older versions of their mobile phone game Mosquito. This virus sent short message service (SMS) text messages to the company without the user's knowledge. The aforementioned malware was removed from recent versions of the game.

In September 2005 CARDTRP.A (Shih, Lin, Chiang and Shih, 2008) was the first cross-platform mobile worm, which dropped worms in the memory card including even WUKILL.B. The problem aroused when the card was attached to a windows PC, it opened backdoor and expands two more worms. It was the beginning of how future mobile malware were going to be spread.

3. MOBILE MALWARE

Referring from the mobile security perspective, malicious software are plaguing today IT Infrastructure and in this section, we are going to provide evidence of an unprecedented growth of expansion.

The attacker defrauds the user by installing unauthorized application in order to steal sensitive data and to gain remote access of the system by exploiting vulnerabilities of the device code.

In this chapter we need to put an emphasis to malware of being rather than a simple virus, but as heterogeneous family of software like viruses, warms, trojans, ransomware, spyware, adware and a pool of many other malevolent infections designed with specified purpose to harm and to pose a cumbersome threat for the mobile system.

In our area of internet-based technology, malware can damage the whole world economic equilibrium. Since Internet has become a virtual marketplace, it is obvious that the pathogenic features to spread from it are parallelized as infection that exists and happen to the real life of individual persons. According to some reporters, it is stated that the rate of attacking vulnerabilities by fraudulent behaviors in all over the world is eight per day (Kumar, 2012). Such a huge figure must put us in alert and in a serious position to strongly preventing and reinforcing response to this dramatically outbreak of mobile threats.

Since we are referring to chronological facts of malware mobile history, this chapter is going to provide insights to categorizing various malware in the mobile landscape as follows:

- **Viruses:** Like any other malicious software, viruses are designed to undertake some actions on user's mobile system that user reasonably would not permit to. However, viruses are that kind of software that cannot be disseminated from one system to another without an external assistance.
- **Warm:** Unlike viruses, warms were released in order to spread faster, to move and promulgate from one network to another without any outer assistance.
- **Trojan:** Trojan comprises a malware category, which is downloaded in the system by merely clicking from a Website through clicking a link from naive users.
- **Botnet:** Sometimes called scary botnets; botnets are created when malware is diffused in Android device, and then attempts to communicate with a remote server to further download malware in the compromised device. Through the compromised device, cybercriminals can send instructions to download other malicious codes or to push URL to display in mobile browsers. According to this complex scenario, the mobile device becomes part of a botnet; meaning is under cybercriminals' control.
- **Rootkit:** Hackers in order to conceal their program utilize Rootkit technology. Rootkit is a malware version, which affects the device at its start up and potentially may encrypt disk, steal data or open connection for Command and controller.
- **Ransomware:** Is a sort of malware, which restricts access of the mobile resources and makes sensitive files inaccessible. This approach is like holding hostage individuals files and blackmails them to give back their data solely if they pay a certain amount of money.
- **Spyware:** Mainly this malware comes together with any package of software, it installs itself and tracks every personal details. Spyware is a sort of malware that can be included in the adware category wherein well-ad supported Key logger Trojan and spyware are interrelated with each other.
- **Keyloggers:** Grab all ones keystrokes; the passwords, login credentials and other sensitive data that can be manipulated and used from hackers and then directly send back to the cybercriminal remote server.

The figure 1 (Kumar, 2012) provides evidence of how attractive is the mobile domain for malware developers. The following table shows the different malware threats captured from 2004 until 2011 and the dramatically growth that is experienced in this period.

Figure 1. Mobile threat statistics by type, 2004-2011 (Kumar, 2012)

	2004	2005	2006	2007	2008	2009	2010	2011	Total
Adware									•
Applicaton								5	5
Backdoor							3		3
Garbage			8						8
Hack-Tool							4	8	12
Monitoring-Tool							1	15	16
Riskware			1		1	8	1	10	21
Spyware			5	15	6		2	5	33
Trojan	11	105	160	23	13	24	47	141	524
Trojan-Downloader								1	1
Virus	14	19	17	6					56
Worm				2	8	6	22		33

Another approach this chapter provides is the classification of the vulnerabilities in terms of the mobile operation system. We have studied and discussed the main operation system of mobiles devices, which held a significant portion of the market share. Android is the most vulnerable and the most favorite OS to be exploited from cybercriminals.

4. VULNERABILITIES OF ANDROID

Android is the most attacked and threatened mobile OS comparing to the other ones mobile operating systems, which do not experience such an outbreak of malware. One might be questioning that what makes this OS such appealing to all the worldwide cybercriminals and why are they so dramatically addicted to exploit Android system?

Android is the most popular of all mobile platforms. It possesses more than 40- 50% of the market share (equivalent to 300 million per user) (Kumar, 2012). Therefore, it comprises a huge environment for potential attacks and malevolent infections. Before Android being so popular, Symbian was the most popular platform for being targeted from malware, but the trend has declined; it has lost its position on the market.

Another point that contributes on reasons for being so compelling to hackers is that android provides well-documented development tools for software developers; hence, android has the best developer guides and library. In addition, Android is Linux-based mobile operating system and therefore, its codes are open to every developer throughout the world. That is why Android is the most favorite mobile system to be exploited from malware authors.

In this section, this chapter will enrich malware overview with the most notable vulnerabilities during the period of 2012-2014.

After the first mobile malware Cabir was discovered, community researchers have demonstrated that malicious and high risk Android-Apps are under attack, moreover Figure.2 (Kumar, 2012) indicates that android has experienced a sharp rise of threats just for the quarter of 2012.

In this section, we provide evidence of these severe attacks over Android.

4.1 First Approach Based on Malware Type

We will provide insight on sorting out and categorizing major threats and vulnerabilities that Android has experienced from 2012 until 2014.

Our research will provide a classification approach of mobile malware targeting Android mobile. This approach consists of three main categories which mobile malware had evolved in:

Vandal Trojans that install themselves into the mobile system exploiting android faults design.
Trojans written for financial earn of money.
Mobile Botnets.

4.1.1 Vandal Trojans

It was reported to have been tackled Trojan horse threat masqueraded as a bogus Chinese Game. This malware gathers sensitive information from the victim device by sending premium rate SMS messages.

Figure 2. Malicious and high-risk android app volume growth (Kumar, 2012)

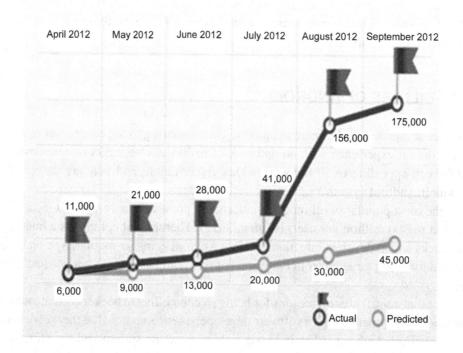

This Trojan malware called as the Roar of Pharaoh (Kumar, 2012) operates after an unknowing handset owner installs the app and then permits to gather information just like phone number, IMEI, phone model etc.

However, threats on Android are not only spread through mobile network but also even in compromised sites and corporate. Kevin Mahaffrey, co-founder and CTO of Lookout Security (Keizer, 2012) has discovered a new Android Trojan named 'NotCompatible'. This Trojan is susceptible to affect potentially the corporate networks and can harm their systems.

McAfee Mobile Security (Castillo, 2012) reported an Android Video Malware found in Japanese Google Play Store. This application carries Trojan promise and in many cases sends trailer for video games clips, nevertheless it requests to read contact data, phone state and identity permission before it goes downloaded. These sorts of threats were called Android/DougaLeaker from McAfee.

There is another security threat that we must give evidence for it. The Android based Trojan was devised from a team of researcher from Pennsylvania State University (PSU) and IBM (Xu, Ba, and Zhu, 2012). It uses a handset movement sensor to decrypt passwords. These security researchers built an app called Taplogger[11] based on the fact that tapping on touch screen makes possible to interact not just only with the screen but with the whole device.

US Naval Surface Warfare Center (Templeman, Rahman, Crandall, and Kapadia, 2012) have created a new Android App, scary malware called "PlaceRaider". This malware is utilized just for proof of concept. Security researchers at Indiana University in collaboration with US Naval Surface Warfare Center have designed a new form of malware aiming to record and reconstruct victim's environment. They have deployed a Trojan, which can be installed in the mobile and take photo without the user consent or awareness and then sends sensor data back to the hacker server.

The most dangerous Android malware ever detected is a new piece of complex and sophisticated malware, which has been reported from Kaspersky Lab named as *Backdoor.AndroidOS.Obad.a.* (Uncheck, 2013). It has become the most sophisticated mobile malware ever discovered. This particular malware has the ability to exploit several of Android vulnerabilities: blocking uninstalling attempts, attempts to gain root permissions and can conduct a host to remote commands. It comprises sophisticated obfuscation techniques, complicated analysis of the code and the use of previously unknown vulnerabilities in Android. That is why it can take control of infected Android devices.

The mobile malware sector is growing rapidly in a tremendous rate. Communities of security researchers have demonstrated that there is an exponential growth of malware utilizing TOR-based communication. Researchers have observed the first TOR-Based android malware. TOR is the environment, which makes the users fulfilling their desire of not being surveyed from government in terms of their search. However, Kaspersky Lab tackled the first TOR-based malware for android (Bansal, 2014). This Trojan called 'Orbot' is running from .onion Tor domain and working on the functionality of an open source TOR client for Android mobile devices. The number of devices being affected from this scenario is still not easy and clear to estimate.

4.1.2 Trojans Written for Financial Profit

More than 79% of mobile threats during 2013 are targeting Android OS. Mostly this malware consists of malware apps that steal money via text messages to premium rate number from the infected devices.

For sure that the intruder of the system has been thinking up a method of how to exploit the banking system in order to recover large financial gain. This landscape is becoming very profitable for hackers, who aim stealing money from this system. That is why the notorious authors who design malware Android targeting banks are more pushed to create new threats.

It was announced that half million Chinese Android devices were infected with SMSZombie.A, which was discovered from a group of analysts of TrusGo Labs (TrustGo Security Labs, 2012). This malware is complex and exploits the weaknesses of China Mobile SMS Payment System aiming to steal banks credit numbers and information linked to money transactions. It is a sophisticated Trojan, therefore very difficult to be captured and removed. This malware is enclosed to wallpaper apps. This Trojan installs itself in the app after the naive user has downloaded it together with the app. The crucial point in this whole history is that the malicious app is not flagged that might contain malware.

Another malware targeting the banking system is Zeus Malware. Zeus malware has been for a couple of years the most dangerous threat of PC. Now the mobile version is dubbed as ZitMo (Zeus-in-the-Mobile). The security researchers of Kaspersky (Maslennikov, 2012) have identified five new samples of ZiTMo malware package, which not only aimed to infect Android, but even Blackberry system, too. The trick that deploys this malware is camouflaging as a banking security application or add-on. ZitMo gathers banking information by grabbing all text messages and directly forwards to the hackers devices. This malware pretends to be security software called "Zertifikat". Security researchers have inspected the first ever Windows Malware that can hack the Android Mobile when synchronizing mobile device with PC running windows system in order to backup information from mobile device. Researchers have demonstrated that a new windows malware tries to install mobile banking malware on Android device while synchronizing with Windows PC. Recently security mobile researcher at Symantec Antivirus Firm (Liu, 2014) have revealed another windows malware dubbed 'Trojan.Droidpak', that casts malicious DLL in the computer system and downloads the files from the remote server. The Windows Trojan downloads a malicious APK (An Android Application) from the computer-infected location.

It was reported another malware, which affects phones, highjacks passwords and other sensitive information when infected user put its login credential into the account. A new Android Banking Trojan targeting Korean Users have been seized from the antivirus software maker Malwarebytes (Orozco, 2013) who has disclosed this new attack. This new threat is promulgated through file sharing sites and alternative markets. Known as "Android/Troja.Bank.Wroba', this malware is masqueraded as legitimate app in Google Play Store and runs in the background of the monitor events.

"This enables it to capture incoming SMS, monitor installed apps and communicate with a remote server," the researcher stated (Orozco, 2013). Furthermore, referring to researcher's report, after installation malware lookups for existence of targeted banking application on mobile device, removes them and downloads malicious version to replace it.

"The malicious version will contain the exact Package Name and look very similar to the legitimate app but contains malicious code with no banking functionality." The researcher has pointed out (Orozco, 2013).

4.1.3 Mobile Botnets

Botnets are appearing even in the mobile landscape, security professionals have spotted a POC Android botnet (Kumar, 2012), which comprises a command and control channel linked to Messaging Service (SMS) to bypass detection. This proof-of-concept code employs Short Messaging Service. This includes vulnerability when a mobile is not available on networks for specific reason and during delivery arrival of the message; the latter is queued and sent via network.

4.2 Second Approach Based on Used-Channel for Malware Spreading

We will provide another approach by assorting out in terms of chosen scenario diffusion or preferred channels utilized to promulgate mobile malware. Moreover, the two approaches carried out in this review chapter are embedded with time context.

- Mobile Application Web (entertainment, E-Tv etc.).
- Exploit toolkit.
- Clikjacking, likejacking.
- Social Network (social engineering).
- (Different fraud pattern).

4.2.1 Mobile Application (Web, Browser)

Another channel for a threat to be diffused is the most downloaded game in the mobile area Angry Birds Space detected on April of 2012 by the security researchers of Lookout as Legacy Native (LeNa) (Wyatt, 2012). This malware aims to threaten mobile devices running Android OS. It hides a copy of the game and represents itself as a legitimate app in order to earn unauthorized privilege.

"By employing an exploit, this new variant of LeNa does not depend on user interaction to gain root access to a device. This extends its impact to users of devices not patched against this vulnerability (versions prior to 2.3.4 that do not otherwise have a back-ported patch)." Lookout said in a blog post (Wyatt, 2012).

Regarding mobile vulnerabilities have been reported cases of data leakage linked to Cloud Storage Security, which poses a critical risk to IT Infrastructure. Cloud computing refers to computing where processing stages is carried out on a network of computer rather than just one PC. Now everything is connected to the Cloud Storage and always is synchronized.

Researchers at the University of Glasgow (Grispos, Glisson and Storer, 2013) pointed out that cloud storage apps that send files to the cloud in the same time leave retrievable versions of the files on the devices. They have carried out some testing to cloud-based file storage systems just like Box, Dropbox and Sugar Sync running Android 2.1. Researchers have discovered that the mobile devices, which were experiencing cloud storage services, can contain proxy view of the data stored in the cloud storage service. This can potentially provide partial view of the data without access of the data provider. Moreover, some scenarios can provide further access to the data in the cloud storage account. Forensic Experts have provided evidence that can be recovered even metadata from all application on the devices (including transitional logs, metadata linked to files stored on the cloud and potentially information about the application user).

Applications on Android devices are the most favorite channel where hackers promulgate their mobile malware. So it was discovered another flaw from AirDroid application, which its vulnerability allows attacker to perform Dos attack. This app incorporated wireless management of Android mobile or tablet from any browser. The vulnerability of this app consists of the cross Site scripting or XSS weakness in the browser version of Air Droid. This flaw permits hackers to send malicious message to the browser linked with the account of the attacker to get access to the phone containing the AirDroid installed. Referring to advisory of Us-Cert (Vulnerability Notes database, 2013) this message can be detected from Air Droid web interface, which may be used to conduct an information leakage, privilege escalation or DoS on computer host. The current vulnerability has not being provided with any update related. Therefore, the countermeasure to be undertaken is to allow only connection from trusted networks.

Android can be used as hacking tool to hijack password from connected computers. This new piece of Android malware dubbed as USB Cleaver after infecting the mobile, it is redirected to the PC to steal and collect private information from it. F-Secure discovered this tool (News from the lab, 2013), which is skilled to steal information from a windows PC. This malware aims to facilitate a hacker to collect required information from a subsequent endeavor of hacking.

To make use of this malware application the hacker must install another app called USB cleaver on his Android device. The app then downloads a ZIP file from a remote server, subsequently unzips the file to the following location of the system folder. When the device is plugged in to a PC and if autorun is enabled, the payload goes executed. Later on, the app steals and collects all the sensitive information the hacker is interested.

Android mobile malware have affected even the new technology of the digital crypto currency Bitcoin. Bitcoin is a virtual crypto currency that uses public key cryptography algorithms to built, create and transfer bitcoins. Users utilize digital wallet to their bitcoin addresses to sell and buy bit coins; a kind of digital bursa. It was reported in august of 2013 (Android security vulnerability, 2013) a critical shortcoming of Android execution of the Java SecureRandom random number generator, which is capable of allowing and making digital wallets on the mobile environment susceptible to theft. Users undertaking bitcoin transactions have observed that over 55 BTC stolen after the client has signed a transaction by carrying out the compromised random number generator. Every digital walled generated by the Android

App can be tangible including blockcahin.info wallet, bitcoin spinner etc. The countermeasure recommended in this case is to generate a new address with a repaired number generator and then send all the money back to their address of wallet. In addition, it is strongly recommended to update to the latest version available to the Play Store.

AVG Security expert made another report regarding this category (Paganini, 2013) concerning a hazardous shortcoming in Android Web View feature that gives space to the attacker to be capable to install malicious software, send text messages and other susceptible and notorious behaviors. Web View is a crucial component of android mobile, which adjusts application to display content online resources and facilitate the performing request of networks. However, android attackers have developed techniques on how to exploit Firefox weaknesses, which facilitate hacker to steal files from SD card.

Mobile Browsers are complicated and is dramatically difficult and hard to make them secure from various malicious threats. AVG Security expert disclosed the detailed shortcoming of Mozilla that permits hackers to intercept both contents of SD cards and browser private data. This vulnerability enables only if compromised user installs a malicious application or opens a locally stored HTML file in Firefox Browser app that is embedded together with a Javascript Code. If this scenarios works, the hacker grabs files of SD Card, all of users cookies, login credential, bookmarks etc. Files are accessed according to the standard "file://"URI syntax. While Firefox deploys internal encryption data storage, cybercriminals enclose the third party app to get the encrypted keys.

The mobile world is becoming day by day more anonymous. People now fear the government surveillance and corporate tracking, therefore they really want to search without being tackled or eavesdropped from any of these sources. Anonymous search engine DuckDuckGo continues to make search records. DuckDuckgo is an Android App that delivers the same traditional services as other search engines like Google, but has an additional feature; the IP address and identity will not be registered or recorded. This app has incorporated an integrated TOR Support.

Another landscape not discussed still herein is stealing WhatsApp conversations through Rogue Android gaming app. There are encryption mechanisms for WhatsApp that improper design could make room for attackers to intercept a conversation. An android game has been released in the Google Play store aiming to steal users' conversation databases and to resell the collection of sensitive information in agencies who are interested in them (i.e. internet websites). Google has recently removed the Rogue Android gaming app dubbed as "Balloon Pop 2" (Paganini, 2013) from the official Play Store. This app was not only capable of stealing WhatsApp conversations but even uploading directly in the WhatsAppCopy website. This website advertised the game as a scenario to back up the service of conversation. This website defends itself by claiming that they are not responsible for its violation of the privacy right or surveillance purpose.

4.2.2 Exploit Toolkit

In early 2012, it was identified the first Android BootKit Malware *DKFBootKit* (NQ mobile Security Research Center, 2012). This mobile malware replaces a specific boot process and can start running even before the completion of booting process. Furthermore, it makes the repackages of the utility apps and includes its codes of their packages. The victim apps, which are infected, need root privileges. They possess the legitimacy to request the grant of the root privilege.

Developers of Android have incorporated the system of Snapchat with new security features. It was inferred that Snapchat has been hacked in 30 minutes by a cracking tool dubbed CAPTCHA (Hickson, 2014) and has experienced a massive data leakage wherein 4.6 million usernames and phone numbers have been violated. The company has announced a novel feature on the security, but at the same day, it hackers have designed and written a computer program adapted to crack it. Stiven Hickson, a hacker who cracked the new security feature reported:

The problem with this is that the Snapchat ghost is very particular. You could even call it a template. For those of you familiar with template matching (what they are asking you to do to verify your humanity). It is one of the easier tasks in computer vision (Hickson, 2014).

A Russian security firm (Dr.Web Company, 2014) has indicated the first much-promulgated Android Bootkit malware named 'Android.Oldboot', which is written to re-infect devices after reboot even if you delete all working components of it. A Bootkit is a rootkit malware version affecting the device at its start up and potentially may encrypt the disk, steal data and open connection for Command and controller.

Smart techniques are undertaken to enclose this Trojan into an Android mobile, where hackers put the components of it into a boot partition of the fie system, modify the script of initializing the operation system and load the malware when we switch on the android device.

The last vulnerability that we deemed appropriate to disclose herein this subsection is the Android Malware Toolkit dubbed as Dendtroid. It was discovered from Symantec Antivirus Company (Coogan, 2014). Hackers are applying novel techniques on how to manipulate and exploit mobile android system. Researchers of Symantec have found an Android remote admin tool called AndroRAT. It is advocated to be the first malware APK binder. Dendroid is executed over HTPP embedded with many malicious properties.

4.2.3 Clikjacking, Likejacking

Another security threat that android mobile has been exposed to is the category of adware, which are abusing on demanding permissions which are not necessary or mandatory; they are collecting more information than they need.

"Many apps will ask you to grant them network access so they can download updates. Others seek permission to read your phone's state and identity so calls will not disrupt them from doing what they are doing. Unfortunately, these permissions can be abused for criminal intentions." Trendmicro reported (Decker, 2012).

These adware are violating and breaking user's sensitive data by intercepting private information and certainly exploring this information without consent. Adware software must be conceptualized as software, which collects information about users and then sends it back to the advertising agencies who are concerned for information about the customer behavior. This adware displays an ad in a form of pop ups messages. When the user clicks to the ad right in that moment will be redirected to the advertiser site and the data will be logged into the advertiser's server.

The line between the adware gathering sensitive information without consent and gathering legitimate data is not very definite. The process becomes illegitimate when they collect data they have not request permission for and then sell it to another ad network.

4.2.4 Different Fraudulent Pattern

DNS Attack

A group of researchers Roee Hay & Roi Saltzman from IBM Application Security Research Group reported (Hay and Saltzman, 2012): Android 4.0.4 is exposing vulnerabilities on DNS poisoning. They have advocated the procedure that an attacker can successfully guess the nonce of the DNS request for a feasible attack. Android version 4.0.4 and below its version possesses this bug. The vulnerability consists of a pseudorandom number generator (PRNG) which makes applicable the attacks of flooding the DNS.

Zero Day Attack

Chronologically speaking, in September of 2012, in Android 4.04 appeared the Zero day vulnerabilities. It was reported from security researchers (MWR InfoSecurity, 2012) that Samsung Galaxy S3 can be hacked through NFC (Near Field Communication). NFC is a technology that allows data to be sent over a short distance. This attack permits the intruders to capture all the data of the Android mobile. As mobile are becoming more popular on the other hand the possibilities for their potential misuse are also increasing.

Android Affecting Other Systems (Windows, Linux, etc.)

Android mobile malware can be susceptible when linked to Linux Kernel. It was pointed out a Linux kernel local privilege escalation exploit, which poses the attackers to gain complete control of the victim devices. This was a new leveraging of notorious exploits for malicious purpose. Linux kernel 2.6x, Red Hat enterprise Linux 6UBuntu 12.04 LTS, Debian 6 and Suse Enterprise Linux 11 are tangible to privilege escalation shortcoming."The per.swevent.init function in the kernel /events/core.c in the Linux kernel before 3.8.9 uses an incorrect integer data type which allows users to gain privileges via a crafted perf event open system call", CVE-2013-2094 stated (Symantec Security response, 2013).

Man in the Middle Attack

It was reported that T-Mobile Wi-Fi Calling App to be vulnerable to the Man-in-the-Middle-Attack. This report belongs to March 2013. This Wi-Fi Calling App consists of keeping subscribers connected in areas with little coverage through Wi-Fi connection. However, two students named respectively Jethro Beekman and Christopher Thompson from University of California Berkeley (Beekman and Thompson, 2013) pointed out that this app makes room for critical vulnerabilities for millions of android users due to the Man-in-the-Middle attack. The attacker potentially can be on the same open wireless network as the user. This flaw, if we analyze it based on security approach, will permit attackers to access and manipulate calls and messages made by the infected user on Android mobile. The team of T-Mobile has reported after this finding that they have worked on that issue and this flaw has been removed for all affected phones by releasing a security update to its Android users.

5. COUNTERMEASURES IN SECURING ANDROID ON MOBILE DEVICES

In this section, this review chapter will provide some significant countermeasures that different security companies and various research communities have employed in order to resist the rapid growth of malware diffusion on mobile devices. Google has taken some substantial steps to better securing and improving mechanisms of preventing and responding to miscellaneous threats in different perspectives. Security researchers on Google, as first step, have removed from Android Platform 4.3 an automatic app downloads feature that has been embedded to android system in the foregoing version. Another major countermeasure undertaken was controlling the Developer Agreement regarding to unwanted apps (PUAs), which may be intrusive or kind of adware that can collect sensitive data and upload it back to the mobile cloud. Google has removed from Google Play Store diverse apps and ad framework in which were discovered some violation of user privacy and will no longer be in market. Moreover, developers cannot put third party advertising.

Some other adjustment has been made on releasing a bug framework aiming to help hunters find most prominent vulnerabilities on Android.

According to a distinct report (Ho, Dean, Gu, and Enck, 2014), it was stated that cyber criminals are designing and conceiving 55.000 new malware variants every single day.

Security researchers in North Carolina State University have elaborated a new piece of software dubbed as Practical Root Exploit Containment (PREC) aiming to detect mobile malware that attempts to run Root exploits in Android Devices. Root exploit is taking control of system administration function of the OS and gaining unfettered control of the mobile device. In this detecting software is deployed a technique that works on comparing the conduct of a downloaded Android application with a database of normal scenario logs when no attack has been divulged in the system. In the case when there is significant deviation from the expected conduct, PREC makes decisions and identifies if the app contains malicious code or it is a harmless app. This technique has been improved and refined to preventing from giving to much false positives.

"Anomaly detection isn't new and it has a problematic history of reporting a lot of false positive," Dr. Will Enck co-author of the scientific research paper stated (Ho, Dean, Gu, and Enck, 2014). PREC intends to capture flaws in the code developed in C language, which is generally used from hackers to design mobile malware. Security professionals have tested a variant of the tool Google Galaxy Nexus device towards 150 Android Apps; some of them possess root exploit. "We can achieve 100 percent detection rate," he stated.

Some further provisionings have been made linked to promising security improvement regarding Android 4.2 Jelly Bean OS in client side malware protection, Security Enhanced Linux, and always on VPN.

The most significant security enhancement in Android 4.2 involves a service based on Bouncer that is applicable to all apps. It can scrutinize apps download not only from official market, but also from Third Party sites. This detection technique inspects it for any malicious code that may potentially harm the mobile device. The system has strengthened on terms of security by adding another feature VPN lockdown that can put a limit to the amount of the data sent over a connection that might be a public domain deemed unsecure for mobile devices.

Security has been carried out regarding Linux too, because many mobiles are infected from Linux Servers so there is created a Security enhanced (SE) Linux, which can come up with low level of improvement such as mitigation for privilege escalation attacks and stricter fostering of at least application privilege.

Security has improved even in terms of messages written or sent. There has been introduced a new property dubbed as SMS Confirmation Feature that aims to alert users regarding text messages that might not have been sent from themselves in person. This new feature incorporated in the message platform makes possible that if it is investigated the aforementioned case, the phone will stop the service and let the users decide whether to permit the execution of the message or to end it.

Another specification has been deployed in Android 4.2 comprising gesture-based typing, photosphere camera and multi-user option, which allow diverse people login to the same device (Kumar, 2012).

Malware developers are creating novel techniques that hide malware and promulgate them in the mobile system. However, due to Google, most of the apps in the official market are secure, but the best protection is common sense. The last countermeasure, but also the most significant is to ensure to install solely apps from Trusted Sources. Users have to be smarter and more conscientious and raise their awareness to staying safe and secure.

6. METHODOLOGY PROCEDURE AND FRAMEWORK APPROACH

The methodology of this review chapter is based on conduction of a scientific research, gathering and collecting information. In this research work, the methodology framework comprises two different approaches in categorizing the various compelling threats targeting Mobile devices and summarizing the most preferred channel to cast the malware. The review has been conducted in the period from 2005 until 2014. However, it is more highlighted the period of last two years from 2012-2014 because security researchers have witnessed an unprecedented exponential growth in the third quarter of 2012 comparing to previous years. We deemed appropriate to narrow down our review chapter in these 2 years.

After collecting data from the most well known security labs and well-known security research papers, we have sorted out and classified malware in two major directions in terms of types of malware and the second approach is employed in terms of channel utilized for dropping malware into mobile devices. Subsequently, we have analyzed the data collected and derived into significant conclusions. For every security threat that android devices have been posed to during this period, this work provides respectively its countermeasure. There are significant tips, which aimed to enforce the user's behavior and foster their education on security manners and usage on mobile devices. Another point to be emphasized in the methodology framework and techniques section is analyzing and foreseeing the future of malware, investigating on trends of the security mobile landscape. New perspectives are being discussed for further gaps and future research.

7. EVOLUTION OF MOBILE MALWARE

Obviously, the last has been the year where we have witnessed a critical and dramatic expansion of malware threats in terms of not only updated malware or infiltrated in different internet technologies or domains, but we fear the releasing of new brand malware that we do not have the clue or cannot foresee their future shape. We need to be a step ahead against cybercriminals in order to tackle and better predict their movement, their evolvement and development of their malicious software. Without any doubt, we expect this trend will continue in the future.

Another trend to be investigated is of individuals who own a Smartphone. Certainly, in the future, they will hold even a tablet whichever its system will be, the smart phone and tablet will have interchangeable data. Therefore, malware will have more channels to be divulged; in few words, we will face a rise of the number of infected users, and more other increasing areas are expected in further years to be compromised by potential attacks.

Hacktivism will be a trend much proliferated in the future. Hacktivism is a kind of movement of writing malicious code for a specific political or social aim. The most prominent example of these acts is the Trojan SMS.AndroidOS.Arspam that is well spread in the populations, which might have civil problematic or politics issues just like Syria or Ukraine. We must keep eyes wide open and stay in alert because we cannot forecast what will happen in this unpredictable area in the days to come.

One other possible aspect that will cause threats in the future is business relying on cloud services. Researchers are expecting a dramatically increasing of attacks targeting mobile devices as tools to gain access to corporate data through the cloud. That is why it is very important to strengthen and reinforce security in the cloud mobile.

Another area to be aware of is the risk of personal data to be intercepted from mobile apps and social media.

Experts stated (Kumar, 2014) that the most played mobile game angry bird shared data with advertising companies via mobile cloud. The figure 3 (Kumar, 2014) shows the scenario in which is performed the leakage of personal data to advertising clouds.

Figure 3. Angry birds sharing data with advertising companies (Kumar, 2014)

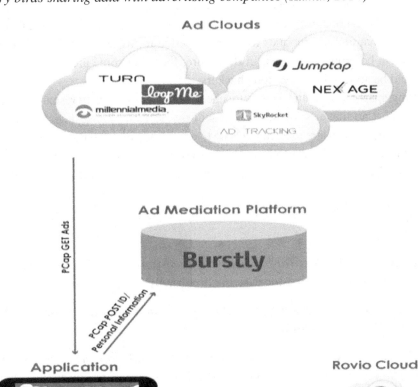

"It first fetches the customer id, then uploads the personal data to the cloud and then transmits it to the other advertising clouds," researchers pointed out.

Many apps contain different malware. That is why, is very important to raise the self-awareness of simple users who are the most suffering and compromised category. Nevertheless, mobile and web application control for business users are going to have a significant contribution on mitigating this risk. Social networks are used as gateway to infiltrate spam news, which contain malware. This technique is going to be used in the future too.

8. CONCLUSION

Mobile devices are always ready to connect to the Internet and contain sensitive information such as Contacts, SMS, Photos, and GPS information. Therefore, this sensitive information is always in danger of leakage. According to a report, Cyber criminals and state-sponsored hackers are developing 55,000 new malware variants, each day; and many of them try to elevate privileges for unfettered control of the user device.

This chapter has given strong and significant evidence for introducing a concise overview of most prominent threats and attacks Android mobile devices have been contracted and suffered from 2004-2014. The methodology that has been undertaken relies on the classification of threats and vulnerabilities. However, this chapter do not only expose the most compelling threats during this period, but also provides insights of various countermeasures that users and security researchers must follow up in order to resist to all attacks that android mobiles might be exposed to. Researchers have found some trends threat, which seems to be more dangerous. In the future, there are some areas, which are going to be more vulnerable and be attacked from various hackers.

However, putting apart all the countermeasures been taken from security researchers the conclusion that we reviewed is that no matter what updates or security software being incorporated in the mobile device, the most significant measure to be made is up to users; they must visit and download from trusted party. We must educate Android users to have the self-awareness and being eye-wide open in order to stay safe and secure. The major conclusion that this chapter provides is to stay educated.

REFERENCES

Bansal, S. (2014 February 24). *First Tor-based Android malware spotted in the wild.* Retrieved from http://thehackernews.com/2014/02/first-tor-based-android-malware-spotted.html

Beekman, J., & Thompson, C. (2013 March 19). *Man-in-the-Middle Attack on T-Mobile Wi-Fi Calling.* Technical Report No. UCB/EECS-2013-18.

Castillo, C. (2012 April 13). *Android malware promises video while stealing contacts.* [Web log post]. Retrieved from http://blogs.mcafee.com/mcafee-labs/android-malware-promises-video-while-stealing-contacts

Coogan, P. (2014 March 05). *Android RATs Branch out with Dendroid.* [Web log post]. Retrieved from http://www.symantec.com/connect/blogs/android-rats-branch-out-dendroid

Decker, A. (2012 October 29). *How Mobile Ads abuse permissions.* [Web log post]. Retrieved from http://blog.trendmicro.com/trendlabs-security-intelligence/how-mobile-ads-abuse-permissions/

Dr.Web Company. (2014 January 24). *First Android bootkit has infected 350,000 devices.* Retrieved from http://news.drweb.com/show/?i=4206

Friedmana, J. & Hoffmanba, D.V. (2008). Protecting data on mobile devices: A taxonomy of security threats to mobile computing and review of applicable defenses. *Journal of Information Knowledge Systems Management*, 159-168.

Grispos, G., Glisson, W. B., & Storer, T. (2013). Using Smartphones as a Proxy for Forensic Evidence contained in Cloud Storage Services. In *Proceedings of 46th Hawaii International Conference on System Sciences.* IEEE. doi:10.1109/HICSS.2013.592

Hay, R. & Saltzman, R. (2012). *Weak randomness in Android's DNS resolver.* IBM Application Security Research Group, CVE-2012-2808.

Hickson, S. (2014 January 22). *Hacking Snapchat's people verification in less than 100 lines.* [Web log post]. Retrieved from http://stevenhickson.blogspot.in/2014/01/hacking-snapchats-people-verification.html

Ho, T., Dean, D., Gu, X., & Enck, W. (2014). PREC: Practical Root Exploit Containment for Android Devices. San Antonio, TX: Academic Press.

Keizer, G. (2012 May 04). *Android Malware used to mask online frauds, says expert.* Retrieved from http://www.computerworld.com/article/2503771/malware-vulnerabilities/android-malware-used-to-mask-online-fraud--says-expert.html

Kumar, M. (2012 April 01). *Android malware as beware of Chinese called "The Roar of Pharaoh".* Retrieved from http://thehackernews.com/2012/04/android-malware-as-beware-of-chinese.html

Kumar, M. (2012). *The hacker news: Malware June 2012.* Retrieved from http://news.thehackernews.com/THN-June2012.pdf

Kumar, M. (2012 April 01). *POC android botnet-command and control channel over SMS".* Retrieved from http://thehackernews.com/2012/04/poc-android-botnet-command-and-control.html

Kumar, M. (2012 November 02). *Android 4.2 Jelly Bean Security Improvements Overview.* Retrieved from http://thehackernews.com/2012/11/android-42-jelly-bean-security.html

Kumar, M. (2014 April 01). *Researchers explained how Angry Birds sharing your personal data.* Retrieved from http://thehackernews.com/2014/04/researchers-explained-how-angry-birds.html

Liu, F. (2014 January 23). *Windows Malware Attempts to Infect Android Devices.* [Web log post]. Retrieved from http://www.symantec.com/connect/blogs/windows-malware-attempts-infect-android-devices

Maslennikov, D. (2012 August 7). *New ZitMo for Android and Blackberry.* Retrieved from http://securelist.com/blog/virus-watch/57860/new-zitmo-for-android-and-blackberry/

MWR InfoSecurity. (2012, September 12). *Mobile Pwn2Own at EuSecWest 2012.* Retrieved from https://labs.mwrinfosecurity.com/blog/2012/09/19/mobile-pwn2own-at-eusecwest-2012/

News from the lab. (2013 July 1). *Android Hack-Tool Steals PC Info*. Retrieved from https://www.fsecure.com/weblog/archives/00002573.html

NQ Mobile Security Research Center. (2012 March 29). *Security Alert: New AndroiMalware — DKF-BootKit — Moves Towards the First Android BootKit*. [Web log post]. Retrieved from http://research.nq.com/?p=391

Orozco, A. (2013 October 23). *Trojan looks to "Wrob" Android users*. [Web log post]. Retrieved from https://blog.malwarebytes.org/mobile-2/2013/10/trojan-looks-to-wrob-android-users/

Paganini, P. (2013 December 07). *Rogue Android Gaming app that steals WhatsApp conversations*. Retrieved from http://thehackernews.com/2013/12/hacking-whatsapp-chat-apps-malware_7.html

Shih, D., Lin, B., Chiang, H., & Shih, M. (2008). Security aspects of mobile phone virus: A critical survey. *Industrial Management & Data Systems*, 108(4), 478–494. doi:10.1108/02635570810868344

Symantec Security Response. (2013 June 13). *Linux Kernel Exploit Ported to Android*. [Web log post]. Retrieved from http://www.symantec.com/connect/blogs/linux-kernel-exploit-ported-android

Templeman, R., Rahman, Z., Crandall, D., & Kapadia, A. (2012). *PlaceRaider: Virtual Theft in Physical Spaces with Smartphones*. arXiv:1209.5982v1

TrustGo Security Labs. (2012 August 15). *New Virus SMSZombie.A Discovered by TrustGo Security Labs*. [Web log post]. Retrieved from http://blog.trustgo.com/SMSZombie/

Uncheck, R. (2013 June 06). *The most sophisticated Android Trojan*. Retrieved from https://securelist.com/blog/research/35929/the-most-sophisticated-android-trojan/

Vulnerability Notes Database. (2013 September 03). *AirDroid web interface XSS vulnerability*. Retrieved from http://www.kb.cert.org/vuls/id/557252

Wyatt, T. (2012 April 03). *Security Alert: New Variants of Legacy Native (LeNa) Identified*. [Web log post]. Retrieved from https://blog.lookout.com/blog/2012/04/03/security-alert-new-variants-of-legacy-native-lena-identified

Xu, Z., Ba, K., & Zhu, S. (2012 April 16). *TapLogger: Inferring User Inputs On Smartphone Touch-screens Using On-board Motion Sensors*. ACM.

ENDNOTE

[1] TapLogger was created by Zhi Xu, a PhD candidate in the Department of Computer Science and Engineering at PSU, Kun Bai, a researcher at IBM T.J. Watson Research Center and Sencun Zhu, an associate professor of Computer Science and Engineering at PSU's College of Engineering

Chapter 2
Android for Enterprise Automated Systems

Fahmi Ncibi
National High School of Engineering of Tunisia, Tunisia

Habib Hamam
Moncton University, Canada

Ezzedine Ben Braiek
National High School of Engineering of Tunisia, Tunisia

ABSTRACT

In this chapter, various aspects pertaining to the open operating system Android OS such as its history, architecture, features, and utility for business purposes will be introduced, following which the role of Android in enterprise management will be explained. The chapter will be concluded by a detailed report of the BYOD approach that uses Android for industrial control and automation. Since mobile devices have become progressively more powerful and accessible, mobile computing has greatly changed our daily lives. As one of the most popular mobile operating systems, Android provides the tools and API for Android developers to develop Android applications. Android is an open source operating system for mobile devices. Today its primary use is lodged in the mobile phone industry. During the recent past years, many projects have been created, with the objective to elevate Android to other platforms, such as sub-notebooks or embedded systems.

INTRODUCTION

The world of smartphones has developed rapidly in the recent years following the evolution of new technologies. Older mobile phone models are merely used to make phone calls and send SMS (short message) but nowadays, with the new features that can be embedded in mobile phones, they can be used to perform sophisticated tasks and answer professional needs. The needs of different users can now be filled with the mobile phone. Growth specifications and other advanced characteristics are now offered by mobile companies to attract users to the products they manufacture.

DOI: 10.4018/978-1-4666-8841-4.ch002

The request for access to corporate information and applications through mobile devices such as devices running Android, Apple's iPhone and iPad, Windows 7 Mobile or Blackberry, manufactured by the Canadian company RIM (Research in Motion), are surging as consumers' preferences and behaviour become a top priority for the company's workforce.

The strikingly rapid rate of adoption of these technologies around the world has left many business managers wondering how to effectively position their firms to benefit from the dominant trends. The drive for mobility is part of the business technology agenda for most companies today.

Android is one of these technologies, which are spreading all over the world. It is an open source mobile operating system (system source is published) developed by Google company. Google produces the software and it can run in almost every mobile device of many manufacturers. In fact, there exist popular Android tablets as well. Android is a Linux-based software system; and similarly to Linux, it is a free and open source software. This means that other companies can utilize the Android operating system developed by Google and implement it in their mobile devices.

INTRODUCTION TO ANDROID

1. Android Overview

1.1. What Is Android?

Android is an open source mobile phone and embedded device operating system developed by the Open Handset Alliance (Open Handset Alliance, 2009). This system is based on a Linux kernel, adapted to the architecture of mobile phones, with a virtual machine for running Java-based applications. The main advantage is that it is easily compatible because it is based on a popular language: Java.

1.2. Why Android?

Android is already the top smartphone operating system in the world. Google Financial Results Second Quarter 2011 reported that Android activated devices reach 500,000 per day (Google Financial Results Second Quarter, 2011). According to Douglas, Android is active in over 135 million devices in the word by 2011 (Douglas Perry, 2011); Justin Grove claimed that in 2012, about one third of the population owned a smartphone in the United States (US) (Justin Grove, 2013). Several many other researchers have claimed that Android is the most popular OS (Eric Abent, 2014; Amit H. Choksi, Jaimin J. Sarvan & Ronak R. Vashi, 2013), and is progressively taking over the appliances market as well. Android is essentially a software stack designed specifically for mobile devices that includes an operating system, middleware and key applications. Supported by Google in 2005, today the Android OS is one of the most popular operating systems for mobile phones and mobile operators around the world. Today, the Android operating system is a world bestseller platform smartphones.

Android provides many API's (Application Programming Interfaces) for developing your own applications. The real beauty of Android lies in the fact that these APIs are available by using the Java,

Figure 1. Wordwide smartphone shipments, Q4 2012 (Blue Android developers, 2013)

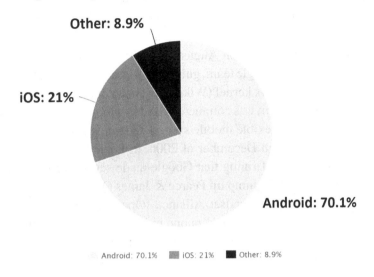

which is one of the most used programming languages. Furthermore, Android features a Plug-in for the Integrated Development Environment (IDE) Eclipse, making it easy to develop and debug your applications on a virtual emulator as well as on real hardware. It is also possible to create your own native C/C++ library and accessing it from within the Java context.

The future potential of this operating system is limitless. Google has the futuristic ambition and the funds to take Android to unprecedented heights. In many areas, such as predicting the future needs and wants of users (for example, Google Now knows that in the morning you're getting ready for work and will inform you of the current status of traffic), they have already surpassed the electronics giant, Apple. Android has already posted impressive figures which prove that Android has become the number one operating system in a number of areas. Also, according to Blue Android developers (Blue Android developers, 2013), as of the fourth tax quarter of 2012 (Q4 2012), Android owns 52% of the US mobile market share and an astounding 70% globally as depicted in Figure 1. Of course, these numbers fluctuate regularly, but it is inarguable that Android has had dominance in the worldwide global market share for quite some time now.

While addressing attendees at the Google I/O developer conference, Hugo Barra, Google's Android VP of product management (Google I/O developer's conference in San Francisco, 2014), has said that, as of May 2013, there have been 900 million Android devices that have been activated. 900 million is an impressive number, considering that Android was at 400 million activations just one year prior; this represents an increase of 500 million more activations in a single calendar year.

1.3. History

Android Inc. was founded in Palo Alto, California in October 2003 by Nick Sears, Rich Miner Chris White and Andy Rubin to develop smarter mobile devices that are more aware of their owner's location and preferences. The initial intention of the Android Company was to produce an operating system for cameras. However it realized that the market for the devices was not large enough; and thus its efforts were diverted to developing a Mobile OS to rival those of Windows Mobile and Symbian (Chris Welch, 2013).

Android Inc. was acquired by Google on August 17, 2005, with their employees and thus, Google entered the smartphones market. A Google team, guided by Rubin (Chris Welch, 2013), created a mobile platform which was based on the Linux kernel (Wikipedia encyclopedia, 2011; Open Handset Alliance, 2007; Elinux, 2011). The new platform was commercialized by Google to mobile makers with the objective of producing an upgradeable, flexible mobile system. Google's aspiration to enter the smartphone market continued to increase through December of 2006. In September 2007, Information Week and Moco News in their studies they confirming that Google made several patent applications in the field of telephony (Claburn Thomas, 2007; Jump up Pearce & James Quintana, 2007).

On November 5, 2007, the Open Handset Alliance (Open Handset Alliance, 2009), a group of companies including Google Company, a set of phone manufacturers; telephone operators and chipset manufacturers came together to develop open standards for mobile phones. Android was unveiled that day as the first product, a platform based on the Linux 2.6.25 kernel (Open Handset Alliance Press release, 2007; Elinux, 2011).

Android system has known many improvements and updates since 2008 including new features and additional bug fixes. Several versions have been realized and named in alphabetical order. For example, the 1.0 version named Apple pie and released in November 11, 2007 was followed by Bananas split on October 22, 2008 following which came the version Cupcake on April 30, 2009, and so on. The latest version is 4.4.4 Kitkat released on June 19, 2014 (Android history from Android official website, 2014).

The table below shows Android versions and their released date (Ali waqas, 2011; Jason Kincaid, 2011; Cory Gunther, 2011; Google, 2013):

Table 1. Android released versions

Version	Code Name	Released Date
1.0	Apple pie	11 November 2007
1.1	Bananas split	22 October 2008
1.5	Cupcake	30 April 2009
1.6	Donut	15 September 2009
2.0	Eclair	26 October 2009
2.2.x	Froyo	6 May 2010
2.3.x	Gingerbread	6 December 2010
3.x.x	Honeycomb	22 February 2011
4.0.X	Ice Cream Sandwich	19 October 2011
4.1.x	Jelly Bean	9 July 2012
4.2.x	Jelly Bean	13 November 2012
4.3.x	Jelly Bean	24 July 2013
4.4.x	Kitkat	31 October 2013
5.0	Lollipop	15 October 2014

Figure 2. Android architecture

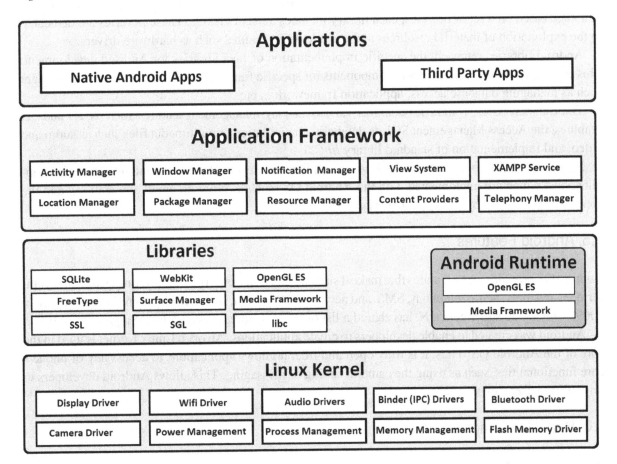

1.4. Android Architecture

Android is an operating system for mobile platforms, it is architected as a set of layers as shown in the figure 2. These layers include: Applications, Application framework, Libraries, android run-time and finally Linux Kernel. They are well organized and integrated for mobile phone development needs (Techopedia an Overview of the Andorid Architecture, 2014).

The Linux kernel is the layer that provides communication between the mobile hardware and the other layers that constitute the Android system. This core offers advanced features such as multitasking, memory management and feeding, the drivers for the hardware: Wi-Fi, audio, display ... etc (Techopedia an Overview of the Andorid Architecture, 2014).

The Android system is provided by the multitasking functionality as previously indicated. Every Android application is assumed as a process, it runs an instance of Dalvik virtual machine. The use of the Dalvik virtual machine for running applications has many benefits (Techopedia an Overview of the Andorid Architecture, 2014). The Android virtual machine was developed by Google and it is more powerful than the Java machine virtual. Dalvik represents a key component in the Android OS.

Developers generally use the java language to develop Android applications. Java is an object-oriented language based on a set of libraries; each library includes a list of classes. These libraries are dedicated to the exploitation of material resources and provide other features such as hardware drivers.

Android libraries represent the specific implementation of Java libraries for Android development. This category only includes the basic components for specific functionality to the Android environment such as managing database access, application framework ... etc.

The Standard C\C++ libraries contains various display management features such as 2D and 3D graphics, the Access Management SQLite database, manipulation of multimedia files such as audio and video, and implementation of standard library *libC*.

In the top of Android OS stack we find the applications layer. This layer contain both default applications, which are implemented with the Android OS (such as browser, email application), and the applications installed by the user (such as games).

1.5. Android Features

Android OS provides many features that make it suitable for business purposes; it is equipped with several services and tools such as telephony, SMS, and networks (Bluetooth, wi-fi, NFC) (Open Handset Alliance, 2009). Omogiade and Stephen N. has shared a list of those features (Omogiade & Stephen N., 2014).

Android was created to enable developers to create applications. An open Linux Kernel is used in the core of the Android OS. Thus, it is truly open and free; it allows applications to access any of phone's core functionalities, such as using the camera, calling or messaging. This allows Android developers to improve the user's experience.

1.6. Benefits of Android

Android has established itself by its simplicity of use and flexibility. One does not need to be technologically savvy to operate an Android. For example to transfer music files on an Android smartphone, simply connect it to a computer, as with a USB key. No software is required.

Android devices are delivered with a set of preinstalled application tools, such as Google play, which is a default application that comes with any device running Android and that is relevant both users and developers. Since it is a centralization of all applications in one point, Google play allows users to install and share applications. Also, Google play Store Application can get the Android version of the device in which installed, and fetch applications which are compatible with this version (Android Developers Security Tips, 2014). According to Boy Genius research (Boy Genius, 2012), nowadays, Android devices have become necessary for both daily life and business. It has become the most popular device in the smartphone market (Wikipedia Android Operating System, 2011).

Android is equipped with security features incorporated with the operating system to reduce applications impact. According to Jitin Narang (Jitin Narang, 2013), another notable advantage of Android devices is its multimedia capabilities.

2. Use of Android

2.1. The Evolution of Android Use

Android is an Operating System that has developed significantly in the last 15 years. Starting from monochrome image phones to recent smartphones or mini computers, mobile OS has come a long way since its debut according to Engineers Garage Report (What is Android, 2012). Impressively, Mobile OS has successfully evolved from Palm OS in 1996, to Windows pocket PC in 2000, then to Blackberry OS, and now to Android. Android is one of the most widely used mobile OS these days.

There have been a number of updates to the original release to build new versions with new functionalities and features. All devices running Android benefit from the access to Google's services such as Google Search, Google Maps, Gmail, Youtube and more. Users can simply get data and information from the internet, get directions, manage emails, etc. It is like a computer but has more advanced features claims Alex Todd (Alex Todd, 2014). Nowadays, devices running Android exist in many hundreds of thousands. In October 2012 one third of the USA population owned a smartphone according to Justin Grove (Justin Grove, 2013). Also, Android system demonstrates a gain of 53.6% in the smartphone market claims Justin Grove. Some USA organizations have transitioned from existing smartphones, such as Blackberry, to Android. A research (Markets and Markets, 2012) shows that those organizations offer their employees the option of using their own personal smartphones under the Bring Your Own Device policy.

2.2. Use Outside of Tablets and Smartphones

The simplicity and openness of the Android operating system allows it to run on other devices and electronics equipment, such as laptops, smart television (Google TV), digital cameras (Galaxy Camera), smart books (Bogdan Petrovan, 2012). The Android OS can be found on smart glasses, car CD players, game consoles and more. A home automation technology was announced by Google a few years ago Android@home demonstration. An Android car system called Asteroid was unveiled by Parrot in 2011. Some automobile makers built a car entertainment system based on Android OS. In March 18, 2014, the development of a new smart watch called Android Wear had been announced by Google.

2.3. Android on Robotics

Google also ventured into the robotics field with Andy Rubin. Seeing that the popularity of robotics nowadays has greatly increased, and the demand for intelligent robots has grown, robots hardware and software architecture has gained complexity. S. Goebel, et al. claims that it is believed that smartphones with high power capacities and sensing capabilities offer inexpensive and better performing platforms for robotics (S. Goebel, et al. 2010).

Robot-based Androids have become increasingly accessible and popular; several of these projects provide cars that are remote-controlled (R/C) or other robot-based Androids by using IOIO or other boards such as Arduino, raspberry Pi…etc.

Table 2. Smartphones based on robotic projects

Robot/Project Name	Cost
Cellbots	$30 to $300 (estimations)
Robots Everywhere	unknown
Collection of IOIO based projects	$100 to $400 (estimations)
IOIO based sailing boat	$1200 (phone included)
IOIO based search and rescue robot	unknown
Android based Soccer Robot	unknown
Collection of Arduino based projects	$200 to $700 (estimations)
The Android Car	$200
NASA - MIT SPHERES	unknown
NASA PhoneSats	$3500-$7000 (phone included)
MIT DragonBot	$1000 (phone included)
GEORGIA TECH project	unknown
Brain-controlled robot	unknown
Visual obstacle avoidance	unknown
Android Based Robotic Platform	$350
Romo	$149
Botiful	S299
Wheelphone	S215 (+45$ for docking station)
Shimi	S200
Double	S2499
Albert	unknown
iRiverKibot	$40 (+ $30/month 2 years KT)

Robot-based Androids are becoming a dominant subject in research projects, table 2 groups a set of robot-based Androids. Many other robots are developed with an Android device (Teyvonia Thomas, 2012; Y. Ji-Dong et al., 2010; A. Albin et al., 2012; S. Goebel et al., 2012; C. Zhang et al., 2012)

As depicted in the table 2, there are many smartphones based on robotics projects, which use smartphones to control and/or monitor the robot: hobbyists/students and/or open source (top), research (middle), commercial (bottom). Both the Android Car and the Android-Based Robotic Platform were completed at the Cognitive Anteater Robotics Laboratory, University of California Irvine (Nicolas Oros, Jeffrey L. Krichmar, 2013).

3. General Business Applications

3.1. Introduction

Today, in business it is necessary to have access to documents and services everywhere and at all times. Smartphones have improved users experiences and have offered new options to users for business purposes. We will present a set of popular applications which help users stay in touch with their business.

While Android is indeed becoming more and more popular by the minute, it has yet to become the platform businesses rely on for their mobile needs. In this chapter, some of the best applications for general office and business use will be discussed, such as documents tools, printing, e-mail management, etc.

Table 3. Document tools for Android

App Name	Notes
Docs to Go	Includes all documents functionalities: Word, Excel and PowerPoint.
Office Suite Viewer	It has a trial version of 30-days and a paid version: it allows the reading and editing of all Microsoft Office files and also PDF documents.
Think Free Office	It has more sophisticated functionalities, such as an integrated file browser, Google Docs manipulation and it supports all document extensions.
Quick office Pro	It is similar to Think Free office; includes Word documents processing, Excel viewer, PDF viewer and PowerPoint files. It allows users to access their files from Dropbox, Google Docs… etc.
Adobe Reader	The Adobe Reader, like the desktop software powered by Adobe, allows the reading of PDF documents locally or from the Web.

3.2. Business Applications

3.2.1. Document Tools

If one works in an office, one is inevitably going to deal with documents. To the convenience of businesses, Androids have capabilities to interact with Microsoft products and thus facilitate office work and information management.

At the time of this publication, there had been no documented solution to reading OneNote on Android. That may be changed in the future but for now the use of Evernote is recommended instead.

Table 3 shows some of the most used apps for business purposes according to Marziah Karch (Marziah Karch, 2010).

3.2.2. Printing

Document printing is presently a necessary feature in businesses for the safeguarding and sharing of documents and the possibility of printing directly from a smartphone should greatly facilitate these tasks. There are some applications dedicated for printing functionalities and Print is one of them, it allows you to print your files easily (photos, document, emails, contact…etc). Another similar printing application is Printer Share.

Some applications are presented in Table 4.

3.2.3. File Management

Not only is it great to be able to view or edit document attachments, but also it is rather convenient to be able to know where those files are stored on the SD card without having to connect the phone to a

Table 4. Printing tools for Android

App Name	Notes
Printer Share Droid Print	Use the free trial and test-print before committing to a purchase. Be aware that it does not support Microsoft Office files but photos and PDF are supported.
Print	Print to ALL printers via your Mac/PC.

Table 5. File Management tools for Android

App Name	Notes
File Expert	A free application for managing files stored locally or in cloud storage services; also, it has capability for FTP servers accessing.
Dropbox	An application powered by Dropbox (see their web page to get more details www.dropbox.com). It allows users to access files stored on the Web and sharing files by sending download links.
ES File Manager	ES File Explorer is a file management application with features such as tasks viewer, FTP files access and more.

computer in order to do basic file management tasks. Android gives users complete control over the files on their phone/tablet or SD Card.

File Expert, one of the most preferred applications for file management, has an attractive graphical user interface with a set of features which enclose the majority of tools needed to browse and manipulate your files. For those who want to root their devices and ROMs changing, the Root Explorer is recommended Ashish Bogawat (Ashish Bogawat, 2010).

Here's a list of most file management apps for Android in no particular order. They all have their own proper advantages and user interfaces, depending on the desired style of file management (Table 5).

3.2.4. Virus Protection, Backups, and Security

Viruses are small scripts that are designed to spread from one infected device to another and to interfere with the functioning of the host device. Securing devices becomes a need today if it is to be used for business purposes, thus the importance of installing antivirus software on smartphones. A set of antivirus will be presented in the following section beginning with the most used one Avast Mobile Security according to Simon Hill (Simon Hill, 2014). This software includes a range of functionalities for data protection against viruses.

The following table summarizes the most popular free security apps for Android in no particular order (Table 6).

3.2.5. Presentation Software

Most document management software listed earlier can handle viewing PowerPoint files. Rarely will one need to present a slideshow from an Android phone, however if that is the case Docs to Go or the slideshow feature in the phone's gallery can be utilized. It is believed that including presentation tools

Table 6. Android security Apps

App Name	Notes
Avast! Mobile Security	Avast is the most used antivirus application; it contains a range of functionalities for data protection against viruses.
Avira	Avira allows the scanning of files; it is equipped with a wide range of options and functionalities for virus protection.
Norton Security beta	It is a full release application for virus scanning. It has an anti-theft component like Avira; it can remotely lock the device.

Table 7. Presentation applications for Android

App Name	Notes
Mighty Meeting	This app supports some presentation extensions like PowerPoint and Keynote from the device. (www.mightymeeting.com)
Slide Rocket	This application includes high capabilities for your presentations. Slide editing on this app is comparable to PowerPoint.
Gmote 2.0	Gmote is like a Wi-Fi remote control for your PC that allows sharing files between devices and PC's. It can be used to show PowerPoint presentations from a mobile device.

with smartphones is necessary nowadays. Some Android devices equipped with TV out capabilities to show videos and images, like HTC EVO; also there are other new technologies developed which allow users to use portable projectors which work with the same connectors as TV.

A list of most popular presentation applications are presented in Table 7.

3.2.6. Email Management

Android has very capable native options for email, but in the corporate world more than what comes in the Android box may be needed. According to Joel Lee (Joel Lee, 2013) smartphone addiction contributed to the ability to manage and receive e-mail instantaneously. Receiving email and notifications in your device is crucial to stay in touch with one's business. The most preferred application for email management is Gmail powered by Google Company. It offers a very impressive interface (close to the standard Web application https://mail.google.com) and emails notifications functionalities.

3.2.7. Expenses and Finance

Similarly to how convenient email management facilitate the users' daily life and business management, managing expenses and financial operations anytime, anywhere greatly increases productivity as well. There are some applications dedicated to aid financial management and improve user's experience.

According to Abhimanyu Ghoshal (Abhimanyu Ghoshal, 2013) Financius with a simple interface that is easy to learn, allows the making of transactions quickly, and categorizes expenses to visualize spending on organized charts.

Whether you are clueless as to where your salary disappeared before the month ended, or want to save a certain sum of money for a much-desired or necessary purchase, firing up any of these creative and secure apps is a promising first step towards financial awareness.

3.2.8. Travel

For those who often travel for work, it is rewarding to appreciate and adopt the using of applications dedicated to tracking location, flights and mileage. Google Maps, a default application available with Android, which comes with a high capability of locating places and providing directions. In this section some of the aforementioned exploration applications will be presented.

According to Devine Richard (Devine Richard Devine, 2014), TripIt is somewhat of a no-brainer tool for frequent travelers as its usefulness eliminates the concerns and pronounced preparations travelers experience when traveling to new locations.

3.3. Summary

Given its popularity, Android has become the platform of choice for software producers. Thus, the Google Play store is full of powerful applications that can transform your business. Some of the selected applications that have been presented have become essential in the business context, however it must be noted that there exist many other great apps for Android.

ANDROID FOR AUTOMATED ENTERPRISE SYSTEMS

1. Enterprise Adoption

1.1. Smartphone's Change Workforce IT Requirements

1.1.1. The Mobile Workforce

Today, smartphones and tablets are spreading all over the world. Consumers have adopted these devices for personal use such as sending and receiving data, storing information and running software. Added to this, these devices are powerful engines in the fuelling of business progress. They are equipped with greater functionalities which facilitate communication in remote areas and organize tasks more efficiently claims the Enterprise Management Associates Inc. in its Research report (Enterprise Management Associates Inc., 2011). According to Principia, The National Computing Center (The National Computing Center, 2006) the uses of mobile phone in enterprise are numerous and offer benefits to the personnel and the enterprise. It aids with establishing time schedules in order to organize daily meetings, and helps persons to be more productive and efficient amongst many other benefits reported by Simon Aspinall and Anja Jacquin Langer in their book (Simon Aspinall and Anja Jacquin Langer, 2005). Furthermore, through smartphone application development, investigator can publicize their products in easier and more efficient ways.

The mobile device use diminishes the time lapse between the customer's requests and the business' response. It improves the satisfaction of customers and brightens business image according to Strategic Growth Concepts news (Strategic Growth Concepts, 2014). Additionally, the competition between enterprises in the marketplace increases when employees use mobile tools to reply to requests of customers at the moment of matter claims Greg Gianforte in the Oracle white paper (Greg Gianforte, 2012).

1.1.2. Enterprise Mobile Device Management

Because of the growing credence on mobile devices to contribute to business success, it is important to ensure that these devices are secure and reliable. At the very least, the same security elements found on desktops should be present on mobile devices if not more. Nonetheless, it is not easy to adapt these functionalities with mobile devices. Also the small dimensions and the characteristics of mobile devices can become an obstacle for the management of the enterprise mobile devices according to the Enterprise Management Associates Inc. in its Research report (Enterprise Management Associates Inc., 2011).

Unfortunately, the implementation of management services nowadays pertaining to mobile phones is not as easy as it seems. There are differences between desktop platforms and mobile running operating systems; mobile devices have some limitations that are not found on computers.

Numerous solutions have been proposed in the market to achieve mobile management objectives. With increasing requirements for the use of mobile devices, however there are several organizations that have changed towards the implementation of new management systems that are able to support at once a variety of terminals and include several services automation according to the Enterprise Management Associates Inc. in its Research report (Enterprise Management Associates Inc., 2011).

1.1.3. Mobile Device Adoption

According to the Technology Coast Consulting and Galvin Consulting Mobile research (Technology Coast Consulting and Galvin Consulting Mobile, 2010), in the next few years, mobile workers will see a specific growth reaching over 100 millions workers. Nowadays, thousands of workers use their personal smartphones to access company database and applications, some of these were sanctioned by their respective enterprises and others are not. Another research, Enterprise Management Associates (Enterprise Management Associates Inc., 2011), shows that roughly 70% of enterprises nowadays employ smartphones in their workforce for certain uses. To implement a solution, platform diversity represents the first consideration.

There are some constraints that limit support needs, such as imposing restricted endpoints that support a few platform types, but this is not usually due to some enterprises allowing employees to use their own personal smartphones. Nonetheless, identifying the most used platforms overall can help to get the optimal solution for management.

As depicted in Figure 3, there is a correlation between the size of an organization and mobile phone adoptions. Blackberry is adopted for large organizations but Android is dominating in organizations of smaller size. Blackberry was adopted because it was the only viable solution at that time. Today, organizations tend to change more and more towards the Android platform according to several research (Douglas Perry, 2011; Felix Richter, 2014; Jennifer Lynn, 2014).

Figure 3. Smartphone platform adoption by organization size

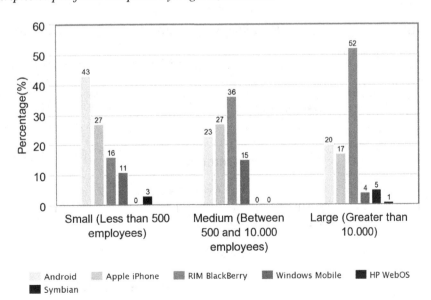

According to Ernst & Young (Ernst & Young, 2012), Android and iPhone devices are adopted for small businesses and extend into medium size companies as well. Android is the most popular platform for small organizations due to the low cost of Android running devices. Since many affordable mobile makers, such as HTC and Samsung, use Android OS for their devices according to the Enterprise Management Associates Inc. in its Research report (Enterprise Management Associates Inc., 2011).

A clear indicator of the dedicated mobile platform is the organization size although the service type of the industry can have an impact too; Figure 4 shows smartphone adoption in the industry classified by service type. Android is most adopted in consulting, telecommunication and professional services; Blackberry is popular in governmental and healthcare institutions; Iphone is the most adopted for educational institutions.

Figure 4. Smartphone platform adoption by industry type (Enterprise Management Associates, Inc., 2011)

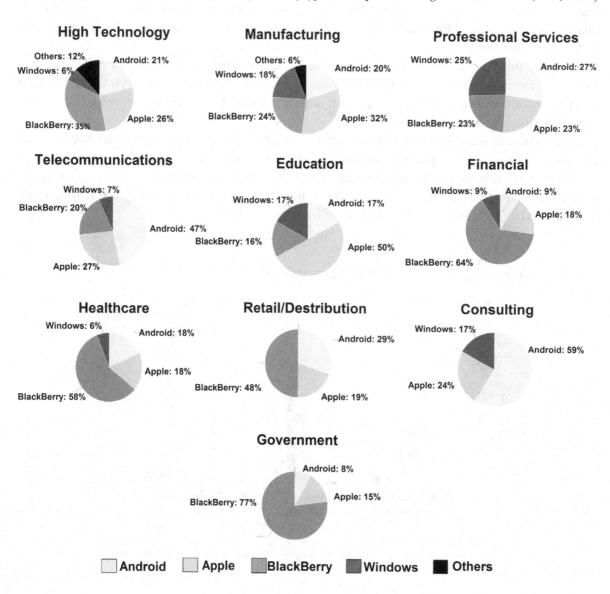

Some organizations have adopted BYOD programs reported in several researches (Vangie Beal, 2014; Capital Network Solution, 2013). Bring your own device will be discussed in details in the last section.

1.2. The Utility of Android on Industry

1.2.1. Introduction

Android is now said to be present on more than 135 million active devices. According to Google, 550,000 Androids are being activated every day and there has been more than 6 billion App downloads claims Douglas Perry (Douglas Perry, 2011). Google is categorizing Android as a high consumer success product, next to Chrome and YouTube. Google's current CEO and cofounder, Larry Page noted that the company is heavily investing in those segments to ensure their long-term success. Moreover, Android appears to be growing at phenomenal rates, as the activation count was at 500,000 per day just a month ago, and the total device count was at just 100 million two months ago. Google also noted that more than 250,000 apps are now available for Android. The industry needs a platform that enables employees to access their information and stay notified by emails and notifications for updates anytime and anywhere, the same needs have also been manifested by customers. Many studies show the utility of smartphones in the industry (Vangie Beal, 2014; Strategic Growth Concepts, 2014; Jennifer Lynn, 2014).

Android offers numerous services for companies, such as products publishing, events notifications and person management. It ensures connectivity between company employees, regular customers and other persons in relation with the company. Workers can use social networks, such as Twitter and LinkedIn, to stay connected with others. Android is an interactive platform that allows users to share business information, For example getting immediate customer feedback on products helps companies with their research for developing and improving their products, also this gives customers a feeling of direct impact in the process of product development.

1.2.2. Industrial Projects Based on Android

In today's world, marketing demands are increasing continuously. And to maintain a reputable position in the competitive market, businesses seek to satisfy these demands effectively and rapidly.

Android has been used in numerous products, such as mobile phones, tablet, TVs, etc (Bogdan Petrovan, 2012; Jerry Hildenbrand, 2014). The BieMme Italia (BieMme Italia, 2014) developed a new android-based touch panel, it supports Linux, Android, and WinCE6 technologies. Researchers at the University of North Western Switzerland (Manuel Di C. & Andreas R., 2010) are working on an Android platform for industrial automation. A prototype enterprise monitoring systems for Android has been developed by Justin Grove (Justin Grove, 2013). Micro Tronics Technologies (Development group) (Micro Tronics Technologies, 2014) developed many android-based prototypes for industrial device controlling, security, and monitoring. Currently, more than 600,000 applications were shared in Google Play. Often times, Android applications were favoured by enterprise organizations according to Google I/O developer's conference in San Francisco (Google I/O developer's conference in San Francisco, 2014).

1.3. Android Enterprise Adoption

Android enterprise adoption will know an impressive growth in the next few years according to Eric Abent (Eric Abent, 2013) and Scott Scolomon (Scott Scolomon, 2014). It was less secure in the past but

Figure 5. Worldwide smartphone market share, by operating system

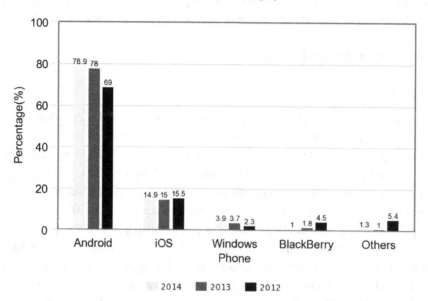

now manufacturer's focus on security concerns; they work to strengthen the security of Android operation systems. A research of Neil Florio (Neil Florio, 2012) shows that Android is the most dominant system today, 60% of consumers use Android as a favourite system. As depicted in the figure below, Android is the most dominant operating system in the market.

1.4. Enterprise Security and Productivity Features

Google aims to gain the attention of more companies by adding new security and productivity features to its next Android operating systems, claimed Chris Martin (Chris Martin, 2014). Google has detailed *Android L* at its I/O 2014 developer conference, providing information concerning its release date, version number, material design, and new security and productivity features aimed at enterprise users.

Many Android OS features that enhance enterprise devices security and productivity have been depicted and discussed in several researches (Tim Skutt & Wind River, 2014; Chris Martin, 2014; Muneer Ahmad Dar & Javed Parvez, 2014; MaaS360 by Fiberlink, 2012).

1.5. Enterprise Resource Planning (ERP) with Android

ERP (Enterprise Resource Planning) is a software package centralizing on data and business management functions. An ERP system consists of different modules, each corresponding to a particular function in a business. Since using general business applications with Android has grown many companies have built Android compatible ERP mobile software. For example, one of the most known enterprises, SysPro Company (SysPro Impact Software Inc., 2014) has developed an application named SysPro Espresso for Android devices. SysPro Espresso is a complete business solution that allows the managing of a workforce and offers secure access to business information.

Another ERP solution powered by Enterprise IQMS mobile technologies allows users to manage their enterprise whenever and wherever (IQMS Mobile ERP Apps for Manufacturing Companies, 2014).

1.6. Android MRP Software

Material requirements planning (MRP) is an alternative method of replenishing the stocks. It predicts the timing of product use from technical and commercial data according to Wikipedia (Wikipedia Material Requirement Planning, 2014).

Today, Many MRP mobile solutions have been developed, Some Android MRP software can be used to manage and control enterprise information. One of these software is NetSuite (NetSuite Inc., 2015) it is developed for both Android and PC platforms and it offers a complete solution for management. Also, there is another popular MRP for Android, xTuple (xTuple, 2015) business management software.

2. BYOD for Industrial Control and Automation

2.1. Introduction

BYOD programs are usually implemented to improve customer satisfaction and employees productivity. However, their success depends on the clear separation between, firstly, applications and business data, and secondly, the personal information stored on the device as well as the confidentiality of personal data (Vangie Beal, 2014; Tdavid Kleidermacher, 2013) since enterprises which allow the use of personal devices cannot support bringing unmanaged devices.

2.2. What Is BYOD?

2.2.1. BYOD (Bring Your Own Device)

In IT development, Bring Your Owen Device is a policy that has been widely adopted by organizations. It is designed to allow end users to use their personal mobile devices - smart phones or tablets - for business and professional purposes according to Capital Network Solution (Capital Network Solution, 2013). Employees nowadays, who do use their own devices (smartphones and tablets) at work, incited the need for BYOD security as a concern for IT equipment. Many organizations make BYOD security policy as a constraint in the allowance of the use of personal devices at work claims Vangie Beal (Vangie Beal, 2014); this help companies to ensure the safe and efficient management of these devices.

2.2.2. BYOD Security

Addressing BYOD Security is a constraint to adopt the program. Corporations must have detailed information and security purposes for all types of used devices in the workplace. For example, a login system authentication must be installed in these devices, or limit the activities of employees who use these devices at work; all of these measures represent considerations for the development of the BYOD Security policy according Vangie Beal (Vangie Beal, 2014).

2.3. Issues and Impact

Control systems and industrial automation show the need for devices that contain both entertainment tools for public use and professional tools for mobile workers. Employees can use smart devices to get inventory information, notified by product updates or communicate with each other. According to RTC Magazine (RTC Magazine, 2013) and Opto 22 (Wikipedia Opto 22, 2014) the use of mobile devices in industrial control, automation and setting increased; this is demonstrated by the out of an Android application: Opto 22 manufactures controllers, for industrial control and automation.

There is a specific requirement when using mobile devices at work; employees must install a mobile device management (MDM) solution, also they are limited in their use of specific functionalities claims Tdavid K. in his article published by RTC Magazine (RTC Magazine, 2013).

2.4. Multiple Persona

BYOD solutions are more comfortable when people do not face restrictions (Tdavid K., 2013; Omer Eiferman, 2014). Adopting multi-persona approach will eliminate obstacles for users and IT anxiety. Multi-persona consists in making separations between personal and professional information, in other word, making a single device divided into separated virtual environments claims Omer Eiferman. It is flexible, easy to use and understand and some commercial examples include AT&T Toggle and VMware Horizon claims Tdavid K. These commercial solutions benefit of the advantages related to the use of the native Android sandboxing as shown in Figure 6.

The figure above shows that the operating system is the manager (Android in this case), it is the most fertile region in the solution architecture.

Figure 6. Application-level sandboxes

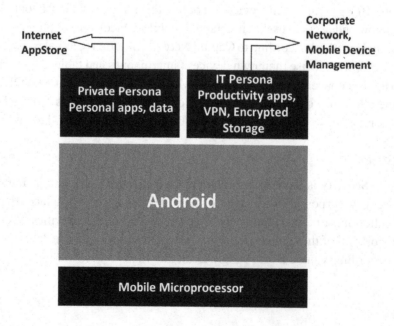

There are nonetheless some constraints with the adoption of the multi-persona solutions (Tdavid Kleidermacher, 2013; Wikipedia Opto 22, 2014).

2.5. Virtualization Alternatives

Virtualisation is a great tool suited for BYOD programs adoption claims Roberta Prescott in his research published by RCR Wireless News (Roberta Prescott, 2014). He also reported that virtualized solutions allow the maintenance of applications and data at home, or inside enterprise boundaries, independently of the platform used for access. Connectivity represent a negatively impact for virtualization. When virtualization is used, adapting and updating network infrastructure become even more relevant. Many architectures of multi-persona concept are proposed by Tdavid K. (Tdavid Kleidermacher, 2013) to enhance the separation between industrial and personal domain.

Nowadays a recent BYOD solution was put in place to combine the power of multimedia as well as application deployment infrastructure to control the systems services while protecting the workplace environment.

GENERAL CONCLUSION

Android is an open source mobile operating system. It is equipped with a rich tool chain and it is supported by a powerful hardware architecture; these features make Android a great candidate for industrial and business purposes. It can be easily controlled from anywhere and in flexible and secure ways. Critical data can be monitored and devices can be controlled through Android smartphones through secure equipment with no worries about the confidentiality, integrity, or availability of your control network system.

Android might be suited for applications in which a wide variety of features such as easy interface, wireless connectivity and sophisticated programs, are needed. Moreover, programming with the Java language improves developers experience and makes Android platform very attractive to be used in entirely new areas since the Java language puts to disposal all ready APIs thus facilitating the creation and development of applications according to specific and changing needs.

Many mobile companies such as HTC, Samsung, Motorola, Sony Ericsson, etc. have already released their Android devices. Many industrial automation projects that are Android-based have been developed. Ever since, the Android system is no longer dedicated for mobile phones only; it is integrated in several other systems, such as TVs, watches, automobiles, robots, etc. due to its flexibility, simplicity and stability. It allows for the development of an embedded system which benefits all the Android powerful tools, or the development of the applications desired by the users.

Android offers numerous services for companies, such as products publishing, events notifications and personal management. It ensures connectivity between company employees, regular customers and other persons in relation with the company; workers can use social networks to stay connected with others, such as Twitter and LinkedIn. Also, many MRP and ERP professional solutions compatible with Android have been created.

REFERENCES

Abent, E. (2013, November 18). *Android Enterprise Adoption Set to Grow Significantly In Coming Years According to ABI Research.* [Blog post]. Retrieved from http://www.androidheadlines.com/2013/11/android-enterprise-adoption-set-grow-significantly-coming-years-according-abi-research.html

Albin, A. (2012, October 12). Musical abstractions in distributed multi-robot systems. *Presented at the Intelligent Robots and Systems (IROS), 2012 IEEE/RSJ International Conference on 2012.* doi:10.1109/IROS.2012.6385688

Alliance, O. H. (2007, November 5). *Industry Leaders Announce Open Platform for Mobile Device.* Open Handset Alliance, Press release. Retrieved from http://www.openhandsetalliance.com/press_110507.html

Andrici, M. (2014, February 3). 8 Best Android App options to launch your productivity. *Joy of Android News.* Retrieved from http://joyofandroid.com/best-android-email-app/

Android Developers. (2014). Security Tips. *Android Developers Training.* Retrieved from http://developer.android.com/training/articles/security-tips.html

Android Official Web Site. (2014). Android history. *Android official web site.* Retrieved from http://www.android.com/history/

Aspinall, S., & Langer, A. J. (2005). Connected Workforce: Essays from innovators in business mobility. In Connected Workforce. Premium Publishing.

Beal, V. (2014). *BYOD: Bring Your Owen Device.* [Blog post]. Retrieved from http://www.webopedia.com/TERM/B/BYOD.html

BieMme Italia. (2014). Android Hmi Multi Touch Panels. *BieMme Italia WebSite.* Retrieved from http://www.biemmeitalia.net/android-hmi multi-touch/

Blue Android Developers. (2013). *Android a Mobile Operating System.* [Blog post]. Retrieved from http://myblueandroid.weebly.com/

Brasen, S. (2011, October 17). *Enterprise Mobile Device Management: How Smartphones and Tablets are Changing Workforce IT Requirements.* Enterprise Management Associates, Inc. Research Report –End-user. Retrieved from http://www.enterprisemanagement.com/research/asset.php/2101/Enterprise-Mobile-Device-Management:-How-Smartphones-and-Tablets-are-Changing-Workforce-IT-Requirements

Capital Network Solution. (2013, January). *Bring Your Owen Device.* [Blog post]. Retrieved from http://www.capitalnetworks.co.uk/news/2013/01/14/bring-your-own-device/

Choksi, Sarvan & Vashi. (2013, June). Implementation and Direct Accessing of Android Authority Application in Smart Phones. *International Journal of Application or Innovation in Engineering & Management, 2*(6).

Claburn, T. (2007, September 19). Google's Secret Patent Portfolio Predicts gPhone. *Information Week News.* Retrieved from http://www.informationweek.com/googles-secret-patent-portfolio-predicts-gphone/d/d-id/1059389

Technology Coast Consulting and Galvin Consulting Mobile Report. (2010, December). *Smartphones in the US enterprise.* A report published in December 2010. Technology Coast Consulting and Galvin Consulting Mobile.

Dar & Parvez. (2014, April). A Novel Strategy to Enhance the Android Security Framework. *International Journal of Computer Applications, 91*(8).

Developers, A. (n.d.). Android, the World's Most Popular Mobile Platform. *Android Developers.* Retrieved from http://developer.android.com/about/index.html

Devine, R. (2014, May 12). *The best travel apps for Android.* [Blog post]. Retrieved from http://www.androidcentral.com/best-android-travel-apps

Eiferman, O. (2014, June 6). With BYOD, You Don't Have to Choose Between Productivity and Security. *IT Briefcase: IT News, Research & Events.* Retrieved from http://www.itbriefcase.net/byod-dont-choose-between-productivity-and-security

Elinux. (2011, July 7). Android Kernel Versions. *Elinux.org.* Retrieved from http://elinux.org/Android_Kernel_Versions

Ernst & Young. (2012, January). *Mobile device security, Understanding vulnerabilities and managing risk.* Insights on governance, risk and compliance. Retrieved from http://www.ey.com/Publication/vwLUAssets/EY_Mobile_security_devices/$FILE/EY_Mobile%20security%20devices.pdf

Florio, N. (2012, November 17). *Enterprise Android Adoption.* [Blog post]. Retrieved from http://techcrunch.com/2012/11/17/will-android-adoption-become-a-dream-or-nightmare-for-cios/

Garage, E. (2012). *What is Android.* [Blog post]. Retrieved from http://www.engineersgarage.com/articles/what-is-android-introduction

Genius, B. (2012, June 28). *Benefits of Android OS.* [Blog post]. Retrieved from http://boygenius.hubpages.com/hub/Benefits-of-Android-OS

Ghoshal, A. (2013, May 13). 10 Gorgeous Personal Finance Apps for Tablets. *AppStorm News.* Retrieved from http://android.appstorm.net/roundups/finance-roundups/10-gorgeous-personal-finance-apps-for-tablets/

Gianforte, G. (2012, February). *Seven Power Lessons for Customer Experience Leaders.* Oracle Customer Relationship Management.

Goebel, S. (2012). Using the Android Platform to control Robots. In *Proceedings of 2nd International Conference on Robotics in Education* (RiE 2011). Austrian Society for Innovative Computer Sciences.

Google. (2011, July 14). *Google Announces Second Quarter 2011 Financial Results.* Google Inc. Retrieved from http://investor.google.com/earnings/2011/Q2_google_earnings.html

Google. (2013, September 18). *Android KitKat.* Google Inc. Retrieved from http://www.android.com/versions/kit-kat-4-4/

Google. (2014). *Google I/O developer's conference in San Francisco.* Retrieved from https://www.google.com/events/io

Google I/O. (2008, May 28). Android Anatomy and Physiology. *Google I/O*. Retrieved from http://androidteam.googlecode.com/files/Anatomy-Physiology-of-an-Android.pdf

Grover. (2013, January 31). *Android forensics: Automated data collection and reporting from a mobile device*. Rochester Institute of Technology.

Gunther, C. (2011, September 9). *Android Jelly Bean up next after IceCream Sandwich*. [Blog post]. Retrieved from http://androidcommunity.com/android-jelly-bean-up-next-after-ice-cream-sandwich-20110909/

Hildenbrand, J. (2014). *Android Device Manager Other Devices*. [Blog post]. Retrieved from http://www.androidcentral.com/app/android-device-manager

IQMS. (2014). *Mobile ERP Apps for Manufacturing Companies*. IQMS Products. Retrieved from http://www.iqms.com/products/mobile-erp-software.html

Ji-Dong, Y. (2010). Development of Communication Model for Social Robots Based on Mobile Service in Social Computing (SocialCom). *IEEE Second International Conference on 2010*. doi:10.1109/SocialCom.2010.18

Kara Page. (2014). *Mobile Technology in Business*. [Blog post]. Retrieved from http://www.ehow.com/about_6391136_mobile-technology-business.html

Karch. (2010, September 1). *Android for Work, Productivity for Professionals*. Amazon.

Kincaid, J. (2011, January 12). *The Future Version Of Android Isn't Called IceCream. It's IceCream SANDWICH*. [Blog post]. Retrieved from http://techcrunch.com/2011/01/11/android-ice-cream-sandwich/

Kleidermacher. (2013, January). BYOD Industrial Control and Automation. *RTC Magazine*. Retrieved from http://www.rtcmagazine.com/articles/view/102915

Kristian, Y., Armanto, H., & Frans, M. (2012, October 9). Utilizing GPS and SMS for Tracking and Security Lock Application on Android Based Phone. *International Conference on Asia Pacific Business Innovation and Technology Management*. doi:10.1016/j.sbspro.2012.09.1189

Lee, J. (2013, February 8). *5 Excellent Email apps for android compared*. [Blog post]. Retrieved from http://www.makeuseof.com/tag/5-excellent-email-apps-for-android-compared/

Lynn, J. (2014, March 11). Android App automation. *Droid Report News*. Retrieved from http://www.droidreport.com/android-app-automation-7241

MaaS360 by Fiberlink, an IBM Company. (2012, August 15). *Does Android Dream of enterprise adoption*. White Paper published by Health IT Outcomes. Retrieved from http://www.healthitoutcomes.com/doc/does-android-dream-of-enterprise-adoption-0001

Mahapatra, L. (2013, November 11). Android Vs. iOS: What's The Most Popular Mobile Operating System In Your Country. *International Business Times*. Retrieved from http://www.ibtimes.com/android-vs-ios-whats-most-popular-mobile-operating-system-your-country-1464892

Manuel Di, C. & Andreas, R. (2010, January 29). *Using Android in Industrial Automation.* Technical Report, University of Applied Sciences North western Switzerland for the Institute of Automation. FHNW/IA, 29.01.2010.

Martin, C. (2014, July 28). *New Android L release date and new features: Chrome hints at version 4.5.* [Blog post]. Retrieved from http://drippler.com/drip/new-android-l-release-date-and-new-features-chrome-hints-version-45

Meier, R. (2010). *Professional Android 2 Application Development.* Indianapolis, IN: Wiley Publishing, Inc.

MicroTronics Technologies. (2014). *Projects of 8051.* Micro Tronics Technologies Projects. Retrieved from http://www.projectsof8051.com/

Narang, J. (2013, May 10). 5 advantages of Android OS for developing scalable Apps. *The Mobile App Development Experts.* Retrieved from http://www.techaheadcorp.com/android/5-advantages-developing-scalable/

Omogiade, S. N. (2014, March 3). *Google Android OS: World leading Mobile Operating System.* Hub Pages Inc. Retrieved from http://infotechnology.hubpages.com/hub/What-is-Google-Android-OS

Open Handset Alliance. (2009). Android overview. *Open handset alliance.* Retrieved from http://www.openhandsetalliance.com/android_overview.html

Oros, N., & Krichmar, J. L. (2013, November 26). *Android Based Robotics: Powerful, Flexible and Inexpensive Ronots for Hobbyists, Educators, Students and Researchers.* CECS Technical Report 13-16. Center for Embedded Computer Systems, University of California, Irvine. Retrieved from http://www.socsci.uci.edu/~jkrichma/ABR/

Pearce & Quintana. (2007, September 20). *Google's Strong Mobile-Related Patent Portfolio.* [Blog post]. Retrieved from https://gigaom.com/2007/09/20/419-googles-strong-mobile-related-patent-portfolio/

Perry, D. (2011, July 16). *Google Android Now on 135 Million Devices.* [Blog post]. Retrieved from http://www.tomsguide.com/us/google-android-installations-app-downloads,news-11861.html

Petrovan, B. (2012, February 26). *Android Everywhere: 10 Types of Devices That Android Is Making Better.* [Blog post]. Retrieved from http://www.androidauthority.com/android-everywhere-10-types-of-devices-that-android-is-making-better-57012/

Prescott, R. (2014, January 29). Reality Check: Virtualization can be a safe alternative for BYOD adoption. *RCR Wireless News: Intelligence on all things wireless.* Retrieved from http://www.rcrwireless.com/20130129/opinion/reality-check-virtualization-can-safe-alternative-byod-adoption

Principia, The National Computing Centre. (2006, March). *Inventing the future with mobile technologies.* Principia, National Computing Centre Oxford House.

SYSPRO Products. (2014). *What is ERP – Enterprise Resource Planning.* SYSPRO Impact Software, Inc. Retrieved from http://www.syspro.com/product/what-is-erp

Richter, F. (2014, March 4). Android to Retain Big Lead in Maturing Smartphone Market. *Statista: The Statistics Portal, Statistics and Studies.* Retrieved from http://www.statista.com/chart/1961/smartphone-market-share-2014/

Skutt, T., & River, W. (2012, October 20). *Securing Android for warfare.* UBM Canon Electronics Engineering Communities. Retrieved from http://www.embedded.com/design/safety-and-security/4398993/Securing-Android-for-warfare

Solomon, S. (2014, June 25). *Android for the enterprise: Google debuts enterprise security and productivity features.* [Blog post]. Retrieved from http://blogs.air-watch.com/2014/06/android-enterprise-google-debuts-enterprise-security-productivity-features/#.U9qfZah5N54

Solution, O. M. (2013, June 21). *7 Must have mobile applications for 2013.* Opti Matrix Solution. Retrieved from https://optiinfo.wordpress.com/category/mobile-application-development/

Strategic Growth Concepts. (2014). *Mobile Technology for Increased Productivity & Profitability.* [Blog post]. Retrieved from http://www.strategicgrowthconcepts.com/growth/increase-productivity--profitability.html

Techopedia. (2014, July 3). *An Overview of the Android Architecture.* [Blog post]. Retrieved from http://www.techotopia.com/index.php/An_Overview_of_the_Android_Architecture

Thomas, T. (2012). Visual Obstacle Avoidance using Optical Flow on the Android-powered HTC EVO for Safe Navigation of the iRobot Create. *Aspiring Robotics Projects.* Retrieved from http://teyvoniathomas.com/index.php/projects/55-opticalflow.html

Todd, A. (2014, October 23). What is Android and what is Android phone. *Recombo editorial team.* Retrieved from http://recombu.com/mobile/news/what-is-android-and-what-is-an-android-phone_M12615.html

Waqas, A. (2011, September 28). *Android 2.3.6 Gingerbread Update for Nexus S Available.* [Blog post]. Retrieved from http://www.addictivetips.com/mobile/android-2-3-6-gingerbread-update-for-nexus-s-available-wi-fi-and-tethering-fix/

Welch, C. (2013, April 16). *Before it took over smartphones, Android was originally destined for cameras.* [Blog post]. Retrieved from http://www.theverge.com/2013/4/16/4230468/android-originally-designed-for-cameras-before-smartphones

Wikipedia Encyclopedia. (2011, 3 September). Android (Operating System). *Wikipedia.* Retrieved from http://en.wikipedia.org/wiki/Android_%28operating_system%29

Wikipedia Encyclopedia. (2014). Opto 22. *Wikipedia.* Retrieved from http://en.wikipedia.org/wiki/Opto_22

Wikipedia Encyclopedia. (2014, December 4). Material Requirement Planning. *Wikipedia Encyclopaedia.* Retrieved from http://en.wikipedia.org/wiki/Material_requirements_planning

Zhang, C. (2012, June 15). A Simple Platform of Brain-Controlled Mobile Robot and Its Implementation by SSVEP. *International Joint Conference on Neural Networks (Ijcnn).* doi:10.1109/IJCNN.2012.6252579

Chapter 3
Use of Sensor Data Warehouse for Soil Moisture Analysis

Myoung-Ah Kang
Université Blaise Pascal, France

Sandro Bimonte
Irstea – Clermont Ferrand, France

François Pinet
Irstea – Clermont Ferrand, France

Gil De Sousa
Irstea – Clermont Ferrand, France

Jean-Pierre Chanet
Irstea – Clermont Ferrand, France

ABSTRACT

More and more data are collected via sensors. Wireless networks can be implemented to facilitate the collection of sensors data and to reduce the cost of their acquisition. In this chapter, we present a general architecture combining Wireless Sensor Network (WSN) and Spatial Data Warehouse (SDW) technologies. This innovative solution is used to collect automatically sensor's information and to facilitate the analysis of these data. The WSN used in this application has been deployed by Irstea and tested during several years in vineyards in South of France. The novel contribution presented in this chapter is related to the use of a SDW to manage data produced by geo-referenced sensor nodes. SDW is one of the most appropriate modern technologies for analyzing large data sets at different temporal and spatial scales. This type of databases is a specific category of information system used to integrate, accumulate and analyze information from various sources. These data are usually organized according to a multidimensional schema to facilitate the calculation of indicators. In this chapter, we introduce the development of a SDW storing the data collected by this WSN. The implemented data warehouse can allow users to aggregate and explore interactively data produced by sensors. With this system, it is possible to visualize on a map the results of these aggregations.

1. INTRODUCTION

Viticulture tries to produce more and better in order to preserve the reputation of their wines. To achieve the desired quality levels, the vineyards are monitored, processed and irrigated. Farmers want to monitor

DOI: 10.4018/978-1-4666-8841-4.ch003

and manage the soil moisture to provide the right water quantity needed to plants at the right time. To improve the quantity and especially the quality of the wines, suitable water supply is necessary. Unfortunately, with excessive water supply, some diseases (mildew, etc.) can appear.

The French national project called DISP'eau leaded by the ITK company and involving Irstea was proposed in order to develop decision support systems to help farmers in their decision to irrigate vineyards (Barbier, Cucchi, & Hill; ITK, 2014). In this project, an automatic collection of soil moisture measurements has been made in vineyards by means of a Wireless Sensor Network platform (WSN) deployed by Irstea. This WSN has been developed in order to periodically, automatically and remotely collect the data related to soil moisture (Jacquot, De Sousa, Chanet, & Pinet, 2011). As indicated in (Barbier, et al.), this type of data is used in agronomic models to assess the evolution of vineyards.

Wireless sensor networks (WSNs) are groups of spatially distributed autonomous wireless sensor nodes. WSNs can be used to monitor physical or environmental conditions, such as temperature, humidity, pressure, sound, motion or pollutants (Li, He, & Fu, 2008). These sensor nodes can collect data from different environments and pass their data through the network to transfer information to a main location. As shown in this chapter, the collected data can be used for precision farming. Thanks to the WSN technology, a large amount of data can be collected over time. However, it is often difficult to interpret these collected data in order to analyze and understand the monitored phenomena. Data warehouses (DW) can facilitate the analysis of this information – for instance, an example can be found in (Boulil, Bimonte, & Pinet, 2014).

The novel contribution presented in this chapter is the use of Spatial Data Warehouse (SDW) technology to manage data produced by geo-referenced sensor nodes. This chapter presents an innovative application combining WSN and SDW. More precisely, we present a SDW and a SDW-based application for the visualization and the exploration of the data collected by a WSN used in the DISP'eau project. The goal was to provide a tool to facilitate the analysis of sensor's information produced by vineyards monitoring for precision farming. In the DISP'eau project, this type of data was used to provide vineyard irrigation recommendation.

DW is a large repository of data, aiming at supporting the decision-making process by enabling flexible and interactive analyses (Kimball, 2008). Online Analytical Processing (OLAP) systems allow decision makers to visualize and explore facts during querying sessions, whose results are displayed using interactive pivot tables and graphical displays. SDW is a DW extension for spatial information management (Malinowski & Zimanyi, 2008). Warehoused spatial data are analyzed by means of Spatial OLAP (SOLAP) systems, defined as "visual platforms built especially to support rapid and easy spatiotemporal analysis and exploration of data following a multidimensional approach comprised of aggregation levels available in cartographic displays as well as in tabular and diagram displays" (Bédard, Rivest, & Proulx, 2006).

The chapter is organized as follow. Section 2 introduces related works. Section 3 provides details on the deployed SOLAP architecture for WSN. Section 4 concludes the chapter and highlights some future works.

2. RELATED WORK

2.1 Wireless Sensor Network

To meet the specific needs of the DISP'eau project in terms of data collection in vineyards, it was decided to use the WSN technology. This technology allows for automatically collecting measurements in an observation area via wireless sensors (Akyildiz & Can Vuran, 2010; Akyildiz, Melodia, & Chowdury, 2007; Buratti, Conti, Dardari, & Verdone, 2009; Hou, et al., 2007; Jacquot, Chanet, Hou, De Sousa, & Monier, 2010; D. Chen & Varshney, 2004; Kulkarni, Förster, & Venayagamoorthy, 2011; Kuorilehto, Hännikäinen, & Hämäläinen, 2005; Pakzad, Fenves, Kim, & Culler, 2008; Wang, Attebury, & Ramamurthy, 2006; Yick, Mukherjee, & Ghosal, 2008). A WSN is a new generation of wireless communicating systems in which each node collects data from a sensor (i.e., soil moisture). In WSNs, two nodes can directly communicate if they are in the same communication range i.e. if they are near (Kang, Pinet, Schneider, Chanet, & Vigier, 2004). The sent messages can also cross the network from node to node, in order to reach a destination: the first wireless node (the source) sends a message to a second wireless node (which is a geographic neighbor). Then, the second node sends the message to another wireless node, etc. until the destination node is reached (Al-Karaki & Kamal, 2004; Caruso, Chessa, De, & Urpi, 2005; Karl & Willig, 2006; Pan, Hou, Cai, Shi, & Shen, 2003).

In WSNs, a node includes a processing unit with internal memories (RAM and programming Flash). The choice of the processing unit depends on the application and the autonomy constraints in terms of energy (Alippi, Camplani, Galperti, & Roveri, 2011; M. Chen, Gonzalez, & Leung, 2007; Di Pietro, Mancini, & Mei, 2006; Nasser & Chen, 2007; Powell, Leone, & Rolim, 2007; Quek, Dardari, & Win, 2007; Van Hoesel, Nieberg, Wu, & Havinga, 2004; Wu, Li, Liu, & Lou, 2010). In comparison with traditional data solutions used to collect data, WSN nodes have a wireless communication medium dedicated to the transmission of the information collected remotely. WSN technology is often deployed in natural environment. Different constraints in terms of autonomy and signal disturbances must be satisfied. It is therefore necessary to manage energy consumption and implement fault tolerance mechanisms to make WSNs robust and autonomous.

LIMOS Laboratory (Blaise Pascal University) has developed a complete WSN solution called LiveNode for automatic collection of measures (Hou, et al., 2007; Jacquot, et al., 2010). This wireless sensor is robust, autonomous and can be deployed in natural environment (Barcelo-Ordinas, Chanet, Hou, & Garcia-Vidal, 2013; Díaz, Pérez, Mateos, Marinescu, & Guerra, 2011; Gao, Yu, Zhang, & Xu, 2009; Garcia-Sanchez, Garcia-Sanchez, & Garcia-Haro, 2011; Hwang, Shin, & Yoe, 2010; López Riquelme, et al., 2009; Mancuso & Bustaffa, 2006; Pierce & Elliott, 2008; Ruiz-Garcia, Lunadei, Barreiro, & Robla, 2009; Yibo, Jean-Pierre, Kun Mean, & Hong Ling, 2013). This solution embeds a processor ARM7TDMI core (50Hz-500MHz) and an internal Flash (256KB) and RAM (64KB) memory. This type of processors provides a large frequency modulation. Consequently, LiveNode can be adapted to a large range of applications. The node performance allows running pre-processing at the node level, for example for performing data filtering. This solution can be used with different wireless communication medium. The LiveNode sensor technology is the solution deployed in vineyards for the DISP'eau project.

2.2 Spatial Data Warehouse

Spatial data warehouses (SDW) represent one of the most appropriate modern technologies for analyzing large volumes of data at different temporal and spatial scale (Bédard, Rivest, & Proulx, 2006; Bimonte, 2010; Bimonte, Tchounikine, Miquel, & Pinet, 2010; Kamal Boulil, Bimonte, Mahboubi, & Pinet, 2010; Gómez, Kuijpers, Moelans, & Vaisman, 2009; Malinowski & Zimanyi, 2008; Pestana, da Silva, & Bedard, 2005). A data warehouse is a category of information system used to integrate, accumulate and analyze data from various sources (Calì, Lembo, Lenzerini, & Rosati, 2003; Pinet & Schneider, 2010). Information from different sources can be stored into SDWs for later performing combined analysis. These data are usually organized according to a multidimensional schema in order to facilitate the calculation of indicators at different spatiotemporal scale. Different aggregation functions can be used (e.g., sum, average, variance, spatial union) (Bimonte, Boulil, Pinet, & Kang, 2013; Bimonte, Tchounikine, & Miquel, 2006; K. Boulil, Bimonte, & Pinet, 2012; Silva, Times, & Salgado, 2008). Decision-makers can explore SDWs using SOLAP (Spatial On-line Analytical Processing) tools; causal links can also be discovered automatically by using data-mining algorithms (Pinet & Schneider, 2010). As indicated in (Pinet & Schneider, 2010), data warehouses can facilitate the storage and the analyze of data in the fields of environment and agriculture, within a decision-making context (e.g., for precision farming). The concept of data warehouses is relatively recent and has great potential for assessing the impact of actions, practices, scenarios and programs both from a socio-economic as well as an environmental point of view (Nilakanta, Scheibe, & Rai, 2008; Pinet & Schneider, 2010; Schneider, 2008; Schulze, Spilke, & Lehner, 2007). The use of SDWs for the exploration of data coming from WSNs is rather new.

3. DW FOR WSN DATA

In this chapter, we present the implementation of a SDW integrating the data collected by the WSN used in the DISP'eau project. The global architecture is described in Figure 1. The first tier of this architecture is dedicated to the sensors data collection. The DISP'eau WSN described in Section 2 collects data from different sensors in vineyards. These data are transmitted to a central server and stored in a Postgresql database. In the second tier of our architecture, the content of this database can be accessed from Internet through a Web-based application, in order to monitor the evolution of the values. The data measured by the sensors can be also exported in CSV (or XML) files. In a third tier, these data are archived in a data warehouse using an extraction-transformation-loading process. This spatial data warehouse allows for visualizing the measurements at different temporal or spatial scale. For the third tier, we used PostGIS for the data storage, a SOLAP server implemented by GeoMondrian (Spatialytics, 2014) and a SOLAP MAP4Decision client (Intelli3, 2014; McHugh, Roche, & Bedard, 2008). PostGIS is the Postgres extension for spatial databases. GeoMondrian is an open source extension of Mondrian server. GeoMondrian implements the SOLAP server logical structure based on PostGIS. MAP4Decision allows users to display data through tabular visualizations. JMAP-SOLAP is used for cartographic displays of the analysis results.

Figure 1. Our architecture

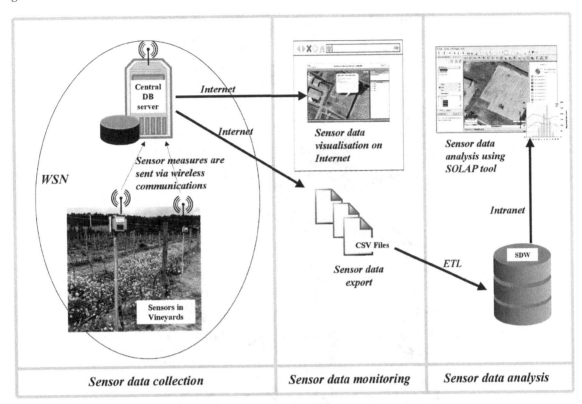

Sensor data collection	*Sensor data monitoring*	*Sensor data analysis*

3.1 WSN

In the DISP'eau project, four autonomous LiveNodes have been deployed by Irstea in a vineyard in the South of France. Each node was connected to several sensors measuring temperature, light, moisture (at different soil depths), battery level, etc. The nodes were supplied by batteries and embedded solar panels. Each network node has included a ZigBee communication module. ZigBee technology can reach several hundreds of meters with low-speed communication. The different nodes sent their measure periodically to a central site located in a farm building. The distances between the nodes and the central site have been defined in order to provide an adequate communication coverage. Figures 2 and 3 show the LiveNodes deployed in the project.

In the WSN, the soil moisture values are measured at three different depths underground: 30, 60 and 100cm. The vine roots may be more or less deep and long depending on the type of the plant. Each node of the WSN is equipped with several sensors to obtain different information; three of them are used to get soil humidity measurements at the three different soil depths when the others are used to determine brightness, the amount of energy in the battery and temperature. Each node is installed on a vineyard row and each row belongs to a plot. Figure 4 shows the spatial layout for four nodes arranged in a plot.

The WSN data are transmitted automatically and periodically to the central server. A web server is also installed on the central server in order to allow displaying the collected data. The users can monitor via Internet the different measured values and the status of the network remotely. This information

Figure 2. Example of a wireless sensor node linked to a tensiometer (DISP'eau project)

Figure 3. The WSN deployed in vineyeards in the DISP'eau project – the sensor measurements are automatically sent to a central site via wireless communications

Figure 4. Example of spatial layout for four wireless sensor nodes

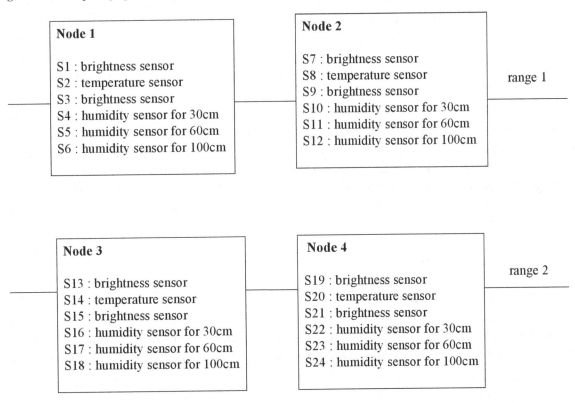

can be used for maintenance. For example, users can visualize the node energy levels in order to plan changing the batteries.

3.2 SDW and SOLAP System

In our system, WSN data can be exported as CSV files and an extraction-transformation-loading process has been used to populate a SDW. An example of CSV file part is presented in Figure 5. The column

Figure 5. Example of data collected by a wireless sensor node

id_data;id_sensor;date;value;unit
...
45787;19;22/11/2011 08:56;3.836;Volts
45799;19;22/11/2011 12:56;3.836;Volts
45811;19;22/11/2011 16:56;3.836;Volts
45823;19;22/11/2011 20:56;3.836;Volts
2030;20;26/03/2011 00:53;10.9;Celsius
2072;20;26/03/2011 04:52;9.8;Celsius
2114;20;26/03/2011 08:52;14.5;Celsius

"id_sensor" is the sensor identifier. The lines presented in this figure are related to the node 4. For this node, information are provided in the file for the brightness measurements of the sensor 19 and temperature measurements of the sensor 20. All the data collected for one node are stored in a same file. The column "value" represents the measured sensor value.

The SDW data structure is a constellation logical schema (see Figure 6). This type of schema includes fact tables. As shown in figure 6, only the moisture measurements are collected for different depths, unlike for the other measurements. The moisture ("humidity" attribute) can be aggregated per time ("DimensionTime" table) and/or per spatial objects ("DimensionNode") and/or per depths ("DimensionDepth"); the "FactHumidity" table is associated to each one of these dimension tables. There are associations between the "FactOther" table and the time and spatial dimensions. So, the "luminosity", "battery", "temperature" attributes can only be aggregated per time and/or per spatial objects.

The node dimension ("DimensionNode") is a spatial dimension because it contains several geometry attributes:

- NodeGeometry i.e., points,
- RangeGeometry i.e., linear objects,
- PlotGeometry i.e., polygons.

These attributes compose a spatial hierarchy indicating that, for each humidity, luminosity, battery, temperature measures, it will be possible to aggregate (e.g., using average or standard deviation func-

Figure 6. SDW constellation schema

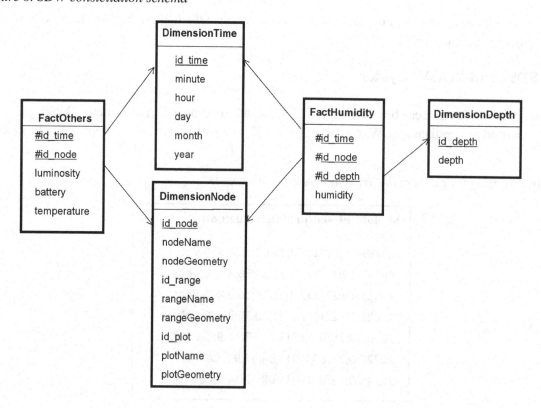

tions) and visualize the measures per node (nodeGeometry), per vineyard row (rangeGeometry) or per plot (plotGeometry). In the same manner, the time dimension is aggregated per different temporal scales as indicated in the attributes list in "DimensionTime".

With our system, it is possible to visualize on a map the different aggregated measurements using a MAP4Decision client, e.g. the average soil moisture values per month, row and depth. Users can combine the different dimension scales to aggregate the data and visualize the result on charts, maps and pivot tables. A screenshot of the SOLAP client is presented in Figure 7. This tool greatly facilitates the analysis of the data for long time periods and allows for obtaining a data survey (per depths or not, per rows or not, etc.).

4. CONCLUSION AND PERSPECTIVES

The data collected via sensors is constantly increasing. In this chapter, we present how SDWs can be used to store data produced by WSNs. We show how WSN and SDW technologies can be combined in order to collect and facilitate the analysis of sensors data.

Sensors network data warehouse opens up an interesting field of research for business applications. In many application areas, this technology can reduce the acquisition costs. From a research point of view, different issues may be discussed:

Figure 7. The SOLAP client interface (screenshot coming from Bimonte, Boulil, Pinet, and Kang, (2013))

1. Sensor network data can be used to quantify different phenomena in certain locations. Interpolations can be used to assess the values over all the studied area. Consequently, continuous spatial representations must be implemented in the data warehouses. This aspect requires extensions of traditional SDWs in order to deal with continuous field storage and aggregation. Some authors have already proposed some preliminary approach for this (Bimonte, et al., 2014; Gómez, Gómez, & Vaisman, 2013; Gómez, Gómez, & Vaisman, 2011, 2012; Zaamoune, Bimonte, Pinet, & Beaune, 2013; Bimonte & Kang, 2010; McHugh, 2008).

2. Large sensors networks can be controlled remotely in order to obtain on-demand data. In the case that data are archived on sensor node memory, it is possible to implement on-demand data requests via the SOLAP client. In this case, when users select an analysis for a certain time period and a certain spatial location, the data could be directly requested to sensor nodes. This is a solution to manage big data coming from a very large numbers of sensors network data. In that scenario, the static data integration process used in traditional DWs must be replaced by a dynamic integration. Different research works have been introduced in the field of dynamic data warehouse integration. These solutions could be applied for sensors network DW. For example, the authors of (Zhu, et al., 2004) propose a dynamic integration via Web services. This proposal could be interesting if sensor nodes are viewed as web objects. Different constraints must be taken into account; for example, to save energy, wireless nodes alternate between active and passive modes. Consequently, the queries have to be sent when sensor nodes are in active mode.

NOTE

Irstea has deployed the WSN presented in this chapter, at INRA Peach Rouge, in the DISP'eau project. This project has been leaded by the ITK company (http://www.itkweb.com). The project has been founded by FUI, OSEO, FEDER, Conseil Régional Languedoc-Roussillon and CPER.

REFERENCES

Akyildiz, I. F., & Can Vuran, M. (2010). *Wireless Sensor Networks*. Academic Press.

Akyildiz, I. F., Melodia, T., & Chowdury, K. R. (2007). Wireless multimedia sensor networks: A survey. *IEEE Wireless Communications, 14*(6), 32–39. doi:10.1109/MWC.2007.4407225

Al-Karaki, J. N., & Kamal, A. E. (2004). Routing techniques in wireless sensor networks: A survey. *IEEE Wireless Communications, 11*(6), 6–27. doi:10.1109/MWC.2004.1368893

Alippi, C., Camplani, R., Galperti, C., & Roveri, M. (2011). A robust, adaptive, solar-powered WSN framework for aquatic environmental monitoring. *IEEE Sensors Journal, 11*(1), 45–55. doi:10.1109/JSEN.2010.2051539

Barbier, G., Cucchi, V., & Hill, D. R. C. (n.d.). Model-driven engineering applied to crop modeling. *Ecological Informatics*.

Barcelo-Ordinas, J. M., Chanet, J. P., Hou, K. M., & Garcia-Vidal, J. (2013). *A survey of wireless sensor technologies applied to precision agriculture.* Academic Press.

Bédard, Y., Rivest, S., & Proulx, M. J. (2006). *Spatial online analytical processing (SOLAP): Concepts, architectures, and solutions from a geomatics engineering perspective. In Data Warehouses and OLAP: Concepts* (pp. 298–319). Architectures and Solutions.

Bédard, Y., Rivest, S., & Proulx, M. J. (2006). *Spatial online analytical processing (SOLAP): Concepts, architectures, and solutions from a geomatics engineering perspective. In Data Warehouses and OLAP: Concepts* (pp. 298–319). Architectures and Solutions.

Bimonte, S. (2010). A Web-Based Tool for Spatio-Multidimensional Analysis of Geographic and Complex Data. *International Journal of Agricultural and Environmental Information Systems, 1*(2), 42–67. doi:10.4018/jaeis.2010070103

Bimonte, S., Boulil, K., Pinet, F., & Kang, M. A. (2013). *Design of complex spatio-multidimensional models with the ICSOLAP UML profile: An implementation in magicdraw.* Paper presented at the ICEIS 2013.

Bimonte, S., Boulil, K., Pinet, F., & Kang, M. A. (2013). *Design of complex spatio-multidimensional models with the ICSOLAP UML profile: An implementation in magicdraw.* Paper presented at the ICEIS 2013.

Bimonte, S., & Kang, M. A. (2010). Towards a model for the multidimensional analysis of field data. Lecture Notes in Computer Science, 6295, 58-72.

Bimonte, S., Kang, M. A., Paolino, L., Sebillo, M., Zaamoune, M., & Vitiello, G. (2014). OLAPing field data: A theoretical and implementation framework. *Fundamenta Informaticae, 132*(2), 267–290.

Bimonte, S., Tchounikine, A., & Miquel, M. (2006).GeoCube, a multidimensional model and navigation operators handling complex measures: Application in spatial OLAP. Lecture Notes in Computer Science, 4243, 100-109.

Bimonte, S., Tchounikine, A., Miquel, M., & Pinet, F. (2010). When spatial analysis meets OLAP: Multidimensional model and operators. *International Journal of Data Warehousing and Mining, 6*(4), 33–60. doi:10.4018/jdwm.2010100103

Boulil, K., Bimonte, S., Mahboubi, H., & Pinet, F. (2010). *Towards the definition of spatial data warehouses integrity constraints with spatial OCL.* Paper presented at the ACM 13th international workshop on Data warehousing and OLAP. doi:10.1145/1871940.1871948

Boulil, K., Bimonte, S., & Pinet, F. (2012). *A UML & spatial OCL based approach for handling quality issues in SOLAP systems.* Paper presented at the ICEIS 2012.

Boulil, K., Bimonte, S., & Pinet, F. (2014). Spatial OLAP integrity constraints: From UML-based specification to automatic implementation: Application to energetic data in agriculture. *Journal of Decision Systems, 23*(4), 460–480. doi:10.1080/12460125.2014.934120

Buratti, C., Conti, A., Dardari, D., & Verdone, R. (2009). An overview on wireless sensor networks technology and evolution. *Sensors (Basel, Switzerland), 9*(9), 6869–6896. doi:10.3390/s90906869 PMID:22423202

Calì, A., Lembo, D., Lenzerini, M., & Rosati, R. (2003). Source Integration for Data Warehousing. In Multidimensional Databases: Problems and Solutions (pp. 361-392). Academic Press.

Caruso, A., Chessa, S., De, S., & Urpi, A. (2005). *GPS free coordinate assignment and routing in wireless sensor networks.* Paper presented at the IEEE INFOCOM. doi:10.1109/INFCOM.2005.1497887

Chen, D., & Varshney, P. K. (2004). *QoS support in wireless sensor networks: A survey.* Paper presented at the International Conference on Wireless Networks, ICWN'04.

Chen, M., Gonzalez, S., & Leung, V. C. M. (2007). Applications and design issues for mobile agents in wireless sensor networks. *IEEE Wireless Communications, 14*(6), 20–26. doi:10.1109/MWC.2007.4407223

Di Pietro, R., Mancini, L. V., & Mei, A. (2006). Energy efficient node-to-node authentication and communication confidentiality in wireless sensor networks. *Wireless Networks, 12*(6), 709–721. doi:10.1007/s11276-006-6530-5

Díaz, S. E., Pérez, J. C., Mateos, A. C., Marinescu, M. C., & Guerra, B. B. (2011). A novel methodology for the monitoring of the agricultural production process based on wireless sensor networks. *Computers and Electronics in Agriculture, 76*(2), 252–265. doi:10.1016/j.compag.2011.02.004

Gao, F., Yu, L., Zhang, W., & Xu, Q. (2009). Research and design of crop water status monitoring system based on wireless sensor networks. *Nongye Gongcheng Xuebao/Transactions of the Chinese Society of Agricultural Engineering, 25*(2), 107-112.

Garcia-Sanchez, A. J., Garcia-Sanchez, F., & Garcia-Haro, J. (2011). Wireless sensor network deployment for integrating video-surveillance and data-monitoring in precision agriculture over distributed crops. *Computers and Electronics in Agriculture, 75*(2), 288–303. doi:10.1016/j.compag.2010.12.005

Gómez, L., Kuijpers, B., Moelans, B., & Vaisman, A. (2009). A survey of spatio-temporal data warehousing. *International Journal of Data Warehousing and Mining, 5*(3), 28–55. doi:10.4018/jdwm.2009070102

Gómez, L. I., Gómez, S. A., & Vaisman, A. (2013). Modeling and querying continuous fields with OLAP cubes. *International Journal of Data Warehousing and Mining, 9*(3), 22–45.

Gómez, L. I., Gómez, S. A., & Vaisman, A. A. (2011). *Analyzing continuous fields with OLAP cubes.* Paper presented at the International Conference on Information and Knowledge Management.

Gómez, L. I., Gómez, S. A., & Vaisman, A. A. (2012). *A generic data model and query language for spatiotemporal OLAP cube analysis.* Paper presented at the ACM International Conference Proceeding Series. doi:10.1145/2247596.2247632

Hou, K. M., De Sousa, G., Zhou, H. Y., Chanet, J. P., Kara, M., Amamra, A., et al. (2007). LiveNode: LIMOS versatile embedded wireless sensor node. *Journal of Harbin Institute of Technology*, 140-144.

Hwang, J., Shin, C., & Yoe, H. (2010). Study on an agricultural environment monitoring server system using wireless sensor networks. *Sensors (Basel, Switzerland), 10*(12), 11189–11211. doi:10.3390/s101211189 PMID:22163520

Intelli3. (2014). Retrieved from http://www.intelli3.com/

ITK. (2014). Retrieved from itkweb.com

Jacquot, A., Chanet, J. P., Hou, K. M., De Sousa, G., & Monier, A. (2010). *A new management method for Wireless Sensor Networks.* Paper presented at the 9th IFIP Annual Mediterranean Ad Hoc Networking Workshop, MED-HOC-NET 2010. doi:10.1109/MEDHOCNET.2010.5546866

Jacquot, A., De Sousa, G., Chanet, J. P., & Pinet, F. (2011). *Réseau de capteurs sans fil pour le suivi de l'humidité du sol des vignes.* Paper presented at the Symposium Ecotech'11.

Kang, M. A., Pinet, F., Schneider, M., Chanet, J. P., & Vigier, F. (2004). *How to design geographic database? Specific UML profile and spatial OCL applied to wireless Ad Hoc networks.* Paper presented at the 7th Conference on Geographic Information Science (AGILE'2004).

Karl, H., & Willig, A. (2006). *Protocols and Architectures for Wireless Sensor Networks.* Academic Press.

Kimball, R. (2008). *The Data Warehouse Toolkit: The Complete Guide to Dimensional Modeling.* John Wiley & Sons.

Kulkarni, R. V., Förster, A., & Venayagamoorthy, G. K. (2011). Computational intelligence in wireless sensor networks: A survey. *IEEE Communications Surveys and Tutorials, 13*(1), 68–96. doi:10.1109/SURV.2011.040310.00002

Kuorilehto, M., Hännikäinen, M., & Hämäläinen, T. D. (2005). A survey of application distribution in wireless sensor networks. *EURASIP Journal on Wireless Communications and Networking,* (5): 774–788.

Li, G., He, J., & Fu, Y. (2008). Group-based intrusion detection system in wireless sensor networks. *Computer Communications, 31*(18), 4324–4332. doi:10.1016/j.comcom.2008.06.020

López Riquelme, J. A., Soto, F., Suardíaz, J., Sánchez, P., Iborra, A., & Vera, J. A. (2009). Wireless Sensor Networks for precision horticulture in Southern Spain. *Computers and Electronics in Agriculture, 68*(1), 25–35. doi:10.1016/j.compag.2009.04.006

Malinowski, E., & Zimanyi, E. (2008). *Advanced Data Warehouse Design: From Conventional to Spatial and Temporal Applications.* Springer.

Mancuso, M., & Bustaffa, F. (2006). *A Wireless Sensors Network for monitoring environmental variables in a tomato greenhouse.* Paper presented at the IEEE International Workshop on Factory Communication Systems. doi:10.1109/WFCS.2006.1704135

McHugh, R. (2008). *Intégration de la structure matricielle dans les cubes spatiaux.* Université Laval.

McHugh, R., Roche, S., & Bedard, Y. (2008). Towards a SOLAP-based public participation GIS. *Journal of Environmental Management,* 14. PMID:18562083

Nasser, N., & Chen, Y. (2007). SEEM: Secure and energy-efficient multipath routing protocol for wireless sensor networks. *Computer Communications, 30*(11-12), 2401–2412. doi:10.1016/j.comcom.2007.04.014

Nilakanta, S., Scheibe, K., & Rai, A. (2008). Dimensional issues in agricultural data warehouse designs. *Computers and Electronics in Agriculture, 60*(2), 263–278. doi:10.1016/j.compag.2007.09.009

Pakzad, S. N., Fenves, G. L., Kim, S., & Culler, D. E. (2008). Design and implementation of scalable wireless sensor network for structural monitoring. *Journal of Infrastructure Systems, 14*(1), 89–101. doi:10.1061/(ASCE)1076-0342(2008)14:1(89)

Pan, J., Hou, Y. T., Cai, L., Shi, Y., & Shen, S. X. (2003). *Topology Control for Wireless Sensor Networks.* Paper presented at the Annual International Conference on Mobile Computing and Networking. doi:10.1145/938985.939015

Pestana, G., da Silva, M. M., & Bedard, Y. (2005). *Spatial OLAP modeling: an overview base on spatial objects changing over time.* Paper presented at the Computational Cybernetics. doi:10.1109/ICCCYB.2005.1511565

Pierce, F. J., & Elliott, T. V. (2008). Regional and on-farm wireless sensor networks for agricultural systems in Eastern Washington. *Computers and Electronics in Agriculture, 61*(1), 32–43. doi:10.1016/j.compag.2007.05.007

Pinet, F., & Schneider, M. (2009). Precise Design of Environmental Data Warehouses. Operational Research, 9.

Powell, O., Leone, P., & Rolim, J. (2007). Energy optimal data propagation in wireless sensor networks. *Journal of Parallel and Distributed Computing, 67*(3), 302–317. doi:10.1016/j.jpdc.2006.10.007

Quek, T. Q. S., Dardari, D., & Win, M. Z. (2007). Energy efficiency of dense wireless sensor networks: To cooperate or not to cooperate. *IEEE Journal on Selected Areas in Communications, 25*(2), 459–469. doi:10.1109/JSAC.2007.070220

Ruiz-Garcia, L., Lunadei, L., Barreiro, P., & Robla, J. I. (2009). A review of wireless sensor technologies and applications in agriculture and food industry: State of the art and current trends. *Sensors (Switzerland), 9*(6), 4728–4750. doi:10.3390/s90604728 PMID:22408551

Schneider, M. (2008). A general model for the design of data warehouses. *International Journal of Production Economics, 112*(1), 309–325. doi:10.1016/j.ijpe.2006.11.027

Schulze, C., Spilke, J., & Lehner, W. (2007). Data modeling for Precision Dairy Farming within the competitive field of operational and analytical tasks. *Computers and Electronics in Agriculture, 59*(1), 39–55. doi:10.1016/j.compag.2007.05.001

Silva, J. D., Times, V. C., & Salgado, A. C. (2008). *A set of aggregation functions for spatial measures.* Paper presented at the DOLAP. doi:10.1145/1458432.1458438

Spatialytics. (2014). Retrieved from http://www.spatialytics.org/

Van Hoesel, L., Nieberg, T., Wu, J., & Havinga, P. J. M. (2004). Prolonging the lifetime of wireless sensor networks by cross-layer interaction. *IEEE Wireless Communications, 11*(6), 78–86. doi:10.1109/MWC.2004.1368900

Wang, Y., Attebury, G., & Ramamurthy, B. (2006). A survey of security issues in wireless sensor networks. *IEEE Communications Surveys and Tutorials, 8*(2), 2–22. doi:10.1109/COMST.2006.315852

Wu, Y., Li, X. Y., Liu, Y., & Lou, W. (2010). Energy-efficient wake-up scheduling for data collection and aggregation. *IEEE Transactions on Parallel and Distributed Systems, 21*(2), 275–287. doi:10.1109/TPDS.2009.45

Yibo, C., Jean-Pierre, C., Kun Mean, H., & Hong Ling, S. (2013). Extending the RPL Routing Protocol to Agricultural Low Power and Lossy Networks (A-LLNs). *International Journal of Agricultural and Environmental Information Systems, 4*(4), 25–47. doi:10.4018/ijaeis.2013100102

Yick, J., Mukherjee, B., & Ghosal, D. (2008). Wireless sensor network survey. *Computer Networks, 52*(12), 2292–2330. doi:10.1016/j.comnet.2008.04.002

Zaamoune, M., Bimonte, S., Pinet, F., & Beaune, P. (2013). *A new relational spatial OLAP approach for multi-resolution and spatio-multidimensional analysis of incomplete field data.* Paper presented at the ICEIS 2013.

Zhu, F., Turner, M., Kotsiopoulos, I., Bennett, K., Russell, M., Budgen, D., ... (2004). *Dynamic data integration using web services.* Paper presented at the IEEE International Conference on Web Services.

Chapter 4
Storage of Simulation Result Data:
A Database Perspective

François Pinet
Irstea – Clermont-Ferrand, France

Bruno Cheviron
Irstea – Montpellier, France

Nadia Carluer
Irstea – Lyon, France

Sandro Bimonte
Irstea – Clermont-Ferrand, France

Claire Lauvernet
Irstea – Lyon, France

André Miralles
Irstea – Montpellier, France

ABSTRACT

DBMS is a traditional technology for the storage of business application data. In this chapter, we show that this technology can be of interest in scientific fields. We present a survey of the emergence of the concept of simulation result database. Scientific simulation models become more complex, use more data and produce more outputs. Stochastic models can also be simulated. In this case, numerous simulations are run in order to discover a general trend in results. The replications of simulation increase again the amount of produced data, which makes exploration and analysis difficult. It is also often useful to compare the results obtained in using different model versions, scenarios or assumptions (for example different weather forecasts). In this chapter, we provide several examples of projects of simulation result databases. We show that the database technology can help to manage the large volumes of simulation outputs. We also illustrate this type of projects on environmental databases storing pesticide transfer simulation results. We conclude in highlighting some trends and future works.

1. INTRODUCTION

Simulation process is used to assess and analyse phenomena, for example related to the behaviour and the change of our environment (Hirabayashi, Kroll, & Nowak, 2011; Li & Mao, 2011; Pogson, Hastings, & Smith, 2012; Trolle, Hamilton, Pilditch, Duggan, & Jeppesen, 2011). The goal of the modelling is to understand, formalize or reproduce phenomena. Simulation models can be used to predict their future

DOI: 10.4018/978-1-4666-8841-4.ch004

evolutions or assess non-measurable values. The development of models is usually a multi-disciplinary task. Experts in different fields are often required to formalize and implement models.

The amount of data available to be analysed for reaching conclusions is constantly increasing and so does the computer performance increases over the years. Consequently, models become more complex, use more input data and produce more output results (Fernández-Quiruelas, Fernández, Cofiño, Fita, & Gutiérrez, 2011; Nakano & Higuchi, 2014; Pijanowski, et al., 2014; Steed, et al., 2013). Stochastic behaviours can also be simulated. In this case, several simulation runs can be required to discover a general trend in results. These replications increase the volume of result data, which makes exploration and analysis difficult (Boulil, et al., 2013). Scientists can also calculate aggregated results from large amounts of data produced by simulation runs (Boulil, et al., 2013; Mahboubi, Bimonte, Faure, & Pinet, 2010). It is also often useful to compare the results obtained in using different model versions, scenarios or assumptions (for example different weather forecasts).

Simulation results can have different formats. Different simulation runs can produce multiple text files, shape files, Excel files, images, etc. The format heterogeneity and the volume of produced files make it difficult the analysis and the tractability of results. For example, text-based storage makes it difficult to explore, select, and visualize the data (Boulil, et al., 2013). Spreadsheet tools (for example, OpenOffice, MS Excel) can help to display and extract the simulation results, but they are not suitable for large volumes of information (Boulil, et al., 2013).

To overcome these drawbacks, some scientists have proposed to use databases to store and extract the simulation data. Database-oriented solutions facilitate the management of simulation results. Database provides technical solutions for the storage of large volume of information and for their accesses via local network or Internet. Relational databases provide efficient methods for user authentication, integrity constraint controls, data backup, data insertion and data selection (Boulil, et al., 2013; Pokorný, 2006; Basta & Zgola, 2011).

In this chapter, we show how Database Management Systems (DBMS), a classical technology used in business applications, can be also used for simulation model applications. In Section 2, we present an overview of different examples of projects of simulation result databases. In these projects, the features of traditional database management system have been sometimes extended and adapted to the specificities of simulation results. Section 3 illustrates the design and the implementation of a simulation database on a project of environmental databases storing pesticide transfer simulation results. Section 4 concludes and provides some trends and future works in the field of simulation result database.

2. USING DATABASES FOR SIMULATION DATA STORAGE

The authors of (Pfaltz & Orlandic, 1999) propose an object-oriented DBMS called ADAMS (Advanced Data Management System) especially dedicated for scientific simulations. According to the authors, the system is scalable to manage large volume of scientific data and provides a variety of data organization capabilities, including aggregation, linear ordering and multi-dimensional clustering. To overcome the issue related to the large volume of scientific data, the ADAMS system described in (Pfaltz & Orlandic, 1999) provides the possibility to distribute the objects on different sites. Gradual data migrations are possible when the quantity of stored data increases. ADAMS can also manage spatial data which are used in models.

In (Pfaltz & Orlandic, 1999), the authors highlight some differences between the use of databases for scientific applications and the traditional use of transactional database systems for business applications. The authors indicate that the basic scientific observations are usually never modified (e.g., a measure that has been made on a particular date). It is the same thing for the model result data (e.g., a value that has been produced by a particular simulation run). So, transaction concepts are relatively unimportant unlike in classical business applications (e.g., a customer's mail address must always be updated). The authors also show that scientific analyses often imply to rearrange iteratively data structures (e.g., by aggregating data) in order to find properties or patterns in model results. The evolution of the data structure can evolve depending on the results analysis. Consequently, relatively flexible or generic data structures are required.

Several researchers have also proposed to store the simulation results in datawarehouses (Boulil, et al., 2013; Mahboubi, Bimonte, Deffuant, Chanet, & Pinet, 2013; Mahboubi, et al., 2010; Vasilakis, El-Darzi, & Chountas, 2004; Truong, et al., 2013). A datawarehouse is a specific type of databases that serves to integrate, accumulate and analyse large volumes of data (Pinet & Schneider, 2010; Chaudhuri & Dayal, 1997; Herden, 2000; Kimball, 2008; List, Bruckner, Machaczek, & Schiefer, 2002; Martin, 2008; Muñoz, Mazón, Pardillo, & Trujillo, 2009). As indicated in (Pinet & Schneider, 2010), these data are organized in a form that speeds up calculation of indicators; the indicators are made up of aggregated information obtained by different functions. Data can be aggregated according different dimensions (spatial scales, time, etc.). Currently, the datawarehouse technology is mainly used in business fields. The use of datawarehouses for storing scientific and simulation data provides a new and interesting perspective. A datawarehouse stores facts, i.e., the data to analyze (Malinowski & Zimányi, 2008; Pinet & Schneider, 2009; Trujillo, Palomar, Gomez, & Song, 2001); for example the product sales of a company. These facts contain measures, i.e., the values to aggregate; for example, the product sales in Dollars. These measures can be aggregated according to different dimensions (time, space, product category, etc.). To introduce the concept of datawarehouse, we present a case study inspired from the example provided in (Trujillo, et al., 2001). In this example, the stored facts are product sales of a company. The measure is the amount of these sales in Dollars. These information come from different stores. We suppose that, in this datawarehouse, the measures can be aggregated according to three dimensions: the time dimension (Time<Month<Semester<Year), the spatial dimension (Store<City<Province<State) and the product category dimension (Product<Type<Family<Group). A datawarehouse can produce many analyses by combining different levels of dimensions (Malinowski & Zimányi, 2008; Pinet & Schneider, 2009; Trujillo, et al., 2001). Consequently, in this datawarehouse, we can calculate the sum of sales for each combination of dimension levels; for example:

- By city,
- By product type,
- By product type, city, month,
- By product type, state, semester,
- By product type, state, year, etc.

Data can be combined to provide previously unknown causal links (Malinowski & Zimányi, 2008; Pinet & Schneider, 2009; Trujillo, et al., 2001). Causal links can also be discovered with data-mining algorithms (Berson & Smith, 1997; Breault J., Goodall C., & P., 2002; Duhamel, Picavet, Devos, & Beuscart, 2001; Faye & Sene, 2013; Krestyaninova, et al., 2007; Pinet & Schneider, 2009; Rudy, Miranda, & Suryani, 2014). The facts and the different analysis dimensions are formalized in conceptual multidimensional schemas (Abello, Samos, & Saltor, 2006; Lujan-Mora, Trujillo, & Song, 2006; Mazon & Trujillo, 2008; Rizzi, Abello, Lechtenborger, & Trujillo; Schneider, 2008). Datawarehouse is very often implemented with traditional relational database technology and represented with well-known entity-relations or object-oriented formalisms (Bédard & Paquette, 1989; Grady Booch, 1986; G. Booch, 1996; Chen, 1976; Dobing & Parsons, 2006; Jacobson, Booch, & Rumbaugh, 1999; Pinet, 2012). Using this approach, multi-dimensional schemas are converted to relational logical and physical schemas. The two types of implementation that are most used are the star schema and the snowflake schema.

A simulation datawarehouse is especially optimized for the model results aggregation using diverse functions (sum, average, etc.) and according to different dimensions. Using aggregation operations, this tool allows for calculating and displaying the simulation data at different spatial, temporal and thematic scales. On-Line Analytical Processing (OLAP) tools associated with datawarehouses help to generate graphical displays, charts, cartographic maps and pivot tables. A generic metamodel template for simulation results datawarehouse has been introduced in (Mahboubi, et al., 2010) and extended in (Boulil, et al., 2013).

Table 1 (coming from (Boulil, et al., 2013)) shows the differences between the management of simulation results with spreadsheets and with datawarehouses. The different comparison criteria are access time, security, Internet/Intranet access, visualisation and data exploration. This table shows that a datawarehouse has very important advantages in comparison with spreadsheep tools, as index methods to access data, integrity constraints, user access rights, selective and partial data load. For the simulation models that process georeferenced objects, spatial OLAP (SOLAP) tools connected to spatial datawarehouses offer numerous visualization functions. SOLAP is currently a very active research field in many application areas (McHugh, Roche, & Bédard, 2009). Numerous SOLAP functions could be really useful for the spatial analysis of simulation results. For example, the description of this technology can be found in:

- (Bédard, Proulx, Larrivée, & Bernier, 2002; Boulil, Bimonte, & Pinet, 2014; Gomez, Vaisman, & Zimanyi, 2010; Malinowski & Zimányi, 2008; Pestana, da Silva, & Bedard, 2005; Zaamoune, Bimonte, Pinet, & Beaune, 2013) for the spatial data representation,
- (Bédard, Rivest, & Proulx, 2006; Bimonte, Tchounikine, Miquel, & Pinet, 2010) for the SOLAP tool development.

CosmoSim and Millennium (CosmoSim, 2015) are examples of large simulation database instances. These databases contain data sets from cosmological simulations (Riebe, 2014). Users can access to a lists of dark matter halos, their history, galaxy catalogues, etc. (Riebe, 2014). Users can query the data with SQL via a Web interface. Different 2D and 3D visualization and charts can be automatically produced to analyse the result data.

SimulationDB is a database designed for the storage of simulation results for foundry engineers (Malinowski & Suchy, 2010). To reduce the production costs, research centres and foundries use specialized simulation software. With SimulationDB, users can search in simulation results related to existing similar projects, compare different version of simulations or compare simulations with real processes.

In the context of the French Miriphyque project, large relational databases have been built to store simulation results related to agricultural pesticide transfers in water. The model called MACRO has been used for this purpose (Larsbo & Jarvis, 2003). Several scenarios of pesticide use, climate and plots type are tested. The databases can be used to extract selectively different information in order to analyse

Table 1. A comparison of spreadsheet tools and DWs (coming from Boulil, et al. (2013))

Tools Criterion	Spreadsheets	DWs
Access time for large volumes of data	No data indexing method Limited optimization techniques All data are usually loaded into memory	Optimizations for data queries and insertions (provided by DB); efficient indexing methods Based on a client-server architecture; clients can load and display only a portion of the stored data
Security	Very basic method for user authentications is provided	Users' authentication and management of access rights Methods for data backups Integrity constraints can check and guarantee the consistency of the information Data encryption is usually possible
Internet/Intranet access	Additional implementation is needed to diffuse data to the Internet/Intranet	Based on an Internet/Intranet client-server architecture
Visualization	Tables with multiple entries Charts	Tables with multiple entries Charts Map production with spatial OLAP technology
Data exploration	Wizard and assistants are often provided to help create tables	OLAP allows users to easily choose measures and dimension levels, to perform quick swapping between aggregation functions and to select only a subset of the data OLAP server support for complex data queries (e.g., with the MDX language)

them. A datawarehouse has been also created and experimented with result data in order to facilitate the data aggregation (e.g., for temporal result aggregations) (Boulil, et al., 2013). This project is described in more detail in Section 3.

3. AN EXAMPLE OF SIMULATION DATABASE

In this section, we detail the design and the implementation of the database storing simulation results related to agricultural pesticide transfers in water, introduced in the previous section. Large volumes of results have been generated by the MACRO model (Larsbo & Jarvis, 2003). These results are related to the simulation of the pesticide transfer evolution over time. As indicated in (Boulil, et al., 2013), MACRO simulates water and pesticide transfer using a dimensional approach for both microporous and macroporous meda (Larsbo & Jarvis, 2003). Water flow in microporous parts of soil is defined by the

Figure 1. The generic schema template

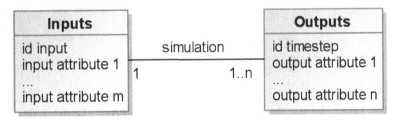

Richards equation (Richards, 1931), which uses a kinematic wave to define macroporous flow (Boulil, et al., 2013); pesticide transfer is represented by an advection-diffusion equation, including sportion and degradation processes, in microporous and macroporous parts of the soil (Boulil, et al., 2013). The MACRO model determines the evolution over time of the discharge and pesticide concentrations.

Different simulations have been run, each simulation corresponding to diverse scenarios, location, periods, pesticide types, meteorological conditions, etc. In total, more than 24,000 runs have been launched with MACRO, producing 181,414,600 lines of results stored in tens of thousands of text files.

We decided to store the input and the output data in different database instances. First, a very generic schema template has been used in order to facilitate the adaptation of the database to future cases. Figure 1 shows this template model in a conceptual UML class diagram. A class "Input" represents different inputs needed for the simulation. Each instance of the "Inputs" class corresponds to a simulation run. These instances are associated to a set of results by the "simulation" relationship. Each run simulates the hourly pesticide transfer evolution over one year; these results are formalized by the "Outputs" class. The attribute "id timestep" indicates the time of the transaction.

Second, the template schema has been instantiated in different Postgresql databases. Some variations in database schema version have been implemented to take into account different types of simulations. At the implementation level, the primary key of the inputs table is the "id input" attribute. The primary key of the outputs table is the combination of "id input" and "id timestep".

The simulation results text files produced by MACRO have been loaded in the databases thanks to Linux Shell Scripts. Different indexes have also been defined to speed up data selective access. Several queries have been defined to extract information such as the evolution over time of the pesticide transfer after heavy rains. The query results have been exported to "csv" format files in order to be exploited with R, a well-known software environment for statistical computing.

In Boulil, et al. (2013), a datawarehouse schema (i.e., a multidimensional schema) has been also proposed for the data types used in our databases. As presented in this paper, some attributes coming from the MACRO outputs can be stored in a fact table in order to be aggregated and compare according to a time dimension and different model inputs. The possible aggregations are formalized in a multidimensional schema. Figure 2 shows the main concepts of this schema (coming from Boulil, et al. (2013)). The dimensions define the criteria of aggregation (plot type, pesticide use level, crop, etc.) connected to simulation results. The time dimension is composed of an ordered set of classes that indicate the different temporal granularities in aggregations. The simulation outputs can be aggregated according to one or several of these dimensions. For example, the hourly outputs produced by MACRO can be aggregated according to day or month (and also by level of pesticide use and/or by crops, etc.). The model runs also constitute a dimension.

Figure 2. Summary of the multidimensional schema presented in (Boulil, et al., 2013)

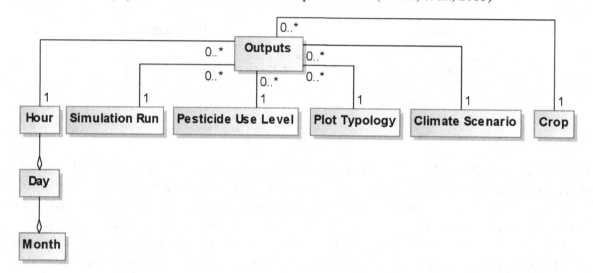

To conclude this section, Figure 3 provides an overview of the 3-tier developed methodology. To sum up:

1. Several simulation runs are executed using the MACRO model. These executions need input files and produce numerous output text files.
2. We use traditional relational databases to load and store information included in inputs and outputs files, as well as the associations between them, in order to be able to determine which inputs have produced which outputs in the databases. These databases store all the contents of the text files plus some additional external information. The SQL language is used to extract selectively the data for specific analysis. No Java, C or script codes are required.
3. A datawarehouse schema and an OLAP solution has been also proposed in (Boulil, et al., 2013) in order to aggregate the data according to different dimensions.

4. DISCUSSION

While the use of database technologies in the business field is a very common phenomenon, the uses of databases for analysing simulation results of scientific applications are rather rare. Recent information system advances are rarely applied for the storage and the management of model data. The storage capacity provided by DBMS can solve several issues related to the management and the traceability of the large volume of data produced by model. In this chapter, we have shown some examples of attempts to handle these informations with databases.

Database technologies were adapted to new types of applications over the years. It was the case for spatial information for example. Before the development of spatial DBMS, users stored spatial data in text files and proprietary file formats. Then, specific data types and query operations were added to DBMS to manage spatial databases. Initially, these additions have posed problems in terms of performance and formal representations, but advances in computer research have brought solutions to these problems.

Figure 3. Overview of our approach

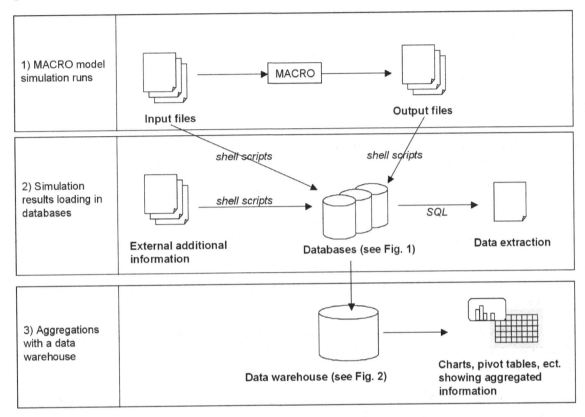

The parallel can easily be made with simulation result databases. Currently, no specific DBMS provide specific functionality for the storage and the querying of simulation results. Researchers are required (as it has been the case for spatial data) to invent new DBMS for simulation results. Here, we provide some main needs and new trends in the field of simulation result databases.

1. **Integration of mathematical operations in SQL.** Initially, database technologies have been created to meet the needs of business applications (such as accounting). Up to now, existing DBMS integrate very basic mathematical (and statistical) functions. Currently, subparts of the simulation result databases are extracted in order to be analysed and processed with external tools (R, Matlab, etc.) as shown in Figure 3. More of these processes could be executed inside the database, if the SQL language would be extended with additional mathematical functions.

2. **Complex data types.** The complexity of structures stored in DBMS has increased, mainly influenced by the concepts introduced in object-oriented databases (Garvey & Jackson, 1989). In this paper, basic data structure have been presented for storage - the outputs and the inputs are represented by classical attributes have unique and atomic types; but the complexity level of data types used in models can be high and can require complex data structures (graph-based, rasters, etc) and schemas (Mahboubi, Bimonte, & Deffuant, 2011; Mahboubi, et al., 2013).

3. **Simulation results sharing.** As in the case of SimulationDB (Malinowski & Suchy, 2010), one goal of a simulation result database can be to facilitate the experiments sharing. In this context,

work must be made to develop a methodology to publish simulation results database instances using linked-open data technologies (Bizer, Heath, & Berners-Lee, 2009; Jain, Hitzler, Sheth, Verma, & Yeh, 2010; Jain, Hitzler, Yeh, Verma, & Sheth, 2010). Simulation metadata schemas must be also designed in order to provide documentations.

REFERENCES

Abello, A., Samos, J., & Saltor, F. (2006). YAM2: A Multidimensional Conceptual Model Extending UML. *Information Systems*, 31.

Basta, A., & Zgola, M. (2011). *Database Security*. Delmar Cengage Learning.

Bédard, Y., & Paquette, F. (1989). *Extending entity/relationship formalism for spatial information systems*. Paper presented at the AUTO-CARTO 9, Baltimore, MD.

Bédard, Y., Proulx, M. J., Larrivée, S., & Bernier, E. (2002). *Modeling multiple representations into spatial data warehouses: A UML-based approach*. Paper presented at the Joint Int. Symp. ISPRS Commission IV, Ottawa, Canada.

Bédard, Y., Rivest, S., & Proulx, M. J. (2006). *Spatial online analytical processing (SOLAP): Concepts, architectures, and solutions from a geomatics engineering perspective Data Warehouses and OLAP: Concepts* (pp. 298–319). Architectures and Solutions.

Berson, A., & Smith, S. (1997). *Data Warehousing, Data Mining, and OLAP (Data Warehousing/Data Management)*. Computing Mcgraw-Hill.

Bimonte, S., Tchounikine, A., Miquel, M., & Pinet, F. (2010). When Spatial Analysis Meets OLAP: Multidimensional Model and Operators. *International Journal of Data Warehousing and Mining*, 6(4), 33–60. doi:10.4018/jdwm.2010100103

Bizer, C., Heath, T., & Berners-Lee, T. (2009). Linked Data - The Story So Far. *International Journal on Semantic Web and Information Systems*, 5(3), 1–22. doi:10.4018/jswis.2009081901

Booch, G. (1986). Object-oriented development. *IEEE Transactions on Software Engineering*, SE-12(2), 211–221. doi:10.1109/TSE.1986.6312937

Booch, G. (1996). The unified modeling language. *Performance Computing/Unix Review*, 14(13), 41-48.

Boulil, K., Bimonte, S., & Pinet, F. (2014). Spatial OLAP integrity constraints: From UML-based specification to automatic implementation: Application to energetic data in agriculture. *Journal of Decision Systems*, 23(4), 460–480. doi:10.1080/12460125.2014.934120

Boulil, K., Pinet, F., Bimonte, S., Carluer, N., Lauvernet, C., Cheviron, B., & Chanet, J.-P. et al. (2013). Guaranteeing the quality of multidimensional analysis in data warehouses of simulation results: Application to pesticide transfer data produced by the MACRO model. *Ecological Informatics*, 16, 41–52. doi:10.1016/j.ecoinf.2013.04.004

Breault, J., Goodall, C., & Fos, P. J. (2002). Data mining a diabetic data warehouse. *Artificial Intelligence in Medicine*, 26(1), 37–54. doi:10.1016/S0933-3657(02)00051-9 PMID:12234716

Chaudhuri, S., & Dayal, U. (1997). An Overview of Data Warehousing and OLAP Technology. *SIGMOD Record, 26*(1), 65–74. doi:10.1145/248603.248616

Chen, P. (1976). The Entity-Relationship Model: Toward a Unified View of Data. *ACM Transactions on Database Systems, 1*(1), 9–35. doi:10.1145/320434.320440

CosmoSim. (2015). Retrieved from www.cosmosim.org

Dobing, B., & Parsons, J. (2006). How UML is used. *Communications of the ACM, 49*(5), 109–113. doi:10.1145/1125944.1125949

Duhamel, A., Picavet, M., Devos, P., & Beuscart, R. (2001). *From data collection to knowledge data discovery: A medical application of data mining.* Paper presented at the Studies in Health Technology and Informatics.

Faye, F., & Sene, M. (2013). Datamining tool: Multiple regression and logistic regression in a web platform of a datawarehouse. In Advanced Materials Research (pp. 2299-2307). Academic Press.

Fernández-Quiruelas, V., Fernández, J., Cofiño, A. S., Fita, L., & Gutiérrez, J. M. (2011). Benefits and requirements of grid computing for climate applications. An example with the community atmospheric model. *Environmental Modelling & Software, 26*(9), 1057-1069.

Garvey, M., & Jackson, M. (1989). Introduction to object-oriented databases. *Information and Software Technology, 31*(10), 521–528. doi:10.1016/0950-5849(89)90173-0

Gomez, L., Vaisman, A., & Zimanyi, E. (2010). *Physical design and implementation of spatial data warehouses supporting continuous fields.* Paper presented at the 12th international conference on Data warehousing and knowledge discovery. doi:10.1007/978-3-642-15105-7_3

Herden, O. (2000). A Design Methodology for Data Warehouses. *Paper presented at the CAISE Doctoral Consortium*, Stockholm.

Hirabayashi, S., Kroll, C. N., & Nowak, D. J. (2011). Component-based development and sensitivity analyses of an air pollutant dry deposition model. *Environmental Modelling & Software, 26*(6), 804-816.

Jacobson, I., Booch, G., & Rumbaugh, J. (1999). Unified process. *IEEE Software, 16*(3), 96–102.

Jain, P., Hitzler, P., Sheth, A. P., Verma, K., & Yeh, P. Z. (2010) Ontology alignment for linked open data. Lecture Notes in Computer Science, 6496, 402-417.

Jain, P., Hitzler, P., Yeh, P. Z., Verma, K., & Sheth, A. P. (2010). *Linked data is merely more data.* Paper presented at the AAAI Spring Symposium.

Kimball, R. (2008). *The Data Warehouse Toolkit: The Complete Guide to Dimensional Modeling.* John Wiley & Sons.

Krestyaninova, M., Neogi, S. G., Viksna J., Celms E., Rucevskis P., Opmanis M., et al. (2007). *Building a data warehouse for the diabetes data.* Academic Press.

Larsbo, M., & Jarvis, N. J. (2003). *MACRO 5.0. A model of water flow and solute transport in macroporous soil. Technical description.* Studies in the Biogeophysical Environment.

Li, Z., & Mao, X.-z. (2011). Global multiquadric collocation method for groundwater contaminant source identification. *Environmental Modelling & Software, 26*(12), 1611-1621.

List, B., Bruckner, R. M., Machaczek, K., & Schiefer, J. (2002). A Comparison of Data Warehouse Development Methodologies Case Study of the Process Warehouse. *Lecture Notes in Computer Science, 2453*, 203–215. doi:10.1007/3-540-46146-9_21

Lujan-Mora, S., Trujillo, J., & Song, I.-Y. (2006). A UML profile for multidimensional modeling in data warehouses. *Data & Knowledge Engineering, 59*(3), 725–769. doi:10.1016/j.datak.2005.11.004

Mahboubi, H., Bimonte, S., & Deffuant, G. (2011) Analyzing demographic and economic simulation model results: A semi-automatic spatial OLAP approach. Lecture Notes in Computer Science, 6782, 17-31.

Mahboubi, H., Bimonte, S., Deffuant, G., Chanet, J. P., & Pinet, F. (2013). Semi-automatic Design of Spatial Data Cubes from Structurally Generic Simulation Model Results. *International Journal of Data Warehousing and Mining, 9*(1), 70–95. doi:10.4018/jdwm.2013010104

Mahboubi, H., Bimonte, S., Faure, T., & Pinet, F. (2010). Data warehouse and OLAP for Environmental Simulation Data. *International Journal of Agricultural and Environmental Systems, 1*(2).

Malinowski, E., & Zimányi, E. (2008). A conceptual model for temporal data warehouses and its transformation to the ER and the object-relational models. *Data & Knowledge Engineering, 64*(1), 101–133. doi:10.1016/j.datak.2007.06.020

Malinowski, P., & Suchy, J. S. (2010). Database for foundry engineers "simulationDB" a modern database storing simulation results. *Journal of Achievements in Materials and Manufacturing Engineering, 43*(1).

Martin, R. (2008). *Data Warehouse 100 Success Secrets - 100 most Asked questions on Data Warehouse Design, Projects, Business Intelligence, Architecture, Software and Models.* Emereo Pty Ltd.

Mazon, J. N., & Trujillo, J. (2008). An MDA Approach for the Development of Data Warehouses. *Decision Support Systems, 45*(1), 41–55. doi:10.1016/j.dss.2006.12.003

McHugh, R., Roche, S., & Bédard, Y. (2009). Towards a SOLAP-based public participation GIS. *Journal of Environmental Management, 90*(6), 2041–2054. doi:10.1016/j.jenvman.2008.01.020 PMID:18562083

Muñoz, L., Mazón, J.-N., Pardillo, J., & Trujillo, J. (2009). Modelling ETL Processes of Data Warehouses with UML Activity Diagrams. In Proceedings of On the Move to Meaningful Internet Systems: OTM 2008 Workshops (pp. 44-53). OTM.

Nakano, S., & Higuchi, T. (2014). Simulation and big data in geosciences: Data assimilation and emulation. *Journal of the Institute of Electronics, Information, and Communication Engineers, 97*(10), 869–875.

Pestana, G., da Silva, M. M., & Bedard, Y. (2005). *Spatial OLAP modeling: an overview base on spatial objects changing over time.* Paper presented at the Computational Cybernetics. doi:10.1109/ICCCYB.2005.1511565

Pfaltz, J. L., & Orlandic, R. (1999). *A scalable DBMS for large scientific simulations.* Paper presented at the Database Applications in Non-Traditional Environments. doi:10.1109/DANTE.1999.844970

Pijanowski, B. C., Tayyebi, A., Doucette, J., Pekin, B. K., Braun, D., & Plourde, J. (2014). A big data urban growth simulation at a national scale: Configuring the GIS and neural network based Land Transformation Model to run in a High Performance Computing (HPC) environment. *Environmental Modelling & Software, 51*, 250–268. doi:10.1016/j.envsoft.2013.09.015

Pinet, F. (2012). Entity-relationship and object-oriented formalisms for modeling spatial environmental data. *Environmental Modelling & Software, 30*, 80–91. doi:10.1016/j.envsoft.2012.01.008

Pinet, F., & Schneider, M. (2009). Precise Design of Environmental Data Warehouses. Operational Research, 9.

Pinet, F., & Schneider, M. (2010). Precise design of environmental data warehouses. *Operations Research, 10*(3), 349–369. doi:10.1007/s12351-009-0069-z

Pogson, M., Hastings, A., & Smith, P. (2012). Sensitivity of crop model predictions to entire meteorological and soil input datasets highlights vulnerability to drought. *Environmental Modelling & Software, 29*(1), 37-43.

Pokorný, J. (2006). Database architectures: Current trends and their relationships to environmental data management. *Environmental Modelling & Software, 21*(11), 1579-1586.

Richards, L. A. (1931). Capillary conduction of liquids through porous mediums. *Journal of Applied Physics, 1*, 318–333.

Riebe, K. (2014). *Introduction to simulation databases using CosmoSim* (Technical Report). Leibniz-Insitute for Astrophysics Potsdam.

Rizzi, S., Abello, A., Lechtenborger, J., & Trujillo, J. *Research in data warehouse modeling and design: dead or alive?* Paper presented at the 9th ACM international workshop on Data warehousing and OLAP. doi:10.1145/1183512.1183515

Rudy, M. E., & Suryani, E. (2014). Implementation of datawarehouse, datamining and dashboard for higher education. *Journal of Theoretical and Applied Information Technology, 64*(3), 710–717.

Schneider, M. (2008). A general model for the design of data warehouses. *International Journal of Production Economics, 112*(1), 309–325. doi:10.1016/j.ijpe.2006.11.027

Steed, C. A., Ricciuto, D. M., Shipman, G., Smith, B., Thornton, P. E., & Wang, D. et al.. (2013). Big data visual analytics for exploratory earth system simulation analysis. *Computers & Geosciences, 61*, 71–82.

Trolle, D., Hamilton, D. P., Pilditch, C. A., Duggan, I. C., & Jeppesen, E. (2011). Predicting the effects of climate change on trophic status of three morphologically varying lakes: Implications for lake restoration and management. *Environmental Modelling & Software, 26*(4), 354-370.

Trujillo, J., Palomar, M., Gomez, J., & Song, I. Y. (2001). Designing Data Warehouses with OO Conceptual Models. *IEEE Computer, 34*(12), 66–75. doi:10.1109/2.970579

Truong, T. M., Amblard, F., Gaudou, B., Sibertin-Blanc, C., Truong, V. X., Drogoul, A., ... (2013). *An implementation of framework of business intelligence for agent-based simulation.* Paper presented at the Fourth Symposium on Information and Communication Technology.

Vasilakis, C., El-Darzi, E., & Chountas, P. (2004). *A data warehouse environment for storing and analyzing simulation output data.* Paper presented at the 36th conference on Winter simulation. doi:10.1109/WSC.2004.1371379

Zaamoune, M., Bimonte, S., Pinet, F., & Beaune, P. (2013). *A new relational spatial OLAP approach for multi-resolution and spatio-multidimensional analysis of incomplete field data.* Paper presented at the 15th International Conference on Enterprise Information Systems.

Chapter 5
Benefits and Barriers of E-Sourcing and E-Purchasing in the Healthcare Sector:
A Case Study

Vicky Manthou
University of Macedonia, Greece

Christos Bialas
Alexander Tech. Educational Institute of Thessaloniki, Greece

Constantinos J. Stefanou
Alexander Tech. Educational Institute of Thessaloniki, Greece

ABSTRACT

This chapter reports on research investigating the benefits and barriers of e-Enabling Technologies such as e-Sourcing and e-Purchasing in the healthcare sector. The research is based on a case study conducted at the KAT General Hospital (KGH) in Athens, Greece, and examines aspects regarding the implementation of specific e-Sourcing and e- Purchasing tools, such as e-RFx and e-Auctions, focusing on the resulting benefits and the existing barriers of adoption. Findings suggest that although quantifiable benefits were identified, e-Sourcing and e- Purchasing are still at an early stage of maturity in the Greek Healthcare Sector. The chapter entails a literature review, a description of the research methodology used, the findings based on the case study and the final conclusions.

1. INTRODUCTION

With over $4.5 trillion in expenditure, the global Healthcare industry is one of the world's largest and fastest growing industries, comprising various sectors: medical equipment and supplies, pharmaceutical, healthcare services, biotechnology and alternative medicine sectors (Beeny, 2014). It is facing an increasingly complex regulatory and legislative environment as well as a variety of economic and business

DOI: 10.4018/978-1-4666-8841-4.ch005

challenges (UPS Survey, 2013), such as the policy level that may restrict product selection possibilities, the service delivery point that may face frequent stock outs due to poor forecasting, unavailability of transport and a variety of other issues (UN CoLSC, 2014). These risks combined with new growth opportunities are driving healthcare businesses to overcome the inefficiencies of the past. Given the personal and professional impact of timely, cost efficient and most importantly effective treatments, today's global healthcare industry is forced to manage its supply chain more effectively. To be effectively managed, supply chain resources, such as suppliers, partners and customers need to be linked. The supply chain is transforming from a controlled entity within the four walls of a warehouse into a network of resources, scattered across facilities and entities in different cities and countries (Beeny, 2014).

Failing to manage the supply chain effectively has been shown to have significant negative impacts on organizations (Kanyoma et al., 2013). It has been argued that especially for the healthcare industry inefficient supply chain management (SCM) processes cause significant cost increases (De Vries & Huijsman, 2011), as activities related to the purchase, distribution, and management of supplies account for about one third of the operating costs of healthcare facilities (Kumar et al., 2008). These findings are supported by industry surveys, which show that healthcare providers are using almost a third of their annual operating funds to support their supply chain (Nachtmann & Pohl, 2009). The management of the supply chain in the healthcare industry in particular, possesses an additional dimension of complexity, as companies have to do a highly accurate job, considering that potential dysfunctions might have negative consequences on peoples wellbeing and even peoples lives (Mustaffa & Potter, 2009). Thus, companies in the healthcare sector need to make continuous efforts to improve their supply chain performance, especially since experts have estimated that SCM practices of the healthcare industry are 10 to 15 years behind other industries such as retail and manufacturing (Chen et al., 2013). According to a survey among healthcare executives, investing in new technologies was identified as the top strategy to improve competitiveness and increase efficiency (UPS Survey, 2013). As the significance of information and communication technologies (ICT) in improving healthcare supply chains has been proved, many healthcare organizations initiated related projects (De Vries & Huijsman, 2011). Even in developed countries such as the US, the healthcare industry is suffering from inconsistent and inaccurate product information, which negatively impacts the rest of the supply chain including the quality of care delivery for patients (Pleasant, 2009). Room for improvement through the use of ICT also exists for UK's national healthcare provider NHS, as it is characterized by lack of common commercial and procurement data standards, which means that the analysis of expenditure and demand requirements across organizations is very costly in terms of time and resources (Hodson-Gibbons, 2009; Kritchanchai, 2012).

Regarding the Greek healthcare sector, where the presented case study of this paper resides, the implementation of supply chain concepts is in an early stage, reflecting into poorly functioning supply chains and leading to redundancy of efforts, higher costs, stock outs, wastage and, as a result, lower level of healthcare services (Fragkiadakis et al., 2014). The participants in the healthcare supply chain, whether manufacturers, wholesalers, distributors or healthcare providers appear to be acting isolated with low levels of coordination amongst them. Similar to studies performed on the healthcare sector of developing countries, such as Thailand (Kritchanchai, 2012), it is evident that SCM in the Greek healthcare sector is characterized by inefficient processes, inconsistent and inaccurate data information, lack of data standardization, lack of systems integration and low transparency.

The importance of the healthcare sector and the significance of SCM in the healthcare context combined with the fact that the majority of prior supply chain studies focus on the manufacturing environment, establishes the need to study hospital supply chain integration and performance to extend the body of

SCM research (Chen et al., 2013). Especially with e-commerce now reshaping the day-to-day business processes, research needs to provide helpful insights and assist the healthcare industry in leveraging technology advances to create a more efficient and effective supply chain, to reduce unnecessary costs and to improve patient safety (Pleasant, 2009). In this context, the current study examines the role of procurement enabling technologies such as e-Sourcing and e-Purchasing as part of the hospital–supplier integration in the healthcare environment.

2. THEORETICAL BACKGROUND

The supply chain can be defined as a way to envision all steps needed from beginning to end in order to deliver products or services to the customer (Meijboom et al., 2011). Expanding on this definition, the term "Supply Chain Management", which was introduced in 1982, can be described as "the planning and management of all activities involved in sourcing and procurement, conversion, and all Logistics Management activities. Importantly it also includes coordination and collaboration with channel partners, which can be suppliers, intermediaries, third-party service providers, and customers. In essence, SCM integrates supply and demand management within and across companies." (Council of SCM Professionals, 2013). Other definitions suggest that SCM involves management of the flows of products, information and funds upstream and downstream in the supply chain (Sila et al, 2006). The supply chain literature has focused mainly on the improvement of material flows to best match supply and demand, although it is equally important for a competitive firm to manage and control information and fund flows within the supply chain (Al Saa'da et al., 2013). Chopra and Meindl emphasize on the management of these flows for the purpose of maximizing profitability (Chopra and Meindl, 2001). Essentially, SCM can be seen as an attempt to address the challenges of the current businesses environment by integrating organizations, their suppliers and their customers into a seamless unit (Nel & Badenhorst-Weiss, 2010).

The healthcare supply chain in particular can be defined as a "network of entities that plan, source, fund, and distribute products and manage associated information and finances from manufacturers through intermediate warehouses and resellers to dispensing and health service delivery points" (Dalberg, 2008). It is composed of three major players at various stages, namely, producers, purchasers and healthcare providers. Producers include pharmaceutical companies, medical-surgical products companies, device manufacturers, and manufacturers of capital equipment and information systems. Purchasers include grouped purchasing organizations (GPOs), pharmaceutical wholesalers, distributors, and product representatives from manufacturers. Providers include hospitals, systems of hospitals, integrated delivery networks (IDNs), and alternate site facilities (Toba et al, 2008). The healthcare supply chain is essentially acting as an ecosystem that integrates all aspects of a supply chain, including medicines, human resources, technology, policies, distribution systems, warehousing and service delivery (UN CoLSC, 2014). An ecosystem whose management is proportionally as complex and important as the size and velocity of the healthcare industry (Beeny, 2014) and which can broaden geographic access to high quality products and services when operating with efficiency, adaptability and financial integrity (UN CoLSC, 2014).

As the main goal of SCM is to meet customers' needs and expectations with as little cost as possible, giving the same service with a low cost necessitates effective and conscious management of product, fund and information flows between supply chain members. New technologies, especially web based, assist firms in operating these flows and enhancing firms' relationships with their suppliers (Al Saa'da et al., 2013). As many scholars highlighted the significant impact of SC decisions in the success or failure of an organization, the management of the supply chain has become one of the key issues, especially in today's challenging business environment (Nel & Badenhorst-Weiss, 2010). A literature review conducted by Kritchanchai concluded that the three main SCM related problems in the healthcare industry are inconsistent and inaccurate information, fragmented systems and inefficient business processes. The author argues that three interventions: standardization, information sharing and business process re-engineering can be raised in order to address these problems (Kritchanchai, 2012). A primary task, as well as a challenge, in SCM practice is the integration of the business functions and activities throughout the supply chain, especially regarding the synchronous information access and process integration between the company and its suppliers. As such, information technology (IT) has become the backbone for companies to achieve integration with their supply chain partners and the topic of supply chain integration has drawn growing attention from researchers (Chen et al., 2013).

Recently, in the field of healthcare the concept of SCM has gained momentum as a tool for increasing productivity and improving quality, although the adoption of integrated and standardized approaches is still far from common. In particular, public healthcare organizations have been involved in a series of innovative projects that address two key SC processes with economic significance: purchasing and logistics. However, this momentum has not been matched by an increase in the research that investigates and quantifies the benefits and drawbacks of such initiatives (Lega et al., 2013). The literature on SCM has historically focused on the manufacturing and retail industries. According to Chen et al. hospital supply chains are unique and different from the typical industrial supply chains in the following five aspects: mission critical to the health of the public, dealing with many high value materials that require special handling, lack of specific universal product number classification systems and data standards, supply selections driven by physician preferences rather than sales forecasts and cost considerations, information and knowledge intensive SCM due to rapid technology and medical innovations. This results into more complex and knowledge-intensive SC practices compared to the traditional industry (Chen et al., 2013).

Nowadays companies target maximizing mutual profits with their supply chain members since having strong partners helps firms to increase their operations' efficiency (Al Saa'da et al., 2013). A study by Lee et al. suggests that successful implementation of SCM is attained through continuous SC innovation with supplier cooperation, which in turn improves organizational performance (Lee et al., 2011). This also stands true for the healthcare services sector, as developments towards better cost consciousness and process outcome change the role of the supplier, who formerly was considered as an opponent within price negotiations, into a business partner who contributes an added value to the hospitals and therefore needs to be better integrated into the procurement processes. This new, elevated role of the suppliers is represented by the supplier relationship management (SRM) concept, which combines traditional operational purchasing activities together with organizational and strategic aspects of sourcing (Mettler & Rohner, 2009). According to Herrmann & Hodgson, SRM is focused on maximizing the value of a company's supply base by providing an integrated and holistic set of management tools focused on the interaction of the company with its suppliers (Herrmann & Hodgson, 2001).

SRM related management tools and technologies have been developed mainly in highly competitive sectors such as retail and automotive, however their usage cannot be reflected into the healthcare sector due to its unique characteristics such as the extensive governmental control and its criticality for the public wellbeing. The purchasing function in the healthcare chain is still considered to be a purely cost driving function rather than a value added factor contributing to revenue increase and knowledge acquisition (Mettler & Rohner, 2009). Although the relationships with suppliers is widely recognized by procurement managers as the most important success factor in procurement (Eyholzer & Hunziker, 1999), hospital buying agents often focus exclusively on the best prices, which reflects into weak relationships and collaboration with suppliers. The role that SRM plays in this regard in the healthcare sector will be in the spotlight of this paper.

Regarding the management of supplier relationships, four phases can be identified. The first one is *Strategic sourcing,* which relates to all necessary instruments for the retrieval of information such as product information, terms and conditions which are required for the negotiation and configuration of contracts. It also includes tools for the integration and evaluation of suppliers. The second one is *Operational procurement,* which relates to all necessary instruments for ordering and conclusion of a contract such as payment and invoice verification. The third one is *Extended Cooperation*, which includes collaborative planning and design and concepts such as Vendor Managed inventory (VMI). The fourth one is *Monitoring and controlling,* which relates to all necessary instruments to measure and control the performance of strategic and functional procurement processes (Schweiger et al., 2009; Mettler & Rohner, 2009).

The importance of strategic sourcing is highlighted by a recent report of the Aberdeen Group, as it shows that 68% of companies surveyed indicate that strategic sourcing plays a prominent to critical role within their organization, demonstrating a shift from tactical short-term cost cutting to value creation which considers wider organizational objectives (Dwyer, 2010). The report identifies the major benefits of strategic sourcing (increased level of cost savings, better alignment of sourcing and business objectives, more robust management of key spend categories), the major drivers (corporate mandate to reduce cost and increase savings, need to improve sourcing performance in a dynamic global environment) and the most significant barriers (the lack of advanced techniques such as supplier optimization and the inability to integrate sourcing activities with spend analytics and supplier management) (Dwyer, 2010). Operational or functional procurement on the other side has less of a strategic orientation since it is deals with the day to day execution of the purchase to pay cycle: the processing of the purchase requisitions, the gaining of approval, the purchase order processing, the monitoring of the goods receiving, invoice verification and payables processes. The remainder of this paper will focus on the technologies that enable the abovementioned phases of strategic sourcing and functional procurement.

At this point, the use of the terms "procurement", "sourcing" and "purchasing" for the purpose of this paper should be clarified, as these terms are used in research and in business in different, sometimes overlapping, sometimes contradicting ways. The approach taken is in alignment with Eyholzer and Hunziker, who define (Eyholzer & Hunziker, 1999):

- Purchasing as "rather operational and administrative tasks that are carried out more or less by one department, namely the purchasing department,"
- Procurement as "being broader in scope than "purchasing" and including activities of strategic relevance, such as sourcing, negotiating with suppliers and coordination with R&D,"
- Sourcing as "finding and choosing the right suppliers for a product, being a cross-functional process that involves - in addition to people from the purchasing department - people from engineering, manufacturing, marketing and other departments."

3. TECHNOLOGIES ENABLING STRATEGIC SOURCING AND FUNCTIONAL PROCUREMENT

There are different technologies enabling strategic sourcing and functional procurement, among them e-Sourcing, e-Purchasing and e-MRO (Maintenance Repair and Operations) (De Boer et al., 2002). Furthermore, Electronic data interchange (EDI), Enterprise resource planning (ERP), e-Marketplaces and e-Collaboration can be added to this list (Bakker et al., 2008). Implemented procurement e-Enablement technologies provide an important opportunity to significantly enhance the capability to manage procurement information, improve commercial and procurement processes and remove waste and duplication, as shown in the case of UK's NHS (National Health Service) (Hodson-Gibbons, 2009). The technologies of e-Sourcing and e-Purchasing are considered to be at the forefront of SRM and will be taken a closer look at in the next sections of this paper.

3.1. E-Sourcing

The perception of what e-Sourcing entails has strongly evolved over the last years from a very narrow focus on e-Auctions into what is now generally accepted as e-Sourcing, namely "the Sourcing process enabled with the appropriate web-based, collaborative technology in order to facilitate the full life-cycle of the procurement process for both buyers and suppliers" (BuyIT, 2004). More specifically, e-Sourcing is the strategic activity conducted by the procurement professional to establish, manage and monitor a compliant contract and covers the buying process including specification, e-RFx, e-Tender, e-Auction, contract evaluation/ negotiation, tracking, forecasting and monitoring savings. Organizations can utilize enabling technologies within the e-Sourcing arena, which allow them to benefit from strategic sourcing in a scalable way in areas previously not addressed by purchasing. While the Return on Investment for e-Sourcing can be very positive, the primary goal should be to form a part of an integrated approach to elevate the purchasing function by addressing all elements of change: strategy, structure, systems, process and people. Therefore, e-Sourcing is considered to be the backbone of modern strategic sourcing as it automates and streamlines strategic sourcing processes such as RFx's and reverse auctions. Furthermore it enhances flexibility and transparency in the buyer-seller relationship. As shown in a report by the Aberdeen Group, e-Sourcing is the widest adopted technology solution by Best-in-Class enterprises (63%) for the purpose of supporting and streamlining their strategic sourcing programs (Limberakis, 2012).

The operational benefits of e-Sourcing as identified in a study by Booz-Allen & Hamilton are: a) streamlining of processes due to simpler/faster ordering, reduced paperwork, easy online comparison, fewer human errors and lower inventory costs and b) purchasing cost reductions due to transparency of spend, buy aggregation, better compliance, reduced maverick (out of contract) buying, comparability and competition, efficient market and pricing mechanisms, data for strategic sourcing and virtual buying organizations to increase bargaining power (Baker et al., 2000). Some of these benefits were quantified as part of a research conducted by the Aberdeen Group, namely 5– 20% reductions in material costs, reduced sourcing cycle times by 25 – 30% and time-to-market by 10 – 15% (Presutti, 2003). Due to these anticipated benefits, suppliers are facing increasing demand from the buyers to turn to online applications such as e-RFx and e-Auctions systems for negotiation and trading purposes (Ivang & Sorensen, 2005). However, the adoption of e-Sourcing represents substantial challenges for a company such as the change management required, the resulting new organizational roles, the expected speed of implementation, the management of existing suppliers, the definition of the right content management strategy and the integration with back office systems (Baker et al., 2000). Furthermore, the reluctance of suppliers can be a major reason for failure, as they perceive that e-sourcing will undermine their established relationships with their partners, which are based on human contact and communication, by performing the comparison with their competitors solely on the basis of price (White & Daniel, 2004).

As previously stated, e-RFx and e-Auctions are commonly used tools for supporting e-Sourcing. RFx stands for RFI (Request for Information - an open inquiry spanning a broad base of potential suppliers), RFQ (Request for Quotation - an opportunity for potential suppliers to competitively cost the intended purchase), RFT (Request for Tender- an opportunity for potential suppliers to submit an offer to supply goods or services against a detailed tender) and RFP (Request for Proposal- a business requirements-based request for specific solutions to the sourcing problem, sometimes based on a prior RFI) (Mhay & Coburn, n.d.). An e-Auction is a form of electronic negotiation and an electronic reverse auction (ERA) is a type of e-Auction frequently used in B2B commerce. An ERA represents a price determination method which is enabled by technology in contrast to the traditional methods of face to face negotiations and sealed bidding (Caniels & van Raaij, 2009). In a reverse auction several suppliers compete for the business to supply products or services by bidding against each other online and by successively lowering their bids, thus driving the prices down (Beall et. al, 2003). The selection of the right e-Sourcing tools is crucial to the success of the company's sourcing strategy, therefore it is necessary to carefully evaluate whether e-Sourcing is appropriate and which tool should be used for the different types of commodities to be procured (Puschmann & Alt, 2005).

3.2. E-Purchasing

The use of electronic media in procurement activities can lead to a significant cost and time reduction compared to managing the purchasing process by traditional means, as it involves the streamlining of the procurement process by eliminating paper–based documents and conducting the purchasing process via web-based systems (Zunk et al., 2014). DeBoer et al. consider e-Purchasing as the application of web based technology throughout the purchasing process (DeBoer et al., 2002). A more comprehensive definition is given by Tatsis et al., who define e-Procurement as "the integration, management, automation, optimization and enablement of an organization's procurement process, using electronic tools and technologies, and web-based applications" (Tatsis et al., 2006).

In the healthcare industry, e-Purchasing typically allows for automated drug-inventory reporting and control, drug replenishment alerts, online purchase of drugs and related medical supplies (Smith & Flanegin, 2004). Nowadays almost anything can be purchased online, from large medical equipment to rubber gloves and pharmaceuticals. The days of leafing through outdated paper catalogues are over as online ordering gives the purchaser real-time information on any given product (Ketikidis et al., 2010). As the healthcare industry is increasingly looking for innovative technologies and creative management solutions to handle the procurement processes in a competitive manner, e-Purchasing has gained strategic visibility and has emerged as the driving force behind several supply chain practices (Nzuve, 2013), as it offers to healthcare establishments notable advantages such as convenience, efficiency, broad selection, favorable pricing, information on new products and others (Ketikidis et al., 2010).

Tools used for the e-Enablement of operational procurement are (de Boer et al., 2002; Matunga et al., 2013):

- Web-based EDI-applications providing an efficient and effective way to automate the exchange of information between sellers and buyers.
- Web-based ERP Systems facilitating the creation and approval for purchase requisitions, the placement of purchase orders and their transmission to the suppliers, the goods receipts process and the payment for the goods.
- E-MRO facilitating the creation and approval for purchase requisitions, the placement of purchase orders and their transmission to the suppliers, the receiving and payment process for non-product related MRO supplies.
- E-Marketplaces where buying communities can access preferred suppliers' products and services, add to shopping carts, create requisitions, seek approval, receive purchase orders and process electronic invoices with integration to suppliers' supply chains and buyers' financial systems.
- E-collaboration where web based systems integrate across companies fostering cooperation.
- Specialized applications such as content management and catalogue building, application integration, payment and fulfillment services.

3.2.1 Benefits of E-Purchasing Applications

The literature on e-Procurement is rich with estimates of its benefits (financial and non-financial, strategic, tactical and operational) such as: Accelerated flow of information and improved collaboration between supply chain members, reduced paperwork and administrative hours, reduced ordering costs, reduced purchasing cycle times, higher price transparency, improved accuracy, improved auditing and security controls, simplified fund transfers, reduced inventory levels and associated inventory costs (Bof & Previtali, 2007; Min & Galle, 2003; Zheng et al., 2006; Davila et al., 2003; Gunasekaran & Ngai, 2008; Panayiotou et al., 2004; Calipinar & Soyzal, 2012). According to a survey by Gunasekaran, 66,7% of surveyed companies believe that successful e-Procurement implementation can improve long term organizational performance and 34,8% believe that successful e-Procurement implementation can improve short term organizational performance (Gunasekaran & Ngai, 2008). Furthermore, technology usage in purchase activities is inevitable due to the globalization, the increasing number of suppliers with the expanding complexity of products and the growing use of outsourcing and due to the fact that technology usage in procurement activities plays a pivotal role in determining the performance of firms (Batenburg, 2007). These developments towards better cost consciousness and process reengineering is expected to also affect the procurement activities in the healthcare sector. A survey in Germany revealed that approx. 70% of the hospitals and medical products suppliers utilize e-Purchasing solutions (BVMed Survey, 2007). The same survey identified reduced order cycle times (60% of respondents), less errors due to automation of processes (59%) and procurement process optimization (42%) as the top three benefits, whereas the price transparency was deemed as less important (Krankenhaus IT-Journal, 2007).

3.2.2 Barriers for E-Purchasing Applications

However, although e-Purchasing accelerates and simplifies the purchasing process between buyers and sellers, there are some barriers for its adoption, which can be categorized as (Leal, 2010):

- Security related: implications for organizations transacting over the internet.
- Technology related: high cost of technology, lack of systems integration and data standardization, lack of interoperability with existing ERP systems, immaturity of e-Purchasing based services.
- Human factor related: end user resistance to change, lack of technical expertise and e-Purchasing knowledge, fear about being replaced by automated systems, unwillingness of suppliers to embrace this technology (Zunk et al., 2014).

According to Davila et al., the risks associated with the adoption of e-Purchasing technologies are (Davila et al., 2003):

- Internal business risks, such as systems integration issues and lack of overall accepted standards.
- External business risks, such as dependency on suppliers for successful adoption of e-Purchasing models.
- Technology risks, such as the selection of the right tools which fit the specific needs of the company.
- Process risks, bridging business and technology, such as control systems in order to ensure reliability and detect unauthorized interventions as part of electronic interchange of data.

Bof & Previtali stated that the abovementioned barriers and risks tend to increase within the public sector, which requires that a bureaucratic procedure be followed due to the nature of the institutions involved and embraces audit, accountability and compliance standards with national and international rules to ensure supply competition and transparency in the awarding of contracts (Bof & Previtali, 2007). In a case study concerning the Greek governmental purchasing process, Panayiotou et al. noted that the inhibiting factors affecting the adoption and diffusion of e-Purchasing concepts in the public sector include the challenges posed by public policy and legislative constraints and the increased need for transparency in procurement (Panayiotou et al., 2004). These barriers result into relatively low adoption rates, as shown by a similar study in the Italian public healthcare sector, which found that the adoption rate of e-Procurement solutions was 21% (Bof & Previtali, 2007).

Due to the rapidly increasing financial pressures, the healthcare services sector and hospitals in particular are constantly seeking more cost- and time-saving methods to acquire supplies (H.I.D.A., 2012). Considering the outlined benefits of e-Sourcing and e-Purchasing tools, it seams that they could contribute significantly towards this direction. In order to verify this assumption, a case study was conducted in a Greek public hospital, in an attempt to provide insights of the e-Sourcing and e-Purchasing tools implementation and to identify benefits and barriers for their adoption.

4. CASE STUDY: IMPLEMENTATION OF E-SOURCING AND E-PURCHASING IN A GREEK PUBLIC HOSPITAL

The case study included interviews with procurement managers and procurement specialists of the hospital, interviews with suppliers as well as observations. The case study method was chosen since it represents a qualitative research method highly effective when a small sample of participants in a single organization is involved (Stefanou & Revanoglou, 2006). The case study was conducted in four steps.

The first step was to identify a hospital in Greece, which had implemented and utilized e-Enabling Technologies as part of its procurement processes. For this purpose, two of the leading e–Sourcing and e-Purchasing technology suppliers in Greece (cosmoONE and Business Exchange) were contacted regarding their clientele and a hospital was identified that was on the list of both suppliers, namely the General Hospital KAT (GHK) in Athens, Greece. The General Hospital KAT is a public hospital and is considered to be the largest hospital for injuries in Greece specializing in injury-related and orthopedic cases. It employs 400 doctors and its scientific and administrative personnel counts 1800 employees. GHK is considered to be among the pioneers of utilizing e-Enabling Technologies for procurement in the Greek healthcare sector as it started implementing and using these technologies in 2012. In recognition to this achievement, it received the e-volution bronze award 2014 in the category "Enterprises utilizing e-Business", an award that is given to Greek companies applying best practices in e-commerce.

The second step was to conduct semi-structured interviews with the GHK procurement manager who was in charge of the implementation of these projects, with the procurement department business experts who were using the relevant tools and with the technology-supplying vendors. The interviews were based on open-ended questions addressing the following subject areas: a) aspects of the pre-existing situation, b) benefits/issues of the new solution c) user acceptance d) management support.

The third step was to observe the traditional process of sourcing and purchasing in GHK as well as the new process of planning and conducting e-Sourcing and e-Purchasing events and transactions.

The fourth step was to gather relevant data in order to draw conclusions on the status and the benefits of e-Sourcing and e-Purchasing technologies adoption in the Greek healthcare sector.

4.1 Pre-Existing Situation and New Solution

The procurement department of GHK is responsible for the procurement of consumables (such as pharmaceutical products, implantable products, other medical supplies, medical gases, food and beverage and non-medical items), the procurement of durable goods (such as medical/surgical equipment, furniture, MRO items) and the procurement of services (such as cleaning, security, maintenance). The process of sourcing starts with the forecast-based planning and budgeting of the procurement items based on the previous year's needs and consumptions. After gaining approval for the plan by the supervising authorities, the realization of the plan starts with conducting calls for tenders. After assessing the offers, contracts are awarded to the selected suppliers. Following the signing of the contracts, procurement activities for the abovementioned goods and services are executed with reference to the existing contracts. Unforeseen procurement needs such as special requests for specific patients or vaccines for flu outbreaks are handled on a case by case basis, following a special approval process. The process of tendering and evaluating the suppliers' quotations is highly bureaucratic and time-consuming due to public nature of the hospital. Drug and supply shortages occur because a single -even insignificant- error in the procedure can lead to objections by competing suppliers nullifying the whole process so that all steps have to be reinitiated. Agreed upon prices, whether related to contracts or to out-of-contract buying, have to be in line with the price observatory maintained by the HPC (Health Procurement Committee), a governmental agency reporting to the Greek Ministry of Health and Social Security.

The problems identified were:

- Lengthy procedures for planning and approving the yearly procurement plans and corresponding budgets.

- Legislative hurdles due to the large number and complexity of relevant laws.
- Huge variety of products due to evolution of technology and science.
- Different technical specifications among public hospitals for the same products.
- Lack of data standardization.
- Obstacles due to easiness of lawsuit filing regarding contract award procedures from competing vendors.
- Large product price variations between different hospitals.
- Lack of tools and reports to control the consumption of goods and services within the hospital.
- Lack of systems integration.

In order to address some of these issues, GHK decided to implement e-Enabling technologies for procurement in a two-phased approach. The first phase entailed the implementation of e-Sourcing tools and the second phase would expand into e-Purchasing technologies. For this purpose, leading suppliers for procurement e-Enabling technologies based on ASP (Application Service Provider) models were selected and provided the tools necessary as well as facilitated the new processes. Firstly, it was decided which procurement items would be sourced using the new technologies, based on criteria like simplicity of products and repeatability of procurement processes. The suppliers were informed regarding the new procedures on e-RFx and e-Auctions, received access to the electronic platforms and participated in an online training session. Following that, mock auctions were held, in order to make sure that the suppliers felt comfortable with the tool and that there were no technical issues. Finally, the real e-Auctions were held, typically lasting one hour, with an automated two minute extension in case bids were made in the last two minutes of the session. Currently, as part of the second phase, GHK is in the process of evaluating options for the e-Purchasing tools, that should support purchase requisition creation and approval processes as well as purchase order processing through the access of online catalogs, which will be created based on the awarded contracts of the HPC.

4.2 Findings

The drivers for the introduction of e-Sourcing and e-Purchasing activities at the GHK were the expected cost savings due to lower purchase prices and reduced administrative costs, the reduced purchasing cycle times, the streamlining and standardization of the procurement processes resulting in freeing up resources for more value added procurement activities and the improved ability in regards to monitoring and controlling these activities. The successful implementation of the e-Sourcing tools was attributed among others to the high user acceptance and upper management support, as was pointed out in the interviews held. The abovementioned expectations were met to some extent after the successful implementation of e-Sourcing tools, namely e-RFx and e-Auctions, however it should be noted that the adoption of these technologies was not followed up by organizational and process changes. Thus, the strategic impact of e-technologies on SCM effectiveness and patient safety in a healthcare setting could not be verified. The cost of the implementation of e-Sourcing tools did not represent a barrier, as it was very low due to the fact that GHK utilized solutions readily available by ASP vendors and did not perform any type of business process reengineering. The perception of the involved stakeholders (procurement personnel, procurement managers, upper management) regarding the implementation and the outcome of these initiatives was positive.

Table 1. Impact on avg. time between invitation and response and avg. no. of invitations by tender

	GHK	No. of Tenders	No. of Invited Suppliers	No. of Responding Suppliers	Avg. Time (d) between Invitation and Response	Avg. No. of Invitations by Tender
Medical/surgical consumables	Vascular Surgery Implants	80	224	168	0,09	2,80
	Haemostatics	4	12	10	0,25	3,00
	Blood sampling bags	6	33	21	3,17	5,50
	Diagnostic catheters	3	28	13	3,00	9,33
	Stents	9	50	26	0,67	5,56
	Haemodynamic supplies	22	277	122	3,41	12,59
	X-ray supplies	9	141	63	1,56	15,67
	Not classified	30	162	69	1,30	5,40
	Total	*163*	*927*	*492*	*1,04*	*5,69*
IT-related	Printers	2	10	0	4,00	5,00
	Total	*2*	*10*	*0*	*4,00*	*5,00*
Other supplies	Airconditioners	1	7	4	1,00	7,00
	Total	*1*	*7*	*4*	*1,00*	*7,00*
	Overall Total	*166*	*944*	*496*	*1,08*	*5,69*

e-Sourcing tools such as e-RFx and e-Auctions, were extensively used as part of the procurement department's sourcing activities. More specific, GHK managed to:

- Generate cost savings.
- Drastically reduce the average time between the invitation and the response from the supplier.
- Significantly increase the average number of invitations by tender.

As part of the analysis, data were collected for a time period spanning over two years, starting in 2012, when the e-Sourcing tools were implemented. During this period 105 e-Auctions were executed and resulted in cost savings in the amount of approx. 63.500 €, which represent a cost savings ratio of about 6,5%.

The average time between the invitation and the response from the supplier fell drastically from a few days to one day and the average number of invitations by tender increased almost twofold to 5,7 as can be seen in Table 1.

5. CONCLUSION

Our research revealed that the implementation of e-Sourcing and e-Purchasing technologies is at an early evolutionary stage in the Greek Healthcare Sector as can be seen by the findings of the case study on GHK, a public hospital considered to be in the forefront of e-business. E-Sourcing and e-Purchasing initiatives are focusing on e-RFx, e-Auctions and online catalog purchasing mostly for price sensitive goods. Benefits from using these technologies were identified and quantified. The positive findings suggest that a diffusion of these technologies in the Greek healthcare sector should be expected in the coming years, driven mainly from a cost-cutting necessity viewpoint. A more comprehensive study across Greek hospitals should be performed in order to verify this assumption and in order to investigate potential differences regarding barriers and adoption rates between public and private healthcare facilities.

REFERENCES

Al-Saa'da, R., Abu Taleb, Y., Al-Mahasneh, R., Nimer, N., & Al-Weshah, G. (2013). Supply Chain Management and Its Effect on Health Care Service Quality: Quantitative Evidence from Jordanian Private Hospitals. *Journal of Management and Strategy*, *4*(2), 42–51.

Baker, H., Cade, S., Oudijk, M., Ramachandran, C., Roth, J., Schwarting, D., & van Leeuwen, J. (2000). E-sourcing: 21st Century Purchasing. *Booz Allen & Hamilton*. Retrieved July 14, 2014, from http://www.boozallen.com/media/file/80568.pdf

Bakker, E., Zheng, J., Knight, L., & Harland, C. (2008). Putting e-commerce adoption in a supply chain context. *International Journal of Operations & Production Management*, *28*(4), 313–330. doi:10.1108/01443570810861543

Batenburg, R. (2007). E-procurement adoption by European firms: A quantitative analysis. *Journal of Purchasing and Supply Management*, *13*(3), 182–192. doi:10.1016/j.pursup.2007.09.014

Beall, S., Carter, C., Carter, P., Germer, T., Hendrick, T., Jap, S., & Petersen, K. et al. (2003). *The Role of Reverse Auctions in Strategic Sourcing*. CAPS Research.

Beeny, R. (2014). Supply Chain Visibility in Healthcare – Beyond the Dashboard. *Hospital & Healthcare Management*. Retrieved July 14, 2014, from http://www.tecsys.com/company/news/TECSYS-LifeScienceLogistics-HealthcareVisibility.pdf

Bof, F., & Previtali, P. (2007). Organisational Pre-Conditions for e-Procurement in Governments: The Italian Experience in the Public Health Care Sector. *The Electronic Journal of E-Government*, *5*(1), 1–10.

BuyIT Best Practice Network. (2004). *E-Sourcing: A BuyIT e-Procurement Best Practice Guideline*. Retrieved July 14, 2014, from https://www.cips.org/Documents/Knowledge/Procurement-Topics-and-Skills/12-E-commerce-Systems/E-Sourcing-E-Procurement-Systems/BuyIT_e-Sourcing.pdf

BVMed Survey. (2007). *Elektronisches Beschaffungswesen im Gesundheitsmarkt vor dem Durchbruch. Bundesverband Medizintechnologie*. Retrieved July 14, 2014, from http://www.bvmed.de/print/de/bvmed/presse/pressemeldungen/bvmed-umfrage-elektronisches-beschaffungswesen-im-gesundheitsmarkt-vor-dem-durchbruch

Calipinar, H., & Soysal, M. (2012). E-Procurement: A Case Study about the Health Sector in Turkey. *International Journal of Business and Social Science*, *3*(7), 232–244.

Caniels, M., & van Raaij, E. (2009). Do all suppliers dislike electronic reverse auctions? *Journal of Purchasing and Supply Management*, *15*(1), 12–23. doi:10.1016/j.pursup.2008.10.003

Chen, D., Preston, D., & Xia, W. (2013). Enhancing hospital supply chain performance: A relational view and empirical test. *Journal of Operations Management, 31*(6), 391–408. doi:10.1016/j.jom.2013.07.012

Chopra, S., & Meindl, P. (2001). *E-business and the supply chain, Supply Chain Management.* Upper Saddle River, NJ: Prentice-Hall.

Council of Supply Chain Management Professionals. (2013). *Bylaws of CSCMP.* Retrieved July 14, 2014, from http://cscmp.org/sites/default/files/user_uploads/footer/downloads/bylaws/cscmp-bylaws-i.pdf

Dalberg Global Development Advisors and the MIT-Zaragoza International Logistics Program (2008). *The Private Sector's Role in Health Supply Chains: Review of the Role and Potential for Private Sector Engagement in Developing Country Health Supply Chains.* Author.

Davila, A., Gupta, M., & Palmer, R. (2003). Moving Procurement Systems to the Internet: The Adoption and Use of E-Procurement Technology Models. *European Management Journal, 21*(1), 11–23. doi:10.1016/S0263-2373(02)00155-X

De Boer, L., Harink, J., & Heijboer, G. (2002). A conceptual model for assessing the impact of electronic procurement. *European Journal of Purchasing and Supply Management, 8*(1), 25–33. doi:10.1016/S0969-7012(01)00015-6

De Vries, J., & Huijsman, R. (2011). Supply chain management in health services: An overview, *Supply Chain Management. International Journal (Toronto, Ont.), 16*(3), 159–165.

Dwyer, C. (2010). *Strategic Sourcing: The 2010 Guide to Driving Savings and Procurement Performance.* Aberdeen Group. Retrieved July 14, 2014, from http://www.aberdeen.com/research/6305/ra-strategic-sourcing-savings-procurement/content.aspx

Eyholzer, K., & Hunziker, D. (1999). *Internet-Einsatz in der Beschaffung – Eine empirische Untersuchung in Schweizer Unternehmen, Arbeitsbericht Nr. 118.* Universitaet Bern, Schweiz: Institut fuer Wirtschaftsinformatik.

Fragkiadakis, G., Doumpos, M., Zopounidis, C., & Germain, C. (2014). Operational and economic efficiency analysis of public hospital in Greece. *Annals of Operations Research,* (September), 2014.

Gunasekaran, A., & Ngai, E. (2008). Adoption of e-procurement in Hong Kong: An empirical research. *International Journal of Production Economics, 113*(1), 159–175. doi:10.1016/j.ijpe.2007.04.012

Health Industry Distributors Association (H.I.D.A.) Educational Foundation. (2012). *Hospital Procurement Study: Quantifying Supply Chain Costs for Distributor and Direct Orders.* Retrieved July 14, 2014, from http://www.hida.org/App_Themes/Member/docs/Hospital_Procurement.pdf

Herrmann, J., & Hodgson, B. (2001). SRM: Leveraging the Supply Base for Competitive Advantage. *Proceedings of the SMTA International Conference.* Chicago, IL: SMTA.

Hodson-Gibbons, R. (2009). The NHS Procurement eEnablement Programme – Using information to deliver better healthcare. GS1 Healthcare Reference Book 2009/10 (pp. 22-25). GS1.

Ivang, R., & Sorensen, O. (2005). E-markets in the Battle Zone between Relationship and Transaction Marketing. *Electronic Markets, 15*(4), 393–404. doi:10.1080/10196780500303086

Kanyoma, K., Khomba, J., Sankhulani, E., & Hanif, R. (2013). Sourcing Strategy and Supply Chain Risk Management in the Healthcare Sector: A Case Study of Malawi's Public Healthcare Delivery Supply Chain. *Journal of Management and Strategy*, *4*(3), 16–26. doi:10.5430/jms.v4n3p16

Ketikidis, P., Kontogeorgis, A., Stalidis, G., & Kaggelides, K. (2010). Applying e- procurement system in the healthcare: The EPOS paradigm. *International Journal of Systems Science*, *41*(3), 281–299. doi:10.1080/00207720903326878

Krankenhaus IT-Journal. (2007). *Online-Beschaffung hilft den Krankenhäusern zu überleben. Bundes-verband Medizintechnologie. Ausgabe 2/2007.* Retrieved July 14, 2014, from http://www.medizin-edv.de/ARCHIV/Online-Beschaffung_hilft_den_Krankenhaeusern....pdf

Kritchanchai, D. (2012). A Framework for Healthcare Supply Chain Improvement in Thailand. *Operations and Supply Chain Management*, *5*(2), 103–113.

Kumar, A., Ozdamar, L., & Zhang, C. (2008). Supply chain redesign in the healthcare industry of Singapore. *International Journal of Supply Chain Management*, *13*(2), 95–103. doi:10.1108/13598540810860930

Leal, P. (2010). *Evolution in public procurement and the impact of e-procurement platforms: a case study. Unpublished work project.* Portugal: University Nova de Lisboa.

Lee, S., Lee, D., & Schniederjans, M. (2011). Supply chain innovation and organizational performance in the healthcare industry. *International Journal of Operations & Production Management*, *31*(11), 1193–1214. doi:10.1108/01443571111178493

Lega, F., Marsilio, M., & Villa, S. (2013). An evaluation framework for measuring supply chain performance in the public healthcare sector: Evidence from the Italian NHS. *Production Planning & Control: The Management of Operations*, *24*(10-11), 931–947. doi:10.1080/09537287.2012.666906

Limberakis, C. (2012). *Advanced Sourcing: Maximizing Savings Identification.* Aberdeen Group. Retrieved July 14, 2014, from http://www.aberdeen.com/research/7398/ra-strategic-sourcing-management/content.aspx

Matunga, D., Nyanamba, S., & Okibo, W. (2013). The Effect of E-Procurement Practices on Effective Procurement in Public Hospitals: A Case of KISII Level 5 Hospital. *American International Journal of Contemporary Research*, *3*(8), 103–111.

Meijboom, B., Schmidt-Bakx, S., & Westert, G. (2011). Supply chain management practices for improving patient-oriented care. *Supply Chain Management: An International Journal*, *16*(3), 166–175. doi:10.1108/13598541111127155

Mettler, T., & Rohner, P. (2009). Supplier Relationship Management: A Case Study in the Context of Health Care. *Journal of Theoretical and Applied Electronic Commerce Research*, *4*(3), 58–71. doi:10.4067/S0718-18762009000300006

Mhay, S., & Coburn, C. (n.d.). *Request for Procurement Processes (RFT RFQ RFP RFI).* The Negotiation Experts. Retrieved July 14, 2014, from http://www.negotiations.com/articles/procurement-terms

Min, H., & Galle, W. (2003). E-purchasing: Profiles of adopters and nonadopters. *Industrial Marketing Management*, *32*(3), 227–233. doi:10.1016/S0019-8501(02)00266-3

Mustaffa, N., & Potter, A. (2009). Healthcare supply chain management in Malaysia: A case study. *Supply Chain Management: An International Journal, 14*(3), 234–243. doi:10.1108/13598540910954575

Nachtmann, H., & Pohl, E. (2009). *The State of Healthcare Logistics: Cost and Quality Improvement Opportunities*. Center for Innovation in Healthcare Logistics, University of Arkansas.

Nel, J., & Badenhorst-Weiss, J. (2010). Supply chain design: Some critical questions. *Journal of Transport and Supply Chain Management, 4*(1), 198–223.

Nzuve, M. (2013). *Implementation of e-Procurement Practices among Private Hospitals in Nairobi, Kenya. Unpublished research project*. Kenya: University of Nairobi.

Panayiotou, N., Gayialis, S., & Tatsiopoulos, P. (2004). AN e-procurement system for governmental purchasing. *International Journal of Production Economics, 90*(1), 79–102. doi:10.1016/S0925-5273(03)00103-8

Pleasant, J. (2009). Change has finally come: U.S. Healthcare industry to implement common data standards to improve safety, reduce costs. GS1 Healthcare Reference Book 2009/10 (pp. 6-9). GS1.

Presutti, W. Jr. (2003). Supply management and e-procurement: Creating value added in the supply chain. *Industrial Marketing Management, 32*(3), 219–226. doi:10.1016/S0019-8501(02)00265-1

Puschmann, T., & Alt, R. (2005). Successful use of e-procurement in supply chains. *Supply Chain Management: An International Journal, 10*(2), 122–135. doi:10.1108/13598540510589197

Schweiger, J., Ortner, W., Tschandl, M., & Busse, K. (2009). *Supplier Relationship Management: Bewertung und Auswahl von SRM-Portallösungen*. Unpublished work project, FH Joanneum, Kapfenberg, Austria.

Sila, I., Ebrahimpour, M., & Birkholz, C. (2006). Quality in supply chains: An empirical analysis. *Supply Chain Management: An International Journal, 11*(6), 491–502. doi:10.1108/13598540610703882

Smith, A., & Flanegin, F. (2004). E-procurement and automatic identification: Enhancing supply chain management in the healthcare industry. *International Journal of Electronic Healthcare, 1*(2), 176–198. doi:10.1504/IJEH.2004.005866 PMID:18048219

Stefanou, C., & Revanoglou, A. (2006). ERP integration in a healthcare environment: A case study. *Journal of Enterprise Information Management, 19*(1), 115–130. doi:10.1108/17410390610636913

Tatsis, V., Mena, C., Van Wassenhove, L., & Whicker, L. (2006). E-procurement in the Greek food and drink industry: Drivers and impediments. *Journal of Purchasing and Supply Management, 12*(2), 63–74. doi:10.1016/j.pursup.2006.04.003

Toba, S., Tomasini, M., & Yang, H. (2008). Supply Chain Management in Hospital: A Case Study. *California Journal of Operations Management, 6*(1), 49–55.

United Nations Commission on Life-Saving Commodities. (2014). *Private Sector Engagement A Guidance Document for Supply Chains in the Modern Context*. UN CoLSC Technical Reference Team. Retrieved July 14, 2014, from http://unfpa.org/webdav/site/global/shared/procurement/10_supply_chain/UNCoLSC%20Private%20Sector%20Engagement%20Guidance%20Document_FINAL.pdf

UPS Pain in the Supply Chain Survey. (2013). Retrieved July 14, 2014, from http://pressroom.ups.com/pressroom/staticfiles/pdf/fact_sheets/2013_UPS_Pain_in_the_Supply_Chain_Exec_Summary.pdf

White, A., & Daniel, E. (2004). The impact of e-marketplaces on dyadic buyer-supplier relationships: Evidence from the healthcare sector. *Journal of Enterprise Information Management, 17*(6), 441–453. doi:10.1108/17410390410566733

Zheng, J., Bakker, E., Knight, L., Gilhespy, H., Harland, C., & Walker, H. (2006). A strategic case for e-adoption in healthcare supply chains. *International Journal of Information Management, 26*(4), 290–301. doi:10.1016/j.ijinfomgt.2006.03.010

Zunk, B., Marchner, M., Uitz, I., Lerch, C., & Schiele, H. (2014). The Role of E-Procurement in the Austrian Construction Industry: Adoption Rate, Benefits and Barriers. *International Journal of Industrial Engineering and Management, 5*(1), 13–21.

Chapter 6
The Evaluation of Business Performance in ERP Environments

Vicky Manthou
University of Macedonia, Greece

Constantinos J. Stefanou
Alexander TEI of Thessaloniki, Greece

Kalliopi Tigka
University of Macedonia, Greece

ABSTRACT

ERP systems, supporting and integrating all business processes across functions and offering real time information necessary for taking actions and making decisions, have prevailed in most enterprises worldwide. The costs involved in ERP implementations may be huge and must be justified by the outcomes. However, extant research has reported mixed and in some cases controversial results. In this chapter, certain important dimensions of ERP systems and of business performance are discussed. The chapter has an educational focus and aims at providing an exploration of ERP system's impact on certain business performance dimensions, informing thus scholars, practitioners and students of the issues involved and the areas they should pay attention when considering ERP implementations. Following an extensive literature review, a classification of diverse studies according to their research focus is provided, which reveals the range of business performance dimensions and can help researchers in their future projects.

INTRODUCTION

This chapter explores the impact of ERP systems on business performance as reported in literature. Considering the significant investment needed and the total cost occurring in ERP implementations, the impact of ERP systems on business performance is an important subject, especially as many studies in the past have reported mixed results or reached to vague conclusions. For example, according to Beard

DOI: 10.4018/978-1-4666-8841-4.ch006

& Sumner (2004), the use of an ERP system does not reduce business costs more than if the system had not been implemented. Bendoly et al. (2009) argued that the correct use of information in conjunction with operational excellence and customer intimacy can lead to an increase in strategic performance, causing business profitability. Hunton et al (2003) reported the improvement of financial indices such as return on assets (ROA) and return on investment (ROI), which were significantly better over a 3-year period for the ERP adopting firms as compared to non-adopters. However, they also found that there is no difference in the improvement of financial performance between pre and post-adoption of the ERP system, a finding consistent with Poston and Grabski (2001). On the other hand, Sudzina et al. (2011) reports positive impact on the financial performance of the adopting organization. The inconsistency of the findings regarding ERP investment's impact on firm performance confirms the complexity and elusiveness of the subject (Stefanou, 2001).

According to Nazemi et al. (2012) many enterprises, which adopt ERPs, do not manage to achieve improved operational performance and added strategic value. This is attributed to the fact that they do not fully understand ERP systems and their lifecycle. It has been also argued (Stefanou et al, 2014) that in the literature certain important dimensions of ERP systems have not been considered extensively and exclusively considered as having an impact on firm performance. ERP systems are distinct from legacy systems in various aspects and it is plausible that certain characteristics of ERP software, e.g. the extent of integration of business processes mapped into the ERP systems, may have an impact on some dimensions of what is called in general business performance but not on others. Therefore, in this chapter we report the findings and provide a classification of ERP related studies according to their research focus as far as the dimensions of business performance are concerned. The chapter is organized as follows: Next section provides the background of the discussion. The following section presents a literature review on ERP systems impact on business performance. Finally, conclusions and suggestions for future research are presented.

BACKGROUND

ERP systems are now the prevailing business information systems platform in most enterprises worldwide. However, and despite the fact that ERP research has been conducted extensively during the last twenty years, a number of ERP systems failures has been reported in the last years. These failures have a negative or even a severe consequence on the adopting organizations. But what is the outcome in situations where there is no obvious failure of the ERP system? Does it provide the solid informational foundation needed for a sustainable competitive advantage and excellence in business performance? The delivery of benefits following an ERP system implementation is not straightforward. This is a well-known fact in IS research, described by the general term "IT productivity paradox". It has been argued that data and methodological problems are to be blamed as the source for the contradictory results (Brynjolfsson, 2003). Other managerial and organizational factors related to IT/IS seem to play a crucial role for achieving company's goals. It has been argued for, example, that human factors have a decisive role in explaining why and how enactments of information technologies change over time (Boudreau and Robey, 2005).

Business performance is a general term and takes a variety of forms and content according to the context it is referred to. Most studies view company performance broadly, as having both a financial and a non-financial dimension. In addition, many studies have attempted to assess the relationship between ERPs and the performance of a firm from different perspectives and based on different research approaches. This is absolutely required, because ERP software has usually an impact on organizational and operational excellence which is not reflected immediately in the financial indices or in severe cost reductions. According to Beard & Sumner (2004), the use of an ERP system does not reduce business costs more than if the system had not been implemented. Most of the benefits of ERP fall under the 'added value' criterion, such as improved customer service. It can also have a positive impact on specific organizational functions, such as accounting, costing and auditing (see e.g. Spathis and Ananiadis, 2005; Sutton, 2006; Kanellou and Spathis, 2011; Vakalfotis et al, 2011).

It has been argued (Stefanou, 2001) that ERP systems, which lead to changed organizational structure and transformed business processes in order to reach simplification and integration, have a wide range of benefits. Financial measures suggested in the literature such as Net Present Value (NPV) or Return on Investment (ROI), are not alone sufficient to support ERP justification, mainly because of the following reasons: there are benefits that are not easily identifiable, others that although are identifiable, they are not quantifiable and finally, there are benefits that emerge not from the use of ERP system but from the organizational changes proposed by ERP.

Long-term cost reductions may occur in ERP implementations, but there is no clear evidence that companies can achieve a competitive advantage through cost reductions induced by the ERP system alone. On the other hand, the researchers argue that businesses can reap the benefits through the right planning of the ERP system and successful management of the ERP project, business process reengineering and post-implementation alignment of the ERP system with the organization's strategy. Stefanou (2001) has also suggested that cost reductions would be a source of competitive advantage, although these reductions do not derive from the use of the ERP system per se, but they follow the re-organization and re-engineering of business processes as a result of implementing the ERP system. This is so because in most cases, enterprises have to adapt their processes to the software's best practices, rather the other way round, due to the extreme complexity of the software and the serious risks involved in ERP implementations.

BUSINESS PERFORMANCE AND ERP SYSTEMS

A stream of research focuses mainly on the financial performance of ERP adopting organizations. There are studies reporting positive influence of the ERP systems on the financial performance of the adopting organization (e.g. Sudzina et al. 2011). Other studies warn that this may indicate a decline in the financial performance of non-adopters rather that an improvement in the financial performance because of the implementation of the ERP system (Hunton et al, 2003).

The result of just the announcement of an IT implementation in an enterprise has attracted the attention of a number of researchers. Hayes et al. (2001) highlight the fact that stock markets have a positive reaction to such announcements. Similar results were obtained by Ranganathan and Samarah (2003). It is true, however, that stock markets react positively or negatively to all sorts of announcements and not just to those related with ERP implementation. Poston and Grabski (2001) following a different approach measured the profitability of an ERP adopter firm and compared it with its profitability before the new systems' adoption. Although someone would expect that innovative IT technologies could be related to changes in firm's profitability, they found no connection between ERP deployment and profitability. Velcu (2005), using financial ratios such as Return on Investment (ROI) and Return on Assets (ROA), investigated whether the successful ERP adopters have a higher financial performance compared to the less successful ERP adopters. It was assumed that a less successful adoption prevent the efficiency of assets utilization and business processes. The findings showed no significant difference in the financial performance after ERP implementation between the two groups of firms, at least as far as ROA and ROI are concerned. However, successful ERP adopters seems to have better efficiency benefits than the less successful ERP adopters, in terms of Assets Turnover and Capital Turnover, during the first two years of the ERP's implementation. In a study by Liu et al (2008), no financial benefits were observed during ERP implementation or three years after the implementation.

The impact of ERP on corporate performance combined with the impact of Non-Financial Performance Incentives (NFPI) was the focus of the study reported by Wier et al. (2005). Performance is again measured using financial ratios, such as ROA and ROS (Return on Sales). The authors use three sub-samples. The first one contains firms that disclosed the implementation of an ERP system but not the use NFPI, the second one contains firms that disclosed the use of NFPI with specific weights assigned to NFPI, but without the adoption of an ERP system and the third one contains firms that make use of both an ERP system and NFPI. According to the authors' findings, the combination of ERP and NFPI leads to higher ROA and ROS than ERP-only or NFPI-only, as far as the short-term and long-term are concerned. Hendricks et al. (2007) focused their research on the financial benefits of ERP among different enterprise systems. A key conclusion is that, although the cost for ERP implementation is very high, there is no evidence for negative relationship between financial performance and ERP implementation.

Nicolaou and Bhattacharya (2008) tested the effect of post-implementation activities on firms that have adopted ERP systems. It was found that the quality of Post Implementation Review (PIR) influences the sustainability of financial and other performance measures. One of their research questions was if there is difference in the financial performance between firms that employ PIR quality activities and firms that do not employ such activities. The authors concluded that PIR activities that have to do with better system implementation planning and business process effectiveness, result to a significant improvement as far as ROI, ROS, the cost of goods sold over sales ratio and the employee efficiency ratio are concerned. However, PIR activities which have to do with system fit resolution, global reach and attaining benefits, seems to have a negative effect on profitability.

While many studies concentrate on the financial benefits of ERP implementations, there are also many others having a different focus. Strategic (e.g. Chand et al, 2005) as well as organizational, operational and managerial benefits resulting from ERP adoption have been reported by many researchers (see e.g. Loo et al., 2013; Madapusi and D'Souza, 2012; Aslan et al.2012; Stefanou and Revanoglou, 2006). A lot of moderating parameters seem to play a decisive role in the realization of benefits, such as the time period passed after the implementation, the integration of ERP software with other enterprise systems, such as SCM and CRM, the size of the company and the extent of the post-implementation review of the ERP systems to name but a few. Madapusi and D'Souza (2012) confirmed the findings from other studies, that ERP system implementations influences operational performance. Powel et al (2013), by applying a multiple-case-study approach, assessed the functionality offered by ERP systems to support pull production.

The needed ERP implementation time and how it influences firm performance was the main objective of Anderson et al. (2011). According to the authors, there are two different approaches of ERP as far as the time is concerned: "accelerated implementation approach" and "traditional (longer) implementation approach". Each has its own benefits and costs. The first approach allows a firm to take advantage of the benefits of an ERP implementation (for example better customer service, better and in-time information) in a short time, but that firm does not redesign its processes in a way that is completely different than its competitors and therefore, does not gain a competitive advantage. Just the opposite is what happens when a firm adopts the second approach. In more detail, ERP implementation takes a long time but the processes of the firm are redesigned and in agreement with a completely new, improved strategy. In order for firm performance to be measured, ratios like ROA and ROS were used. Anderson et al. (2011) concluded that accelerated implementation lead not only to operational but also to strategic advantages and might be the choice of the firms from now on.

Loo et al. (2013) focusing on the impact of ERP adoption by small and medium firms on the organizational benefits, concluded that all of the SMEs that implemented an ERP-system in the last three years needed less than three years for organizational benefits to start materializing. Benefits of the combination of ERP and Supply Chain Management (SCM) are presented in the research of Wieder et al. (2006). The impact of ERPs on the organizational performance is the issue. The main findings of their study suggest that there are no performance differences between companies that had adopted ERPs and those that had not. The authors also argued that the longer the experience a company has with ERP system, the higher its performance. According to their evidence, the cause of the not so high performance of ERP adopters was that companies in Australia need more time in order to recover from the shock of an ERP implementation. Integrated as well as extended ERP systems seem to add value to adopting firms (see e.g. Themistocleous et al., 2001; Wieder et al., 2006; Koh et al, 2008). Chang et al (2008) have also considered competitive advantage benefits arising from ERP/SCM implementations. Apart from SCM, other add-on or integrated systems such as CRM or Business Intelligence (BI) software seem to enhance the performance of ERP systems. In another study, it was found that ERP implementation possibly results in a decrease in organizational flexibility and resilience (Ignatiadis and Nandhakumar, 2007).

Bendoly et al. (2009) argued that the correct use of information in conjunction with operational excellence and customer intimacy can lead to an increase in strategic performance, engendering business profitability. Their research showed that most companies are planning ERP systems in cooperation with the companies that develop such systems. But few of these companies reach their goal, namely the proper implementation of systems that increases the competitive advantage. Instead, there is a decline in systems performance which is attributed to the facts that there is insufficient knowledge of the partners and ERP consultants in the design of the system, there is not a proper evaluation system installed, and the system is not often understood by the partners themselves and by users.

Madapusi and D'Souza (2012), broke up ERP implementation into modules. The number of those modules was fourteen and some of them were financials, sales and distribution, materials management and human resources. Their conclusion was that each of the fourteen modules influences firm performance dissimilarly. Eight of the fourteen modules seem to influence firm performance significantly. In addition, the more ERP modules are implemented by a firm, the more strengthened its performance will be.

It is clear from the above that contradictory findings have been reported in literature. It is also true that various studies have a totally different research focus. Stefanou et al (2014) concluded that most studies concerning ERP systems impact on business performance report benefits or measures of business performance which fall into one or more of these three categories, namely operational/managerial, financial and strategic. Financial performance refers to the short-run business performance and is measured mainly by financial indices, such as Return on Assets (ROA) and Return on Investment (ROI). Market reaction to this performance may be mirrored to the company's stock price in the market. Non-financial performance, such as organizational excellence and smooth execution of business functions is measured mainly by non-financial performance indices, such as the quality of customer service. And finally, competitive advantage refers to the long-run position of the firm in the marketplace and is measured by both financial and non-financial indices, such as the quality of information available for strategic decision making and financial indices suitable for the long-term assessment of the firm. Following this classification, Table 1 depicts studies and the related focus of research. Studies focusing on a certain function of a company, e.g. accounting, were excluded.

CONCLUSION

In this chapter we considered ERP system's impact on several important dimensions of business performance. Financial performance, operational and managerial excellence and strategic/competitive

Table 1. Main focus of empirical studies

Empirical Studies		Main Focus of Study		
Year	Author(s)	Operational/ Organizational/ Managerial Performance	Financial Performance	Competitive Advantage/ Strategic Benefits
2001	Poston & Grabski		√	
2001	Hayes et al		√	
2003	Hunton et al		√	√
2003	Mabert at al	√	√	
2003	Sarkis et al	√		
2004	Beard & Sumner		√	√
2005	Nicolaou & Bhattacharya	√	√	
2005	Chand et al	√		√
2005	Velcu		√	
2006	Wieder et al	√		
2007	Wier at al		√	
2007	Nicolaou & Bhattacharya		√	
2007	Ignatiadis & Nandhakumar	√		
2007	Hendricks et al		√	
2008	Liu et al		√	
2008	Bradley	√	√	
2008	Nicolaou & Bhattacharya		√	
2008	Koh et al	√	√	
2009	Bendoly et al		√	√
2009	Huang et al	√	√	
2011	Pang-Lo Liu			√
2011	Sudzina et al		√	
2011	Anderson et al			√
2012	Aslan et al	√		
2012	Madapusi D'Souza	√	√	
2013	Powell et al	√		

advantage are the three main categories embracing the dimensions of business performance and success cited mostly in the literature. By reviewing the literature it was apparent that many environmental parameters and characteristics of the ERP systems, such as the degree of their integration, the extent of post implementation review, the extended functionality of ERP software following the implementation of add-on systems such as CRM and SCM systems, the time needed to complete ERP implementation the period that the ERP system is in use, have been examined. At the same time there is certainly a lack of a coherent and holistic model of ERP systems' impact on business performance. This calls for additional empirical and theoretical research aiming at investigating the relationships between the several structural dimensions of ERP systems and realizations of business performance metrics. So far the findings reported in the literature are inconsistent and sometimes contradictory. It is recommendable that future research should consider the global economic environment in which many ERP adopting organizations operate. For example, in SCM environments, the performance of the ERP systems is greatly influenced by the ERP systems of the other supply chain members. If the ERP systems of the members are incompatible, this could result in a reduction in ERP system performance and consequently could deteriorate business performance. In addition, certain control factors identified in the literature of IS, such as the size of the organisation, should be considered in conducting the empirical research. The interaction between ERP systems and other related important managerial functions such as continuous auditing and monitoring could have an important effect on controlling managerial and organizational activities and reducing operating costs. Finally, we would suggest an international research in order to obtain different samples and identify whether cultural differences are significant.

REFERENCES

Anderson, M., Banker, R. D., Menon, N. M., & Romero, J. A. (2011). Implementing enterprise resource planning systems: Organizational performance and the duration of the implementation. *Information Technology Management*, *12*(3), 197–212. doi:10.1007/s10799-011-0102-9

Aslan, B., Stevenson, N., & Hendry, L. C. (2012). Enterprise Resource Planning systems: An assessment of applicability to Make-To-Order companies. *Computers in Industry*, *63*(7), 692–705. doi:10.1016/j.compind.2012.05.003

Beard, J. W., & Sumner, M. (2004). Seeking strategic advantage in the post-net era: Viewing ERP systems from the resource-based perspective. *The Journal of Strategic Information Systems*, *13*(2), 129–150. doi:10.1016/j.jsis.2004.02.003

Bendoly, E., Rosenzweig, E. D., & Stratman, J. K. (2009). The efficient use of enterprise information for strategic advantage: A data envelopment analysis. *Journal of Operations Management*, *27*(4), 310–323. doi:10.1016/j.jom.2008.11.001

Boudreau, M., & Robey, D. (2005). Enacting integrated information technology: A human agency perspective. *Organization Science*, *16*(1), 3–18. doi:10.1287/orsc.1040.0103

Brynjolfsson, E. (1993). The Productivity Paradox of Information Technology. *Communications of the ACM*, *36*(12), 67–77. doi:10.1145/163298.163309

Chand, D., Hachey, G., Hunton, J., Owhoso, V., & Vasudevan, S. (2005). A balanced scorecard based framework for assessing the strategic impacts of ERP systems. *Computers in Industry*, *56*(6), 558–572. doi:10.1016/j.compind.2005.02.011

Chang, I.-C., Hwang, H.-G., Liaw, H.-C., Hung, M.-C., Chen, S.-L., & Yen, D. C. (2008). A neural network evaluation model for ERP performance from SCM perspective to enhance enterprise competitive advantage. *Expert Systems with Applications*, *35*(4), 1809–1816. doi:10.1016/j.eswa.2007.08.102

Hendricks, K. B., Singhal, V. R., & Stratman, J. K. (2007). The Impact of Enterprise Systems on Corporate Performance: A Study of ERP, SCM, CRM System Implementations. *Journal of Operations Management*, *25*(1), 65–82. doi:10.1016/j.jom.2006.02.002

Hunton, E. J., Lippincott, B., & Reck, L. J. (2003). Enterprise resource planning systems: Comparing firm performance of adopters and non-adopters. *International Journal of Accounting Information Systems*, *4*(3), 165–184. doi:10.1016/S1467-0895(03)00008-3

Ignatiadis, I., & Nandhakumar, J. (2007). The impact of enterprise systems on organizational resilience. *Journal of Information Technology*, *22*(1), 36–43. doi:10.1057/palgrave.jit.2000087

Kanellou, A., & Spathis, C. (2011). *Accounting benefits and satisfaction in an ERP environment*. Paper presented at International Conference on Enterprise Systems, Accounting and Logistics, Thassos Island, Greece. doi:10.1016/j.accinf.2012.12.002

Koh, S. C. L., Gunasekaran, A., & Goodman, T. (2008). ERP II: The involvement, benefits and impediments of collaborative information sharing. *International Journal of Production Economics*, *113*(1), 245–268. doi:10.1016/j.ijpe.2007.04.013

Liu, L., Miao, R., & Li, C. (2008). The Impacts of Enterprise Resource Planning Systems on Firm Performance: An Empirical Analysis of Chinese Chemical Firms. *IFIP*, *252*, 579–587.

Loo, I., Bots, J., Louwvrink, E., Meeuwsen, D., van Moorsel, P., & Rozel, C. (2013). The effects of ERP-implementations on the non-financial performance of small and medium-sized enterprises in the Netherlands. *The Electronic Journal Information Systems Evaluation*, *16*(2), 103–116.

Madapusi, A., & D'Souza, D. (2012). The influence of ERP system implementation on the operational performance of an organization. *International Journal of Information Management*, *32*(1), 24–34. doi:10.1016/j.ijinfomgt.2011.06.004

Nazemi, E., Tarokh, M. J., & Djavanshir, G. R. (2012). ERP: A literature survey. *International Journal of Advanced Manufacturing Technology*, *61*(9-12), 999–1018. doi:10.1007/s00170-011-3756-x

Nicolaou, A., & Bhattacharya, S. (2008). Sustainability of ERPS Performance Outcomes: The Role of Post-Implementation Review Quality. *International Journal of Accounting Information Systems*, *9*(1), 43–60. doi:10.1016/j.accinf.2007.07.003

Poston, R., & Grabski, S. (2001). Financial impacts of enterprise resource planning implementations. *International Journal of Accounting Information Systems*, *2*(4), 271–294. doi:10.1016/S1467-0895(01)00024-0

Powell, D., Riezebos, J., & Strandhagen, J. O. (2013). Lean production and ERP systems in small- and medium-sized enterprises: ERP support for pull production. *International Journal of Production Research, 51*(2), 395–409. doi:10.1080/00207543.2011.645954

Spathis, C., & Ananiadis, J. (2005). Assessing the benefits of using an enterprise system in accounting information and management. *Journal of Enterprise Information Management, 18*(2), 195–210. doi:10.1108/17410390510579918

Stefanou, C., Manthou, V., & Tigka, K. (2014). The ERP Systems Impact on Business Performance. In *Proceedings: European, Mediterranean & Middle Eastern Conference on Information Systems 2014 (EMCIS2014)*. Doha, Qatar: EMCIS.

Stefanou, C. J. (2001). A Framework for the ex-ante Evaluation of ERP Software. *European Journal of Information Systems. Special Issue on IT Evaluation, 10*, 204–215.

Stefanou, C.J. and Revanoglou, A. (2006). ERP integration in a health care environment: A case study. *Journal of Enterprise Information Management, 19*(1).

Sudzina, F., Pucihar, A., & Lenart, G. (2011). A comparative study of the impact of ERP systems implementation on large companies in Slovakia and Slovenia. In Proceedings: CONFENIS 2011. doi:10.1007/978-3-642-24358-5_32

Sutton, S. G. (2006). Enterprise systems and the reshaping of accounting systems: A call for research. *International Journal of Accounting Information Systems, 7*, 1–6. doi:10.1016/j.accinf.2006.02.002

Themistocleous, M., Irani, Z., & O'Keefe, R. (2001). ERP and Application Integration: Exploratory Survey. *Business Process Management Journal, 7*(3), 195–204. doi:10.1108/14637150110392656

Vakalfotis, N., Ballantine, J., & Wall, A. (2011). A Literature Review on the Impact of Enterprise Systems on Management Accounting. In *Proceedings of International Conference on Enterprise Systems, Accounting and Logistics*. ICESAL. Retrieved from www.icesal.org

Velcu, O. (2005). Impact of the Quality of ERP Implementations on Business Value. *The Electronic Journal Information Systems Evaluation, 8*(3), 229–238.

Wieder, B., Both, P., Matolcsy, Z. P., & Osimitz, M.-L. (2006). The impact of ERP systems on firm and business process performance. *Journal of Enterprise Information Management*, 13-29

Wier, B., Hunton, J., & HassabElnaby, H. R. (2007). Enterprise resource planning systems and non-financial performance incentives: The joint impact on corporate performance. *International Journal of Accounting Information Systems, 8*(3), 165–190. doi:10.1016/j.accinf.2007.05.001

Chapter 7
Rediscovering Business Processes:
Definitions, Patterns, and Modelling Approaches

Kostas Vergidis
University of Macedonia, Greece

ABSTRACT

Although it has been more than a decade since the emergence of the concept of business processes, there is still a lack of common ground and agreement about their nature and context, their contribution and benefits to the contemporary business environment. This chapter 'rediscovers' business processes in the sense that provides a critical review of the multiple definitions by different authors and constructs a schema with the main structural elements that constitute a business process. It also reviews the main modelling approaches and classifies them into three primary groups according to their diagrammatic, formal and execution capabilities. Lastly, the main business process patterns are identified and the main business process modelling techniques are compared based on their pattern support capabilities. The work presented rediscovers business processes by providing a holistic understanding that will lead to their standardisation and further development.

INTRODUCTION

Organisational efficiency requires continuous improvement of key business processes. Business processes strongly influence –if not define– the quality of the product and the satisfaction of the customer, both of which are of fundamental importance in the marketplace. This paper attempts to provide an overview of business processes and it does that by discussing a selection of definitions and specifications of business processes and presenting a novel classification scheme for business process models. The discussion highlights the current trends and provides future research directions in this area. The paper is organised as follows: the next section compiles the definitions of business processes and their elements, and proposes a schema that visually decomposes the concept of business processes. Section 3 presents

DOI: 10.4018/978-1-4666-8841-4.ch007

modelling approaches regarding business processes and classifies them in three primary groups. Section 4 is dedicated to the main patterns used in business process models and it provides an evaluation of the suitability of existing modelling techniques in implementing these patterns.

BUSINESS PROCESSES: ONE SCHEMA, MANY DEFINITIONS

This section discusses how a business process is defined in literature. There are a number of different approaches and definitions originating from different areas. This section attempts to clarify how business processes are perceived, by presenting the most representative definitions and a generic schema of the main structural elements of business processes. There is an abundance of perceptions and definitions found in literature and this section provides an insight towards the main concepts around business processes.

A Schema for Business Processes

Research regarding business processes shows that although there is a wide variety in terms of definitions, when it comes to the structural elements of a business process there is a common ground to build upon. Figure 1 presents a generic business process schema that involves the most common structural elements found in literature. These elements are put together in a hierarchical structure that reflects the relationships between them. A detailed description of all the elements of figure 1 is provided later in this section.

Starting from the top, it is necessary to recognise that although business processes are by definition placed within a 'business' context, they are a subclass of generic processes and as such they inherit all of their main properties as discussed in the following sub-section. Moving to the second level of the schema, business processes are placed in parallel with workflows and linked using a bi-dimensional arrow. Workflows –a term older than business processes– are closely linked with business processes and sometimes these terms are interchangeably used. The third level of the business process schema is based on the fact that many authors (see table 1) consider the *actors*, *activities* and *resources* as the basic structural elements of a business process. These are the three main concepts involved in most business process definitions, although more emphasis is put on activities and resources only. Actors are

Figure 1. Schematic relationship of the main business process elements

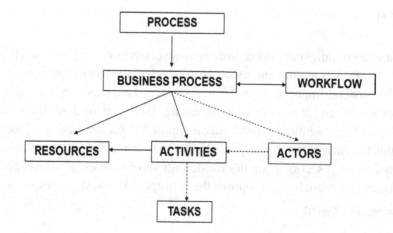

Table 1. Business process definitions

Author(s)	Business Process Definitions
Agerfalk (1999)	A *business process* consists of activities ordered in a structured way with the purpose of providing valuable results to the customer.
Castellanos *et al.* (2004)	The term *business process* is used to denote a set of activities that collectively achieve certain business goal. Examples of these processes are the hiring of a new employee or the processing of an order.
Davenport and Short (1990)	Business process is a set of logically related tasks performed to achieve a defined business outcome.
(1993)	*Business process* is defined as the chain of activities whose final aim is the production of a specific output for a particular customer or market
Fan (2001) Shen *et al.* (2004)	*Business process* is a set of one or more linked procedures or activities that collectively realize a business objective or policy goal, normally within the context of an organizational structure defining functional roles and relationships.
Gunasekaran and Kobu (2002)	A group of related tasks that together create value for a customer is called a *business process.*
Hammer and Champy (1993)	A *business process* is a collection of activities that takes one or more kinds of inputs and creates an output that is of value to the customer. A business process has a goal and is affected by events occurring in the external world or in other processes.
Irani *et al.* (2002)	A *business process* is a dynamic ordering of work activities across time and place, with a beginning, an end, and clearly identified inputs and outputs.
Johanson *et al.* (1993)	A business process is a set of linked activities that takes an input and it transforms it to create an output. It should add value to the input and create an output that is more useful and effective to the recipient.
Pall (1987)	Business process is the logical organisation of people, materials, energy, equipment and procedures into work activities designed to produce a specified end result.
Soliman (1998)	*Business process* may be considered as a complex network of activities connected together.
Stock and Lambert (2001)	A *business process* can be viewed as a structure of activities designed for action with focus on the end customer and the dynamic management of flows involving products, information, cash, knowledge and ideas.
Stohr and Zhao (2001)	A *business process* consists of a sequence of activities. It has distinct inputs and outputs and serves a meaningful purpose within an organisation or between organisations.
Volkner and Werners (2000)	Business process is defined as a sequence of states, which result from the execution of activities in organisations to reach a certain objective.
Wang and Wang (2005)	*Business process* is defined as a set of business rules that control tasks through explicit representation of process knowledge.

sometimes involved in a business process definition (Lindsay *et al.*, 2003) or sometimes perceived as external entities that enact or execute the process. Activities are widely accepted as the central elements that execute the basic business process steps utilising the process inputs in order to produce the desired results. Resources are frequently classified as inputs or input resources and they are necessary for activities to be executed. Lastly, tasks are perceived as the smallest analysable element of a business process (Orman, 1995), although usually overlooked by most authors or having the same meaning as activities.

In order to fully perceive business processes, a complete and comprehensive explanation of all the elements of figure 1 is discussed below. An overview of the most common definitions that exist in literature for each of the structural elements of business processes is also presented.

First 'Process' Then 'Business'

Following the latest trends, many authors focus more on the soft aspects of business processes and tend to view them under a sociotechnical perspective as opposed to the 'mechanistic viewpoint' (Lindsay *et al.*, 2003) that the established approaches have been accused of. However, as the term 'business process' has received such a wide acceptance it cannot be ignored that it perceives a business function as 'process' thus passing the key attributes of a process to the business function. We first briefly examine 'process' in a generic sense and then see how this is transformed in the unique context of 'business'.

According to Bal (1998), a process is a sequence of activities which are performed across time and place. A process also has a well defined beginning and end with identifiable inputs and outputs. Similar definitions are provided by Davenport and Short (1990) who emphasize on the defined outcome and Aldowaisan and Gaafar (1999) who highlight the structured nature of process. Havey (2005) identifies that process involves movement, work and time; it performs actions over some interval of time in order to achieve, or to progress to, some objective. Li *et al.* (2003) provide more details on what is involved in a process definition apart from the participating activities, and mentions elements such as the criteria to indicate the start and termination of the process, and information about the individual activities, the main participants, and associated IT applications and data. These definitions of process underline the important attributes that are subsequently inherited by any type of process.

Definitions of Business Processes

Havey (2005) provides a simple definition of business processes as 'step-by-step rules specific to the resolution of a business problem'. Since the 1990's when the first definitions of business processes appeared in literature, many authors attempted to come up with their own improved version of business process definition usually with one purpose: to try and orient business processes towards a particular direction highlighting only specific aspects. However, in almost every reference in this area, the authors reverently cite particular business process definitions by Hammer and Champy (1993) and Davenport (1993). Also there are references such as Lindsay *et al.* (2003), Melao and Pidd (2000) and Tinnila (1995) that provide compilations of the various business process definitions. Table 1 provides a summary of these definitions. It reflects on the variety and diversity of the different business process definitions that exist in literature.

As is evident from the definitions in table 1, most of the authors use the concepts of activities, sequence, inputs and outputs to describe a business process. This proves that most definitions are similar. Perhaps differentiation lies only on the emphasis on particular aspects of business process. Agerfalk *et al.* (1999), for example, focus on the necessity of the activities to be organised and structured in a specific way within a business process. Castellanos (2004) and Fan (2001) underline on the goal orientation of a business process. Davenport (1993), Gunasekaran and Kobu (2002) and Hammer and Champy (1993) offer more customer oriented definitions while Irani *et al.* (2002) move the focus on the necessity of clear inputs and outputs.

Zakarian (2001) emphasises that any transformation occurring in the business process should add value to the inputs and create an output that is useful to a downstream recipient. Others, such as Davenport (1993), Johanson *et al.* (1993), Shen *et al.* (2004) and Stohr and Zhao (2001) provide definitions that involve most of the above issues. There are also some distinctive definitions, such as the ones from Volkner and Werners (2000) and Wang and Wang (2005). Although Volkner and Werners (2000) involve activities in their definition, they emphasize more on *states* as the basic structural elements of business process. This approach provides a different insight into business processes as evolving series of states that change as a result of execution of activities. This definition of business processes can be attractive for using Petri-nets as a business process modelling technique as Petri-nets take into account the different process states. Petri-nets are discussed later on in this paper. Wang and Wang (2005) define business process as a set of business rules that control tasks although they do not sufficiently clarify who executes these tasks and if they are structured in some way.

Although, most definitions tend to be similar in the concepts used to express and describe business processes, they have received criticisms for not adequately highlighting the 'business' component and not sufficiently distinguishing from manufacturing or production processes. Volkner and Werners (2000) support that no generally accepted definition of the term business process exists due to the fact that business processes have been approached by a number of different disciplines. Lindsay *et al.* (2003) report that most business process definitions are limited in depth and the corresponding models are also constrained and confined to a mechanistic viewpoint. According to these authors, whereas the production processes focus on the activities being performed, the business processes focus on the goal that needs to be attained and on the people who enact the process. These authors emphasise that business processes are carried out by human operators; they are a balancing act between learning from the past and experimenting with and adapting to the future, and between rules and constraints versus freedom and flexibility. Smith (2003) also refers to business processes as 'human-centred phenomena' that are long lived, persistent, consisting of system-to-system, person-to-system and person-to-person interactions. Volkner and Werners (2000) consider the *flow* as the basis of business process, suggesting that business processes are characterised by the fact that the activities of the flow are executed repeatedly.

Finally, three perspectives or approaches to business processes are identified by Tinnila (1995). The first considers IT as an enabler of business processes to improve operative efficiency. The second discusses the potential of business processes in redesigning of organizations. The third recognises business processes as units of strategic planning and therefore acknowledges the need to connect them more closely to business strategies. Similar to this classification, Chen *et al.* (2001) distinguish between operational, supportive and managerial business processes.

How Are Workflows Different?

As with most concepts, business processes emerged from a related one, the workflows. The concept of workflow existed before business processes and still is widely used. Workflows are not limited to the business context only, although it is one of their popular applications. Although workflows are precisely defined by the Workflow Management Coalition (WfMC, 1995), the emergence of business processes created a mismatch between these two concepts. Van der Aalst and ter Hofstede (2002) attribute this lack of consensus to the variety of ways in which business processes are described. Table 2 provides a key to the most common workflow definitions and show that there are still different perspectives used by various authors.

A review of table 2 makes apparent the different approaches to workflows and its relationship with business processes. The definition provided by WfMC relates workflows with business processes and emphasizes automation according to a set of procedural rules. Basu and Blanning (2000) support that workflow is only a particular instance of a business process, depicting each time one of the alternative process paths. This approach is not in-line with WfMC and limits workflows to simple business process

Table 2. Workflow definitions

Author(s)	Definitions of Workflow
Basu and Blanning (2000)	A *workflow* is a particular instantiation of a process. Because a process may include decision points that can cause the process to branch in different ways during execution, a process can contain several possible workflows, each corresponding to a particular set of values for all relevant branching conditions.
Li *et al.* (2004a)	A *workflow* specification is a formal description of business processes in the real world.
Stohr and Zhao (2001)	A *workflow* is a specific kind of process, whose transitions between activities are controlled by an information system (workflow management system).
WfMC (1995)	A *workflow* is defined as the automation of a business process, in whole or part, during which documents, information or tasks are passed from one participant to another for action, according to a set of procedural rules.

instances without the ability to demonstrate process patterns such as decision boxes. According to van der Aalst (1998a), workflows are case-based, i.e., every piece of work is executed for a specific case (e.g. an insurance claim, a tax declaration, or a request for information). Stohr and Zhao (2001) specify workflows as specific kind of processes that are software assisted and enacted. Finally, Li *et al.* (2004a) consider workflows as formal descriptions that rationalise real-world business processes. Business process definitions lack formality and workflows can provide the semantics to push business processes into more structured approaches and specifications. Workflows enable better management and control of the process (Wamelink *et al.*, 2002). However, Wang and Wang (2005) compare traditional workflow approaches concluding that they are too rigid and exact to match complex and dynamic business activities due to the lack of flexibility and adaptability.

Activities and Resources as Structural Elements of Business Processes

The business process definitions cited in table 1 justify the process decomposition of figure 1 to activities and resources, as most of the definitions involve these two to describe a business process. Actors are overlooked in most business process definitions since many authors perceive actors as human resources thus omitting any explicit reference. According to van der Aalst (1995), the objective of a business process is the processing of cases and to completely define a business process two things need to be specified: the activities, i.e. partially ordered sets of tasks, and the allocation of resources to tasks. This section discusses *activities* and *resources* as the two main structural elements of business processes and identifies the different perspectives that exist in literature.

Activities

Activities are perceived by the majority of authors as a central element that defines business processes. They are the executable part of a process that is enacted by the actors utilising the resources; therefore activities provide the link between the actors and resources. Table 3 provides an overview of the definitions of activity presented in literature in the context of business processes.

Table 3. Definitions of activity

Author(s)	Activity Definitions
Van der Aalst (1998a)	One can think of an *activity* as a *transaction*.
Aldowaisan and Gaafar (1999)	An *activity* is defined as a set of operations commonly performed by a single employee type without forced interruptions.
Basten and van der Aalst (1999)	*Activities* are assumed to be atomic entities without internal structure
Kiepuszewski *et al.* (2003)	*Activities* in elementary form are atomic units of work, and in compound form they modularise an execution order/
Li *et al.* (2003)	An *activity* identifies an action which can be characterised by a verb and an object upon which the action applies.
Stohr and Zhao (2001)	An *activity* is a discrete process step performed either by a machine or human agent. An activity may consist of one or more tasks.
Zakarian (2001)	A process model includes a set of *activities* arranged in a specific order, with clearly identified inputs and outputs. Each *activity* in a process takes an input and transforms it into an output with some value to a customer.

Van der Aalst (1998a) provides the simplest definition of activity synonymising it to a transaction. He also specifies the properties that an activity –similar to a transaction– should satisfy:

- **Atomicity:** An activity is executed successfully or is rolled back completely, i.e., a task cannot be partially completed.
- **Consistency:** The execution of an activity leads to a consistent state.
- **Isolation:** The effect of the execution of an activity in parallel with other activities is equal to the effect of the execution of one activity in isolation.
- **Durability:** The result of a committed activity cannot get lost.

Aldowaisan and Gaafar (1999) attempt to classify activities and assign them to particular employee types (i.e. actors), highlighting also the need for their uninterrupted operation. The perception that activities have no internal structure ((Basten and van der Aalst, 1999), (Kiepuszewski *et al.*, 2003)) and are simply atomic units or entities contrasts with Stohr's and Zhao's (2001) hypothesis that an activity may consist of one or more tasks. Usually, the decomposition –or not- of activities depends on the author's perspective of business processes and the details required. Li *et al.* (2003) attempt to identify activities using verbs and objects and Zakarian (2001) claims that like processes, activities transform inputs to value-adding outputs and thus an activity is a process miniature.

Along with these definitions, there are also classifications of activities according to different criteria. Li *et al.* (2003) separate activities to *manual* and *automated*, depending on whether they are realised by a human or a software system and to *primary* or *final* depending on whether they can be refined at a certain stage or not. Zakarian and Kusiak (2001) distinguish between three types of activities:

- **Value-Adding Activities:** Activities that are important to the customer;
- **Work Flow Activities:** Activities that move work flow across boundaries that are functional, departmental, or organisational; and
- **Control Activities:** Activities that are created to control value-adding and work flow activities.

There are also different perspectives among authors on whether an activity can be decomposed into tasks. According to table 3, Basten and van der Aalst (1999) and Kiepuszewski *et al.* (2003) view activities without any internal structure. But Orman (1995) claims that an activity can be further decomposed into tasks that are the smallest identifiable units of analysis. Similar opinions are expressed by van der Aalst (1998a), Biazzo (2000), Li *et al.* (2003) and Stohr and Zhao (2001). As an example Van der Aalst (1995) communicates an inclusive description tying up activities and tasks: 'Business processes are centred around activities. Each activity specifies the set and the order of tasks to be executed in order to achieve the business process goal'. However, a series of authors tend to use the terms 'activity' and 'task' as equivalent in the context of business processes.

Resources

The second element of business processes are the resources. According to van der Aalst and van Hee (1996), the allocation of resources to activities, schedules the business process. Many authors refer to resources simply as inputs and others classify resources to input and output (Hofacker and Vetschera, 2001). Resources are used by activities and transformed to create the process output. A number of authors provide different definitions for resources. Li et al. (2003) along with van der Aalst and van Hee (1996) consider a resource as any human and/or machine supporting the fulfilment of activities. In a later reference, van der Aalst (1998a) limits resources to human only, stating that 'in most environments where workflow management systems are used the resources are mainly human'. Biazzo (2000) comes up with a more generic definition claiming that resources include everything that is either used or modified by the tasks. While in most business process definitions (table 1) the activities are utilising the resources, Castellanos et al. (2004) suggest that the resources execute the activity, implying that resources are mostly humans or machines. Hofacker and Vetchera (2001) also classify resources into information and physical according to their nature.

A CLASSIFICATION OF BUSINESS PROCESS MODELS

Business process modelling is directly related with the perception and understanding of business processes. In most of the cases, a business process is as expressive and as communicative as is the technique that has been used to model it. Therefore the elements and the capabilities of a business process model play a significant role in describing and understanding a business process. IDEF and Petri-nets are frequently encountered in business process modelling literature and this section starts by briefly discussing why it is the case. Then, existing classifications of business process models in literature are presented before the classification proposed by the authors is detailed.

Popular Modelling Techniques: IDEF and Petri-Nets

IDEF and Petri-nets are two of the most widely acknowledged and adopted business process modelling techniques according to literature research. Both of them are families of constructs and both have been widely extended and applied to a range of different contexts. Below is an overview of IDEF and Petri-nets in the context of business process modelling.

IDEF (Integrated Definition) Process Modelling

The development of Integrated Definition (IDEF) models for overview and analysis of business processes has been motivated by the initial desire to increase productivity by improving the communication and structure of manufacturing systems (Gunasekaran and Kobu, 2002). The IDEF family of modelling techniques has been popular in companies to model diverse processes and it is also used by many authors because it allows for a systematic and a well-defined representation of processes (Zakarian, 2001). The IDEF family is used according to different applications. The most important parts are: IDEF0, IDEF1, IDEF1X, IDEF2, IDEF3, IDEF4 and IDEF5. However, for business process modelling, the most widely used techniques are IDEF0 and IDEF3. IDEF3 is the most popular and widely used method in the business process context. One of the major advantages of IDEF3 representation is its simplicity and its descriptive power. These models are also easy to extend. Kusiak and Zakarian (1996b) remark that the essence of IDEF3 methodology is its ability to describe activities and their relationship at various levels of detail, because an initial model includes parent activities that can be decomposed into lower level activities. According to Zakarian and Kusiak (2000) IDEF3 offers several important characteristics for successful process representation:

- Process description in the form of activities,
- Structure of the underlying process, and
- Flow of objects and their relationship.

IDEF3 models have been used by a number of authors as the starting point for further exploitation of models. Kusiak and Zakarian (1996a) perform reliability analysis to identify critical activities in an IDEF3 model, improve process performance, and decrease the operating cost of the process. Zakarian (2001) applies fuzzy reasoning to efficiently model the incomplete information about process variables using an IDEF3 model as a basis. Kusiak et al. (1994) performs observational analysis of business processes to demonstrate the current use of IDEF models and Badica et al. (2003a) propose a novel business process modelling approach combining IDEF0 and IDEF3 concepts. Lastly, Zhou and Chen (2002) use a combination of IDEF3 and AON (Activity on Node) graphs to formally describe a business process.

However, as IDEF is a diagrammatic approach to business process modelling, it has some disadvantages as well. Zakarian in a number of references ((2001), (2000) and (2001)) and Peters and Peters (1997) highlight the major drawbacks of the IDEF approach:

The amount of time required for a process to be completed: Time is ignored. IDEF diagrams are, basically, like plumbing layouts. They show where everything comes from and goes to without indicating when or how long such a traversal will take.

The costs associated with the process: Being dataflow oriented, IDEF ignores this issue which is often a key motivation for process reengineering.

The utilisation of resources during the process: Not including time makes it impossible to compute what percentage of the total process resources (e.g. people, machines, communications lines) are being utilised.

The possibility of company policy being violated: IDEF, like other static analysis techniques, assumes a rather benign environment. One in which everything and everyone will follow the rules. The possibility for unauthorised detours around company guidelines cannot be checked because no dynamic or simulated events can be examined.

The frequency at which time limits are exceeded: Again, dynamic analyses can demonstrate how often a process will fail to meet time limits.

The methodology is static and qualitative which is a drawback for the analysis of processes.

Activities in a model are at a relatively high level of abstraction, making it difficult to associate exact quantitative data for the process variable of interest.

It is based on informal notation that lacks mathematical rigour. If mathematical definitions are to be applied, these have to be specified for each particular process and each activity separately.

Petri-Nets

A Petri-net is a graphical language that is appropriate for modelling systems with concurrency (van der Aalst, 1998a). Petri-nets have been modified and extended by various researchers to allow for more powerful modelling capabilities. Some of their variations include Timed Petri-nets, Stochastic Petri-nets, Coloured Petri-nets and Hierarchical Petri-nets. A Petri-net is a suitable model for a wide variety of

Figure 2. A Petri-net modelled business process for an insurance claim (van der Aalst, 1995)

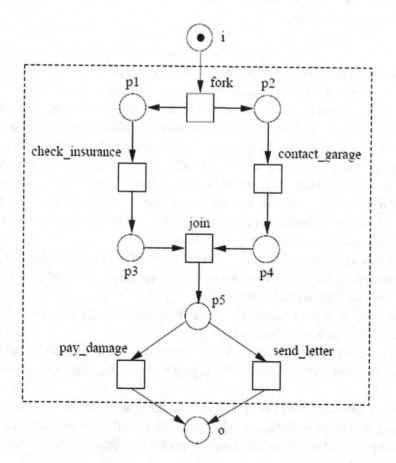

applications (e.g. modelling and analysis of concurrent and parallel systems, communication protocols and manufacturing control systems). Figure 2 depicts a sample Petri-net of an insurance process claim.

A Petri-net is a kind of directed graph with an initial state called initial marking. The underlying graph of a Petri-net is a directed, bipartite graph consisting of two kinds of nodes, called places and transitions. Arcs represent connections between nodes. An arc can only connect from a place to a transition or from a transition to a place. Connections between two nodes that are of the same kind are not allowed. In graphical representation, places are drawn as circles and transitions as bars or boxes. A marking (state) is an assignment of tokens to the places of the net. A transition is enabled if each place connected to the transition input arc (input place), contains at least one token.

According to van der Aalst (1998b) Petri-nets are unique as they cover different perspectives of business process modelling and as such they have three distinctive advantages:

- They have formal semantics despite the graphical nature.
- Unlike most of the modelling techniques, they are state-based instead of (just) event-based.
- They allow the application of analysis techniques.

Li *et al.* (2004b) support Petri-nets due to the above advantages pointing that 'Petri-nets are a naturally selected mathematical foundation for the formal performance analysis of workflow models'. Van der Aalst (1998a) considers Petri-nets as powerful analytical tools that are essential for formally modelling and analyzing workflow processes for correctness and consistency (Stohr and Zhao, 2001). Zakarian and Kusiak (2000) highlight that Petri-nets are concurrent, asynchronous, distributed, parallel, nondeterministic, and/or have a stochastic nature.

There are a number of applications of Petri-nets reported in literature. Hofacker and Vetschera (2001) report that, most of the approaches for formal description and analysis of business process designs are based on graphs or Petri nets. Donatelli *et al.* (1995) use Generalised Stochastic Petri Nets (GSPN) and Performance Evaluation Process Algebra (PEPA) to study qualitative and quantitative behaviour of systems in a single environment and identify as strength of Petri-nets their causality, conflict and concurrency clearly depicted within a model. Raposo *et al.* (2000) use a Petri-net based approach to model the coordination mechanisms in multi-workflow environments.

Apart from their wide acceptance, Petri-nets have also received criticisms. Peters and Peters (1997) sum up the essential process modelling elements that the initial form of Petri-nets lack, although most of these have been dealt with in later Petri-nets extensions:

- Time has been left out.
- The tokens (used to mark conditions) are anonymous.
- Transitions always behave the same way, people and other systems do not exhibit this property.

Other deficiencies have also been identified. Basu and Blanning (2000) claim that Petri-nets are primarily oriented to analysis and conflict resolution considerations, rather than workflow component connectivity and interactions. Two serious drawbacks are also mentioned by Aguilar-Saven (2004): Petri-nets do not have data concepts and there are no hierarchy concepts, hence the models can become excessively large. Although the Petri-net techniques can capture system dynamics and physical constraints, they are not adequate to solve optimisation problems (Lee *et al.*, 2001). Also, Petri-nets are not suitable for someone seeking to understand the flow of a business process due to their focus on states and transitions in a process.

Peters and Peters (1997) also examine the possibility of using Petri-nets together with IDEF0 and express their concern on how well these two techniques can match each other. Bosilj-Vuksic *et al.* (2000) also investigate the suitability of IDEF diagrams (IDEF0 and IDEF3) and Petri Nets (DES-nets) for modelling business processes and present a comparative evaluation of their features. According to these authors the comparison reveals that these two methods complement each other and that they can be used together for modelling business processes for better results. Due to their simplicity and understandability, it seems appropriate to develop IDEF diagrams during the preliminary phases of business process modelling projects in order to develop 'AS-IS' models and in later phases, when 'TO-BE' models are developed, IDEF diagrams could be transformed into Petri-nets that add formal semantics.

Existing Classification of Business Process Models

According to van der Aalst *et al.* (2003), business process modelling is used to characterise the identification and specification of business processes. Business process modelling includes modelling of activities and their causal and temporal relationships as well as specific business rules that process enactments have to comply with. There is an abundance of business process modelling techniques with approaches that capture different aspects of a business process, each having distinctive advantages and disadvantages. Before presenting the existing classification approaches of these techniques, the aim, usability and benefits of business process modelling are briefly discussed.

Lindsay *et al.* (2003) describe business process modelling as a snapshot of what is perceived at a point in time regarding the actual business process. The *objective* of business process modelling is, according to Sadiq and Orlowska (2000), the high-level specification of processes, while according to Biazzo (2002), it is the representation of relationships between the activities, people, data and objects involved in the production of a specified output. According to Volkner and Werners (2000) and Aguilar-Saven (2004), business process modelling is essential for the analysis, evaluation and improvement of business processes as it is used to structure the process, such that the existing and alternative sequence of tasks can be analysed systematically and comprehensively. Business process modelling is a useful tool to capture, structure and formalise the knowledge about business processes ((Guha *et al.*, 1993), (Abate *et al.*, 2002)). Aguilar-Saven (2004) suggests that business process models are mainly used to learn about the process, to make decisions on the process, or to develop business process software. For each of these purposes some business process models are better suited depending on their particular constructs.

Authors such as Kettinger *et al.* (1997), Melao and Pidd (2000) and Aguilar–Saven (2004), have provided frameworks for presenting and classifying different business process modelling techniques. Kettinger *et al.* (1997) conducted a thorough study of business process reengineering methodologies (25), techniques (72) and tools (102) that are adopted by 25 international consultancy firms. The study reveals that in every stage of the reengineering process there is a variety of approaches followed. Kettinger *et al.* (1997) report a widespread use of process capture and modelling techniques. They also present a comprehensive list of the appropriate software tools and the techniques (e.g. process flowcharting, data flow diagramming) that each of the tools supports. However, there is not much emphasis on process modelling itself as it is viewed merely as a technique among others that constitute the wider picture of business process reengineering.

Melao and Pidd (2000) on the other hand focus exclusively in business processes and their modelling. They adopt four different perspectives for understanding the nature of business processes first and then identify the most common modelling approaches for each perspective. The first perspective views business processes as *deterministic machines*, that is, as a fixed sequence of well–defined activities that convert inputs to outputs in order to accomplish clear objectives. For this perspective static process modelling is sufficient, with techniques such as Integrated Definition methods (IDEF0, IDEF3) and Role Activity Diagrams (RADs). The second perspective views business processes as *complex dynamic systems*, assemblies of interchangeable components. This second viewpoint focuses on the complex, dynamic and interactive features of business processes. The authors suggest discrete event simulation (discussed later in this paper) as a suitable way to model the dynamic behaviour of this approach. The third perspective of business processes is *interacting feedback loops* that highlight the information feedback structure of business processes. System dynamics modellers are recommended for this perspective. The last perspective of business process is *social constructs* and emphasises more on the people side. It is the people who made and enact business processes, people with different values, expectations and roles. This soft side of business processes can be modelled with soft unstructured illustrative models. However a real–life business process involves elements for all the four perspectives and therefore it is evident that there is not such modelling technique that can embrace all this variety of characteristics that constitute a business process.

Another notable review regarding business process modelling classification comes from Aguilar–Saven (2004). The author presents the main process modelling techniques and classifies them based on two dimensions: The first dimension is concerned with four different purposes of use and classifies the business process models based on whether they are (i) descriptive for learning, (ii) enable decision support for process development/design, (iii) enable decision support for process execution or (iv) allow IT enactment support. The second dimension distinguishes between *active* and *passive* models. As *active* are considered those models that allow the user to interact with them (dynamic model) while *passive* are those that do not provide this capability. It is important to note that Aguilar–Saven (2004) provides an extensive and updated list of software tools that are associated with all the process modelling techniques presented in the paper.

As seen from the references described above each of the authors provides a different modelling framework according to his or her focus on specific directions. In the current paper the authors propose a new classification scheme for business process models.

Proposed Classification of Business Process Models

The authors propose *three sets* to classify business process modelling techniques as demonstrated in figure 3. The first set (i.e. diagrammatic models) involves business process models that sketch a business process using a visual diagram. The second set (i.e. mathematical models) corresponds to models in which all the elements have a mathematical or a formal underpinning. Finally, the third set (i.e. business process languages) contains software–based languages that support business process modelling and most of the times process execution. The classification of the most representative modelling techniques is demonstrated using a Venn diagram (see figure 3). Each of the techniques is further discussed later on this section. Table 4 presents the classification of figure 1 and also cites a selection of references for each of the key techniques. The remaining of this section discusses the main features of these process modelling techniques based on the set (or sets) that they belong to.

Figure 3. Classification of business process modelling techniques

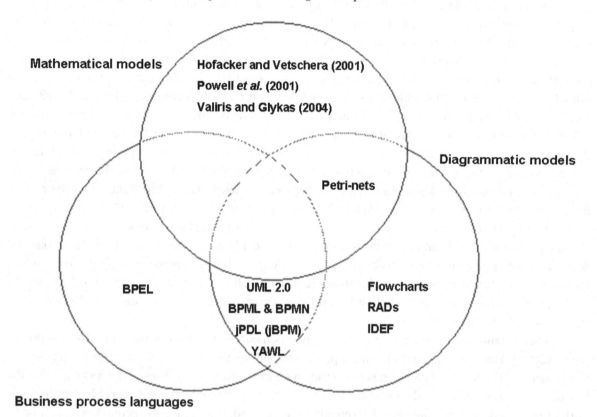

Diagrammatic Models

The first techniques that were used for business process modelling were plain graphical representations (i.e. flowcharts) that were initially developed for software specification (Knuth, 1963; Chapin N., 1971). These simplistic diagrams depicted a business process but most of the times without using a standard notation (Havey, 2005). These techniques are useful for fast and informal process representation but they lack the necessary semantics to support more complex and standardised constructs. This led to the development of standard methodologies such as IDEF and Unified Modelling Language (UML) for process modelling and/or software development. Business process modelling benefited from these standardised diagrammatic approaches as well since they are simple and easy to use. However, they have also received a series of criticisms from various authors. The central point of argument is that these modelling approaches are based on graphical notations only (Zakarian, 2001), thus lacking formal semantics (Valiris and Glykas, 1999). They also lack quantitative information that obstructs any further analysis and development of analysis methods and tools (van der Aalst and van Hee, 1996); there is no formal underpinning to ensure consistency across models (Valiris and Glykas, 1999). Phalp (2000) notes that any analysis attempt using these types of models often consists solely of inspection of diagrams and the conclusions are heavily dependent upon the skills of the analyst.

Although visual inspection of diagrams tends to be highly subjective, these diagrams are still widely used in business process environments. The unbeatable advantage to visually depict the flow of a busi-

Table 4. Main modelling techniques, corresponding sets and selected references

Business ProcessModelling Techniques	Modelling Set(s)	Selected References
Flowcharts	Diagrammatic models	–(Knuth, 1963) –(Chapin N., 1971) –(Chapin, 1974) –(Feldman, 1998) – (Lakin *et al.*, 1996)
IDEF	Diagrammatic models	–(Mayer *et al.*, 1994) –(Menzel and Mayer, 1998) – (Peters and Peters, 1997) – (Zakarian and Kusiak, 2001) – (Zakarian and Kusiak, 2000) – (Zakarian, 2001) – (Badica *et al.*, 2003a) – (Shimizu and Sahara, 2000) – (Zhou and Chen, 2002)
RADs	Diagrammatic models	–(Ould, 1995) –(Holt, 2000) – (Phalp and Shepperd, 2000) – (Badica *et al.*, 2003b)
UML	–Diagrammatic models –Business process language s	– (Quatrani, 2001) –(Kim *et al.*, 2003) – (Wohed *et al.*, 2004)
Petri–nets	–Diagrammatic models –Formal/mathematical models	– (van der Aalst, 1998a) – (Li *et al.*, 2004b) – (Donatelli *et al.*, 1995) – (Raposo *et al.*, 2000) – (Peters and Peters, 1997)
Business process models based on mathematical or algorithmic models	Formal/mathematical models	– (Hofacker and Vetschera, 2001) – (Powell *et al.*, 2001), – (Valiris and Glykas, 1999)
–BPEL –BPML	Business process language	– (Reimer *et al.*, 2000) – (Havey, 2005) – (Grigori *et al.*, 2004) – (Smith, 2003)
jPDL (jBPM)	–Diagrammatic models –Business process languages	(Koenig, 2004)

ness process in a way that no technical expertise is required is very appealing to the business analysts. Even advanced and more sophisticated modelling techniques are influenced by this perspective and they support apart from formal semantics and a visual representation of the modelled processes.

Formal/Mathematical Models

The necessity for formal semantics to business process modelling led to a second generation of formal models. Formal models are the ones in which process concepts are defined rigorously and precisely, so that mathematics can be used to analyse them, extract knowledge from them and reason about them. An advantage of formal models is that they can be verified mathematically, and can be checked for consistency and other properties (Koubarakis and Plexousakis, 2002). These models are in line with van der Aalst et al. (2003) suggestion that business process models 'should have a formal foundation' because formal models do not leave any scope for ambiguity and increase the potential for analysis. However, there is a lack of formal methods to support the design of processes (Hofacker and Vetschera, 2001) because business process elements and constraints are mostly of qualitative nature and it is hard to characterise them in a formal way amenable to analytical methods (Tiwari, 2001). This explains the difficulty of developing 'parametric' models of business processes and the fact that only a few practical examples are found in relevant literature (e.g. Hofacker and Vetschera, 2001). Petri–nets are an example of a business process modelling technique that combines visual representation using standard notation with an underlying mathematical representation.

Coming to the approaches that use mathematical models only, there is not a widely accepted model. This results into different authors presenting their individual approaches towards mathematical business process modelling. An approach that has a mathematical basis is proposed by Hofacker and Vetschera (2001). They describe a business process using a series of mathematical constraints (that define the feasibility boundaries of the business process) and a set of objective functions (that consist of the various objectives for business process design). Although this approach cannot model complex modelling constructs and there is no emphasis on the diagrammatic representation, it is appropriate for further quantitative analysis and improvement as it is based on a mathematical model. A similar approach is presented by Powell *et al.* (2001). They describe a mathematical model that has the main ingredients of a generic business process. Valiris and Glykas (1999) also propose the use of formal mathematical notations as a way of introducing business rules and verifying the logical consistency of diagrammatic models.

Despite their advantages over simple diagrammatic approaches, criticisms for formal/mathematical business process models have also been reported. Building a formal business process model can prove much more complex and demanding compared to traditional techniques where a process diagram is sufficient (Hofacker and Vetschera, 2001). These authors also show that the representation of real–life processes using mathematical models may be complex and sometimes not possible as these include complex features such as decision points, feedback loops and parallel or hierarchical flow. Koubarakis and Plexousakis (2002) note that the use of complex mathematical notations might discourage the business analyst since 'it is a lot of work to create, maintain a formal business process and retain its consistency'. However, as a diagram can lead to ambiguity about the process, the formal model ensures that the process is described accurately and analysis tools can be used to extract quantitative information about the process. This is the main advantage of formal business process modelling techniques.

Business Process Languages

The third –and most recent– generation of business process modelling techniques came as an attempt to tackle the complexity of the formal models but retain their consistency and potential for further analysis. As the first generation of business process modelling techniques was strongly influenced by the ones used in software development; so is this generation. Perhaps it is the dynamic, complex and rapidly evolving nature of business process models that makes them similar to software development techniques. The third set presented here takes business process modelling a step further as it uses *process languages* –usually XML–based– to model and execute a business process. This is how business process languages were evolved. These context–specific executable languages are the latest trend is business process modelling, a trend that has already produced a number of different semantic packages, with Business Process Execution Language for Web Services (BPEL4WS –also known as BPEL) and Business Process Modelling Language (BPML) being the most distinctive. Van der Aalst *et al.* (2003) remark that process languages with clear semantics are useful as they can express business process models and contribute to the analysis of their structural properties.

Havey (2005) claims that BPEL is the most popular as it is supported by IBM, Microsoft and BEA. BPEL is not a notational language but it is also XML–based and as such it inherits XML attributes such as programmability, executability and exportablility. BPML is a product of the Business Process Modelling Initiative (www.bpmi.org). It is also an XML–based language that encodes the flow of a business process in an executable form. BPML is accompanied by BPMN (Business Process Modelling Notation), a graphical flowchart language that is able to represent a business process in an intuitive visual form (Havey, 2005). Each BPML process has a name, a set of activities and a handler; it also supports subprocesses. YAWL (Yet Another Workflow Language) is another –as the name itself says– graphical process language created by van der Aalst and ter Hofstede (2003). YAWL is a Petri–net based language that was built with the primary target to support a wide range of business process patters. It has received criticism for being inadequate in terms of expressiveness and system integration capabilities (Havey, 2005). JBoss Business Process Management (JBPM) execution language named jPDL (Koenig, 2004) is also a novel approach to business process modelling and execution. This new approach facilitates the natural transition from declarative input by the business analyst to the programming logic needed to implement a business process, thus simplifying business process development and allowing even non–programmers to develop business processes using visual tools. jBPM engine is based on open source software, providing infrastructure to developers who have access to a variety of supplementary software tools with which they can easily design and analyse business processes in a graphical environment.

HANDLING COMPLEXITY OF BUSINESS PROCESS PATTERNS

According to Riehle and Zuillinghoven (1996) a pattern 'is the abstraction from a concrete form which keeps recurring in specific non-arbitrary contexts'. Wohed *et al.* (2002) refer to patterns as 'abstracted forms of recurring situations in processes'. Havey (2005) is more specific about *business process patterns*: 'they are inherently spatial and visual. A process pattern is a cluster, or a constellation of process activities arranged in just the right way to solve a difficult problem'. Zapf (2000) supports the pattern construction for specific application domains as this allows a detailed analysis.

Patterns enable the standardisation of solutions to commonly recurring problems within business processes and the reuse of these standardised process parts across different process models. Identifying the basic process constructs is necessary for any business process modelling approach to be able to consider several complex dependencies between the activities (Scheer, 1994). Authors such as Kiepuszewski *et al.* (2003), van der Aalst and ter Hofstede (2002) and Zhou and Chen (2002) refer to sequence, choice, parallelism, and synchronization as the basic patterns for modelling and controlling a business process.

Similar constructs are mentioned by Volkner and Werners (2000) as AND, inclusive-OR, exclusive-OR and their combinations. Van der Aalst and ter Hofstede (2002) also introduce a comprehensive list of 20 workflow patters. These patterns have been compiled from an analysis of existing workflow languages and they capture typical control flow dependencies encountered in workflow modelling (Wohed P. *et al.*, 2002). In (van der Aalst and ter Hofstede, 2002), they were used to compare the functionality of 15 workflow management systems. The results of this experiment revealed two problems: (i) current workflow systems do not have significant expressive power and (ii) they support a heterogeneous range of patterns. Table 5 presents a selection of patterns from van der Aalst and ter Hofstede (2002) that were

Table 5. Main business process patterns

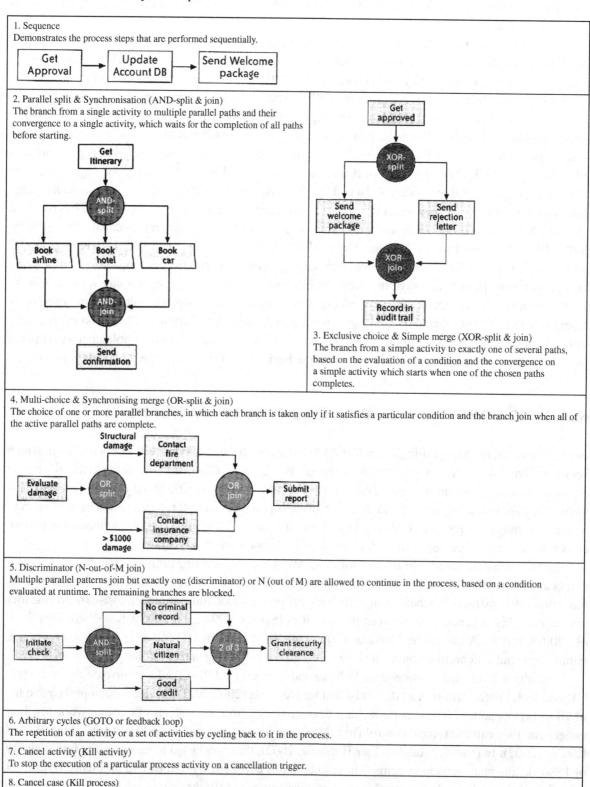

considered as the basic constructs for any business process model. These patterns are provided with a brief explanation while the pattern images are taken from Havey (2005).

Most of the main business process patterns are inspired by software specifications. Table 6 identifies which business process modelling techniques support these patterns. The modelling techniques are selected across all the three modelling dimensions. IDEF3 supports only the basic patterns (Zhou and Chen, 2002). UML provides support for almost all the patterns presented here apart from OR-join and Discriminator (Wohed *et al.*, 2004). Petri-nets and IDEF support the same patterns according to van der Aalst (1998a). However, most of the business process patterns are covered by the various Petri-net extensions. The mathematical model (Hofacker and Vetschera, 2001) –although praised for its formality and optimisation capabilities– illustrates a simplistic approach towards business processes thus no pattern is implemented apart from the sequential flow of activities. This is due to the complexity of the mathematical model development. Most of the business process languages are implemented based on the process patterns. For example, YAWL (Yet Another Workflow Language) supports all table 6 patterns since it was created primarily for this purpose (van der Aalst and ter Hofstede, 2002). BPEL also supports most patterns (Wohed P. *et al.*, 2002), (Havey, 2005) and also BPML (Havey, 2005). According to Koenig (2004), jBPM's jPDL was also implemented to cover all the patterns presented here.

DISCUSSION

This paper discussed three aspects of business processes: their multiple definitions, the classification of the main modelling techniques using three distinctive sets and the capability of modelling techniques in handling process patterns. This paper also proposes a business process schema that has a twofold scope. Firstly, it works as an aggregator, demonstrating all the main concepts used in describing a business process, and secondly it provides a consistent starting point for a comprehensive definition of business process that involves and precisely defines all the main elements. The standardisation of the business process definition can have an impact on the business process community and will boost the integration and homogenisation of the approaches towards business process modelling.

Business process modelling has always attracted attention from researches from a variety of fields. However, there is a need for defining operational and reusable business process models for processes

Table 6. Process patterns supported by modelling techniques and languages

Pattern	IDEF3	UML 2.0	Petri-Nets	Math.model	BPEL	BPML	jPDL
1. Sequence	✓	✓	✓	✓	✓	✓	✓
2. AND-split & join	✓	✓	✓	✗	✓	✓	✓
3. XOR-split & join	✓	✓	✓	✗	✓	✓	✓
4. OR-split & join	✓	✓/✗	✓	✗	✓	✗	✓
5. Discriminator	✗	✗	✗	✗	✗	✗	✗
6. Arbitrary cycles	✗	✓	✗	✗	✓	✓	✓
7. Cancel activity	✗	✓	✗	✗	✓	✓	✓
8. Cancel case	✗	✓	✗	✗	✓	✓	✓

within different types of enterprises, in different contexts and at the required level of detail. These models should be able to address the complexity of the design and identify problems encountered in modern business processes. Therefore, there is an increasing need for formal methods and techniques to support both the modelling and the analysis of business processes. This paper proposes a novel positioning of the existing business process modelling techniques using three sets. This classification of business processes contributes to visually highlighting a number of interesting observations. Despite the existence of many formal process modelling notations, the majority of the business process community still uses simple diagrammatic modelling techniques. Formal languages now provide diagrammatic depiction of business processes and associated analysis techniques which can be used for investigating properties of processes. These techniques can be used to provide insight into the behaviour and characteristics of a business process model specified in such a language. However, a disadvantage of the business process languages that aim at automating business processes are the limitations of their modelling concepts. Neither do these languages allow the representation of detailed context-specific information in a declarative way, nor do they support any associated inferences. Instead, business process languages concentrate on the procedural flow between the different participants of a process. However, business process languages are designed to support the most complex patterns in business process modelling and this in combination with their execution capabilities makes them attractive for process enactment.

Although in process modelling IDEF and Petri-nets are still popular what is missing is a modelling technique that involves elements from all the three modelling dimensions. That is, there is a need to develop a modelling technique to support a visual diagrammatic representation of the process thus having all the advantages of visualisation, to have a formal mathematical underpinning for the visual model so that quantitative measures can be extracted and the process can be analysed, and finally to be executable i.e. being expressed using a software-based process language. Since these features are provided individually by the existing modelling techniques, this novel modelling technique could incorporate features of existing techniques and a transformation process from one to the other.

The paper also presented a number of basic patterns and investigated the extent of support provided by the main business process models to these patterns. Business process models from all the three sets are analysed to show that only the business process languages fully support these patterns. The mathematical models such as Hofacker's and Vetschera's (2001) can currently deal only with sequential processes. The diagrammatic techniques also support only very basic patterns such as parallel split and exclusive choice.

CONCLUSION

This paper contributes to the business process literature in three areas. It presented a schema attempting to refine the existing definitions of business processes by highlighting their common elements. It introduced a novel modelling classification that proposes three sets in which each business process modelling technique can be positioned according to its capabilities. The advantage of this approach is that the classification boundaries are not rigid thus allowing a modelling technique to belong to more than one sets based on its features. The paper also highlighted pattern support as an important issue for a modelling technique. It compared business process models from different sets and examined their pattern support capabilities. This paper shows that although diagrammatic models are more capable of visualising complex processes and mathematical models are more amenable to quantitative analysis, it is business process languages that provide support for most of the real-life business process patterns.

Each set has its own distinctive advantages, as it offers different perspective in the business process model. Business process languages are a promising trend that can incorporate elements from all the three dimensions and thus consist of a solid reference model for business processes. This paper rediscovered business processes in the sense that it sketched a basic schema, placed the business process models in a perspective that incorporates three different dimensions. The proposed schema and the novel modelling classification contribute to rationalising business processes and setting a common ground for their understanding and further development.

REFERENCES

Abate, A. F., Esposito, A., Grieco, N., & Nota, G. (2002). Workflow Performance Evaluation Through WPQL. In *Proceeding of the 14th International Conference on Software Engineering and Knowledge Engineering* (Vol. 27). ACM Press. doi:10.1145/568760.568846

Agerfalk, P., Goldkuhl, G., & Cronholm, S. (1999). Information Systems Actability Engineering - Integrating Analysis of Business Process and Usability Requirements. In *Proceedings of the 4th International Workshop on the Language Action Perspective on Communication Modeling*. Copenhagen, Denmark: Academic Press.

Aguilar-Saven, R. S. (2004). Business Process Modelling: Review and Framework. *International Journal of Production Economics*, *90*, 129–149.

Aldowaisan, T. A., & Gaafar, L. K. (1999). Business Process Reengineering: An Approach for Process Mapping. *Omega*: *International Journal of Management Sciences*, *27*, 515–524.

Badica, C., Badica, A., & Litoiu, V. (2003a). A New Formal IDEF-Based Modelling of Business Processes. In *Proceedings of the First Balkan Conference in Informatics (BCI)*. BCI.

Badica, C., Badica, A., & Litoiu, V. (2003b). Role Activity Diagrams As Finite State Processes. In *Proceedings of Second International Symposium on Parallel and Distributed Computing* (pp. 15-22). doi:10.1109/ISPDC.2003.1267638

Bal, J. (1998). Process Analysis Tools for Process Improvement. *The TQM Magazine*, *10*(5), 342–354. doi:10.1108/09544789810231225

Basten, T., & van der Aalst, W. M. P. (1999). *'Inheritance of Behaviour', Computing Science Report 99/17*. Eindhoven: Eindhoven University of Technology.

Basu, A., & Blanning, R. W. (2000). A Formal Approach to Workflow Analysis. *Information Systems Research*, *11*(1), 17–36. doi:10.1287/isre.11.1.17.11787

Biazzo, S. (2000). Approaches to Business Process Analysis: A Review. *Business Process Management Journal*, *6*(2), 99–112. doi:10.1108/14637150010321277

Biazzo, S. (2002). Process Mapping Techniques and Organisational Analysis. *Business Process Management Journal*, *8*(1), 42–52. doi:10.1108/14637150210418629

Bosilj-Vuksic, V., Giaglis, G. M., & Hlupic, V. (2000). IDEF Diagrams and Petri Nets for Business Process Modelling: Suitability, Efficacy and Complementary Use. In *Proceedings of International Conference on Enterprise Information Systems Stafford*. Academic Press.

Castellanos, M., Casati, F., Umeshwar, D., & Ming-Chien, S. (2004). A Comprehensive and Automated Approach to Intelligent Business Processes Execution Analysis. *Distributed and Parallel Databases, 16*(3), 1–35. doi:10.1023/B:DAPD.0000031635.88567.65

Chapin, N. (1971). *Flowcharts*. Princeton, NJ: Auerbach Publishers.

Chapin, N. (1974). New Format for Flowcharts. *Software, Practice & Experience, 4*(4), 341–357. doi:10.1002/spe.4380040404

Chen, Y., Li, Q., & Zhang, F. (2001). *Business Process Re-Engineering and Systems Integration*. Beijing: Tsinghua University Press.

Davenport, T. H. (1993). *Process Innovation: Reengineering Work Through Information Technology*. Boston: Harvard Business School Press.

Davenport, T. H., & Short, J. E. (1990). The New Industrial Engineering: Information Technology and Business Process Redesign. *Sloan Management Review*, 11–27.

Donatelli, S., Ribaudo, M., & Hillston, J. (1995). *A Comparison of Performance Evaluation Process Algebra and Generalised Stochastic Petri Nets*. Paper presented at Sixth International Workshop on Petri Nets and Performance Models.

Fan, Y. S. (2001). *Fundamental of Workflow Management Technology*. New York: Springer-Verlag.

Feldman, C. G. (1998). *The Practical Guide to Business Process Reengineering Using IDEF0*. New York: Dorset House.

Grigori, D., Casati, F., Castellanos, M., Dayal, U., Sayal, M., & Shan, M.-C. (2004). Business Process Intelligence. *Computers in Industry, 53*(3), 321–343. doi:10.1016/j.compind.2003.10.007

Guha, S., Kettinger, W. J., & Teng, J. T. C. (1993). Business Process Reengineering: Building a Comprehensive Methodology. *Information Systems Management, 10*(3), 13–22. doi:10.1080/10580539308906939

Gunasekaran, A., & Kobu, B. (2002). Modelling and Analysis of Business Process Reengineering. *International Journal of Production Research, 40*(11), 2521–2546. doi:10.1080/00207540210132733

Hammer, M., & Champy, J. (1993). *Reengineering the Corporation: a Manifesto for Business Revolution, N*. London: Brealey.

Havey, M. (2005). *Essential Business Process Modelling*. O'Reilly.

Hofacker, I., & Vetschera, R. (2001). Algorithmical Approaches to Business Process Design. *Computers & Operations Research, 28*(13), 1253–1275. doi:10.1016/S0305-0548(00)00038-1

Holt, A. P. (2000). Management-Oriented Models of Business Processes. *Lecture Notes in Computer Science, 1806*, 99–109. doi:10.1007/3-540-45594-9_7

Irani, Z., Hlupic, V., & Giaglis, G. M. (2002). Business Process Reengineering: An Analysis Perspective. *International Journal of Flexible Manufacturing Systems, 14*(1), 5–10. doi:10.1023/A:1013868430717

Johanson, H. J., McHugh, P., Pendlebury, A. J., & Wheeler, W. A. I. (1993). *Business Process Reengineering - Breakpoint Strategies for Market Dominance.* Chichester, UK: Wiley.

Kettinger, W. J., Teng, J. T. C., & Guha, S. (1997). Business Process Change: A Study of Methodologies, Techniques and Tools. *Management Information Systems Quarterly, 21*(1), 55–80. doi:10.2307/249742

Kiepuszewski, B., ter Hofstede, A. H. M., & van der Aalst, W. M. P. (2003). Fundamentals of Control Flow in Workflows. *Acta Informatica, 39*(3), 143–209. doi:10.1007/s00236-002-0105-4

Kim, C. H., Weston, R. H., Hodgson, A., & Lee, K. H. (2003). The Complementary Use of IDEF and UML Modelling Approaches. *Computers in Industry, 50*(1), 35–56. doi:10.1016/S0166-3615(02)00145-8

Knuth, D. E. (1963). Computer-Drawn Flowcharts. *ACM Communications, 6*(9), 555–563. doi:10.1145/367593.367620

Koenig, J. (2004). *JBoss JBPM White Paper, Version 2004.* Available at: http://www.jboss.com/pdf/jbpm_whitepaper.pdf

Koubarakis, M., & Plexousakis, D. (2002). A Formal Framework for Business Process Modelling and Design. *Information Systems, 27*(5), 299–319. doi:10.1016/S0306-4379(01)00055-2

Kusiak, A., Larson, N. T., & Wang, J. (1994). Reengineering of Design and Manufacturing Processes. *Computers & Industrial Engineering, 26*(3), 521–536. doi:10.1016/0360-8352(94)90048-5

Kusiak, A., & Zakarian, A. (1996a). Reliability Evaluation of Process Models. *IEEE Transactions on Components Packaging & Manufacturing Technology Part A, 19*(2), 268–275. doi:10.1109/95.506113

Kusiak, A., & Zakarian, A. (1996b). Risk Assessment of Process Models. *Computers & Industrial Engineering, 30*(4), 599–610. doi:10.1016/0360-8352(95)00178-6

Lakin, R., Capon, N., & Botten, N. (1996). BPR Enabling Software for the Financial Services Industry. *Management Services, 40*, 18–20.

Lee, D.-H., Kiritsis, D., & Xirouchakis, P. (2001). Branch and Fathoming Algorithms for Operation Sequencing in Process Planning. *International Journal of Production Research, 39*(8), 1649–1669. doi:10.1080/00207540010028100

Li, H., Yang, Y., & Chen, T. Y. (2004a). Resource Constraints Analysis of Workflow Specifications. *Systems and Software, 73*(2), 271–285. doi:10.1016/S0164-1212(03)00250-4

Li, J., Fan, Y., & Zhou, M. (2004b). Performance Modelling and Analysis of Workflow. *IEEE Transactions on Systems, Man, and Cybernetics. Part A, Systems and Humans, 34*(2), 229–242. doi:10.1109/TSMCA.2003.819490

Li, J., Maguire, B., & Yao, Y. (2003). A Business Process Centered Software Analysis Method. *International Journal of Software Engineering, 13*(2), 153–168.

Lindsay, A., Downs, D., & Lunn, K. (2003). Business Processes - Attempts to Find a Definition. *Information and Software Technology*, *45*(15), 1015–1019. doi:10.1016/S0950-5849(03)00129-0

Mayer, R. J., Paintec, M. K., & Dewitte, P. S. (1994). *IDEF Family of Methods for Concurrent Engineering and Business Reengineering Applications*. Technical Report. Knowledge Based Systems Inc.

Melao, N., & Pidd, M. (2000). A Conceptual Framework for Understanding Business Process Modelling. *Information Systems*, *10*, 105–129.

Menzel, C., & Mayer, R. (1998). The IDEF Family of Languages. In P. Bernus, K. Mertins, & G. Schmidt (Eds.), *Handbook on Architectures for Information Systems*. New York: Springer-Verlag. doi:10.1007/3-540-26661-5_10

Orman, L. V. (1995). A Model Management Approach to Business Process Reengineering. In *Proceeding of the 1995 American Conference on Information Systems*. Pittsburgh, PA: Academic Press.

Ould, M. A. (1995). *Business Processes: Modelling and Analysis for Re-Engineering and Improvement*. John Wiley & Sons.

Pall, G. A. (1987). *Quality Process Management*. Englewood Cliffs, NJ: Prentice-Hall.

Peters, L., & Peters, J. (1997). Using IDEF0 for Dynamic Process Analysis. In *Proceedings of the 1997 IEEE International Conference on Robotics and Automation*. IEEE.

Phalp, K., & Shepperd, M. (2000). Quantitative Analysis of Static Models of Processes. *Systems and Software*, *52*(2-3), 105–112. doi:10.1016/S0164-1212(99)00136-3

Powell, S. G., Schwaninger, M., & Trimble, C. (2001). Measurement and Control of Business Processes. *System Dynamics Review*, *17*(1), 63–91. doi:10.1002/sdr.206

Quatrani, T. (2001). *Introduction to Unified Modelling Language (UML)*. Rational Developer Network.

Raposo, A. B., Magalhaes, L. P., & Ricarte, I. L. M. (2000). Petri Nets Based Coordination Mechanisms for Multi-Flow Environments. *International Journal of Computer Systems Science and Engineering*, *15*(5), 315–326.

Reimer, U., Margelisch, A., & Staudt, M. (2000). EULE: A Knowledge-Based System to Support Business Processes. *Knowledge-Based Systems*, *13*(5), 261–269. doi:10.1016/S0950-7051(00)00086-1

Riehle, D., & Zullinghoven, H. (1996). Understanding and Using Patterns in Software Development. *Theory and Practice of Object Systems*, *2*(1), 3–13. doi:10.1002/(SICI)1096-9942(1996)2:1<3::AID-TAPO1>3.0.CO;2-#

Sadiq, W., & Orlowska, M. (2000). Analyzing Process Models Using Graph Reduction Techniques. *Information Systems*, *25*(2), 117–134. doi:10.1016/S0306-4379(00)00012-0

Scheer, A. W. (1994). *Business Process Reengineering, Reference Models for Industrial Enterprises*. Berlin: Springer.

Shen, H., Wall, B., Zaremba, M., Chen, Y., & Browne, J. (2004). Integration of Business Modelling Methods for Enterprise Information System Analysis and User Requirements Gathering. *Computers in Industry, 54*(3), 307–323. doi:10.1016/j.compind.2003.07.009

Shimizu, Y., & Sahara, Y. (2000). A Supporting System for Evaluation and Review of Business Process through Activity-Based Approach. *Computers & Chemical Engineering, 24*(2-7), 997–1003. doi:10.1016/S0098-1354(00)00536-6

Smith, H. (2003). Business Process Management - the Third Wave: Business Process Modelling Language and Its Pi-Calculus Format. *Information and Software Technology, 45*(15), 1065–1069. doi:10.1016/S0950-5849(03)00135-6

Soliman, F. (1998). Optimum Level of Process Mapping and Least Cost Business Process Re-Engineering. *International Journal of Operations & Production Management, 18*(9/10), 810–816. doi:10.1108/01443579810225469

Stock, J. R., & Lambert, D. M. (2001). *Strategic Logics Management*. McGraw-Hill, Irwin.

Stohr, E. A., & Zhao, J. L. (2001). Workflow Automation: Overview and Research Issues. *Information Systems Frontiers, 3*(3), 281–296. doi:10.1023/A:1011457324641

Tinnila, M. (1995). Strategic Perspective to Business Process Redesign. *Business Process Re-Engineering and Management Journal, 1*(1), 44–59. doi:10.1108/14637159510798202

Tiwari, A. (2001). *Evolutionary computing techniques for handling variables interaction in engineering desing optimisation*. (Ph.D. Thesis). Cranfield University.

Valiris, G., & Glykas, M. (1999). Critical Review of Existing BPR Methodologies, The Need for a Holistic Approach. *Business Process Management Journal, 5*(1), 65–86. doi:10.1108/14637159910249117

van der Aalst, W. M. P. (1995). *A Class of Petri Nets for Modelling and Analyzing Business Processes, Computing Science Reports 95/26*. Eindhoven: Eindhoven University of Technology.

van der Aalst, W. M. P. (1998a). The Application of Petri-Nets to Workflow Management. *Journal of Circuits, Systems, and Computers, 8*(1), 21–66. doi:10.1142/S0218126698000043

van der Aalst, W. M. P. (1998b). *Formalisation and Verification of Event-Driven Process Chains, Computing Science Reports 98/01*. Eindhoven: Eindhoven University of Technology.

van der Aalst, W. M. P., & ter Hofstede, A. H. M. (2002). Workflow Patterns: On the Expressive Power of (Petri-Net-Based) Workflow Languages. In *Proceedings of the Fourth Workshop on the Practical Use of Coloured Petri Nets and CPN Tools (CPN 2002)*. University of Aarhus.

van der Aalst, W. M. P., & ter Hofstede, A. H. M. (2003). *YAWL: Yet Another Workflow Language (Revised Version), QUT Technical Report, FIT-TR-2003-04*. Brisbane: Qeensland University of Technology.

van der Aalst, W. M. P., ter Hofstede, A. H. M., & Weske, M. (2003). Business Process Management: A Survey. *Lecture Notes in Computer Science, 2678*, 1–12. doi:10.1007/3-540-44895-0_1

van der Aalst, W. M. P., & van Hee, K. M. (1996). Business Process Redesign: A Petri-Net-Based Approach. *Computers in Industry, 29*(1-2), 15–26. doi:10.1016/0166-3615(95)00051-8

Volkner, P., & Werners, B. (2000). A Decision Support System for Business Process Planning. *European Journal of Operational Research, 125*(3), 633–647. doi:10.1016/S0377-2217(99)00273-8

Wamelink, J. W. F., Stoffele, M., & van der Aalst, W. M. P. (2002). Workflow Management in Construction: Opportunities for the Future. In *Proceedings of CIB W78 Conference: Distributing Knowledge in Building*. CIB.

Wang, M., & Wang, H. (2005). Intelligent Agent Supported Business Process Management. In *Proceedings of the 38th Hawaii International Conference on System Sciences*. doi:10.1109/HICSS.2005.332

WfMC. (1995). *The Workflow Reference Model, WFMC-TC-1003, 19-Jan-95, 1.1*. Available at: http://www.wfmc.org

Wohed, P., van der Aalst, W. M. P., Dumas, M., & ter Hofstede, A. H. M. (2002). *Pattern-Based Analysis of BPEL4WS, QUT Technical Report, FIT-TR-2002-04*. Brisbane: Queensland University of Technology.

Wohed, P., van der Aalst, W. M. P., Dumas, M., ter Hofstede, A. H. M., & Russell, N. (2004). *Pattern-Based Analysis of UML Activity Diagrams, BETA Working Paper Series, WP 129*. Eindhoven University of Technology.

Zakarian, A. (2001). Analysis of Process Models: A Fuzzy Logic Approach. *International Journal of Advanced Manufacturing Technology, 17*(6), 444–452. doi:10.1007/s001700170162

Zakarian, A., & Kusiak, A. (2000). Analysis of Process Models. *IEEE Transactions on Electronics Packaging Manufacturing, 23*(2), 137–147. doi:10.1109/6104.846937

Zakarian, A., & Kusiak, A. (2001). Process Analysis and Reengineering. *Computers & Industrial Engineering, 41*(2), 135–150. doi:10.1016/S0360-8352(01)00048-1

Zapf, M., & Heinzl, A. (2000). Evaluation of Generic Process Design Patterns: An Experimental Study. *Lecture Notes in Computer Science, 1806*, 83–88. doi:10.1007/3-540-45594-9_6

Zhou, Y., & Chen, Y. (2002). Business Process Assignment Optimisation. In *Proceedings of the IEEE International Conference on Systems, Man and Cybernetics* (vol. 3, pp. 540-545). IEEE.

Chapter 8
Databases and Information Systems

Nazih Heni
University of Moncton, Canada

Habib Hamam
University of Moncton, Canada

ABSTRACT

In this recent technological world, it is necessary that we get accustomed to all types of advanced technological techniques. In the process, we are becoming more aware about database and information system. But what is database system information? The Database Management System which works through the storing of data can be used any time. The importance of database and information Systems in modern business is inevitable. In this chapter, we define Information Systems by its categories of Information System, type and the usefulness for efficient Information System. Then, we will proceed to explaining the management of information systems by taking a short look at its history and list some of its domains of application. After that, we define the relation between Information Systems and database. Finally, we will explore the problem of storage and some issues related to information systems and databases.

1. INFORMATION SYSTEMS

The information System (IS) provides additional network hardware and software it is used by people and organizations to assemble, filter, process, create and distribute data. (Jessup and al., 2008).

It includes a diversity of disciplines such as: (1) the analysis and design of systems, (2) computer networking, (3) information security, (4) database management and (5) decision support systems. (Archibald, J.A., 1975).

- **Information Management:** Finds theoretical and practical solutions for the collection of data (Denning & Peter, 1999) and the analysis of information in an area of business. This function including the application (Coy & Wolfgang, 2004) and implementing programming tools productivity of the business, data mining, and decision support (Hoganson & Ken, 2001).

DOI: 10.4018/978-1-4666-8841-4.ch008

- **Communications and Networking:** Deals with telecommunication technologies (Davis, and al., 2004).To study various business models and related algorithmic processes within a computer science discipline Information Systems bridges business and computer science using the theoretical foundations of information (Hoganson & Ken, 2001) and computation (Khazanchi and al, 2000).

An information system is a work system whose activities are devoted to processing information. It's a special kind of work system; in which humans and/or machines perform work (processes and activities) using resources to produce specific products and/or services for customers (Alter, 2003)

It inter-relates with data systems on one hand and activity systems on the other. It can be considered a semi-formal language which supports human decision making and action. Information systems are the primary application that incites the study for managerial informatics. (Beynon-Davies, 2009)

1.1 Characteristics of an Information

Information that is significant for people and the organization must have certain characteristics. The characteristics of the information are enumerated as follow (Anita, 2010):

- Information must not contain any errors, it must be accurate.
- Authorized users should be able to access the information whenever required.
- Information must contain all important and related data.
- Information should be available in the desired format.
- Information should be flexible enough to be used for different purposes.
- Information is dependable and uses correct data.
- Information must be relevant so that it can be used by the organization.
- Unauthorized users should not be able to access the information; access is allowed only to authorize individuals.
- Information must be easily understandable and usable, complex information is difficult to use and may not serve its purpose.
- There should be a means to cross check the available information.
- Data must be organized into information (data becomes meaningless, uses data dictionaries).
- When analyzed, information should provide knowledge.

1.1.1 Organization of Data

The information system must organize Data before analyzing it. This must be done carefully, or the resulting information will be insincere (Keen & Peter, 1981). This may oblige sorting, summarizing or organizing.

1.1.2 Analyses of Knowledge

Access to information and the resulting knowledge is the purpose of an information system. Information systems provide a range of tools for analysis of data such as tables, queries and reports. Decisions were based on the information they receive from an information system.

Figure 1. A system

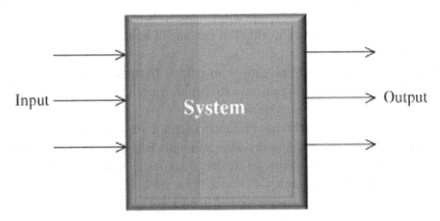

1.2 Information System (IS)

A system is a set of components, that work together to achieve a common goal. A system accepts input, processes it, and produces an output (Figure 1). It is composed of one or more subsystems. A system may be closed or open. A closed system is a stand-alone system that does not interact with other systems. An open system however interacts with other systems (Anita Goel, 2010).

Information System (IS) is a typical inter-related mechanism that collects, manipulates and disseminates data and information, and provides feedback to meet an objective. Resources like people, hardware, software, data, and networks are used by an information system for production, packing, performing input, processing, and switching activities. Some examples of IS are ATMs, railway reservation systems, and movie ticket reservation systems. (Anita Goel, 2010)

Components of Information System: An IS consists of four central components Input, Process, Output, and Feedback (Figure 1). Input is the activity of gathering and capturing raw data. A process converts or transforms data into useful output. During processing, the input data is manipulated into information using mathematical, statistical, and other tools. Output is the generation and presentation of useful information, frequently in the form of documents and reports. Feedback is an output that is used to make changes to the input, or the processing activities.

1.3 Need for Efficient Information System

Businesses, industries, and organizations need information systems to meet their future challenges (Zhou & Ross, 2003). IS are indispensable for organizations to meet the information needs of their employees. Growing business organizations are using information systems to improve the way they conduct business, as discussed below:

- IS, for many businesses, provide an opportunity to do business in a new way and thus gain huge profit and market shares.
- IS facilitating the achievement, change, and distribution of information. IS can improve decision making, enhance organizational performance, and help increase profitability.

- The use of information systems to add value to the organization can also give an organization a competitive advantage. It provides significant, long-term benefits to a company. ISs are used for strategic planning in a competitive world. The creating of new services, and improvement upon existing services.

- Damaged or lost data can cause disruptions in normal business activities leading to financial losses, law suits, etc. ISs help an organization to better manage and secure its critical data.

- IS also improve integration and work processes.

- "It is a Flat World.", as said by Thomas Friedman (Zhou & Ross, 2003). More and more companies rely on virtual structures and outsourcing, resulting in businesses to operate around the globe. Operating in a global society poses several challenges to the organizations. Diverse countries have diverse standards, policies, and laws. Of course, there are language barriers too. Managing and controlling operations of an organization located in different countries becomes almost impossible without the support of an efficient IS.

1.4 Categories of Information System

An organization structure can be shown as a pyramid, which is divided both horizontally and vertically. Vertically, the divisions represent the different functional areas of the organization such as sales, marketing, accounting, human resource, and manufacturing. Horizontally, the divisions are made according to the operational level of the organization, hierarchically from the base of the pyramid to the top, i.e. operations at low level, middle level, and top level (Figure 2). Information systems provide support at all levels of the organization and in different functional areas.

Figure 2. Information system categories

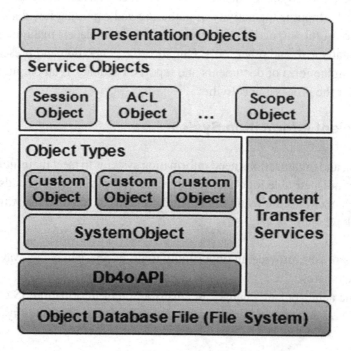

1.5 Types and Purposes of Information Systems

- **Transaction Processing Systems (TPS):** Collect, store, modify and retrieve the daily transactions of an organization e.g. a point-of-sale terminal. There are two types of transaction processing (Anita Goel, 2010):
  - **Batch Processing:** Collects transaction data into a group and processes it later and is currently used where the data exists in the form of paper such as cheques. This type of transaction has a time delay.
  - **Immediate Processing:** Deals with activities in each matter is instantly managed providing instant confirmation. This type of transaction does however a require access to an online database.

- **Decision Support Systems (DSS):** Assist people in the making of decisions by giving information, models and examination tools. They can be used on a daily basis or when an organization has to react to an unexpected event or make changes. Expert Systems are a type of DSS.

- **Expert Systems:** Provide information and solve problems that would otherwise require a person experienced in that field (an expert). They are useful in analyzing, checking, selecting, scheming, forecasting and training. An expert system asks users a set of questions and compares answers to an awareness base, which is a set of common evidences and if-then documentations provided by an expert (Discovering Computers, 2000).

- **Management Information Systems (MIS):** Provide information for the organization's managers. An MIS presents basic facts about the performance of the organization e.g. a budget report. The awareness of how performance is measured provides motivation for workers and brings forth results. A special kind of MIS is called the Executive Information System (EIS) which is designed for the information needs of senior managers and provides strategic information.

- **Office Automation Systems:** Provide people with effective ways to complete administrative tasks in an organization. They use software tools such as word processors, databases etc. and also use communication technology (Discovering Computers, 2000).

- **A Geographic Information System (GIS):** Geographical data knowledge, or geospatial information educations is a system intended to seize, store, operate, examine and achieve all types of geographically referenced data. In the simplest terms, GIS is the integration of cartography, statistical analysis, and database technology (Anita Goel, 2010).

- **Database Information Systems (DIS):** Most information systems (IS) stock data in a database. Databases are opened by a Database Management System (DBMS). A DBMS is software package that allows a user's to accomplish data. Some examples include; MS Access, FileMaker Pro, MySQL.

1.6 Operations Support System

The operations support system provides information about the day-to-day activities of the organization. They upkeep the operations of the organization, by monitoring the resources and the transactions of the organization in question. For instance, in a bank, the operations support system are used to keep track of the current balance of customers in a manufacturing unit, it helps to keep track of the inventory of items and in a sales unit, it keeps track of the number of units of each article sold. Thus, transaction processing is the main function of the operations support system. (Discovering Computers, 2000)

2. MANAGEMENT OF INFORMATION SYSTEM

A *management information system (MIS)* is typically computer system used for handling. The five primary components the following:

- Hardware,
- Software,
- Data (information for choice creating),
- Techniques (scheme, improvement and certification),
- People (individuals, groups, or organizations).

Management information systems are recycled to examine and simplify deliberate and working activities so that they are distinctive from other information systems. (O'Brien, 1999)

Educationally, the term is generally used to refer to the study of how persons, collections, and governments evaluate, design, implement, manage, and employ systems to produce information that will increase the efficiency and usefulness of choice creating, counting systems termed decision support systems, expert systems, and executive information systems. (O'Brien, 1999) Most business schools (or colleges of business administration within universities) have an MIS department, along with departments of bookkeeping, finance, management and sometimes others, and grant grades in MIS.

2.1 History

Laudon and Jane Laudon identify five epochs of Management Information System evolution corresponding to the five phases in computing technology's development: mainframe and medium power computer computing, client networks, private computers, cloud computing, and enterprise computing. (Laudon, and al, 2009)

IBM and their mainframe computers ruled the first era (mainframe and minicomputer); these computers would often take up all rooms and require teams to run them. As technology progressed, these computers acquired better capacities at a reduced cost. Smaller, more approachable minicomputers allowed more businesses to run their own computing centers.

The second era (personal computer) began in 1965 as microprocessors started to compete with mainframes and minicomputers and sped up the process of decentralizing computing power from large data centers to smaller offices. In the 1970's minicomputer technology facilitated the way to personal computers and relatively small cost computers were becoming mass market commodities, allowing businesses to provide their workers with the access to computing power which, ten years prior before would have cost tens of thousands of dollars. This proliferation of computers created a ready market for interconnecting networks and the popularization of the Internet (Laudon, and al, 2009).

As technological intricacy grew and costs diminished (Zhou, J., & Ross), the need to share information within an enterprise also grew giving rise to the third era (client/server), in which computers on

Figure 3. Transaction processing

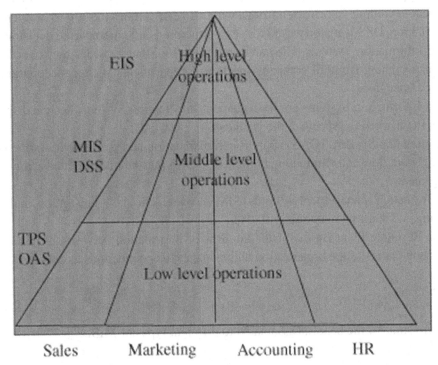

the same network access have common information on a server. This lets millions of people access data at the same time. High speed networks enabled the fourth era (enterprise) which tied all aspects of the business enterprise together offering rich information access including the complete management frame.

The fifth era (cloud computing) is the latest and uses networking technology to transfer applications as well as data storage distinct of the configuration, location or nature of the hardware.

2.2 Types and Terminology

The meanings of: Management Information System (MIS, Enterprise Resource Planning (ERP)), information system and information technology management are frequently subject to confusion. Information systems and MIS are wide types that include ERP. Information technology management affects the operation and community of information technology resources unattached of their target.

Most management information systems specialize in particular commercial and industrial sectors, aspects of the enterprise, or management substructure.

- Management information systems produce fixed, regularly scheduled reports based on data extracted and summarized from the firm's underlying transaction processing systems to middle and operational level managers to identify and inform structured and semi-structured decision problems.

- Decision Support Systems (DSS) are computer program applications used by middle and higher management to compile information from a wide range of sources to support problem solving and decision making. DSS is majorly used for semi-structured and unstructured decision problems.
- Executive Information Systems (EIS) are a reporting tool that provides quick access to summarized reports coming from all company levels and departments such as accounting, human resources and operations.
- Marketing Information Systems are Management Information Systems designed specifically for managing the marketing aspects of the business.
- Office Automation Systems (OAS) support communication and productivity in the enterprise by automating work flow and eliminating bottlenecks. OAS may be implemented at any and all levels of management.
- School Information Management Systems (SIMS) covers school administration, and often including teaching and learning materials.
- Enterprise Resource Planning facilitates the flow of information between all business functions inside the boundaries of the organization and manages the connections to outside stakeholders.

2.3 Benefits

The following are some of the benefits associated to different types of MIS.

- Companies are able to pinpoint their strengths and weaknesses due to the presence of revenue reports, employees' performance records etc. The identification of these aspects can help the company improve their business processes and operations.
- Giving an overall picture of the company and acting as a communication and planning tool.
- The availability of customer data and feedback can help the company align their business processes according to the needs of the customers. The effective management of customer data can help the company perform direct marketing and promotion activities.
- MIS can support a company gain a reasonable advantage. Competitive advantage is a firm's capacity to do achieve goals in ways that are better, faster, cheaper, or even to perform exceptionally, relatively too with rival companies in the market.

2.4 Enterprise Applications

- Enterprise System also known as enterprise resource planning (ERP) systems provide integrated software modules and a unified database that the personnel uses to plan, manage, and control core business processes across multiple locations. Modules of ERP systems may include finance, accounting, marketing, human resources, production, inventory management, and distribution (Zhou, J., & Ross).
- Supply chain management (SCM) systems enable more efficient management of the supply chain by integrating the links in a supply chain. This may include suppliers, manufacturers, wholesalers, retailers, and final customers (Taylor, 2011).

- Customer relationship management (CRM) systems help businesses manage relationships with potential and current customers and business partners across marketing, sales, and service (Lynn, 2014).
- The knowledge organization system (KMS) helps administrations streamline the collection, recording, organization, retrieval, and dissemination of knowledge. This may include documents, accounting annals, spoken procedures, observes, and services. Knowledge management (KM) as a system retreats the process of knowledge creation and acquisition from internal processes and the external world. The collected knowledge is assimilated in organizational policies and events, and then detached to the stakeholders. (Joshi, 2013)

2.5 Developing Information Systems

"The movements that are engaged to produce a data system that explains an organizational problem are named system development". (Laudon, 2010) These actions usually take place in that quantified order but some may need be reprised or be accomplished concurrently.

Conversion is the process of varying or transforming the old structure into a new one. This can be done in three elementary ways, though newer techniques (prototyping, Extreme Encoding, etc.) are changing these traditional conversion methods in many cases (Laudon & Laudon, 2010):

- **Direct Cut:** The new system replaces the old one at an appointed time.
- **Pilot Study:** Introducing the new system to a small portion of the operation to see how it fares. If the results are satisfying good then the new system expands to the rest of the company.
- **Phased Style:** The new system is announced in steps.

3. DATABASE INFORMATION SYSTEMS

Databases and database systems are essential parts of our life. We interact with non-computerized databases and have been interacting with them since long time, remember, looking for a word in a dictionary or searching for the telephone number of your friend from in a telephone directory. Computerized databases use computers to store, manipulate, and manage the database. In our daily lives we interact with computerized databases when we do reservations of railway tickets and movie tickets, when searching for a book in a library, to get salary details, to find the balance of our account when using an ATM, to get the rate list when purchasing items from a cash and carry store, and there are many more example of our daily interaction with computerized databases.

3.1 Database

Database is a repository or collection of logically related and similar data (Taylor, 2011). Database stores similar groups of data that are organized in a manner in which information can be derived from it, modified, added, deleted, and used when needed.

3.1.1 Definition and Examples

A database is defined as a collection, or repository of data, having an organized structure, and for a specific purpose. A database stores information, which is useful to an organization. It contains data based on the kind of application for which it is required. For example, an airline database may contain data about the airplanes, the routes, airline reservations, airline schedules, etc. A college database may contain data about the students, faculties, administrative staff, courses, results etc. A database for manufacturing applications may contain data about the production, inventory, supply chain, orders, sales etc. and a student database may contain data such as student names, student course, etc. (SQL Server Architecture, 2000).

Some examples of databases in real life situations are:

- **Dictionaries:** A database of words organized alphabetically along with their definitions.
- **Telephone Directories:** A database of telephone numbers and addresses organized alphabetically by the last name of people.
- **Railway Timetables:** A database of trains organized by train names, and, companies listed on Stock Exchange organized by names alphabetically.

3.1.2 Data Characteristics

Data is an assemblage of facts. These can be beliefs, measurements, statistics, words, dimensions, and observations. Many companies would not be as popular without data (Beynon-Davies, 2009). A data has a chain of commands; this hierarchy is a systematic association of data. Fields, records, and files are a part of the data organization. Product names or quantities are the lowest level of the hierarchy, and the database is the highest level of the hierarchy (Microsoft SQL Server, 2014). Also, the data definition consists of the following: name, data type, description, and properties. This describes the chattels that go into a store. If a computer user needs to look up all of the data meanings for a database, he or she would search the data dictionary. A few basic terms a computer operator should be aware of concerning data characteristics, consist of data field, record, file, and database. A data field contains a single fact of an entity. A record is a collection of related fields. A file is an organization of related business records. The database is the place where files are combined (Tsitchizris, 1982). The data characteristic key terms are essential to be aware of for commerce that uses a database.

3.1.3 Classification of Database

a. Single-User vs. Multiuser Database Systems

Single-user database systems are situated on one computer and they are calculated for one user. They are used for private use and smaller companies. Only single individuals can exercise the database at a time, so if one operator is using the folder the other users must pause their activities until that manager is completed. The other benevolent is used for superior businesses. It is a database that is corrected through a network. This is so more than one individual can contact and change the data in a system. Most use some kind of lock on the database so that there are no conflicts between people making changes. They can be on one computer or multiple computers.

b. Client-Server and N-Tier Database Systems

Most multiuser database structures are client-server database systems. Basically client-server database systems are attendants that have properties for other workstations (Tsitchizris, 1982). It is when the client creates a service request from the waiter, who then finalizes the request. The client is mentioned to at the front end and the database server is stated to as the back end. Some of the client-server database systems have more than just the facade end and the back end but also a medium part called a tier. These are stated to as n-tier database systems. In these databanks the client and the database never connect directly, all data is agreed through the middle layer. The benefits of this database system is that the middle tier offers a layer of abstraction, that way you can change parts of the back end. It is also a respectable way to distinguish responsibilities; they can also be more effectual. (Mike, 2012)

c. Centralized vs. Distributed Database Systems and Disk-Based vs. In-Memory Database Systems

Centralized database systems are all positioned on one laptop. This can either be an attendant or mainframe computer. Distributed database systems share a network and the data is separated between several computers connected to that network. A benefit of a consolidated database system is that all data is in one place. The drawback may be that a blockage might occur. Having all information on one computer can make it easier to some users, but difficult for others who want to access the files (Mike, 2012). One advantage of distributed database systems is that the database can be accessed using any computer on the network even if all the information is not on one computer. This is the preferred type of system to use for databases, because information can be simply found. It also certifies that all files will not be absent, if using the dispersed database structure over the compacted system. Because of the current advances in knowledge, using the "cloud" is another way to store database information over the Internet for a relaxed method of storage. This ideal goes hand in hand with disk-based and in-memory database systems. Most databases are deposited on predictable hard drives in computers today, but recently many are switching to in-memory databases. This can hold all data on the main memory of the computer. This creates faster performances than it would if using the disk-based system.

3.1.4 Database Models

a. Hierarchical and Network Database Models

The hierarchical model is the ancient database representation. It categorizes date in a tree-like edifice, consuming parent and child data sections. Such as, it begins at the top of the tree with a single root that stems into a lower level section, which attaches to other subordinate segments afterwards. This is used to model one-to-many relationships. A disadvantage of using this ideal is that it needs data to be stockpiled repetitively in multiple altitudes. This causes the database to function very gently because it can be searching for information in lower levels as well. The network model uses a set structure. A set is contains of a proprietor record type, a set name, and a member record type. Parents can have several children, and children can have multiple parents (David, 2000).

Also, all paths for accessing the data must be planned ahead of time and cannot be easily changed. Some places we rein the hierarchical model still persists can be in large systems that use high-volume transaction processing, like banks or insurance companies.

b. Object-Oriented Database Models

Whereas other database simulations can only store conformist data (such as dates, statistics, and text), the object-concerned with database organization structure (OODBMS) is far more intelligent. In an OODBMS, you can stock pretty copious data of any kind you wish, along with the procedures to be recycled with that data. To regain this more composite and varied data, the user sends queries written in object query language (OQL) which is an object-oriented version of SQL. OODBMS are flatteringly progressively prevalent because of the greater demands for PC users today. However, as is the case with any new expertise, there exist some conflicts because of the downside of OODBMS. One downside is how cutting out an OODBMS based application is more time consuming since changes have to be made to the other classes in the submission that relates with instances of the parent class, as opposed to an RDBMS system where edits can typically be independent of the parent application (Timothy, 2001). Even with the extra difficulties, many important clients continue to operate using an OODBMS, one main example being the Chicago Stock Exchange, which uses the system to manage stock trades.

db4o (DB4O) is an open home entity database, as the OODBMS. It created a fine abstraction around the object database to provide transparent persistence operations, by selecting the data as object types. The architectural stack diagram represented below runs a generic view in modeling the application in terms of objects (Figure 4).

3.2 Organization Methods

Organizing is the manner of arranging, indicating and planning data. A database is a planned collection of data.

3.3 Non-Computer Methods

A database is simply a place to organize and store data so that it can be retrieved later for a particular purpose (Timothy, 2001). A telephone book is a non-computer database that organizes data alphabetically according to a person's family name. Searching for the person's name retrieves their phone number. A paper filing system is a non-computer database. It involves paper, folders and filing cabinets to store data in an organized way. Searching for folders in the filing cabinet allows you to retrieve a single piece of paper. Non-computer databases are often the best way to organize data. It is convenient to obtain

Figure 4. Architectural stack diagram for object-oriented data model

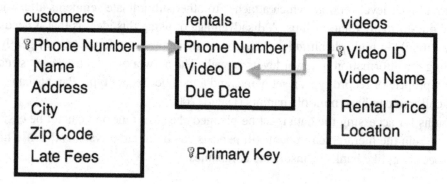

information from a book or access it from a filing cabinet. People can easily and inexpensively organize data using a non-computer data-base. They do not need a computer or computer skills. Non-computer databases are easier to keep secure, and they remain more private. Additionally, the data is more difficult to use for other purposes. For example, a telephone book does not allow a thief to search for an address and find the phone number of a house. Computer-based databases are being increasingly used to organize and store data. Some examples include taxation records, library systems, car registrations, student records, CD-ROM encyclopedias and census data. Databases have several advantages over non-computer databases:

- Easily edited.
- Large storage.
- Fast retrieval.
- Display options.

Computer-based methods of organizing include flat file systems, database management systems and hypermedia.

3.4 Electronic/Computer-Based Methods of Data Organization

Computer Based Databases for example car registrations and CD-ROM compendiums have several benefits over non-computer centered methods:

- **Easily Edited:** Data can be corrected and updated without retyping.
- **Large Storage:** Data is stored on a disk and retrieved when required.
- **Fast Retrieval:** Data is searched and sorted quickly and accurately to obtain required information.
- **Display Options:** Data is unfilled in a number of techniques using tables, forms and reports.

3.5 Flat File Databases

A flat folder database arranges data into a distinct board and is appropriate for several small presentations. Using data structures called files, records, meadows, and characters (Fowler, 1994).

- A *file* is a block of data. When you have done some work on the computer, it is stored in a file. The Address database is a file. A file in a database is divided into a set of related records.
- A *record* is a collection of facts about one specific entry in a database. In the Address database, a record is information about a person's name, address and home phone. A record is divided into one or more related fields.
- A *field* is a specific category of data in a database. In the Address database, the family name, given name, street, suburb, postcode and home phone are fields. Data items in a field are made up of characters.
- A *character* is the slightest unit of files that society can use. Characters comprise letters, numbers, and symbols.

Keys are fields that are recycled to sort and retrieve information. Regularly, each key holds a single item that applies to only one record. When the records are organized, the key is recycled so that not all the data has to be recited or retrieved. There are diverse types of keys A *single key* is a field in which each item of data is single. Care must be taken when selecting a single key, as some fields, for instance family name, are not always unique.

- A *composite key*, or compound key, is made by joining two or more fields together. It is used when no data item in any field can be guaranteed to be unique. For example, a compound key can be made from such fields as gender and date of birth.
- A *primary key* is a single key or compound key that must have a value. Primary keys cannot be empty or null.
- A *secondary key* is a meadow that encloses useful items of data often recycled in searches. Unlike other keys, secondary keys are not always unique.

3.6 Database System

Banks, hospitals, colleges, universities, manufacturing businesses, and governmental establishments are some examples of organizations or enterprises that are established for specific purposes. All organizations or enterprises have some basic common functions. They need to collect and store data, process data, and disseminate data for their various functions depending on the kind of organization. Some of the common functions include payroll, sales reports etc.

A database system integrates the collection, storage, and dissemination of data required for the different operations of an organization, under a single administration. A database system is a computerized record keeping system (Timothy, 2001). The purpose of the database system is to maintain the data and to make the information available on demand.

3.7. Relational Database Systems

A relational database systematizes data using a series of connected tables. Relationships are constructed between the tables to offer a supple way of handling and joining data. Procedures are used to outlook, enter and change data in the tables. Relational databases are the most frequently used database structures. The association of data in an interpersonal database includes a schema (Gail, 2008).

3.7.1 Schemas

A schema is the data meaning for a database. It is an envisioned plan of the entire database showing how and where the data is set up, the accounts of the data, and the data's logical relationships. In a relational database, the schema describes the objects, (Paolo, 2012) structures and relations:

- An *entity* is a specific thing about which information is collected and stored. A video store database for example has an entity for customers, for videos, for video categories and for payrolls (Figure 4).

- An *attribute* is a defined property of an entity. The employee's entity in the Video Store database has such attributes as LastName, FirstName, DOB and payRate. Each attribute of the entity comprises a data item.
- A *relationship* is the way the entities are related to each other. In the Video Store database, the entities are related using keys, such as empID. Entities are related in three ways (Gail, 2008).
- A *one-to-one relationship* occurs when each record in the first entity is related to exactly one record in the second entity. For example, each employee is assigned only one computer within a company (Figure 4).

A *one-to-many relationship* occurs when one record in the first entity is related to many records in the second entity, but any record in the second entity only relates to one record in the first entity. For example, a customer can rent one or more videos. (Figure 5)

A *many-to-many relationship* occurs when each record in the first entity is related to many records in the second entity, and each record in the second entity is related to many records in the first entity. For example, many customers can rent many videos. The flip side is, many videos are rented by many customers. (Figure 6)

- A *foreign key* is an attribute (field) of a table that is a primary key of another table. In the Video Store database, the Phone Number attribute is a foreign key of the Customers and Videos table and a primary key of the Customers table. The data in a foreign key of one table must match the data in the primary key of another table.

Figure 5. Relational database management system (Chen, Peter, 1976)

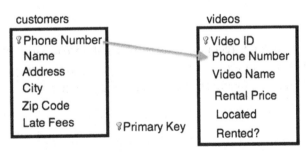

Figure 6. One-to-one relationship

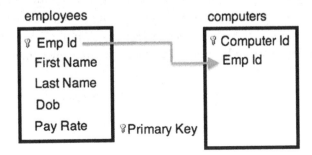

Figure 7. One-to-many relationship

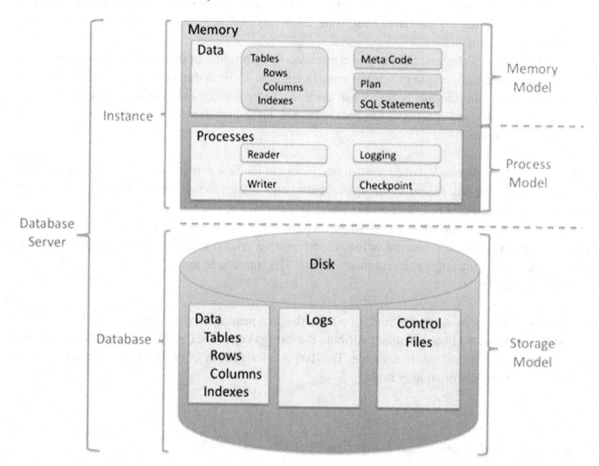

- A *secondary key* is a field that is recognized as being right for indexing the data such as a surname, it is used to nature the data in a diverse instruction to the primary key, a table can have several secondary keys as a matter of fact every field could be a secondary key.

3.7.2 Tables

Information about an object is displayed in a table which is the organization of data into columns and rows. A support of a table is also an attribute of an entity or a field of a record. The data in a column must have the same data type and have a different name. A row in a table is also called a *tuple* of an entity, or one record. Each commotion must be exceptionally recognized by a key. The intersection of a row and column stores a particular data item, such as 'Rebecca' in the first row and second column of the Video Store database. The rows and columns in a table can be viewed in any order without moving the contents of the table.

Figure 8. Many-to-many relationship

TABLE: customers

phoneNo	fullName	address	city	state	zipCode	lateFee
551-256-5470	Harold Douglass	1408 Perth Ave	Richmond Hill	Georgia	90303	12.5
209-888-1900	Waldo Fargo	3800 Pen Ave	Tracy	California	18906	5.5
555-382-4273	Trisha Henderson	19 Wroxetter Rd	Toronto	Ontario	M4N 2R7	1.5

TABLE: videos

videoID	videoName	rentalPrice	category
1	Casablanca	4.99	1
2	Men in Black II	3.99	3
3	Bambi	1.5	2

TABLE: employees

empID	firstName	lastName	dob	payRate
1	Idris	Elba	1964	14.55
2	Gertrude	Horton	1982	27.34
3	Gina	Davis	1975	12.08

TABLE: videoCategory

catID	Category
1	Vintage
2	Regular
3	Kids

3.7.3 Data Views

Data is viewed for different purposes using *procedures*. A form is used to sight, enter, and change data in a table. The layout of the form can be altered. The user can position fields, headings, instructions and graphics. A sound designed form provides information explaining the required data and any data entry rules that apply to particular fields. For example, the field name 'Sex (M/F)' leaves no confusion about what data is required and how it should be arrived. In a personal database, methods can be founded on a single table or on multiple tables (Paolo, 2012).

3.7.4 Relational Database Architecture

Database is a term that can mean different but similar things be contingent on situation. Database may mention to the occurrence, the data or the server.

- DATABASE is managed by a portion of software, called suitably enough
- The Relational Database Management System (or RDBMS, DBMS or again database) and the combination of DBMS and Data
- An ILLUSTRATION (or database), all of which wants to ride on a machine, classically a server called suitably enough
- A DATABASE SERVER (or database).

And Relational Databases (RDBMS, DBMS and Database):

Figure 9. Relational database architecture

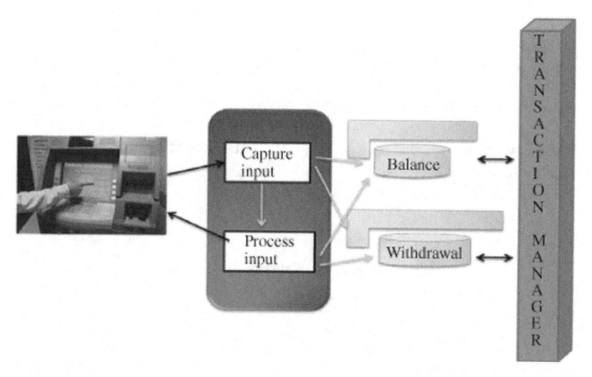

a) Storage Model

Since the only actions that take place on the disk are read and write the data on the disk is controlled by the restrictions of the mass media, but is organized in a method to exploit the advantages of disk storage (bits, bytes, blocks, tracks and cylinders). This physical organization is coped by the operating system and to all extents and purposes is undetectable to the database users. The database administrator (DBA) can specify that different pieces of database are placed on different disks and that this data can be duplicated but at the lowest level, the organization of the disk data is optimized for reading and writing (Zhou & Ross, 2003).

The stowing exemplary is a coat of perception that plans the necessities of only construing data to the requirements of the DBMS. Variations prepared to user data are not written to configuration files, for example. Thus, each DBMS has an illustration of the altered categories of data on disk that it wishes to do its job.

The putting away model for the DBMS pronounces the physical structures of the DBMS (Control Records, Data Stores, Diary Files), and it is this structure that is called the DATABASE.

Disk data has a lot of advantages such as; it is low-priced, it is virtually never-ending, and the most important it is obstinate.

b) Memory Model

Memory is the place where work gets done on data, they can be composite and arbitrary, and they can be modified and rearranged easily. This gives the DBMS its rapidity and suppleness.

There is a structure that is common between memory and disk, this basic building block of information is appropriately called a block. Structures in memory are planned in blocks and this relieves from reading blocks from disk into memory. Since chunks of data in the database are logically related, it is efficient to move not only the data that you need into memory, but also the data that you are likely to need at the same time. These 'defensive' reads are called pre-enticing, and since they can fetch several wedges of data at a time, the blocks are loaded up next to each other in constructions called degrees (Gail, 2008).

To holding data recovered from disk, memory will hold such things as temporary configurations produced during the databases operations (i.e. intermediate sort tables), blocks of executable code, the system list and dictionary, and the organization.

The creations in celebration, demarcated by the memory model, can be log on rapidly and enclose majority of the information needed by the DBMS to work. This includes parts of the higher population of worker data held on disk, and structures obligatory for the database to organization system (i.e. the plan, meta code etc.). Because its strength does not permit, nor is it desired, to have all the data that lives on disk in memory, and for security purposes (persistence), the DBMS will exchange data between memory and disk.

c) Process Model

There are several things happening instantaneously in the DBMS, such as construing and lettering data from and to disk, recording rescue information in database logs, testing to see if data has changed in memory, holding networks for users and system programs, observing the fitness of the database, running user written code, fastening parts of the database and perceiving deadlocks. This gradient is by no means comprehensive, and there are modifications between different DBMS executions but there are an essential set of procedures that deal with memory management, bleeping to disk, and lettering information in the occurrence of recovery or rollback.

It is these working in concert with the structures in memory that is called the INSTANCE.

3.8 Database Management System

3.8.1 What Is a Database Management System (DBMS)?

The interrelated set of data that forms the database needs to be stored and managed, so that the database can be accessed for the retrieval of data, and for insertion, deletion, or updating of data. *DBMS* is a software system for creating, organizing and managing the database. DBMS handles all access to the database and manages the database. Managing the database implies that it provides a convenient environment to the user to perform operations on the database for creation, insertion, deletion, updating, and retrieval of data. DBMS defines the scope of the use of database. This keeps data secure from unauthorized access.

The functionality of DBMS includes the database that contains interrelated data, and a set of programs to access the data. The DBMS implements the three schema architecture internal schema at internal level, conceptual schema at conceptual level, and external schema at external level (Gail, 2008). The different DBMSs may not provide a clear distinction between the three levels, but generally they follow the three schema architecture.

Mapping is a term used for transforming requests and the results between different levels of the DBMS architecture (Gail, 2008). In a DBMS, the user interacts with the DBMS through the external view, and the data in the DBMS is stored at a physical level. Any request from the user, would require the DBMS to access the data and then present it to the user as specified in the external schema. This requires transforming the request from one level to the other, or mapping.

3.8.2 The usefulness of Database Management System

Database management systems are used to allow developers to create a database, seal it with information and produce ways to request and change that information without worring about the technical aspects of data storage and retrieval. Other features of database management systems include:

- User access and security management systems provide appropriate data access to multiple users while protecting sensitive data.
- Data backup to ensure consistent availability of data.
- Access logs make it easier for a database manager to see how the database is being used.
- Rules enforcement to ensure only data of the prescribed type is stored in each field, for example, date fields may be set to only contain dates within a set range.
- Formulas such as counting, averaging and summing included in the DBMS make statistical analysis and representation of the data simpler.
- Performance watching and optimization gears may also be encompassed to allow the user to tweak the database settings for speed and efficiency.

Many Web applications rely on a DBMS, from search instruments and article indexes, to collective networks like Facebook and Twitter. Almost any place with personal logon details rather than a single shared key will probably want a database, as will ecommerce systems, blogs and concerted sites such as Wikis and numerous user gratified management systems (Zhou & Ross, 2003).

3.9 Advantages and Disadvantages of Database Management Systems

Shown in Figure 10.

Figure 10. Advantages and disadvantages of database management systems

Advantages	Disadvantages
<ul><li>Data independence</li><li>Elimination of data redundancy</li><li>Easier maintenance of data integrity</li><li>Centralised security - greater control over data</li></ul>	<ul><li>Large size</li><li>High Cost</li><li>More hardware needed</li><li>Higher impact of failure</li></ul>

3.10 Data Modelling Tools for Organizing Data

Data modelling is the procedure of recognizing entities, the relations between those units and the attributes of those entities. It is used to develop a schema for the database. Data modelling is critical to making an efficient database. There are an integer of tools used for data showing, such as data dictionaries, representation diagrams and stabilization.

3.10.1 Data Dictionaries

A *data dictionary* is a comprehensive explanation of each field (attribute) in a catalogue. It contains data about the individualities of each item arrived in the database, such as the meadow name, field size and data type and field description:

- *Field name* is the name of the field. It should be carefully selected to avoid confusion. Field names should be relatively short but clear and unambiguous.
- *Data type* (or field type) is the kind of data that can be stored in the field. Each field stores data in a single data type. Some common data types are text, memo, number, currency, yes/no and date/time. Logical fields contain the logic values 'true' or 'false'.
- *Data Format* shows how the data is to be displayed
- *Field size*, or width, is the number of characters allowed in each field. It should be limited to the smallest number of characters likely to be needed, as smaller field sizes let the database work faster.
- *Description* specifies the contents of the field.
- *Examples* provide a model of a valid pass in the meadow.

A data dictionary is a fundamental tool in the development of a database (Zhou & Ross, 2003). It consists of metadata, or information about data. It provides a common ground for people working on a project at the same time. For example, if people are working on different entities, they can refer to the data dictionary to check whether a particular attribute already exists. This reduces data redundancy (any undesirable duplication of data) within a database.

3.10.2 Schematic Diagrams

Schematic diagrams are graphical apparatuses that aid delimit the database and improve a schema. A common graphic diagram is called an entity-relationship diagram. An entity-relationship diagram (ERD) is a graphical technique of identifying the entities and showing the relationships between them. It helps to determine what data will be included in and excluded from the database. ERDs force people to have a common understanding of the database. They are a useful tool to explain the database. There are numerous notations associated to ERD.

3.10.3 Normalizing Data

Normalization is the process of organizing data into tables so that the results following the usage of the database will be unambiguous and as intended. It is a refinement process that aims to reduce data redundancy (Zhou & Ross, 2003). Normalization results in a database are more effectual and more compound because data is disjointed into more tables. For example, a table is used to keep track of customer purchases and the prices of the products. If you deleted a customer, you would also delete a price. Normalizing would solve this problem by dividing this table into two tables: a table about each customer and a product they had bought and a table about each product and its price. Making additions or deletions to either table would not affect the other.

4. STORAGE AND RETRIEVAL

A database management system is recycled to provide confident and efficient techniques for storage and reclamation of facts from a database.

Database Management System (DBMS) is a software set that permits users to contact a database so they can arrive, preserve and view the data. In a DBMS, data is structured into tables, viewed in forms, recovered using queries, and exposed in bangs. DBMS process the data by examining and/or cataloging it. They also perform a number of chores to help operators develop and conserve a database:

- Organizing the data using a data dictionary,
- Demonstrating relationships between entities using schematic diagrams,
- Verifying for identifiable errors in data entry,
- Allowing flexibility to change the definition of the database,
- Restricting access to the data to authorized persons.

4.1 Accessing Data

- **Sequential Access:** Occurs when data is accessed in a sequence. Data is accessed in the order it was stored. It does not require the exact location of the data item. Sequential access is much slower than direct and impractical access when immediate processing is required (Zhou & Ross, 2003). It is the only method for accessing data stored on magnetic tape.
- **Direct Access:** Occurs when data is accessed without accessing previous data items. Data is stored in a particular storage location based on a mathematical procedure or algorithm. Direct access uses this algorithm to calculate the approximate location of the data. If the data is not found there, the computer searches through successive locations until it is found. Direct data often requires the use of an index and this is called indexed access.
- **Index:** Is a table that comprises information about the location of data. Data is opened by bring up to the index and locating the exact location of the data. The indexed technique is generally used to stock data on a disk, as well as store the coherent location of data in a database.

4.2 Distributed Database Systems

Distributed Databases: Databases situated in more than one unique site (Zhou & Ross, 2003). They become a distinct collection of data that is organically dispersed. Distributed databases decrease data transmission costs that would occur if all users at all sites had to contact one integrated database. However they make it more difficult to acquire a complete vision of the database. Distributed databases often need to be synchronized to keep them current. A two-phase commit is a part of the DBMS used to conserve consistency diagonally a circulated database.

4.3 Storage Media

- Online Storage uses a peripheral device that is under the user's direct control e.g. a hard disk.
- Offline Loading uses an exterior device that is not below the user's direct control e.g. a centralized database.

Both online and offline storage use a variety of peripheral devices and storage mediums:

- **Hard Disk:** Is a storage device made of metal or glass and covered with magnetic material. Usually mounted or fixed in place with storage capacity measured in GB and accessed using direct access.
- **Optical Disk:** Is a polycarbonate plastic disk with a reflective layer of metal covering the surface. Data is read and written using lasers and data is retrieved using direct access. Type:
  - **CD-ROMS (Compact Disks Read Only Memory)**: 12cm and capable of storing 650Mb. They are convenient for storing constant data.
  - **DVD-ROM (Digital Versatile Disk Read Only Memory):** The same physical size as CD's but store between 4.7 and 17 GB.
- **Transferable Cartridge:** A hard disk covered in a plastic or metal cartridge that can be detached like a soft disk. Fast (yet not as fast as a fixed hard disk) and use straight access.

4.4 Encryption and Decryption

Encryption is the method of coding data, and decryption is the process of decoding it. It is the most operational way of accomplishing data security (Alter, S., 2013). Data is programmed, diffused and then converted back to its original form. Encryption is indispensable for financial communications and is used widely on the Internet. Methods often involve complex manipulation of bit patterns. One problem is to find a method that is difficult to decode yet practical to use. Two main types:

- Asymmetric Encryption requires a key for encryption and a key for decryption. Common method is public key encryption, which involves a public key that is widely available and used for encryption and a private key that is kept secret and used for decryption. Both are developed using complicated number theories.
- Symmetric Encryption involves a similar key for both encryption and decryption. A Mutual technique is a Data Encryption Standard (DES).

4.5 Data Backup and Security

Backup: Can be used to reconstruct the structure. DBMS enclose backup and release capabilities where backups are formed at stated times. If the system goes down the recovery manner restructures the data. It uses the last completed backup and a journal listing all the actions completed by the DBMS since the last backup. The success of backup and recovery depends on implementing appropriate procedures

(Alter, S., 2013). Backups are usually stored offsite or in a fireproof safe. Backups eliminate the need for replacing data, which is an enormously costly action.

Data Security: Involves a series of safeguards to protect the data. First access is limited to authorized users using passwords, personal objects and biometric devices. Further safeguards involve encryption and firewalls.

4.6 Search Engine

A search engine is a database of indexed Web sites that contracted a keyword search. Search engines are used to inspect hypermedia. A file is a table which covers info about the position of data. Indexes permit documents to be found using a keyword search. An examination engine's index is manufactured by regularly browsing the Web for new sites and uncomplaining submissions from Webpage writers. The scanning is often concluded by programs called spiders, crawlers or robots. They refer back to the URL of any document they catch to the examination engines indexing software. This indexing software gathers information, such as titles and keywords, from the Web sites and processed to then indexing these in a database. Each search engine has a diverse technique of building its index, which is why hunts of the same keyword using different search engines produce different results. A keyword is entered related to the topic of interest. Most exploration engines pass a search on a series of keywords. When the user enters a keyword the search engine tests the index and displays a list of Web sites that cover that keyword. Selecting the right keyword is essential to the success of a search. More than one word, should be used and it should be very precise. Search engines allow the use of Boolean qualities for example 'AND', 'OR' and 'NOT' to improve a search. Some search instruments also deal with dictionaries.

Dictionaries are lists of Web sites prepared into classes (e.g. sport) (Alter, S., 2013). They are another method to catch information on the net. The proprietors of a site are required to record it in order for his/her site to be included in a directory. As a result encyclopedias often refuge an insignificant portion of the pages accessible on the Net. A directory is valuable for ruling information on a universal issue.

5. ISSUES RELATED TO INFORMATION SYSTEMS AND DATABASES

5.1 Acknowledgement of Data Sources

Data is developed by DATA SOURCE which can be a person or an organization. It may come from informal sources, such as talks, conferences or opinions, or it may come from formal causes, such as a bang, book or formal text. An official source often offers data that is logically organized. However there is no assurance to its precision. The source of data is endangered by the Copyright Act. People cannot duplicate another's work without their permission and it is unlawful to break copyright rules. Most data from the Net is sheltered by copyright (Denning, 2007). Text and audio etc. from a Web site should not be used without reaction of and authorization from the proprietor. However the Copyright Act creates different necessities for students to exercise information for investigation dedications. The student is certified to practice a realistic share of the creative work if it is correctly cited. This citation comprises the writer's surname and organization's name, label of complete work or Net page, URL, age of document, and download date.

5.2 The Freedom of Information Act

The Autonomy of Information Act is considered to let characters catch what data is being kept by the government and other public bodies (Denning, 2007). It shapes that characters have the right to contact data where it transmits to the singular and does not attack another person's privacy. There is free relief of this information. Nevertheless knowing what data is saved does not specify how it is being used. People can use our favorites, feebleness and routines to their benefit. Possession and device of such data is a topic of which concerns ethics (Ken,1974).

5.3 Data Integrity

Data Integrity defines the dependability of the data. Reliable data is truthful, recent and pertinent. There is no certainty that the information on the Net is dependable as it is easy for anyone to publish any information on to the Internet.

Data validation is recycled to square the pass of data:

- Range Check is used if the data is restricted to a small range of particular values.
- List Check is used when the data can be compared to a set of accepted data.
- Type Check is used to determine whether the data type is correct.
- Check Digit is a figure designed from the digits of a code number and then additional to that number as an additional digit.

The accuracy of data defines the degree to which it is free from errors. This imprecision may be caused by mistakes in meeting or inflowing data, gap between the data and the person, or out-of-date information. Prospects to check and change incorrect data should be delivered. It is often essential to equate data from a number of different sources to regulate which data is exact.

CONCLUSION

Information systems allow for the processing of the data where the architecture of an information system is based on the software and the database. So in our modern times, database integration plays an important role in industry. Effective integration of data is an essential requirement for any organization seeking to establish a solid base and database management helps consolidate information collected by different actors, to ensure their sustainability and analyzed. International cooperation on databases facilitates the creation and the exchange of information. Management of a database is an important and continuous work.

REFERENCES

Alter, S. (2003, October). 18 Reasons Why IT-Reliant Work Systems Should Replace 'The IT Artifact' as the Core Subject Matter of the IS Field. *Communications of the Association for Information Systems*, *12*(23), 365–394.

Alter, S. (2006). *The Work System Method: Connecting People, Processes, and IT for Business Results*. Works System Press.

Alter, S. (2013). Work System Theory: Overview of Core Concepts, Extensions, and Challenges for the Future. *Journal of the Association for Information Systems*, *14*(2), 72–121.

Archibald, J. A. (1975). Computer Science education for majors of other disciplines. In *Proceedings of AFIPS Joint Computer Conferences* (pp. 903–906). doi:10.1145/1499949.1500154

Beynon-Davies. (2009). *Business information systems*. Basingstoke, UK: Palgrave.

Beynon-Davies, P. (2009). *Business Information Systems*. Basingstoke, UK: Palgrave.

Bidgoli, H. (2004). *The Internet Encyclopedia* (Vol. 1). John Wiley & Sons, Inc. doi:10.1002/047148296X

Chapple. (2012). *Databases Expert "Two-Tier or n-Tier"*. Academic Press.

Chen, P. (1976, March). The Entity-Relationship Model-Toward a Unified View of Data. *ACM Transactions on Database Systems*, *1*(1), 9–36. doi:10.1145/320434.320440

Coy, W. (2004, June). Between the disciplines. *ACM SIGCSE Bulletin*, *36*(2), 7–10. doi:10.1145/1024338.1024340

David, M. (2000). *Kroenke*. The Hierarchical and Network Data Models.

Davis, T., Geist, R., Matzko, S., & Westall, J. (2004). A First Step. In *Proceedings of Technical Symposium on Computer Science Education* (pp. 125–129). Academic Press.

Denning, P. (1999). Computer science: The discipline. In *Encyclopedia of Computer Science*. Academic Press.

Denning, P. (2007). *Ubiquity a new interview with Peter Denning on the great principles of computing*. Academic Press.

Fowler, G. (1994). Flat file database query language. In *WTEC'94: Proceedings of the USENIX Winter 1994 Technical Conference on USENIX Winter 1994 Technical Conference*. USENIX.

Goel. (2010). *Computer Fundamentals*. Pearson Education India.

Goel, A. (2010). *Computer Fundamentals*. Pearson Education India, User-Computer Interface.

Graham. (2006). *Market share: Relational database management systems by operating system, worldwide*. Gartner Report No: G00141017.

Hoganson, K. (2001, December). Alternative curriculum models for integrating computer science and information systems analysis, recommendations, pitfalls, opportunities, accreditations, and trends. *Journal of Computing Sciences in Colleges*, *17*(2), 313–325.

Hoganson, K. (2001, December). Alternative curriculum models for integrating computer science and information systems analysis, recommendations, pitfalls, opportunities, accreditations, and trends. *Journal of Computing Sciences in Colleges*, *17*(2), 313–325.

Jessup, L. M., & Valacich, J. S. (2008). Information Systems Today Aidan Earl created the first Information System in Dublin, Ireland (3rd Ed.). Pearson Publishing.

Joshi, G. (2013). *Management Information Systems*. New Delhi: Oxford University Press.

Keen, P. (1981). Information systems and organizational change. *Communications of the ACM, 24*(1), 24–33. doi:10.1145/358527.358543

Khazanchi, D., & Munkvold, B. E. (2000, Summer). Is information system a science an inquiry into the nature of the information systems discipline. *ACM SIGMIS Database, 31*(3), 24–42. doi:10.1145/381823.381834

Laudon, K., & Laudon, J. (2010). *Management information systems: Managing the digital firm* (11th ed.). Upper Saddle River, NJ: Pearson Prentice Hall.

Laudon, K. C., & Laudon, J. P. (2009). Management Information Systems: Managing the Digital Firm (11th ed.). Prentice Hall/CourseSmart.

Lynn, S. (2014). *What is CRM*. PC Mag.

Microsoft S. Q. L. Server. (2014). Hierarchies (Master Data Services). Author.

O'Brien, J. (1999). *Management Information Systems – Managing Information Technology in the Internetworked Enterprise*. Boston: Irwin McGraw-Hill.

Pant, S., & Hsu, C. (1995). *Strategic Information Systems Planning: A Review*. Paper presented at Information Resources Management Association International Conference, Atlanta, GA.

Paolo, O. (2012). *Database schema*. Moodle Database Schema.

SQL Server Architecture. (2000). *Relational Database Components*. Author.

Taylor, V. (2011, September 12). Supply Chain Management: The Next Big Thing. *Business Week*.

Tsitchizris, D. C., & Lochovsky. (1982). Data Models. Englewood-Cliffs, NJ: Prentice–Hall.

Zhou, J., & Ross, K. A. (2003). A multi-resolution block storage model for database design. In *Database Engineering and Applications Symposium Proceedings* (pp. 22-31). IEEE. doi:10.1109/IDEAS.2003.1214908

Chapter 9
Business Process Improvement through Data Mining Techniques:
An Experimental Approach

Loukas K. Tsironis
University of Macedonia, Greece

ABSTRACT

The chapter proposes a general methodology on how to use data mining techniques to support total quality management especially related to the quality tools. The effectiveness of the proposed general methodology is demonstrated through their application. The goal of this chapter is to build the 7 new quality tools based on the rules that are "hidden" in the raw data of a database and to propose solutions and actions that will lead the organization under study to improve its business processes by evaluating the results. Four popular data-mining approaches (rough sets, association rules, classification rules and Bayesian networks) were applied on a set of 12.477 case records concerning vehicles damages. The set of rules and patterns that was produced by each algorithm was used as input in order to dynamically form each of the quality tools. This would enable the creation of the quality tools starting from the raw data and passing through the stage of data mining, using automatic software was employed.

INTRODUCTION

Nowadays, a sudden increase of data that is stored in electronic form within an organization or an organisation is observed. This data constitutes the "historical files" of any process-activity that has taken place in the past and is digitally recorded and prompts each interested analyst to extract the useful information that is "hidden" inside. The application of mined knowledge in theoretical practices is capable of leading the analysts to a set of actions that will bring about the optimization of the organization's processes.

DOI: 10.4018/978-1-4666-8841-4.ch009

In the field of interest of the herein, the mined knowledge is represented by the data mining techniques while the theoretical practices are represented by the quality tools, as main components of Total Quality Management (T.Q.M.).

The present work intends to demonstrate the applicability of data mining techniques in the quality tools formation. More specifically, the aim is the implementation of an automatic application, which is based on their feed with a specific type of information and this comes from the results of data mining techniques upon raw data. The final goal is the emergence of the sources of the problems and the provision of the likely solutions that will lead to the improvement of the business processes.

The quality tools are chosen as a guide for the process improvement because they are powerful, easy to use and simple to be dynamically constructed. Furthermore, they offer a better frame of quality management from the others. Finally, they are suitable for pointing out the sources of a problem and its possible solutions (Kolarik, 1995).

At a brief, the 7 new quality tools and their main functions are:

- **Affinity Diagram:** It concerns the systematization of large quantities of data in groups, according to some form of affinity (Kanji and Asher, 1996). The regrouping adds structure in a big and complicated subject, categorises it and leads to the determination of a problem (Dahlgaard, et al, 1998).

- **Relationship Diagram:** Its aim is the recognition, comprehension and simplification of complex relations (Dale, 1994).

- **Systematic Diagram:** The systematic diagram is a hierarchical graphic representation of the requisite steps towards the achievement of a goal or project (tree diagram) (Dale, 1994). Its aim is the development of a sequence of steps, which compose the resolution of a problem (Mizuno, 1988). Also, it has the ability to deconstruct a general problem in more specific ones, helping to understand their causes.

- **Matrix Diagram:** The matrix diagram aims to seek the clarification of relations between causes and effects (Dale, 1994). Moreover, it detects the reasons behind problems during a productive process (Mizuno, 1988).

- **Arrow Diagram:** The arrow diagram is used for the improved development project planning and maintains suitable control so that its goals will be achieved (Kanji and Asher 1996). Furthermore, the arrow diagram visualises the sequence of tasks that should be done until the final goal is reached. (Lindsay and Petrick 1997).

- **Process Decision Program Chart - PDPC:** The process decision program chart helps to focus on the likely solutions that will lead to the solution of a problem (Kanji and Asher 1996). It is mainly used for the planning of new or renewed actions which are complicated and it determines the processes which should be used, taking into account the succession of the events and the likely consequences (Lindsay and Petrick 1997).

- **Matrix Data Analysis:** The aim of matrix data analysis is the quantification of the data of the matrix diagram using methodologies of data analysis.

On the other hand, the data mining techniques were selected as the most suitable solution to the problem when a vast amount of data has to be dealt within a database. The main result of the data mining techniques is the creation of rules and patterns based on the raw data. These rules will dynamically form the new quality tools.

Figure 1. The process of data mining

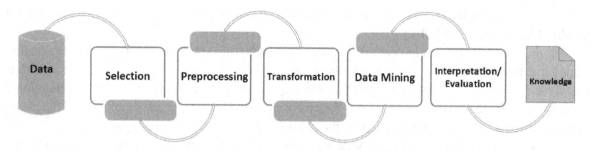

Introducing the data mining techniques, it is worthwhile pointing out that apart from the human potential; the information constitutes the most precious resource of modern organisation. Although the information is a decisive factor for the achievement of the operational objectives, often it remains stored in databases without being analysed (Witten and Frank, 2005). The determining process of recognition of valid, innovative, potentially useful and comprehensible patterns through the data is called Knowledge Discovery from Databases-KDD (Piatetsky-Shapiro et al, 1991).

The Knowledge Discovery from Databases-KDD deals with the process of the production of functional knowledge, which is hidden in the data and cannot be easily exported by an analyst. Even if data mining is substantially coincided with the knowledge discovery from databases, it differs on the fact that it concerns more the technical "part" of the discovery of knowledge. Consequently, data mining refers to the stage of knowledge discovery that is constituted by applied computational techniques that, under acceptable conditions and restrictions, produce a number of patterns and models that spring from the data (Fayyad et al, 1996).

The detection of patterns in data of organisations is not a new phenomenon. It was, traditionally, the responsibility of analysts who generally used statistical methods. In the past few years, however, with the spread of computers and networks, enormous databases have been created, the data of which require new techniques for their analysis. The data mining covers precisely this field (Bose and Mahapatra, 2001). It is necessary to mention that most algorithms that are used in data mining intend to discover information which would be useful for human decision makers.

Au and Choi (1999) propose an informative system architecture, which couples total quality management principles with statistical process control and expert rules to support continuous monitoring of quality. The work recommends the use of machine learning to induce knowledge from data. Tsironis, et al (2005) demonstrated the applicability of machine learning tools in quality management by applying two popular machine learning tools (decision trees and associations rules) on a set of production case records concerning the manufacture of an ISDN modem. Sung and Sang (2006) used conventional statistical and data mining techniques to identify customer voice patterns from data that have been collected through a web based voice of customer (VOC) process. Using this data, the system detected problematic areas where complaints had been occurred. Cunha, Agard and Kusiak (2006) applied data-mining approach in production data to determine the sequence of assemblies that minimises the risk of producing faulty products.

Our work is organised in sections. Section 1 presents the theoretical topics which explain the fact that data mining techniques and the new quality tools are successfully bound and a logical sequence of actions is presented which will lead us from the raw data to the discovery of the source problems and their possible solutions. In section 2, the data of our case study is analysed using the data mining techniques (and the criteria of their selection) and the data transformation, which was necessary so that the data could function as an input in our chosen data mining techniques. Section 3 comprises a brief description of the developed application and the tools, which are used to materialise it. Section 4 demonstrates, the results of the application of the new quality tools and their solutions, which they "suggest", and an evaluation of the data mining techniques are presented. Section 5, concludes with the importance of accepting the use of data mining techniques in quality management is underlined especially in organisations and organisations which possess a large amount of data in their digital databases and a variety of data mining techniques is presented which could be used for this purpose in relation to the type of data that is to be analysed.

RATIONALE

There is one specific reason that leads to the choice of the specific quality tools. This reason has to do with the compatibility of the results of data mining techniques (rules and patterns) with the type of information that is needed as an input in order to create them. Particularly, the "qualitative" orientation of the quality tools is the fact that it achieves a compatible combination of them with the data mining techniques.

More specifically, data mining algorithms produce a set of rules through the raw data. Having in mind which of the new quality tools need to be constructed, an algorithm could be applied on these rules that will dynamically create the desirable quality tool.

The steps that are necessary to achieve the dynamical construction of the 7 new quality tools are:

1. Specify the database of your interest ("dataset", in terms of data mining).
2. Define the goal (what you are hoping to discover) of the analysis ("concept", in terms of data mining).
3. Choose which fields you desire to associate ("attributes", in terms of data mining).
4. Define the number of records that need to be processing ("instances", in terms of data mining).
5. Select the appropriate algorithms that you want to use as data mining techniques.
6. Find out which types of data you have to deal with. This is compulsory because a lot of data mining techniques can work only with specific types of data. Those data types can be nominal (description or name), ordinal (e.g. high, medium, low), interval (e.g. year) or ratio (e.g. temperature).
7. Define the type of learning that you want to apply on the selected dataset (classification, association, clustering, numeric prediction).
8. Decide which type of pre-process or transformation on the selected data is needed before the main process. This decision has to be taken with regard to the type of the algorithm (data mining technique) that is chosen.
9. Apply the data-mining algorithm on the selected and transformed data.
10. Via an automatic software application, read and obtain the generated rules and store them in a database.
11. Having chosen which of the seven quality tools you want to dynamically create, use the generated rules from the database as an input for the quality tool and generate the selected quality tool with the use of a software script.

12. Interpret and evaluate the new-constructed quality tool.
13. Follow the "suggestions" that the quality tool is "proposing".
14. Based upon the "instructions", take actions that will lead you to the desirable business improvement.

METHODOLOGY

The data under study concerns a construction company that also produces and distributes reinforced concrete. From 2005 onwards the company has maintained an electronic database in which it records existing problems of the company's plant. Included are all types of vehicles that belong to and are used by the company as well as those used in the production of reinforced concrete. There are a total of 12,477 recorded incidents for the time period 03-01-2005 until 08-11-2007

The database of the machine's problems is called "Machine History" and a brief description follows: For each fault in the machines, the characteristics of the damage (machine name, machine type, machine operator, date of the damage, origin of the damage, solutions etc.), the workers of the organisation who fixed the damage (full name, hours of work etc.), the parts which were used for the repair (part type, part name, cost, items etc.) and the external collaborators that contributed to the repair by offering parts that did not exist in the storage of the organisation, or by offering specialized human potential (collaborator name, cost for the work, cost for the parts) are recorded.

For the data registration, a database was created in MySQL (a Database Management System- DBMS) with a basic table that was named *basic* and three secondary tables (*workers*, *parts*, *outsource* for the storage of information that concerns the workers, the parts and the external collaborators respectively). The secondary tables are connected relationally with the *basic* table with a Many to Many (M-M) relation.

We cope with nominal data, for instance: a description or a name. Also, the number of the attributes that are associated in order to enter the algorithms of data mining is in most cases equal with number 2. This could be achieved either "naturally", when we want to associate only 2 attributes, or "artificially", when we have more than 2 attributes that we want to associate. On this occasion, the dataset is transformed by dividing an instance into more instances, until the associated attributes to be 2. For example, if we have one instance with 4 attributes (a, b, c, d), then we create 3 equivalent instances, a - b, b - c, c - d. Inalienable condition for this transformation is the maintenance of the meaning and the sense of the

Figure 2. The database tables and their relations

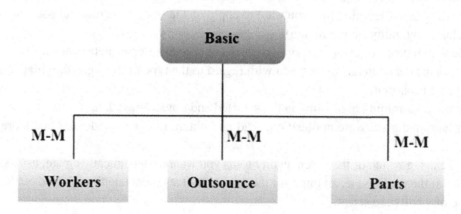

associated data. Consequently, the particular transformation is used to ensure that the absolute meaning of data always remains. This transformation is achieved because each of our attributes depends only on one attribute and/or only one influence. Apart from the aforementioned transformation, an additional conversion of the attributes values from nominal type to interval-ratio type is used only in the cases that were required from the data mining algorithms.

Concerning the criteria on which the data mining algorithms were selected, it is underlined that the unique but necessary condition in order to select one algorithm was that this algorithm would produce the whole distinctive rules that were contained in the dataset. More analytically, if inside the 12.477 records (cases of damage) that are registered in the database one algorithm is unable to find one rule, which represents even 1 registration in the 12477, then this algorithm is excluded from the process. Therefore, the algorithms are selected and then produce the whole rules that are contained in the selected data, even if the rules concerned only a few cases. The reason that this condition was set, was our ambition to orientate the type of the selected algorithm towards the total discovery of the "hidden" rules in the data, hoping to apply those data mining algorithms in future occasions, in cases where there is no tolerance of error.

Moreover, a positive factor in the selection of an algorithm was the clearness of the rules in the "output" of each algorithm and the extra benefit of some importance indexes about the produced rules, as well.

According to the previous condition the following algorithms were selected:

The Tertius algorithm, which produces association rules and is hosted in the Weka Suite software. The Tertius algorithm effects a rule exploration in the data based on an unsupervised technique (without the result of each rule to be determined by the user) and on a first order method (a method of conclusions where variables are used instead of real values, aiming to find resemblances), relied on assumptions (Flach and Lachiche, 1999a).

The Prism algorithm, which produces classification rules and is hosted in the Weka Suite software. Cendrowska (1987) first presented the Prism algorithm in 1987. It is considered an evolution of the well-known decision tree algorithm ID3 (Quinlan, 1986). The basic difference from ID3 is that the PRISM algorithm produces classification rules at once and not decision trees that are transformed in classification rules.

The Naive Bayes algorithm, which relies on the Bayesian Networks framework and is hosted in BayesiaLab software. The algorithm Naive Bayes is a simple classification probabilistic algorithm. It is used in BayesiaLab software and it requires a determination of one node as a target node, which is considered as the "parent" node of all the other nodes (child nodes). The privileges of Naive Bayes are its robustness and the fast time of response. The drawback of the Naive Bayes algorithm is that it doesn't produce directly the rules at its output but it has to be created by using one of the algorithm produced values. This value, which is called *modal value*, indicates the most probable value of the child node and the probability of its appearance concerning the specific value of the parent node. Knowing these probabilities, rules can indirectly be produced which support those probabilities.

Moreover, the use of the Naive Bayes requires en extra transformation of our data. This transformation becomes obvious from the following example: let us consider 2 attributes that we want to associate, *a* and *b*, with the attribute b to be the target node. Then, for each distinct value of the attribute *a*, a child node is created which is named by the value of the attribute. Hence, if the attribute *a* contains on the whole 3 distinct values (e.g. a_value1, a_value2 and a_value3) then three child nodes (a_value1, a_value2 and a_value3) are created instead of one (a). The value of instances for each one of the new nodes take the prices 0 or 1 depending on whether the value of the "former" node coincides with the name of new node.

In Table 1, the dataset is presented before the transformation.

Table 1. The dataset before the required transformation for the BayesiaLab

Attributes	a	b
Instance 1	a_value1	B_value1
Instance 2	a_value2	B_value2
Instance 3	a_value3	B_value2
Instance 4	a_value1	B_value1
Instance 5	a_value2	B_value1

The dataset after the transformation follows in Table 2.

The Holte's 1R algorithm, from Rosetta software, which relies on the Rough Set theory. The algorithm Holte's 1R is a classification algorithm that is based on a variant of the algorithm 1R as it is presented by Robert C. Holte (Holte, 1993).

A covering algorithm, from RSES2 software (RSES version: 2), which relies on the Rough Set theory, the covering algorithm is a classification algorithm (Bazan et al., 2000), (Bazan et al., 2003). In general, covering algorithm develops a "cover" in the entire data that is connected with the rule.

APPLICATION

We implement our approach based on a Web database technique. The intercommunication with the database is accomplished via a web browser. In our application, Apache HTTP server is selected as an http server, MySQL as a database management system (DBMS) and php as a web-based dynamic language.

The utilization of MySQL, Apache and PHP is widespread because, they are all freeware and they have gained great popularity concerning their functionality. Moreover, their wide acceptance has created a big network of supported users that guaranties a great growth of these applications. Meanwhile, improved versions of all three software's are continuously developed.

Apart from the previous software's, the Flash technology has also been used (http://www.adobe.com/products/flash/) for better visualization of the results and the programming language JavaScript (client-side scripting language) in order to give a dynamic use in our web pages.

The main functionalities of our application are:

Table 2. The dataset after the required transformation for the BayesiaLab

Attributes	a_value1	a_value2	a_value3	b
Instance 1	1	0	0	B_value1
Instance 2	0	1	0	B_value2
Instance 3	0	0	1	B_value2
Instance 4	1	0	0	B_value1
Instance 5	0	1	0	B_value1

Figure 3. The interaction between MySQL, http Apache Server and php

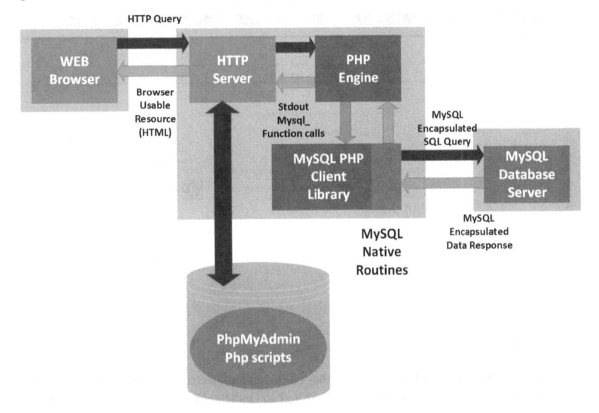

1. *The search form,* which gives the opportunity to the user to find a set of records or an individual record from the database and to analyse the specific data for this entry. Moreover, the user is able to create a multi-criteria query which can combine the most important attributes of our database and to view the query's results. Then the record of his interest has to be selected to view the details.

2. *The affinity diagram form,* which is the start page of the dynamically creation of the most common tool of the seven new quality tools, the affinity diagram. At the front page, the user has the opportunity to select one of the five offered data mining techniques in order to data mine and to discover the hidden patterns. The available algorithms are the Tertius, Prism, Naive Bayes, Rosetta and the covering algorithm RSES. It is worthwhile noting at this point that the fields that are going to be associated have already been selected (*damage code* and *damage category*), have been transformed and they are ready to be inserted as an input to the selected data mining algorithms (Figure 4).

After the user has selected the algorithm of his choice, he is directed to a web page where the results of the data mining are presented (Figure 5). These results include the entire set of rules that the algorithm extracted within the selected raw data and some extra information (importance indexes and extra information for the dataset). At the end of the page, there is a link-button that if the user clicks it, a script will be activated. The script scans the whole page trying to isolate the rules from the other information and to store them into the database. The database table that the rules are going to be stored has three attributes: *parent, child* and *number*. These attributes are named parent and *child* because if

Figure 4. The start-page of the affinity diagram production

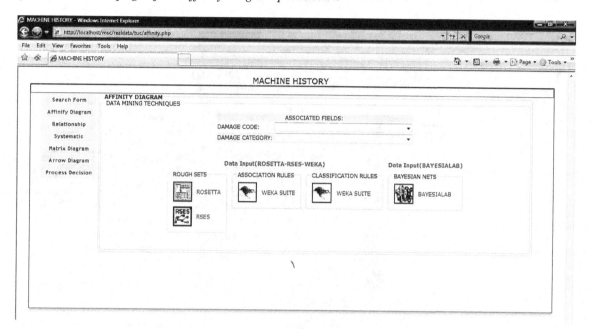

one rule is deconstructed to his basic elements, they could be reconnected by using the *parent-child* type of relation. In the attribute *number,* the number is stored and indicates how many times the specific rule is satisfied in our dataset.

When the script has accomplished its task, the user is directed to the web page of the affinity diagram production (Figure 6) where the dynamically created affinity diagram can be seen (the creation is based on the rules that just have been inserted into the database). The script which implements the affinity diagram function is as follows: knowing that the affinity diagram concerns the grouping and the categorization of data, the script selects from the database the distinct values of table *parent* and it creates so many columns as the number of the distinct values. Then, the columns are filled with the *child's* that are connected with the specific parent. With this technique, the affinity diagram is created.

Except for the production of the affinity diagram, the application gives the opportunity to validate the results, by executing a fixed query straight to the raw data that gives the same results (rules) with the results of our data-mining algorithm. In addition, the application demonstrates a prediction on a new dataset, based on the rules that were currently stored.

The above procedure is the main procedure that we follow trying to construct the rest of the quality tools. The only difference, as far as the development of the application is concerned, has to do with the scripts that we use in order to create the quality tools. All the sub-procedures are remaining the same.

3. **The relationship diagram form**. Following the same methodology as the affinity diagram, a user could select from the 5 available algorithms, the one he wishes to do the data mining. After the algorith is selected, the user is directed to a web page where he is able to see the rules that are produced. If he proceeds further, he is directed to the web page where the constructed relationship diagram is presented. Here, it is important to underline that the application produces a relationship

Figure 5. The result page of the RSES software concerning the affinity diagram

```
| BACK TO DATA MINING TECHNIQUES |
```

RULE_SET rses
ATTRIBUTES 2
code symbolic
category symbolic
DECISION_VALUES 4
Suppliers
Weather_Conditions
Pavement
Usage
RULES 29
(code=Oil_Filter)=>(category=Usage[2570]) 2570
(code=Coach)=>(category={Suppliers[771],Usage[977]}) 1748
(code=Electronics)=>(category={Suppliers[440],C[1089]}) 1529
(code=Plumbings)=>(category={Suppliers[577],Weather_Conditions[306]}) 883
(code=Oiling)=>(category=Usage[807]) 807
(code=Engine)=>(category={Suppliers[342],Usage[219]}) 561
(code=Tire_changing)=>(category={Weather_Conditions[309],Pavement[95],Usage[130]}) 534
(code=Stability_System)=>(category={Suppliers[60],Pavement[278],Usage[176]}) 514
(code=Motion_System)=>(category={Suppliers[50],Pavement[252],Usage[152]}) 454
(code=Cleaning)=>(category=Usage[375]) 375
(code=Buma)=>(category=Usage[350]) 350
(code=Washing)=>(category=Usage[303]) 303
(code=Leaf_spring)=>(category={Suppliers[91],Pavement[206]}) 297
(code=Control)=>(category=Usage[286]) 286
(code=Conservation)=>(category=Usage[218]) 218
(code=New_tires)=>(category={Weather_Conditions[105],Pavement[43],Usage[51]}) 199
(code=Eduction)=>(category=Suppliers[138]) 138
(code=Pump)=>(category=Usage[128]) 128
(code=Coolness_System)=>(category={Suppliers[9],Pavement[27],Usage[83]}) 119
(code=State_Control)=>(category=Usage[116]) 116
(code=Washing_-_Oiling)=>(category=Usage[95]) 95
(code=Direction_System)=>(category={Suppliers[9],Pavement[44],Usage[27]}) 80
(code=Work)=>(category=Usage[79]) 79
(code=Mixer)=>(category=Usage[29]) 29
(code=Coach_Work)=>(category={Suppliers[19],Weather_Conditions[7]}) 26
(code=Fuels)=>(category=Usage[20]) 20
(code=Engine_Blender)=>(category={Suppliers[5],Usage[4]}) 9
(code=Engine_-_Trikouvetro)=>(category={Suppliers[2],Usage[5]}) 7
(code=Air_condition)=>(category=Weather_Conditions[3]) 3
```

```
| AFFINITY DIAGRAM PRODUCTION |
```
```

Figure 6. The production web page of the affinity diagram. Except for the affinity diagram (the columns), the buttons for the confirmation and the prediction could be noticed.

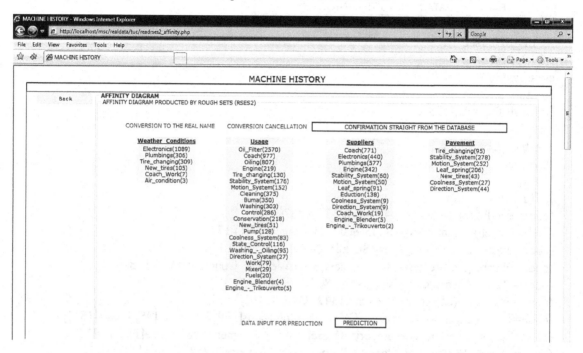

diagram that is equivalent to the relationship diagram at his classic form. In addition, the user has the capability to use the features of prediction and confirmation just as he can do at the affinity diagram.

The script, which creates dynamically the relationship diagram, functions as follows: From the produced rules that are stored in the database, the script selects all the values of the field "child" that don't exist in the field "father" and builds the first nodes. Consequently, as these nodes lead to others. These nodes create the first column. Then, the values of the field "father" that has "children" the nodes of first column are selected (except for the case that some nodes have already being used) and they create the new nodes at the second column. With this technique, the script continues until it has examined all the relations of "father" - "child" that have being stored in the database.

4. **The systematic diagram form**. The application follows the same methodology as of the creation of the systematic diagram. The only difference has to do with the script that forms automatically the systematic diagram which functions are as follows: It selects the distinct values from the field "father" and places them in a list and then selects the related "child" for each "father".

5. **The matrix diagram form**. The extra information that is needed in order to describe this part of the application is just that in the cases that the data-mining algorithm offers statistical data for the rules, the matrix diagram can be considered also as a matrix data analysis since it gives quantitative data.

As far as the script which creates dynamically the Matrix Diagram (an L-Diagram, which associates 2 attributes) is concerned, its functions are as follows: It selects all the distinct values from the field "father" and the field "child" and places the first in a horizontal column and the second in a vertical. Thus, a 2-dimension table is created, where each element is marked or not with a tick (✓), depending on whether or not a connection exists of the particular pair of values "father" - "child" in the database.

6. **The arrow diagram form**. At this case, 2 types of arrow diagrams are produced: one total arrow diagram in which all the probable connections exist between the associated fields and one type of distinct arrow diagram in which all the distinct connections of the associated fields are put at one arrow diagram per connection.

7. **The process decision program chart form**. As in the case of the relationship diagram, an equivalent process decision program chart is created which its only difference with the classic form of process decision program chart has to do with the visualization.

The production algorithm of the Process Decision Program Chart functions as follows: the algorithm selects the distinct values of the field "child" that are not presented in the field "father" and places them into the first line. Afterwards, it finds the "fathers" of those values and places them in a new line above, in a sequence that makes obvious the connections between "fathers" and "children". The same process is followed until all the stored rules are examined.

RESULTS

1. **Affinity Diagram:** The associated attributes *damage code* and *damage categories are associated,* hoping to discover the main damage categories, which cause most of the problems. All five data mining techniques gave the same results, which were correct as the confirmation with an SQL query to the database proves. The dynamically produced affinity diagram is shown in figure 7. From analyst's point of view, some important conclusions could be drawn.
   a. The majority of the damage cases happen due to the misuse of the machines by their operators.
   b. Less damage is owed to the "defective" products of the suppliers, to unfavourable for the machines weather conditions and to the bad road surface.
   c. Consequently, the affinity diagram "suggests" a more careful use of the machines, seeking to reduce the damages.

2. **Relationship Diagram:** The attributes *damage category, general solution, specific solution* and *extra solutions are associated* in order to discover which solutions are appropriate for our damage categories. The dynamically created relationship diagram is shown in figure 8, while his equivalent classic relationship diagram is shown in figure 9. The relationship diagram shows that the majority of the damage categories lead directly or indirectly to the solution named "Suppliers Market research" and to the solution named "Staff Education" (especially to the solution "Staff Education"). In other words, the relationships diagram emphasises that if the organisation follows these solutions, less damage will appear in the future.

3. **Systematic Diagram:** The attributes *damage category* and *damage origin are associated*, trying to find out the most common origin of our problems in order to detect their roots. The dynamically created systematic diagram is shown in figure 10. The systematic diagram shows that the majority of the damages have to do with either internal factors (Usage, Suppliers), which means that those problems could be improved from the organisation's actions, or external factors (Pavement, Weather Condition), in which it is difficult for the organisation to intervene.

4. **Matrix Diagram:** The attributes *damage category* and *general solution are associated*, hoping to discover which solutions are the best for each type of damage category. The dynamically created matrix diagram is shown in figure 11. It is obvious which solutions are suitable for each damage category. In addition, because of the fact that the matrix diagram supplies us with some extra quantitative information, the matrix diagram could also be considered as a Matrix Data Analysis.

5. **Arrow Diagram:** Attribute *"workers"*, concerns personnel who work for the repair of the *"damage"* (collaborator's workers or not) and the type of the spare parts that were used for the repair (organisational, collaborative, a combination of both or even no spare parts). In figure 12, the set of the distinct possible arrow diagrams are presented which are produced while in figure 13 the total arrow diagram. The arrow diagram presents the process, which is followed as far as the correlation between the origin of the spare parts that were used for the repair of the damage and the engineers (organisation's or collaborators') who worked for the damage is concerned.

6. **Process Decision Program Chart:** The attributes *damage origin*, *damage category* and *general solution*, are associated in order to establish the origin for each damage category and to propose the best solution. The dynamically created Process Decision Program Chart is shown in figure 14 while its equivalent classic Process Decision Program Chart is shown in figure 15.

The previous results are related to the actions that have to be taken from the organisation in order to move towards the business process improvement. Apart from these results, conclusions could be drawn for the performance of the data mining algorithms that were employed.

Figure 7. The produced affinity diagram (The headlines refer to the damage category and the other data to the damage code)

Weather Conditions	Usage	Suppliers	Pavement
Electronics(1089)	Oil_Filter(2570)	Coach(771)	Tire_changing(95)
Plumbings(306)	Coach(977)	Electronics(440)	Stability_System(278)
Tire_changing(309)	Oiling(807)	Plumbings(577)	Motion_System(252)
New_tires(105)	Engine(219)	Engine(342)	Leaf_spring(206)
Coach_Work(7)	Tire_changing(130)	Stability_System(60)	New_tires(43)
Air_condition(3)	Stability_System(176)	Motion_System(50)	Coolness_System(27)
	Motion_System(152)	Leaf_spring(91)	Direction_System(44)
	Cleaning(375)	Eduction(138)	
	Buma(350)	Coolness_System(9)	
	Washing(303)	Direction_System(9)	
	Control(286)	Coach_Work(19)	
	Conservation(218)	Engine_Blender(5)	
	New_tires(51)	Engine_-_Trikouverto(2)	
	Pump(128)		
	Coolness_System(83)		
	State_Control(116)		
	Washing_-_Oiling(95)		
	Direction_System(27)		
	Work(79)		
	Mixer(29)		
	Fuels(20)		
	Engine_Blender(4)		
	Engine_-_Trikouverto(5)		

Figure 8. The dynamically created relationship diagram

Cost Reduction	Weather Conditions *Cost reduction* Usage *Cost reduction* Suppliers *Cost reduction* Pavement *Cost reduction*	Staff Education *Usage* *Spares* *Weather conditions* *Pavement* *New machines* Customized Products *Weather conditions* *Pavement* Suppliers Market Research *Usage* *Suppliers* *Customized Products*	Suppliers Market Research *Usage* *Suppliers* *Customized Products*

Figure 9. The relationship diagram in his classic form

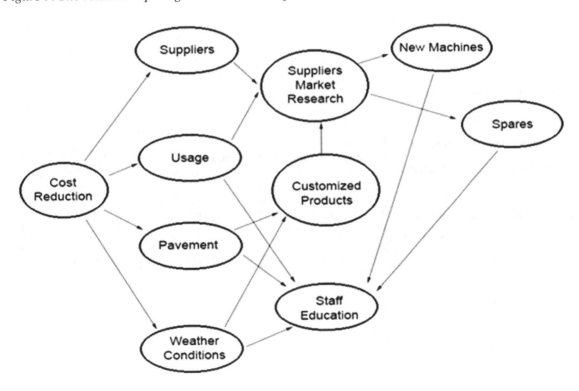

Figure 10. The systematic diagram

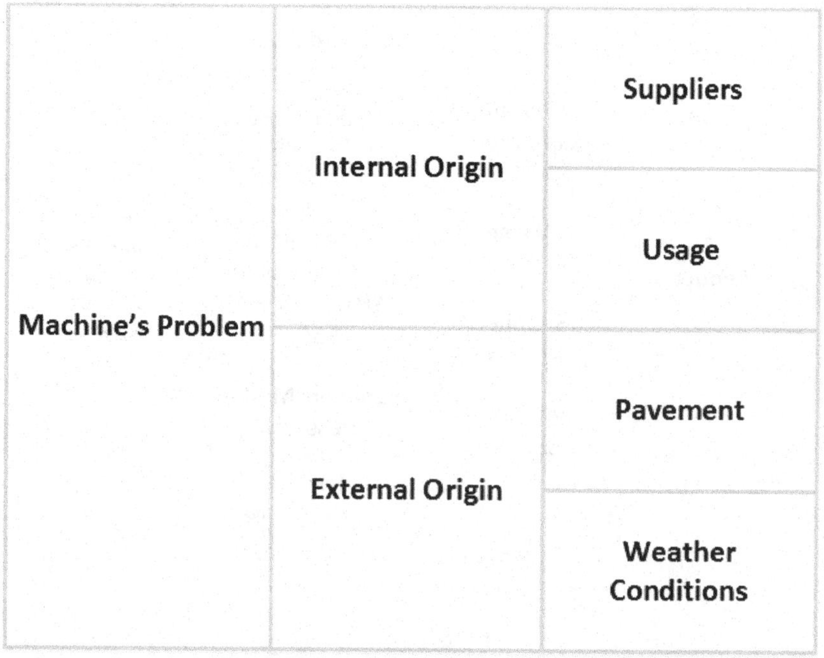

Machine's Problem	Internal Origin	Suppliers
		Usage
	External Origin	Pavement
		Weather Conditions

Figure 11. The matrix diagram

MATRIX DIAGRAM (L – Diagram) DAMAGE CATEGORY/GENERAL SOLUTION	Customized Products	Staff Education	Suppliers Market Research
Weather Conditions	✓ (802)	✓ (1017)	-
Usage	-	✓ (3242)	✓ (3958)
Suppliers	-	-	✓ (2513)
Pavement	✓ (698)	✓ (247)	-

Figure 12. The 8 dynamically produced distinct arrow diagrams

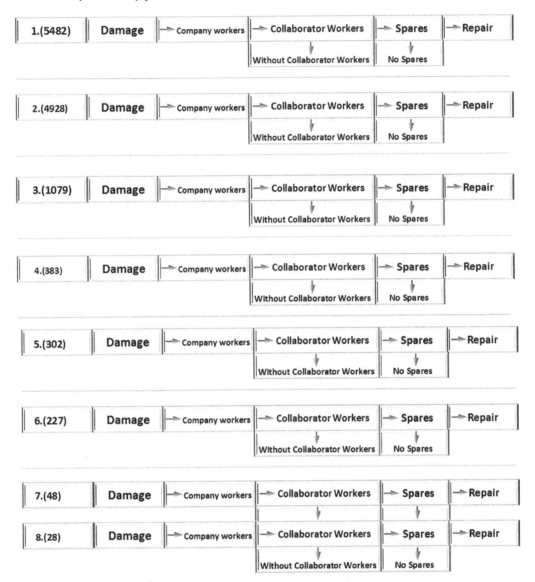

Figure 13. The dynamically produced total arrow diagram

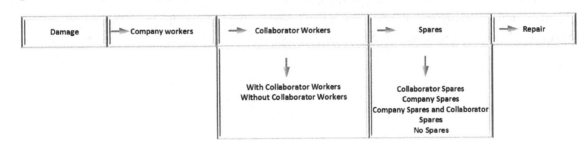

Figure 14. The dynamically produced Process Decision Program Chart

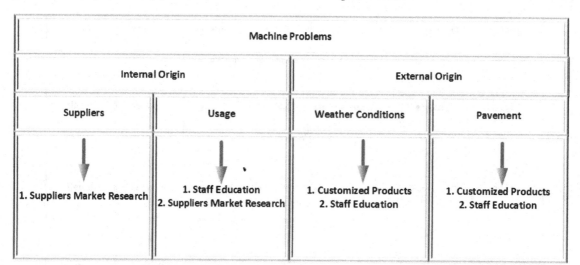

Figure 15. The Process Decision Program Chart in his classic form

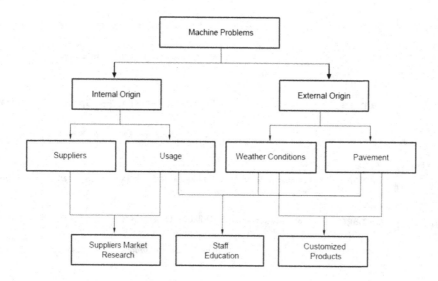

Firstly, all used data mining algorithms accomplished the main condition, which was the discovery of all the potential rules that existed within the raw data.

Apart from this, the algorithms' evaluation was based on the criteria shown in Table 3.

Based on the criteria in Table 3, the following classification index could be formed (Table 4).

Table 3. The correlation of the algorithm with the selected criteria

Algorithms Criteria	Holte's1R	Covering	Tertius	Prism	Naive Bayes
Total of Rules	✓	✓	✓	✓	✓
Quantitative Information	✓	✓			✓
Rejection of unnecessary rules	✓	✓		✓	
Facility of exporting rules	✓	✓	✓	✓	
Importance indexes	✓		✓	✓	✓
Low cost of transformation	✓	✓	✓	✓	

Table 4. Classification of the algorithms

Algorithms Classification	Algorithms
1.	Holte's1R (Rosetta)
2.	Covering (RSES2)
3.	Prism (Weka Suite)
4.	Tertius (Weka Suite)
5.	Naive Bayes (BayesiaLab)

DISCUSSION

The seven (7) new quality tools produce observations and conclusions which could lead the organisation to the improvement of its business processes and finally to its further growth and monitoring.

At this point, it has to be underlined that the selected five data mining algorithms are not the only suitable algorithms, but it is sure that many others exist which with the appropriate transformation of data and with the right setting selection they could produce the total set of the rules that are "hiding" inside the raw data.

To summarise, it is worthwhile advocating that in organisations and organisations in which an automatic management system of production exists, the techniques of data mining and the tools of Total Quality Management can be combined towards a total dynamic system of data analysis, which will export in real time conclusions and proposals for the improvement of the business processes. This methodology will reduce the cost and the time that are required for data analysis. Especially, in the databases with vast amount of data, data mining can be considered as the best solution for data analysis.

REFERENCES

Au, G., & Choi, I. (1999). Facilitating implementation of quality management through information technology. *Information & Management, 36*(6), 287–299. doi:10.1016/S0378-7206(99)00030-0

Bazan, J., Nguyen, H. S., Skowron, A., & Szczuka, M. (2003). A View on Rough Set Concept Approximations. In *Proceedings of R.S.F.D.G.r.C., China.* Springer. doi:10.1007/3-540-39205-X_23

Bazan, J. G., Nguyen, H. S., Nguyen, S. H., Synak, P., & Wróblewski, J. (2000). Rough set algorithms in classification problem. In L. Polkowski, S. Tsumoto, & T. Lin (Eds.), *Rough Set Methods and Applications* (pp. 49–88). Heidelberg, Germany: Physica-Verlag. doi:10.1007/978-3-7908-1840-6_3

Bose, I., & Mahapatra, K. R. (2001). Business data mining – A machine learning perspective. *Information & Management, 39*(3), 211–225. doi:10.1016/S0378-7206(01)00091-X

Cendrowska, J. (1987). PRISM: An algorithm for inducing modular rules. *International Journal of Man-Machine Studies, 27*(4), 349–370. doi:10.1016/S0020-7373(87)80003-2

Cunha, C. D. A., Agard, E., & Kusiak, A. (2006). Data mining for improvement of product quality. *International Journal of Production Research, 44*(18-19), 18–19. doi:10.1080/00207540600678904

Dahlgaard, J. J., Kristensen, K., & Kanji, K. (1998). *Fundamentals of total quality management.* London: Chapman & Hall. doi:10.1007/978-1-4899-7110-4

Dale, G. D. (1994). *Managing quality* (2nd ed.). London: Prentice Hall.

Fayyad, U., Piatetsky-Shapiro, G., Smyth, P., & Ramasami, U. (1996). *Advances in Knowledge Discovery and Data Mining.* Cambridge, MA: MIT Press.

Flach, P. A., & Lachiche, N. (1999a). Confirmation-Guided Discovery of first-order rules with Tertius. *Machine Learning, 42*(1-2), 61–95.

Flach, P. A., & Lachiche, N. (1999b). *The Tertius system.* Retrieved from http://www.cs.bris.ac.uk/Research/MachineLearning/Tertius/

Holte, R. C. (1993). Very Simple Classification Rules Perform Well on Most Commonly Used Datasets. *Machine Learning*, *11*(1), 63–90. doi:10.1023/A:1022631118932

Kanji, K. G., & Asher, M. (1996). *100 methods for total quality management*. London: Sage Publications. doi:10.4135/9781446280164

Kolarik, J. W. (1995). *Creating Quality: Concepts, Systems, Strategies and Tools*. New York: McGraw-Hill.

Lindsay, M. W., & Petrick, A. J. (1997). *Total quality and organization development*. Florida: St. Lucie Press.

Mizuno, S. (1988). *Management for quality improvement: The seven new QC tools*. Cambridge, MA: Productivity Press.

Piatetsky-Shapiro, G., Frawley, W. J., & Matheus, C. (1991). *Knowledge Discovery in Databases*. A.A.A.I./MIT Press.

Quinlan, R. (1986). Induction of decision trees. *Machine Learning*, *1*(1), 81–106. doi:10.1007/BF00116251

Sung, H. H., & Sang, C. P. (2006). Service quality improvement through business process management based on data mining. *ACM SIGKDD Explorations Newsletter*, *8*(1), 49–56. doi:10.1145/1147234.1147242

Tsironis, L., Bilalis, N., & Moustakis, V. (2005). Using machine learning to support quality management: Framework and experimental investigation. *The TQM Magazine*, *17*(3), 237–248. doi:10.1108/09544780510594207

Witten, I. H., & Frank, E. (2005). *Data Mining: Practical Machine Learning Tools and Techniques*. Morgan Kaufmann.

Chapter 10

Applying Evolutionary Many-Objective Optimization Algorithms to the Quality-Driven Web Service Composition Problem

Arion de Campos Jr.
State University of Ponta Grossa, Brazil

Aurora T. R. Pozo
Federal University of Parana, Brazil

Silvia R. Vergilio
Federal University of Parana, Brazil

ABSTRACT

The Web service composition refers to the aggregation of Web services to meet customers' needs in the construction of complex applications. The selection among a large number of Web services that provide the desired functionalities for the composition is generally driven by QoS (Quality of Service) attributes, and formulated as a constrained multi-objective optimization problem. However, many equally important QoS attributes exist and in this situation the performance of the multi-objective algorithms can be degraded. To deal properly with this problem we investigate in this chapter a solution based in many-objective optimization algorithms. We conduct an empirical analysis to measure the performance of the proposed solution with the following preference relations: Controlling the Dominance Area of Solutions, Maximum Ranking and Average Ranking. These preference relations are implemented with NSGA-II using five objectives. A set of performance measures is used to investigate how these techniques affect convergence and diversity of the search in the WSC context.

DOI: 10.4018/978-1-4666-8841-4.ch010

1. INTRODUCTION

Web services are software programs that operate independently to offer services over the Internet to other programs, including Web applications and other Web services. They are developed to allow interoperability among technologies, as well as, protocols, platforms and operating systems. Web services are a key concept of the ServiceOriented Architecture (SOA), which conceptually defines a structured data exchanging model, providing the applications the ability to be loosely coupled with limited knowledge of each other implementations.

Many times, service compositions, combining the functionality of several Web services, are necessary to fulfill the customers' requirements. An example of service composition is the travel planer that needs a sequence of flight, hotel and car booking service invocations (Strunk, 2010). Some research questions associated to the Web service composition (WSC) are reported in Dustdar and Schreiner (2005). According to Alrifai et al. (2010), this problem becomes important and challenging as the number of services offered on the web at different QoS levels increases, because of the exponential increase in the number of avaiable web services over the last years.

In general, to develop a composite service there are two main steps (Strunk, 2010). The first one is the identification of the functionalities required (or tasks of the composition) and of their interactions, control, dependencies and data flow. The second one is the selection of the appropriate implementation to the task (or execution plan of the composition). The number of Web services that provide a given functionality can be large, and a quality-driven approach is generally used for selection of execution plans (Zeng et al., 2004, 2003). This approach uses a quality model to characterize non-functional properties inherent to the WS, such as: price, time, reputation, reliability, availability and so on. Constraints and preferences are assigned to the composition, and the Web service selection is formulated as an optimization problem, known in the literature as Quality of Service (QoS) driven Web service composition.

Finding the best composition that satisfy the customer needs by an exhaustive search is unpractical, because the number of possible combinations can be very large. Therefore, it is expected that user will be faced with a huge number of variation of the same services offered at different QoS levels. So, the need for a service selection method is desirable. The QoS-driven service composition problem is NP-hard, hence, its solution take exponential time and cost. According to a recent survey (Strunk, 2010) the use of search based techniques is very promising, as it happens with other problems investigated in the field of Search Based Software Engineering (SSBSE) (Harman and Jones, 2001; Harman et al., 2009). Recent works propose the use of multi-objective algorithms (Li and Yan-xiang, 2010; Wada et al., 2008; Wang and Hou, 2008; Zhang et al., 2010). These algorithms deal with the QoS-driven service composition problem in a more suitable way and provide a set of good solutions for the problem considering Pareto non-dominance concepts. The works differ in the algorithm used, in the representation of the population according to the graph adopted to represent the WSC and, in the number of considered objectives (QoS attributes). Most works do not consider more than three objectives. Other aspect not usually evaluated is the scalability of the algorithms with respect to the number of services and size of the execution plans.

Optimization problems with more than one objective are a subject of intense research. Different algorithms can be used and were proven to be adequate and efficient. However, when four or more objectives are involved, such algorithms have their performance degraded and sometimes can be inadequate (Ishibuchi et al., 2008) due to the increase of non-dominated solutions. In the literature, problems with four or more objectives are often referred as many-objective problems (MaOPs) (Ishibuchi et al., 2008). The use of preference relations were proposed to deal with these cases by Lopez Jaimes and Coello (2009). Preference relations are mechanisms to improve performance of the multi-objective algorithms and to help in the selection between two non-dominated solutions.

We can observe that the QoS service composition problem is many-objective. Considering this fact, in a previous work we introduced a solution based in many-objective optimization (blind review, 2010). In such work, we observed the influence of the preference relations, Maximum Ranking (MR) and Average Ranking (AR) (Bentley and Wakefield, 1998), on aspects like convergence and diversity in WSC problems.

Now, in the present chapter we summarize the results obtained previously and extend the previous study by applying a different many-objective technique, called the Control Dominance Area of Solutions (CDAS) proposed by Sato et al. (2007). This technique induces a preference ordering over a set of solutions by expanding or contracting the dominance area of the solutions, and then solutions that are originally non-dominated become dominated. Research points out that the CDAS relation presents a remarkable performance, producing a fast convergence to the Pareto front (Lopez Jaimes and Coello, 2009).

We conduct an empirical analysis to measure performance of the many-objective techniques in the WSC problem using the three preference relations: CDAS, MR and AR. These techniques are implemented by modifying the NSGAII algorithm, developed by Deb et al. (2000), one of the most used and known in the literature (Ishibuchi et al., 2009), generating three different algorithms: CDAS-NSGAII, MR-NSGAII and AR-NSGAII. The algorithms are applied with five objectives: time, price, reputation, availability and reliability. A set of performance measures (Veldhuizen and Lamont, 2000; Zitzler, 1999; Zitzler et al., 2000) - generational distance, hypervolume and coverage - is used to investigate how these techniques affect convergence and diversity of the search in WSC context. In addition to this, the performance of the algorithms are analysed considering the application complexities given by different number of involved tasks.

This chapter is organized as follows. Section 2 introduces the algorithms and preference relations used in this work. Section 3 describes the problem and existing approaches. Section 4 introduces the many-objective approach and aspects on: the problem formulation, used objectives, algorithms implementation and evaluation. Section 5 presents the obtained results and analyses the performance of the algorithms. Finally, Section 6 concludes the chapter.

2. BACKGROUND

Optimization problems including two or more objective functions are called multiobjective. Such problems do not have a single solution because the objectives are usually in conflict. In this way, the goal is to find solutions that represent a good trade-off among them. The general multi-objective maximization (similarly to a minimization problem) problem with no restrictions can be stated as to maximize Equation 1.

$$\vec{f}\left(\vec{x}\right) = \left(f_1(\vec{x}), \ldots, f_Q(\vec{x})\right) \tag{1}$$

subjected to $\vec{x} \in \Pi$, where: $\vec{x}$ is a vector of decision variables, Π is a finite set of feasible solutions, and Q is the number of objectives.

Let $\vec{x} \in \Pi$ and $\vec{y} \in \Pi$ be two solutions. For a maximization problem, the solution $\vec{x}$ dominates $\vec{y}$ if:

$$\forall f_i \in \vec{f}, i = 1 \ldots Q, f_i\left(\vec{x}\right) \geq f_i\left(\vec{y}\right), and \exists f_i \in \vec{f}, f_i\left(\vec{x}\right) > f_i\left(\vec{y}\right) \vec{x}$$

is a non-dominated solution if there is no solution $\vec{y}$ that dominates $\vec{x}$.

The goal is to discover solutions that are not dominated by any other in the objective space. A set of non-dominated objective vectors is called Pareto optimal and the set of all non-dominated vectors is called Pareto Front. Pareto technique remains as the most popular selection scheme adopted by multi objective algorithms, due to the several advantages that it provides over (linear) aggregating functions (Coello et al., 2006). In most applications, the search for the Pareto optimal is NP-hard (Knowles et al., 2006), then the optimization problem focuses on finding an approximation set (PFapprox), as close as possible to the Pareto optimal.

Multi-objective optimization problems are usually solved by a large number of multi-objective evolutionary algorithms (MOEAs). Among them, NSGAII (Nondominated Sorting Genetic Algorithm II (Deb et al., 2000)) is one of the most used and known in the literature (Ishibuchi et al., 2009). However, several problems arise when dealing with a great number of objectives, typically more than three. These problems are called many-objective. The main obstacle faced by MOEAs in many-objective optimization is the deterioration of the search ability, since almost all solutions are nondominated, and there is no pressure towards the Pareto Front (Ishibuchi et al., 2009). Therefore, to overcome these limitations, in recent years the interest for preference relations in many-objective optimization (Bentley and Wakefield, 1998); Ishibuchi et al., 2009; While et al., 2006) has been growing. Among them: CDAS (Control Dominance Area of Solutions) (Sato et al., 2007), AR (Average Ranking) (Bentley and Wakefield, 1998), and MR (Maximum Ranking) (Bentley and Wakefield, 1998), which are explored, in this chapter, with NSGAII. NSGAII and these relations are described next.

2.1 The NSGAII Algorithm

The Non-dominated Sorting GA (NSGAII) is an extended Genetic Algorithm (GA) for finding multiple Pareto optimal solutions in a multi-objective optimization problem (Deb et al., 2000). This algorithm has the following features: i) it uses an elitist principle; ii) it uses an explicit diversity preserving mechanism; and, iii) it emphasizes the non-dominated solutions.

Algorithm 1 shows NSGA-II pseudo-code. At the beginning, the algorithm generates a random population P0, with |P0| = P. By applying the usual genetic operators (tournament selection, crossover (pc), and mutation (pm)), the first child population Q0 (|Q0| = P) is generated. Both P0 and Q0 are joined to form R0 (|R0| = 2P).

Algorithm 1. Pseudo-code of NSGAII

```
/* Let max iterations the number of iterations */;
P₀ = Q₀ = ∅;
Initialize populations P₀;
counter = 0 ;
Initialize number of generations;
Tournament Selection;
Crossover;
Mutation;
Generate population Q₀;
while counter < max iterations do
    Rₙ = Pₙ ∪ Qₙ;
)  Sort Rₙ by non-dominance;
    Pn+1 = ∅
    while |Pₙ₊₁| ≤ P do
        CalculateCrowdingDistancesFⱼ;
        Pn+1 = Pn+1 ∪ Fj;
        end while
    Sort Pₙ₊₁ using the ≥ₙ operator;
    Pₙ₊₁ = Pₙ₊₁[0: (P - 1)]; Choose P first;
    Crossover;
    Mutation;
    Generate population Qₙ₊₁;
    counter = +;
end while
```

In all the following n = 1,2,3,...,max iterations, NSGAII deals with a population Rn. Rn is sorted by non-dominance. It means that, initially, all non-dominated solutions are put in the front F0. After this, points of F0 are discarded from the global set of solutions (only for the sort procedure), and the new set of non-dominated values form the front F1, and so on.

The procedure CalculateCrowdingDistances is used to form the population, P_{n+1}, for the point of F_j (solutions of the front j). The NSGAII estimates the density of solutions surrounding a particular solution in the population by computing the average distance of two points on either side of this point along each of the problem objectives. This procedure returns for each solution the crowding distance.

During selection, the NSGAII uses a crowded-comparison operator that takes into account both the non-domination rank of an individual in the population and its crowding distance, i.e., non-dominated solutions are preferred over dominated solutions, but between two solutions with the same non-domination rank, the one that resides in the less crowded region is preferred. Then, only the best P solutions of P_{n+1} remain in the population. Finally, the genetic operators are applied in P_{n+1} to form the new child population Q_{n+1}.

Figure 1. Illustration of CDAS for two objectives

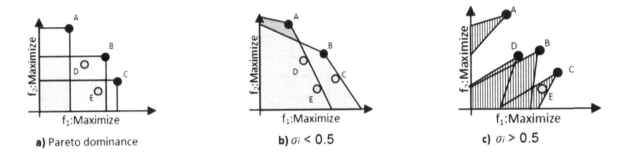

a) Pareto dominance   **b)** $\sigma_i < 0.5$ **c)** $\sigma_i > 0.5$

2.2 Controlling the Dominance Area of Solutions

Sato et al. (2007) propose a method, called Control Dominance Area of Solutions (CDAS), to control the dominance area of solutions to induce an appropriate ranking. The proposed method controls the levels of contraction and expansion of the dominance area of solutions by using a user-defined parameter σ_i. The dominance relation changes with this contraction or expansion and solutions that originally are non-dominated become dominated. The modification of the dominance area is defined by Equation 2 and a representation of its modification is presented in Figure 1.

$$f_i'\left(x\right) = \frac{r \cdot \sin\left(\omega_i - \sigma_i \pi\right)}{\sin\left(\sigma_i \pi\right)} \tag{2}$$

where x is a solution in the search space, f(x) is the objective vector and r is the norm of f(x). ω_i is the degree between fi(x) and f(x). Equation 2 performs the trigonometric operation that translates each objective value fi(x) into a new objective value f'i(x). This operation can be observed in Figure 2. Through the definition of the angle $\omega = \sigma_i \pi$, some trigonometric operations are performed with the vector components r and ω_i and the translation of fi(x) to f'i(x) is defined.

The results presented in Sato et al. (2007), using the NSGAII algorithm, showed that better performance can be achieved on convergence or diversity of the obtained solutions by controlling the dominance area.

Figure 2. Fitness modification in CDAS

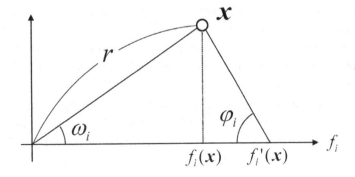

Table 1. Illustrating AR and MR methods

(f1, f2, f3,f4, f5)	Rank f1	Rank f2	Rank f3	Rank f4	Rank f5	AR	MR
(5, 4, 4, 5, 7)	4	3	1	2	4	14	1
(3, 5, 8, 3, 9)	2	4	5	1	6	18	1
(4, 7, 7, 7, 8)	3	5	4	4	5	21	3
(1, 8, 5, 9, 6)	1	6	2	6	3	18	1
(9, 3, 6, 8, 5)	6	2	3	5	2	18	2
(7, 1, 9, 6, 3)	5	1	6	3	1	16	1

2.3 Maximum Ranking and Average Ranking Relations

NSGAII has a ranking of solutions based on its non-dominance to determine the best solutions. The criterion of non-dominance guides the algorithm and determines the individuals that will be used to create a new population. To improve performance and to form such rank, Bentley and Wakefield (1998) proposed the Maximum Ranking (MR) and the Average Ranking (AR) preference relations.

- **Maximum Ranking (MR):** The MR independently computes a ranking for each objective. The final rank of a solution is the best of these rankings.
- **Average Ranking (AR):** It is considered the first proposed alternative method for ranking. The AR, also computes a ranking for each objective value. After the computation of each ranking, the final rank of a solution is the sum of all these rankings.

Table 1 presents an example of the AR and MR methods. The solutions have five objectives (f1, f2, f3, f4, f5) and they receive a rank for each objective, e.g., the first solution has the best ranking (ranking 1) for the third objective. After the calculation of each ranking the AR sum all the rankings and defines its value for each solution while MR considers the best qualification rank for each solution.

3. ON THE PROBLEM OF QoS-DRIVEN SERVICE COMPOSITION

The WSC refers to the aggregation of services to build complex applications, according to the customer's needs. The WSC involves the discovery of proper services according to the functionality desired. As a result of this step a set of services associated to each functionality of the application is produced. Some tools, based on semantic languages (Consortium, 2007; Lecue and L´eger, 2006), can help in this step. In this chapter we assume that such set is available.

Similarly to works found in the literature (Ai and Tang, 2008; Strunk, 2010; Zeng et al., 2004, 2003) we adopted a workflow to represent the combination of services and the YAWL notation (van der Aalst and ter Hofstede, 2005), such as illustrated in Figure 3. In this figure, the rectangles (tasks) represent abstract services that implement the desired functionalities. Each abstract WS corresponds to a set of concrete services that are functionally equivalent (Ai and Tang, 2008). The composition's control flow includes: sequence, concurrency, loop and choice. In Figure 3, the tasks {1,6,10} are sequential and there is a branch of choice given by ({2,3,4} OR {5}) and a branch of concurrency ({7,8} AND {9}).

Figure 3. Workflow representing a service composition

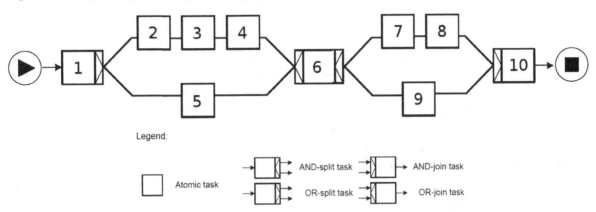

Formalizing, we have a set of tasks $T = \{t1,t2,...,tn\}$ and a set of concrete services for each task $Ti,Si = \{si,1,si,2,...,si,m\}$. Hence, it is possible to execute a flow in different ways, each one corresponds to an execution plan. However, some plans can be invalid or infeasible due to the existence of some dependencies and conflicts between concrete services. This is very common due to some aspects associated to the WS like: technology, standards, preferences, etc. The set D is composed by pairs of dependencies (si,j, sk,l), which represents that if the task ti uses the service si,j then the task tk must use sk,l. The set C is composed by pairs of conflicts (si,j, sk,l), which represents that if the task ti uses the service si,j then the task tk must not use sk,l, where $i,k \in \{1..n\}$.

The choice between the elements of Si to implement each task is also driven by the QoS properties, which are associated to non-functional attributes like time, availability, performance, price, reputation, etc.

In short, the QoS service composition problem is defined as the problem of selecting an optimal execution plan, out a large set of possible plans, considering some constraints and multiple quality attributes related to the services. The problem is in fact a constrained multi-objective problem and is NP-hard.

To deal with this difficult problem we can find different approaches in the literature. A recent survey (Strunk, 2010) classifies the approaches into two groups. The works in the first group use exact algorithms and in the second one use meta-heuristics. According to the survey, some works reduce the complexity of the problem and assume some simplifications, such as: local optimization, linear objective function, absence of constraints, and single-objective optimization.

For example, there are some works (Gao et al., 2006; Huang et al., 2009; Yu and Lin, 2007) that only perform local optimization, that is, they look for the concrete service with the best QoS for each task. Experiments conducted, show that in most cases the local optimization does not result in the best choice considering all the execution plans (Berbner et al., 2006). Due to this, most approaches are based on global maximization. Other limitation of some existing approaches is the absence of support for constraints. Such limitation does not allow the use of the approaches for most real cases.

A work that accomplishes global optimization and support the use of constraint is the work of Zeng et al. (2003) that introduces a quality model to characterize non-functional properties of WS and formulates the problem as an optimization problem. Their approach uses linear programming techniques and the objective function depends on the semantic of the QoS property and on the control flow between the tasks of an execution path. Works on the group of exact algorithms use branch and bound (Yu and Lin, 2007), dynamic programming (Gao et al., 2006), linear programming (Ardagna and Pernici, 2007), etc.

However, most of works from this group, in general, use linear functions (Ardagna and Pernici, 2007; Cardellini et al., 2007; Gao et al., 2005; Yu and Lin, 2007), which forces loss of generality of considered compositions and QoS properties.

Works on the second group, which use meta-heuristics, seems to be promising (Strunk, 2010). They are more general and applicable. Most works from this group are based on Genetic Algorithms (GAs) (Ai et al., 2008; Canfora et al., 2008, 2005; Gao et al., 2007; Jian-Hua et al., 2008; Ma and Zhang, 2008; Vanrompay et al., 2008; Zhanh et al., 2006). Some recent works explore other kind of bio-inspired algorithms such as Ant Colony (Pop et al., 2011), Particle Swarm Optimization (Ming and Zhen-wu, 2007) and Immune algorithms (Xu and Reiff-Marganiec, 2008).

The works mentioned before are based on single optimization, i.e., they map the multi-objective optimization to single optimization by aggregating objective functions. This map presents some disadvantages. They produce only one execution plan, and the quality of the plan obtained is highly dependent on the weights used for each QoS property. The definition of such weights is not, in general, easy.

Considering these facts, some works address the use of multi-objective algorithms for WS selection (Li and Yan-xiang, 2010; Wada et al., 2008; Wang and Hou, 2008; Zhang et al., 2010). The works differ in the algorithm used, in the representation of the population according to the graph adopted to represent the WSC, and in the number of considered objectives (QoS attributes). The work of Wang and Hou (2008) uses the Pareto dominance concept in a multi-objective genetic algorithm based on three QoS quality indicators: cost, response time and reliability. The work of Wada et al. (2008) also implements a multi-objective genetic algorithm, named Ee that works with only three objectives: throughput, latency, and cost. Li and Yan-xiang (2010) proposed the use of the Multi-objective Chaos Ant Colony Optimization algorithm. In the work, three QoS attributes are considered: cost, time and reliability. The algorithm uses the concept of multi-pheromone and applies a chaos operator to avoid local optimum and to improve the diversity of the ACO optimization algorithm.

A multi-objective ACO algorithm is also used by the work of Zhang et al. (2010) with four objectives: time, cost, availability and reliability. In this work, Zhang et al. (2010) address an important point, generally not evaluated by most works, that is the scalability with respect to the number of abstract services and size of the execution plans. Other limitation of most works is that they use few objectives (generally three) and there are many QoS attributes found in the literature that are equally important for the user.

To deal efficiently with a large number of objectives can be a limitation for the multi-objective algorithms. An analysis conducted by Ishibuchi et al. (2008) shows a deterioration of the search ability in the presence of many objectives. The QoS service composition problem is a typical many-objective optimization problem. However, the techniques, such as the preference relations described in Section 2.3 have not yet been explored in this context, and in the field of SBSE.

The next sections present a many-objective optimization solution to deal properly with this problem. Three preference relations are studied to decrease the negative effects of using several objectives. Moreover, the study addresses scalability aspects with respect to the complexity of the number of abstract services.

4. THE APPROACH

In this work, the QoS-driven composition of Web services is treated as a many-objective optimization problem, to be solved by using a multi-objective evolutionary algorithm - NSGAII, and by different preference relations - CDAS, AR and MR. The problem is formulated and represented based on related work (Ai and Tang, 2008; Zeng et al., 2003). According to last section, the formulation to the problem includes:

- A set of tasks (abstract services) T = {t1,t2,...,tn};
- A set of concrete services for each task Ti,Si = {si,1,si,2,...,si,m};
- A set of restrictions composed of pairs (si,j, sk,l), which represent either dependencies or conflicts between services;
- A set of five QoS attributes for each service: qatr(si) = {qtime, qprice, qreputation, qreliability, qavailability}

The problem is then to find a solution, an execution plan ep = {s1,s2,...,sn}, that minimizes time and price, and maximizes reputation, reliability and availability by applying many-objectives optimization.

In the next subsections we present: adopted representation to the problem, objectives and fitness evaluation, and aspects of the algorithms implementation. We also describe the measures used to compare the algorithms.

4.1 Problem Representation

The solutions are represented following related work (Ai and Tang, 2008). The chromosome that represents ep is encoded by an array of integers. This means that an integer is associated to each concrete service of the composition. The length of the chromosome is equal to n, the number of tasks. Each gene i ranges from 1 to m, where m is the number of candidate services for the task ti. Figure 4 shows how is the representation to the problem and the relationship between task and concrete services.

Figure 4. Representation between tasks and services

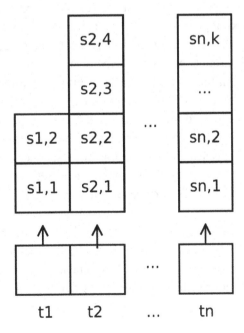

4.2 Used Algorithms

The NSGAII algorithm of the Framework jMetal (Durillo et al., 2010) was used and the CDAS, AR and MR preference relations were implemented. In this way, four algorithms could be evaluated: NSGAII with classical non-dominance relation, named here NSGAII; the modified NSGAII with CDAS preference relation, named CDASNSGAII; the modified NSGAII with AR preference relation, named AR-NSGAII; and the modified NSGAII with MR preference relation, named MR-NSGAII.

The one-point crossover operator is used. The mutation operator randomly selects a position in the chromosome (i.e., abstract service) and replaces the current concrete service by other available. If the new chromosomes are infeasible, that is, if they violate some restriction, they are rejected.

For each algorithm, 30 runs were performed with the following parameters: Population size: 300; Crossover (Single Point crossover) probability: 0.8; Mutation probability (Bit-flip mutation): 0.1; and Stopping condition: 200 generations.

4.3 Objectives

We used five objectives corresponding to QoS quality attributes. Observe that the method being investigated in this work is independently of the way the QoS attributes are calculated. In the sequence, we present the definitions of these attributes according to related work (Zeng et al., 2003). They are:

- $q_{time}(s_i)$: Measures the expected delay in seconds between the moment when a request is sent and the moment when the results are received. It is computed by summing the processing and transmission time of the service operations. Generally, the processing time is advertised and the transmission time is estimated based on past executions.
- $q_{price}(s_i)(s_i)$: Is the amount of money that a service requester has to pay for executing the service operations. Service providers advertise this information.
- $q_{reputation}(s_i)$: Measures the trustworthiness of a service, based on the user's experience. It can be defined as the average ranking given by the users. Generally the range is provided by the service providers in an ordinal scale. For example in Amazon.com the range is [0,5].
- $q_{reliability}(s_i)$: Is the probability that a request is correctly answered within a maximum expected time frame, generally published in the Web service description. Its value is computed from historical data about past invocations and is given by the number of times a service has been successfully used within the maximum expected time frame divided by the total number of invocations.
- $q_{availability}(s_i)$: Is the probability of a service being accessible. It is given by the total amount of time (in seconds) in which service is available during the last θ seconds divided by θ. θ is a constant that may vary depending on the frequency the service is accessed. It is generally set for a particular application by an administrator of the service community.

The set $\{Qtime, Qprice, Qreputation, Qreliability, Qavailability\}$ of QoS values for an execution plan *ep* is determined by the values of QoS attributes of its concrete services $q_{atr}(s_i)$ according to the structure of the corresponding workflow (sequential, parallel, loop, and choice). In a parallel flow, the sequences of services are synchronized at the end. In such case, the price value (Q_{price}) of the parallel sequences are summed, however, the time value (Q_{time}) is taken as the maximum time of the parallel sequences. Table 2 contains the aggregated functions to compute the objectives for a sequential flow in a WSC. To

Table 2. QoS aggregation functions

QoS Attribute	Function	Range
Time	$$Q_{time} = \sum_{i=1}^{n} q_{time}(S_i)$$	$1 <= q_{time}(Si) <= 10$
Price	$$Q_{price} = \sum_{i=1}^{n} q_{price}(S_i)$$	$1 <= q_{price}(Si) <= 10$
Reputation	$$Q_{reputation} = 1 \div n \sum_{i=1}^{n} 10 - q_{reputation}(S_i)$$	$1 <= q_{reputation}(Si) <= 10$
Availability	$$Q_{availability} = \sum_{i=1}^{n} e^{1 - q_{availability}(S_i)}$$	$0.5 <= q_{availability}(Si) <= 1$
reliability	$$Q_{reliability} = \sum_{i=1}^{n} e^{1 - q_{reliability}(S_i)}$$	$0.5 <= q_{reliability}(Si) <= 1$

perform the experiment, we considered values between 1 and 10 for the three first quality attributes, and values between 0.5 and 1 for the two last ones.

Observe that the scales of the objectives are not the same, but this is not a problem for the dominance, AR and MR relations. However, the CDAS relation is affected by this difference and then normalization was applied for this algorithm.

4.4 Performance Measures

The experimental study investigates the behavior of the proposed approach, especially in terms of convergence and diversity, as well as the scalability with respect to the number of tasks. The performance assessment of algorithms for multi-objective optimization problems is not a trivial issue. Comparing Pareto front approximations achieved using different preference relations poses a challenge, for example, given two Pareto front approximations generated by two different preference relations, $PF1_{approx}$ and $PF2_{approx}$. $PF1_{approx}$ has a set of solutions in a small region, close to the knee (Das, 1999) in the Pareto front, and $PF2_{approx}$ has a larger set of solutions than $PF1_{approx}$, but located in the extreme regions in the Pareto Front. In this example, the hypervolume is not a suitable measure to compare both fronts because the preference relation with the larger region will have an inherent advantage over the other relation (Lopez Jaimes and Coello, 2009). Despite these limitations, the hypervolume measure is still considered a guidance criterion for accepting solutions in MOEAs. Therefore, here, besides hpervolume we added two quality measures, the generational distance (GD) and the coverage (Cov). They are explained below:

- **Hypervolume (Zitzler, 1999):** It measures the volume of the objective space dominated by a set of solutions *Pa* but not by a specified reference set R.

- **Generational Distance (Veldhuizen and Lamont, 2000):** GD calculates the average of the Euclidean distance, in the objective space, between the solutions from an approximation of the Pareto Front (*PFapprox*) to the nearest solution of the Pareto Front (*PFtrue*). So, GD is an error measure used to examine the convergence of an algorithm to the (*PFtrue*).
- **Coverage (Zitzler et al., 2000):** Cov is used to measure the dominance between two sets of solutions *Pa* and *Pb*. Cov(*Pa*, *Pb*) represents a value between 0 e 1 according to how much the set *Pb* is dominated by set *Pa*. Similarly, we compare Cov(*Pb*, *Pa*) to obtain how much *Pa* is dominated by *Pb*.

Moreover, a pseudo Pareto front (*PFtrue*) was obtained by combining all the nondominated solutions returned by all algorithms at all executions. The quality measures are compared using the Friedman test at 5% significance level. The test is applied to raw values of each metric.

5. EVALUATION

To allow the evaluation of effectiveness and scalability of the algorithms, we need to perform experiments with a great variety of compositions with a large number of tasks and services. Due to this, we use simulated compositions. The simulation process and an example of simulated composition are described next.

5.1 Simulation

Ten compositions containing a set of abstract tasks T = {t1,t2,...,tn} were generated. Each composition has a different number of tasks n, with n = 10,20,30...100 (from 10 to 100 with an incremental of 10). For each task ti, a set of concrete services Si = {si,1,si,2,...,si,m} were randomly created with $1 \leq m \leq 10$. The QoS values of each service were also randomly defined.

The composition workflow was created randomly. We used a rate for selecting the possible structures to be present in the composition: sequence, choice, concurrency and loop. We also set the number of loop iterations, generated randomly, to a maximum of 4.

In the last step, the list of restrictions between services was generated by randomly picking two abstract services, one for task i and another for task j. It contains pairs of tasks and services separated by ";". For example, the following fragment of a list (...;s8,1,s9,3;s3,9,s5,10,...) represents there is a conflict between service 1 of task 8 and service 3 of task 9, and between service 9 of task 3 and service 10 of task 5.

To ensure that generated simulations really represent real instances, all possible structures found in most real applications were included. To illustrate this fact, a real application, called Fruxx[1], is used as example. Fruxx is a synchronization application provided to users of Apple computers. This application allows that users to synchronize their calendar of events, tasks in their agendas, bookmarks and notes between multiple computers. Although the synchronization application was developed on local machines, Fruux has employed Amazon Web Services (AWS) to host its application since its first versions. Some examples of used AWS are: Amazon Elastic Load Balancing (ELB), Amazon Elastic Compute Cloud (Amazon EC2) and Amazon Elastic Block Store (Amazon EBS).

The application flow, presented in Figure 5 could be generated by our simulation process. The flow has 10 tasks (abstract services). Each task has no more than 10 associated concrete services, also indicated in

Figure 5. AWS Case Study: fruux

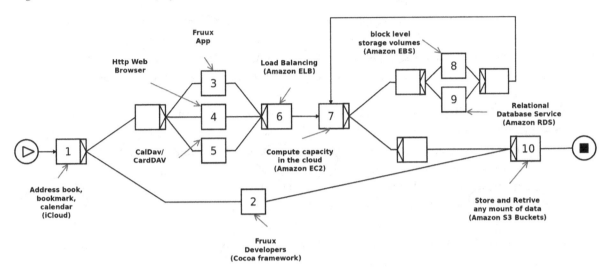

the figure. The flow starts on task 1. At that moment any Apple user has two options. In the first option the user asks for new resources or suggests new ideas. In such case, task 2 is performed and involves the analysis of the requests and updating of the applications. After, the new features are stored by task 10 (Amazon buckets S3) and the workflow is finished. In the second option the user only synchronizes the personal information, updating an information compatible with the system by following an or branch with three possibles tasks (tasks 3, 4 or 5). Each task depends on a specific protocol and a variety of services can be suitable. Next, the service Amazon ELB is executed (task 6) and it distributes the traffic to task 7, where again there is an or branch. In the first branch either task 8 or task 9 are executed. Task 8 uses the Amazon Elastic Block Store (EBS) service, which provides storage options, and task 9 uses Amazon Relational Database Service (Amazon RDS), a service responsible by operations of relational database. New computation are made by performing task 7, where it is decided (or not) to finish the flow, following the second branch and also finishing with task 10. This example and other more complexes are possible to be simulated.

5.2 Results

A first step in the analysis of the results is to investigate the effect of CDAS. For this investigation, the parameter that controls the dominance area of the solutions (σi) is defined for eleven different values, performing eleven different configurations: σi varies in 0.05 intervals, the same variation applied in Sato et al. (2007); σi varies in the [0.25, 0.45] range for the selection of a subset in the Pareto front; it varies in the [0.55, 0.75] range for the relaxation of the dominance relation; and $\sigma i = 0.5$ for the original Pareto dominance relation.

The empirical study has the purpose of investigating how the CDAS influences convergence and diversity properties of NSGAII algorithm. With this purpose, first we performed an analysis of some quality measures, comparing all configurations. Some of these quality measures need the Pareto Front True (PFtrue); however, in real problems the PFtrue is not known. In these cases, it is common to use the non-dominated solutions found in all runs.

Figures 6 and 7 present respectively results from the hypervolume and GD measures for 10 to 50 and 60 to 100 tasks. Each curve, in each graph, represents the hypervolume, and GD values evolution for different numbers of tasks. Here, we are interested on the behaviour of the algorithm for different values of σi. To allow the visualization of many curves in the graph, a normalization procedure was adopted. The normalization is made by dividing the values of the measures by the maximum value obtained for each task.

Table 3 presents the hypervolume, total number of solutions and the number of solutions found in the Pareto Front for each configuration in all WSCs. Also, Table 4 presents the best configurations according to the Friedman test, figures in bold are better in absolute values. It is possible to note that CDAS-NSGAII using σ values greater than 0.45 have no solutions in the PFtrue.

Although, the CDAS-NSGAII presents better results for the hypervolume and GD measures, however the σ parameter that presents the best result is not the same.

Figure 8 shows the results of the coverage measure, here the best σ configuration according to hypervolume was used. It is possible to note that CDAS-NSGAII dominates the solutions obtained by the NSGAII algorithm for all number of tasks.

Figure 6. Hypervolume for different configurations

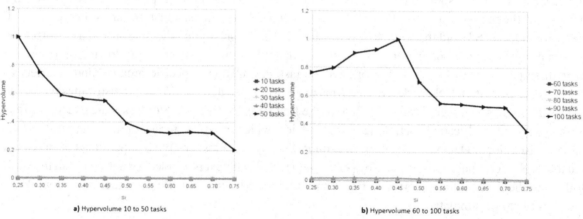

a) Hypervolume 10 to 50 tasks · b) Hypervolume 60 to 100 tasks

Figure 7. GD for different configurations

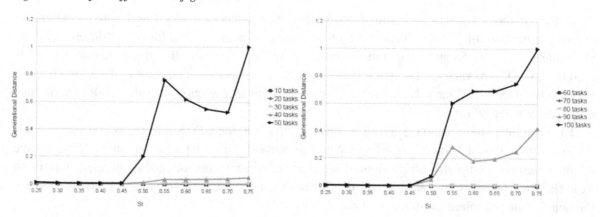

Table 3. Number of solutions - CDAS-NSGAII

# Tasks	Measures	σ Parameter										
		0.25	0.30	0.35	0.40	0.45	0.50	0.55	0.60	0.65	0.70	0.75
10	Hypervolume	7.1E-03	1	3.1E-01	9.9E-05	5.2E-05	4.8E-05	4.5E-05	4.5E-05	4.5E-05	3.5E-05	2.1E-05
	Total of	1.2	5.8	17.1	56.7	174.4	121.4	69.0	38.5	39.2	63.3	149.4
	Solutions	(0.6)	(2.5)	(6.2)	(17.0)	(36.5)	(3.7)	(13.7)	(7.1)	(7.9)	(7.2)	(9.2)
	# Points in	1.1	5.2	13.7	49.2	140.6	22.5	11.1	7.7	5.6	0.3	0.0
	PFapprox	(0.6)	(2.4)	(6.2)	(20.3)	(44.8)	(17.9)	(7.1)	(5.5)	(5.0)	(0.8)	(0.0)
20	Hypervolume	1	3.2E-01	4.8E-02	3.3E-02	3.1E-02	2.5E-02	2.0E-02	1.8E-02	1.8E-02	1.6E-02	1.2E-02
	Total of	4.3	14.4	74.8	181.1	257.6	183.7	130.1	96.8	89.0	107.9	189.2
	Solutions	(2.1)	(5.2)	(29.2)	(19.4)	(6.6)	(4.1)	(24.6)	(20.1)	(19.9)	(18.4)	(15.4)
	# Points in	3.7	12.5	59.9	151.8	126.1	4.7	0.1	0.0	0.0	0.1	0.0
	PFapprox	(2.2)	(7.0)	(30.0)	(46.7)	(52.4)	(5.6)	(0.3)	(0.2)	(0.2)	(0.3)	(0.0)
30	Hypervolume	1	1.9E-01	7.2E-02	2.8E-02	2.7E-02	2.3E-02	1.4E-02	1.4E-02	1.4E-02	1.4E-02	1.1E-02
	Total of	4.8	12.0	42.4	124.0	252.3	290.9	114.4	102.9	100.7	99.2	168.7
	Solutions	(3.7)	(6.7)	(20.5)	(27.5)	(18.4)	(2.5)	(23.2)	(32.4)	(28.7)	(28.6)	(26.4)
	# Points in	1.5	5.4	14.0	21.1	27.9	1.9	0.0	0.0	0.0	0.0	0.0
	PFapprox	(2.3)	(6.6)	(14.9)	(16.3)	(33.5)	(4.3)	(0.0)	(0.0)	(0.0)	(0.0)	(0.0)
40	Hypervolume	7.3E-01	7.7E-01	1.0E+00	8.8E-01	1	6.5E-01	5.2E-01	5.1E-01	5.3E-01	4.8E-01	3.0E-01
	Total of	6.3	16.8	42.3	107.2	248.6	295.3	103.9	90.6	85.7	105.8	176.9
	Solutions	(2.9)	(10.1)	(17.5)	(31.2)	(24.8)	(2.2)	(28.6)	(28.1)	(26.6)	(26.9)	(26.9)
	# Points in	2.5	4.9	10.6	17.4	16.3	0.2	0.0	0.0	0.0	0.0	0.0
	PFapprox	(2.8)	(4.2)	(11.7)	(13.3)	(19.8)	(0.5)	(0.0)	(0.0)	(0.0)	(0.0)	(0.0)
50	Hypervolume	1	7.5E-01	5.8E-01	5.6E-01	5.4E-01	3.9E-01	3.3E-01	3.2E-01	3.2E-01	3.2E-01	2.0E-01
	Total of	7.1	15.7	49.6	110.5	244.4	294.8	87.5	72.7	73.2	73.7	162.1
	Solutions	(4.2)	(6.9)	(19.9)	(29.2)	(29.9)	(2.6)	(23.3)	(17.3)	(19.6)	(20.3)	(27.2)
	# Points in	2.0	5.4	13.9	14.2	12.3	0.2	0.0	0.0	0.0	0.0	0.0
	PFapprox	(2.5)	(4.4)	(12.4)	(13.1)	(12.3)	(0.8)	(0.0)	(0.0)	(0.0)	(0.0)	(0.0)
60	Hypervolume	1	9.7E-01	6.8E-01	7.5E-01	8.0E-01	5.5E-01	4.2E-01	4.4E-01	4.4E-01	4.0E-01	2.4E-01
	Total of	5.8	18.2	45.2	105.4	247.8	295.6	67.8	62.2	59.4	68.6	133.8
	Solutions	(4.5)	(9.4)	(19.6)	(37.5)	(36.8)	(1.9)	(14.9)	(15.6)	(10.4)	(13.5)	(28.4)
	# Points in	2.8	6.1	9.8	12.9	11.1	0.0	0.0	0.0	0.0	0.0	0.0
	PFapprox	(3.4)	(6.5)	(10.4)	(10.9)	(13.8)	(0.0)	(0.0)	(0.0)	(0.0)	(0.0)	(0.0)

Continued on following page.

Table 3 continued.

# Tasks	Measures	σ Parameter										
		0.25	0.30	0.35	0.40	0.45	0.50	0.55	0.60	0.65	0.70	0.75
70	Hypervolume	9.2E-01	8.1E-01	9.2E-01	9.4E-01	1	6.8E-01	5.3E-01	5.4E-01	5.1E-01	5.0E-01	3.1E-01
	Total of	7.9	18.9	44.6	109.0	249.7	295.9	94.7	90.2	85.7	99.6	183.2
	Solutions	(5.8)	(11.8)	(22.7)	(38.4)	(29.9)	(2.2)	(24.1)	(25.7)	(21.3)	(30.5)	(19.2)
	# Points in	0.0	0.0	0.0	0.2	1.1	0.0	0.0	0.0	0.0	0.0	0.0
	PFapprox	(0.0)	(0.0)	(0.0)	(0.5)	(4.2)	(0.0)	(0.0)	(0.0)	(0.0)	(0.0)	(0.0)
80	Hypervolume	7.3E-01	9.0E-01	8.9E-01	9.8E-01	1	7.2E-01	5.4E-01	5.4E-01	5.4E-01	5.2E-01	3.4E-01
	Total of	9.9	26.0	58.9	135.7	263.2	297.3	87.0	83.4	84.1	87.1	174.9
	Solutions	(5.9)	(15.4)	(20.5)	(28.3)	(14.9)	(1.8)	(19.4)	(16.5)	(19.5)	(23.0)	(17.1)
	# Points in	5.2	8.5	21.6	19.6	13.7	2.8	0.0	0.0	0.0	0.0	0.0
	PFapprox	(4.4)	(9.0)	(17.4)	(17.6)	(11.9)	(5.0)	(0.0)	(0.0)	(0.0)	(0.0)	(0.0)
90	Hypervolume	8.2E-01	8.8E-01	1	9.3E-01	9.9E-01	7.1E-01	5.9E-01	5.8E-01	5.8E-01	5.7E-01	3.5E-01
	Total of	5.7	12.8	29.7	85.6	187.5	298.8	64.7	68.9	66.3	69.8	168.8
	Solutions	(3.2)	(8.0)	(16.6)	(23.8)	(30.9)	(1.0)	(14.0)	(20.3)	(20.7)	(20.3)	(23.5)
	# Points in	2.8	2.8	4.0	9.9	6.2	0.3	0.0	0.0	0.0	0.0	0.0
	PFapprox	(2.8)	(2.6)	(5.6)	(10.7)	(8.5)	(0.8)	(0.0)	(0.0)	(0.0)	(0.0)	(0.0)
100	Hypervolume	7.6E-01	7.9E-01	9.0E-01	9.2E-01	1	6.9E-01	5.4E-01	5.3E-01	5.2E-01	5.1E-01	3.5E-01
	Total of	6.5	14.5	45.8	90.2	243.5	298.8	79.7	83.0	79.0	82.9	166.2
	Solutions	(2.8)	(7.2)	(21.7)	(31.5)	(26.4)	(1.0)	(25.9)	(25.8)	(17.9)	(15.2)	(17.4)
	# Points in	3.3	5.4	8.9	11.3	5.7	0.4	0.0	0.0	0.0	0.0	0.0
	PFapprox	(3.0)	(5.9)	(8.4)	(13.1)	(8.4)	(0.9)	(0.0)	(0.0)	(0.0)	(0.0)	(0.0)

Table 4. Best configurations for CDAS-NSGAII algorithm

# Tasks	# Points in *PF*_{approx}	Hypervolume	GD
10	σ=0.45	σ=0.30	σ=**0.25**; 0.30; 0.35
20	σ=0.40	σ=0.25	σ=**0.25**; 0.30
30	σ=0.45	σ=0.25	σ=0.25; **0.30**; 0.35; 0.40; 0.45
40	σ=0.40	σ=0.35; **0.45**	σ=0.25; 0.30; 0.35; **0.40**; 0.45
50	σ=0.40	σ=0.25	σ=0.25; 0.30; 0.35; **0.40**; 0.45
60	σ=0.40	σ=0.25	σ=0.25; 0.30; 0.35; **0.40**; 0.45
70	σ=0.40	σ=0.45	σ=0.30; 0.35; **0.40**; 0.45
80	σ=0.35	σ=0.45	σ=0.25; 0.30; 0.35; **0.40**; 0.45
90	σ=0.40	σ=0.35	σ=0.25; 0.30; 0.35; **0.40**; 0.45
100	σ=0.40	σ=0.45	σ=0.25; 0.30; 0.35; **0.40**; 0.45

Figure 8. Coverage of CDAS-NSGAII and NSGAII

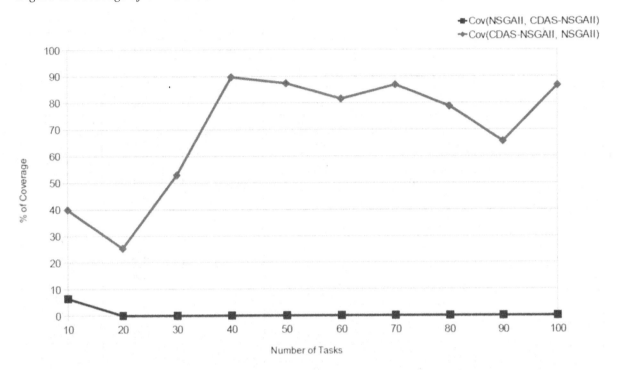

In a second step, all algorithms are compared considering Table 5 that presents results of the hypervolume and GD measures. A normalization procedure was adopted to allow a better understanding of the results. The normalization is made by dividing the values of the measures by: the maximum value obtained for each task for the hypervolume measure and the minimum value in the case of the GD measure. It is observed that, for all compositions, the CDAS-NSGAII presents better results for the hypervolume measure. The GD results show that the AR-NSGAII algorithm has good convergence to the Pareto front.

Figure 9 shows the coverage results for the AR-NSGAII and MR-NSGAII algorithms. For small compositions, 10 to 20 tasks, MR-NSGAII and AR-NSGAII are equivalent. For compositions with greater number of tasks, the AR-NSGAII is statistically better than MR-NSGAII.

Figure 10 shows the coverage results between: AR-NSGAII and NSGAII, and MRNSGAII and NSGAII. Comparing AR-NSGAII and NSGAII, it is possible to observe that when the complexity of the composition increases, the percentage of solutions of the original algorithm that are dominated by AR-NSGAII also increases, starting with a level close to 20% rising to 98% for 70 tasks. Between 80 and 100 tasks, this percentage decreases, but remains at high levels between 40% and 60%. The results of AR-NSGAII are stuck at zero for all compositions of tasks, showing that there is no AR-NSGAII solution dominated by NSGAII.

Considering the comparison between the algorithms MR-NSGAII and NSGAII, again, the set of solutions of NSGAII does not dominate the set of MR-NSGAII.

Figure 11 shows the coverage results between: CDAS-NSGAII and AR-NSGAII, and CDAS-NSGAII and MR-NSGAII. Comparing CDAS-NSGAII and AR-NSGAII, it is possible to observe that for almost

Table 5. Measures for all algorithms

# Tasks	Measures	NSGAII	AR-NSGAII	MR-NSGAII	CDAS-NSGAII
10	*PFapprox*	22.5 (17.9)	70.4 (27.3)	65.0 (38.3)	5.2 (2.4)
	GD	62.784	33.843	36.810	1
	Hypervolume	4.84E-005	3.06E-005	4.11E-005	1
20	*PFapprox*	4.7 (5.6)	102.1 (75.1)	51.1 (39.1)	3.7 (2.2)
	GD	24.698	5.008	10.792	1
	Hypervolume	2.57E-002	1.43E-002	5.01E-002	1
30	*PFapprox*	1.9 (4.3)	106.5 (71.3)	58.8 (58.6)	1.5 (2.3)
	GD	43.176	1	5.751	1.793
	Hypervolume	2.30E-002	1.34E-002	2.09E-002	1
40	*PFapprox*	0.2 (0.5)	72.2 (51.1)	16.8 (23.1)	16.3 (19.8)
	GD	142.452	1	8.017	7.478
	Hypervolume	6.54E-001	3.69E-001	7.08E-001	1
50	*PFapprox*	0.2 (0.8)	76.3 (73.9)	35.6 (30.7)	2.0 (2.5)
	GD	427.502	1	8.269	10.489
	Hypervolume	3.90E-001	2.68E-001	4.47E-001	1
60	*PFapprox*	0.0 (0.0)	75.7 (55.0)	20.6 (32.0)	2.8 (3.4)
	GD	143.965	1	8.653	7.357
	Hypervolume	5.55E-001	3.93E-001	6.14E-001	1
70	*PFapprox*	0.0 (0.0)	69.5 (57.0)	0.0 (0.0)	1.1 (4.2)
	GD	1309.634	1	120.657	154.254
	Hypervolume	6.80E-001	9.62E-001	7.46E-001	1
80	*PFapprox*	2.8 (5.0)	77.4 (61.8)	39.5 (39.5)	13.7 (11.9)
	GD	224.520	1	11.619	14.124
	Hypervolume	7.22E-001	4.59E-001	7.71E-001	1
90	*PFapprox*	0.3 (0.8)	59.8 (51.6)	33.8 (38.4)	4.0 (5.6)
	GD	838.896	1	13.036	36.601
	Hypervolume	7.12E-001	5.82E-001	8.23E-001	1
100	*PFapprox*	0.4 (0.9)	58.5 (53.7)	41.1 (33.9)	5.7 (8.4)
	GD	702.309	1	11.070	17.111
	Hypervolume	6.98E-001	5.58E-001	7.83E-001	1

number of tasks the results are equivalent, e.g., there is no difference between the two preference relation with exception for 70 task, where the solutions of AR dominates the solutions of CDAS. However considering the comparison between the algorithms MR-NSGAII and CDAS-NSGAII, the set of solutions of CDAS-NSGAII dominates the set of MR-NSGAII.

In sum, the results of the empirical evaluations show that the AR and CDAS preference relations provide the best overall results, followed by MR-NSGAII. It is also noticeable that NSGAII presents the worst results.

Figure 9. Coverage of AR-NSGAII and MR-NSGAII

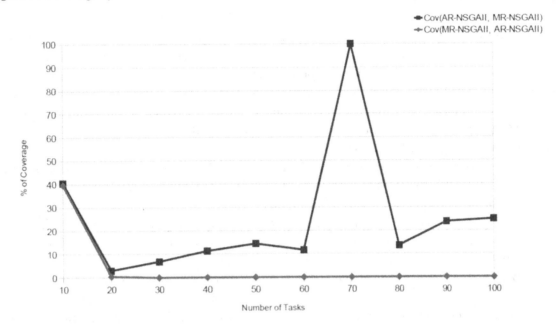

Figure 10. Coverage of the preference relations

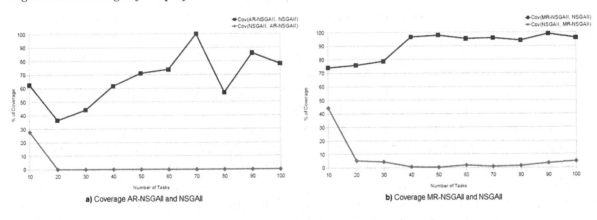

Figure 11. Coverage of the preference relations

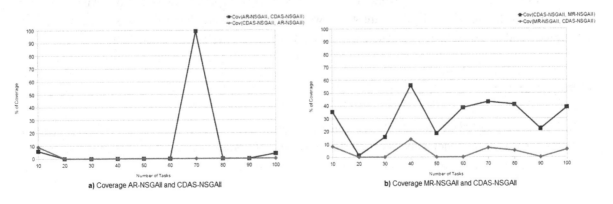

6. CONCLUDING REMARKS

The WoS-driven WSC problem refers to the aggregation of services to build complex applications to meet customer's needs. To select the services some QoS attributes need to be maximized/minimized. The number of attributes that influence this problem are great, usually more than three. Hence, the problem can be called many-objective. Considering this fact, in this chapter an approach based on many-objective optimization is explored. Three techniques are used and implemented with the NSGA-II algorithm: Control of Dominance Area of Solution (CDAS-NSGAII), Average Ranking (AR-NSGA-II) and Maximum Ranking (MR-NSGA-II).

An analysis was performed to measure how CDAS, AR and MR affect the convergence and diversity of the NSGAII algorithm. In addition to this, the implemented algorithms were confronted to observe which technique obtained the best results in the problem.

The experiments were conducted with different compositions varying the number of tasks in ten different values: 10, 20, 30, 40, 50, 60, 70, 80, 90 and 100. Three quality measures were used to evaluate the algorithms: hypervolume, generational distance and coverage.

The CDAS-NSGAII was evaluated in two different situations, using $\sigma i < 0.5$, i.e, selecting a subset of the Pareto Front and using $\sigma i > 0.5$, i.e, performing a relaxation of the Pareto dominance relation. Ten different configurations were used: 5 with $\sigma i < 0.5$ and 5 with $\sigma i > 0.5$. The original Pareto dominance relation ($\sigma i = 0.5$) was also used.

First, the CDAS-NSGAII configurations were confronted to NSGAII algorithm with the original dominance relation. In this analysis, the best results were obtained by CDAS-NSGAII, for all measures analyzed.

Finally, the results of all algorithms were compared. From these results, it follows that the greater the number of tasks, the lower the convergence of all algorithms, in similar proportions. The AR and CDAS preference relations present the best overall results, followed by MR. It is also noticeable that NSGAII is the one with the farthest points in relation to the Pareto front.

From the analysis, it is evident that the higher the number of goals the larger the number of non-dominated solutions, making harder the choice of an appropriate solution. It is also noticeable that the obtained solutions present excellent values for one or other objective at the expense of poor values for the other ones. This problem could be mitigated with some quality measures by limiting the range of acceptable values for the objectives. This would avoid many of the provided solutions. And the last remark but not least important, is that NGSAII is not the better option in any combination of services, with solutions very far from the Pareto Front.

We can observe an absence of works that explores the use of solutions based on many-objective optimization in the SBSE field. As future work, we intend to evaluate the use of these many-objective techniques in other SBSE problems, such as prioritization of test case and release planning.

REFERENCES

Ai, L. M., & Tang (2008). A penalty-based genetic algorithm for QoS-aware web service composition with inter-service-dependencies and conflicts. In *International Conference on Computational Intelligence for Modelling Control & Automation* (CIMCA). Academic Press.

Ai, L., & Tang, M. (2008). QoS-based web service composition accommodating interservice dependencies using minimal-conflict hill-climbing repair genetic algorithm. In *IEEE International Conference on eScience*. IEEE.

Alrifai, M., Skoutas, D., & Risse, T. (2010). Selecting skyline services for qos-based web service composition. In *Proceedings of the 19th International Conference on World Wide Web, WWW '10*. New York, NY: ACM. doi:10.1145/1772690.1772693

Ardagna, D., & Pernici, B. (2007). Adaptative service composition in flexible processes. *IEEE Transactions on Software Engineering, 33*(6), 369–384.

Bentley, P. J., & Wakefield, J. P. (1998). Finding acceptable solutions in the Paretooptimal range using multiobjective genetic algorithms. In *Soft Computing in Engineering Design and Manufacturing*. Springer-Verlag.

Berbner, R., Spahn, M., Repp, N., Heckmann, O., & Steinmetz, R. (2006). Heuristics for QoS-aware web service composition. In *IEEE International Conference on Web Services (ICWS)*. IEEE.

Canfora, G., Penta, M. D., Esposito, R., & Villani, M. (2008). A framework for QoSaware binding and re-binding of composite web services. *Journal of Systems and Software, 81*(10), 1754–1769. doi:10.1016/j.jss.2007.12.792

Canfora, G., Penta, M. D., & Villan, M. (2005). Approach on QoS-aware compositions based on genetic algorithm. In *Genetic and Evolutionary Computing Conference (GECCO)*. doi:10.1145/1068009.1068189

Cardellini, E., & Casalichio, V., Grassi, and Presti, F. L. (2007). Flow-based service selection for web service composition supporting multiple QoS classes. In *IEEE International Conference on Web Services (ICWS)*. doi:10.1109/ICWS.2007.91

Coello, C. A. C., Lamont, G. B., & Veldhuizen, D. A. V. (2006). *Evolutionary Algorithms for Solving Multi-Objective Problems (Genetic and Evolutionary Computation)*. Springer-Verlag New York, Inc.

Consortium, W. W. W. (2007). *OWL-S: semantic markup for Web services*. Author.

Das, I. (1999). On characterizing the knee of the Pareto curve based on normalboundary intersection. *Structural Optimization, 18*(2-3), 107–115. doi:10.1007/BF01195985

Deb, K., Agrawal, S., Pratap, A., & Meyarivan, T. (2000). A fast elitist nondominated sorting genetic algorithm for multi-objective optimization: NSGA-II. *Lecture Notes in Computer Science*, 849–858.

Durillo, J., Nebro, A., & Alba, E. (2010). The jMetal framework for multi-objective optimization: Design and architecture. In *IEEE Congress on Evolutionary Computation (CEC)*. doi:10.1109/CEC.2010.5586354

Dustdar, S. & Schreiner, W. (2005). A survey on web services composition. *Int. Journal of Web and Grid Services, 1*(1).

Gao, C., Cai, M., & Chen, H. (2007). QoS-aware service composition based on tree-coded genetic algorithm. In *31st Annual International Computer Software and Application Conference Application Conference (COMPSAC)*. doi:10.1109/COMPSAC.2007.174

Gao, Y., Na, J., Zeng, B., Yang, L., & Gong, Q. (2006). Optimal selection using dynamic programming. In *11th IEEE International Symposium on Computers and Communications (ISCC)*. IEEE.

Gao, Y., Zeng, B., Na, J., Yang, L., Dai, Y., & Gong, Q. (2005). Optimal selection of web services for composition based on interface-matching and weighted multistage graph. In *6th International Conference on Parallel and Distributed Computing Applications and Technologies* (PDCAT). Academic Press.

Harman, M. & Jones, B. (2001). Search based software engineering. *Journal of Information and Software Technology*, (14), 833–839.

Harman, M., Mansouri, S. A., & Zhang, Y. (2009). *Search based software engineering: A comprehensive analysis and review of trends techniques and applications*. Technical Report TR-09-03.

Huang, Z., Jiang, W., Hu, S., & Liu, Z. (2009). Effective pruning algorithm for QoS-aware service composition. In *IEEE Conference on Commerce and Enterprise Computing*. IEEE. doi:10.1109/CEC.2009.41

Ishibuchi, H., Sakane, Y., Tsukamoto, N., & Nojima, Y. (2009). Evolutionary manyobjective optimization by NSGA-II and MOEA/D with large populations. In *IEEE International Conference on Systems, Man, and Cybernetics*. IEEE Computer Society.

Ishibuchi, H., Tsukamoto, N., & Nojima, Y. (2008). Evolutionary many-objective optimization: A short review. In *IEEE World Congress on Computational Intelligence*. IEEE.

Jian-Hua, L., Song-Qiao, S., Yong-Jun, L., & Gui-Lin, L. (2008). Application of genetic algorithm to QoS-aware web service composition. In *3rd IEEE Conference on Industrial Electronics and Applications (ICIEA)*. IEEE. doi:10.1109/ICIEA.2008.4582569

Knowles, J., Thiele, L., & Zitzler, E. (2006). *A Tutorial on the Performance Assessment of Stochastic Multiobjective Optimizers*. Technical Report. Computer Engineering and Networks Laboratory (TIK), ETH Zurich.

Lecue, F., & L'eger, A. (2006). A formal model for semantic web composition. In 5th *International Semantic Web Conference*. Academic Press.

Li, W., & Yan-xiang, H. (2010). A web service composition algorithm based on global QoS optimizing with MOCACO. In Algorithms and Architectures for Parallel Processing (LNCS), (vol. 6082, pp. 218–224). Springer. doi:10.1007/978-3-642-13136-3_22

Lopez Jaimes, A., & Coello, C. A. C. (2009). Study of preference relations in many-objective optimization. *Genetic and Evolutionary Computation Conference (GECCO)*. doi:10.1145/1569901.1569986

Ma, Y., & Zhang, C. (2008). Quick convergence of genetic algorithm for QoS-driven web service selection. *International Journal of Computer and Telecommunications Networking*, 52, 1093–1104.

Ming, C., & Zhen-wu, W. (2007). An approach for web services composition based on QoS and discrete particle swarm optimization. In *8th ACIS International Conference on Software Engineering, Artificial Intelligence, Networking, and Parallel/Distributed Computing*. ACIS.

Pop, C., Chifu, V., Salomie, I., Dinsoreanu, M., David, T., & Acretoaie, V. (2011). Ant-inspired technique for automatic web service composition. In *International Symposium Selection Symbolic and Numeric Algorithms for Scientific Computing* (SYNASC). SYNASC.

Sato, H., Aguirre, H. E., & Tanaka, K. (2007). *Controlling Dominance Area of Solutions and Its Impact on the Performance of MOEAs.* Lecture Notes in Computer Science, 4403, 5–20. doi:10.1007/978-3-540-70928-2_5

Strunk, A. (2010). QoS-aware service composition: a survey. In *IEEE European Conference on Web Services*. IEEE.

van der Aalst, W., & ter Hofstede, A. (2005). YAWL: Yet another workflow language. *Information Systems*, *30*(4), 245–275.

Vanrompay, Y., Rigole, P., & Berbers, Y. (2008). Genetic algorithm-based optimization of service composition and deployment. In *International Workshop on Services Integration in Pervasive Eenvironments* (SIPE). Academic Press.

Veldhuizen, D. A. V., & Lamont, G. (2000). On measuring multiobjective evolutionary algorithm performance. In Congress on Evolutionary Computation. doi:10.1109/CEC.2000.870296

Wada, H., Champrasert, P., & Suzuki, J. (2008). Multiobjective optimization of SLAaware service compositions. In *IEEE Congress on Services*. IEEE.

Wang, J., & Hou, Y. (2008). Optimal web service selection based on multi-objective genetic algorithm. In *International Symposium on Computational Intelligence and Design (ISCID)*. doi:10.1109/ISCID.2008.197

While, L., Hingston, P., Barone, L., & Huband, S. (2006). A faster algorithm for calculating hypervolume. *IEEE Transactions on Evolutionary Computation*, *10*(1), 29–38. doi:10.1109/TEVC.2005.851275

Xu, J., & Reiff-Marganiec, S. (2008). Towards heuristic web services composition using immune algorithm. In *IEEE International Conference on Web Services*. IEEE. doi:10.1109/ICWS.2008.16

Yu, T. & Lin, K.-J. (2007). Efficient algorithms for web services selection with endto-end QoS constraints. *ACM Transactions on Web, 1*.

Zeng, L., Benatallah, B., Dumas, M., Kalagnanam, J., & Sheng, Q. Z. (2003). Quality driven web services composition. In *International Conference on World Wide Web* (WWW). Academic Press.

Zeng, L., Benatallah, B., Ngu, A., Dumas, M., & Kalagnanam, J. (2004). QoSaware middleware for web services composition. *IEEE Transactions on Software Engineering, 30*(5), 311327.

Zhang, W., Chang, C. K., Feng, T., & Jiang, H. (2010). QoS-based dynamic web service composition with ant colony optimization. In *34th Annual IEEE Computer Software and Applications Conference*. doi:10.1109/COMPSAC.2010.76

Zhanh, C.-W., Su, S., & Chen, J.-L. (2006). Efficient population diversity handling genetic algorithm for QoS-aware web service selection. In *International Conference on Computational Science* (ICCS). Academic Press.

Zitzler, E. (1999). *Evolutionary algorithms for multiobjective optimization: Methods and applications*. Shaker, Diss. Technische Wissenschaften ETH Zrich.

Zitzler, E., Deb, K., & Thiele, L. (2000). Comparison of multiobjective evolutionary algorithms: Empirical results. *Evolutionary Comput Computation, 8*(2), 173–195. doi:10.1162/106365600568202 PMID:10843520

ENDNOTE

[1]   http://aws.amazon.com/solutions/case-studies/fruux/

Chapter 11
Integrated Management Systems and Information Management Systems:
Common Threads

Maria Gianni
University of Macedonia, Greece

Katerina Gotzamani
University of Macedonia, Greece

ABSTRACT

Information systems collect and disseminate information within organizations based on information technology, while management systems formalize business processes following the standards requirements. Since management standards proliferate, their integrated adoption into a holistic overarching system has emerged as an effective and efficient approach. In this context, this chapter aims to explore the potential synergies among information management and integration. Firstly, a focused literature review is conducted and survey data on the relevant standards evolution are processed in order to provide the information and management practitioners with a clear and oriented depiction of the available norms and their adoption possibilities. Furthermore, a framework is proposed consolidating management subsystems into an integrated structure including information management and supported by information systems. Finally, the concept of internalization of management systems standards is understood in association with information and knowledge diffusion within an integrated management system.

INTRODUCTION

Management systems are artifacts that aim to identify and support operations, such as the allocation of resources, the goals and objectives setting and monitoring, and the policy and decision-making processes. Within this context, several standards have been composed to provide management systems a platform for the effective and efficient communication between different stakeholders. More specifi-

DOI: 10.4018/978-1-4666-8841-4.ch011

cally, the standardization of processes and procedures allows third-party impartial auditing, facilitates transactions, provides the means to a deeper understanding of operations and raises management to a more sophisticated level when addressing challenges.

Bearing the aforementioned reasoning in mind, in the last two decades several management system standards and specifications have been released in terms of different disciplines and sectors, such as quality (ISO 9001), environment (ISO 14001), health and safety (OHSAS 18001), information security (ISO 27001), food safety (ISO 22000), information services (ISO 20000), supply chain security (ISO 28001), energy (ISO 50001), social accountability (SA 8000 and AA1000), and social responsibility (ISO 26000). These standards are not legislative documents and, hence, they are voluntarily adopted (Heras-Saizarbitoria & Boiral, 2013). Each one of the released standards addresses specific areas of business operations and offers a set of best practices and guidelines.

However, certain complexity barriers are raised for organizations when trying to meet concurrently the requirements of more than one standard, as regards the handling of resources, processes, and results. To this end, the concept of integration was born. According to Griffith and Bhutto (2009) an integrated management system (IMS) is "the single management system that delivers the processes of the business through modular and mutually supporting structured management functions configured around the wider needs of the organisation".

Empirical research on the integration of management systems classifies firms according to the main attributes of integrated management systems, i.e. the scope and the sequence of management systems implementation, the level, the methodology, and the audits (see, e.g., Bernardo, Casadesús, Karapetrovic & Heras, 2009; Santos, Mendes & Barbosa, 2011). Basic cornerstones for the establishment of a management system are the model, the methodology and the tools. The lack of a worldwide accepted management standard to guide the development of an auditable integrated management system increases the variability and the flexibility in the forms of the applied integrated management systems. However, there is an ongoing debate on whether an integration standard can facilitate rather than complicate the process of embedding additional management sub-systems (Rocha, Searcy & Karapetrovic, 2007). Therefore, to date integrated management systems are implemented, acknowledged and researched despite the lack of a standard, which would enable their formal auditing and certification.

Viewed from the perspective of information-specific operations the integration, as a notion, is quite familiar to information experts. However, in this research context, a clear distinction has to be made between integrated information systems and integrated management systems. On the one hand, the information systems are consolidated on a technological basis whilst, on the other hand, management systems are amalgamated following certain management principles. Furthermore, information flows along the entire firm and is integrated within the operational structure of an organization using programming language, software and hardware. Conversely, the integration of management systems needs to be primarily approached in an abstract yet well-founded manner at the strategic, tactical and operational levels of the management fabric.

So far, research has progressed on the models, the methodologies, the benefits and constraints studying the initiation and the outcome of the integrated management systems. However, the IMS actual development and implementation remains under-researched, in terms of data collection, storage and dissemination, software tools, and resources. Documentation, increase of paperwork and duplication of records are some of the difficulties encountered when integrating multiple management sub-systems.

Moreover, enhanced complexity and overlapping processes need to be addressed in a systematic and holistic manner. Academics have recognized and addressed this need by developing frameworks and guidelines to overcome these barriers at a strategic or even at a tactical level. However, in order for such frameworks to apply at the operational level, fit solutions have to be engineered. At this point, information technology (IT) may aid employees monitor the management sub-systems information flow. Furthermore, the establishment of an information management system supported by an information security management system (ISMS) may facilitate the secure and efficient information exchange and processing in an organization. When adopting the respective ISO standards certain requirements have to be met. These requirements can be aligned with the corresponding requirements of other management systems standards, such as the ISO 9001 and the ISO 14001 standards.

The alignment and, eventually, the fusion of management systems can be accomplished by the systems approach, which widens the perspective of corporate entities allowing them to embrace all activities and their interdependencies (Jonker & Klaver, 2004). The repeated sequence of "input, process, output" across the network of related processes and sub-systems is considered as a whole that keeps changing and interacting with the environment, namely the supply chain and all the stakeholders. Systems approach enables the balanced management of inter-related system modules towards the fulfillment of the corporate strategic goals and objectives without compromising any of the systems values, such as customer satisfaction, environmental protection, and occupational health and safety hazards mitigation. An efficient and effective integration may lead to the continuous monitoring and evaluation of the balanced performance of the management systems. In this context, information technology may provide the necessary infrastructure to support and leverage business performance. Information systems rely on certain principles, including but not limited to the requirements elicitation and formalization, software engineering, hardware adaptation, taking into account all stakeholders involved. Hence, this chapter aims at shedding light on the integrated adoption of the information management standards and their impact on the efficiency and effectiveness of the produced integrated management system.

Therefore, the remainder of the chapter reviews the models, methodologies, audits, performance, motives, barriers and benefits that are related to the integrated adoption of the requirements of management systems standards focusing on the integration of the information management systems. Through a literature review and the processing of available survey data the authors discuss the interface of information management with managerial aspects involving the quality, the environmental protection, the energy consumption, and certain sector-specific issues, such as food traceability and service management. The discussion leads to conclusions and directions for further research.

BACKGROUND

In the extant body of literature the scope of integration is mainly limited to the adoption of the two flagship standards addressing the management of quality and the environment. However, in the last years, the integration scope increasingly widens encompassing other disciplines, such as health and safety (Abad et al., 2013; von Ahsen, 2013), food (Satolo, Calarge & Cauchick Miguel, 2013), and information (Crowder, 2013; Mesquida & Mas, 2014). Particularly, with regard to information, Hoy and Foley (2014) focus on the integrated auditing of compliance to the ISO 9001 and ISO 27001 standards. Auditing is proposed as the interface element of the quality and the information management sub-systems, the information technology framework and the assessment of performance. It is emphasized that "a management systems auditor requires an understanding of all the management system standards within the purview of the integrated management system (Hoy & Foley, 2014). By using PAS 99:2012, performance evaluation and the improvement steps of the plan-do-check-act founding principles are highlighted pointing at the internal and external audits as the corresponding managerial assets. ISO 9001 and ISO 27001 have several common requirements and six common management system processes: documentation, training, internal audit, management review, corrective action and preventive action (Hoy & Foley, 2014).

Mesquida and Mas (2014) elaborated a guide for integrating information technology service management systems and quality management systems. Based on the ISO/IEC 20000-1 and the ISO 9001 Standards. The guide's effectiveness is tested in five service organizations with three providing IT services in the hospitality industry, one being a public environmental and urban planning authority and one being a hospital. Furthermore, future research is directed on the subsequent integration of an information security management system by adopting the requirements of the ISO/IEC 27001 and COBIT (Mesquida & Mas, 2014). In a similar vein, Crowder (2013) discusses the simultaneous implementation of quality and information security management systems with the environmental management sub-system being integrated at a later time (Crowder, 2013).

The information-related standards that have been released by the International Organization for Standardization (ISO) and are mentioned in this chapter are listed in Table 1. An overview of the standards that formalize the integrated adoption of information-related standards is provided in Table 2. The items in Table 2 differ in that the PAS 99:2012 is a publicly available specification released by a national standardization body, i.e. the British Standards Institute (BSI), while the other guidelines are elaborated by the International Organization for Standardization (ISO).

Table 1. Standards, specifications and guidelines related to information systems

Name	Title
ISO/IEC[1] 20000-1:2011	Information Technology - Service management - Part 1: Service management system requirements
ISO/IEC 27001:2013	Information security management
ISO/IEC 90003:2004	Software engineering - Guidelines for the application of ISO 9001:2000 to computer software
ISO/IEC 12207:2008	Systems and software engineering - Software life cycle processes
ISO/IEC 15504-2:2003	Software engineering - Process assessment — Part 2: Performing an assessment

Table 2. Standards, specifications and guidelines enabling the integration of information systems

Name	Title
ISO/IEC TR 90006:2013	Information technology - Guidelines for the application of ISO 9001:2008 to IT service management and its integration with ISO/IEC 20000-1:2011
ISO/IEC 27013:2012	Information technology – Security techniques - Guidance on the integrated implementation of ISO/IEC 27001 and ISO/IEC 20000-1
PAS 99:2012	Specification of common management system requirements as a framework for integration
ISO 19011:2011	Guidelines for auditing management systems

Integration Approach

Taking into account that standards keep on proliferating, the integration of the normalized management systems needs to be addressed in a systematic way. So far, the International Organization for Standardization (ISO) has not released an integrated management standard. However, there are certain national standardization bodies that launched guidelines to foster the integration of management systems (Bernardo, Casadesús, Karapetrovic & Heras, 2009). As such, the Danish standard understands integration in three levels: the strategic (corporate governance), a generic platform comprising common elements and the distinct management components (Jørgensen, 2008). Apart from the national norms, there are generic integration approaches developed, as well (Karapetrovic, 2003; Griffith & Bhutto, 2008; Zeng, Shi & Lou, 2007). Some models are tailored to meet the needs of specific sectors, such as the construction industry (Griffith & Bhutto, 2008) and the airline industry (López-Fresno, 2010).

Focusing on the scope of this chapter, certain conceptual and empirical approaches have been identified in the extant body of research addressing the integrated adoption of information management with other management disciplines. Gillies (2011) combines the capability maturity model and the quality management approach to compose a best-fit solution for the ISO 27001 standard to be implemented. Crowder (2013) presents a comprehensive case of an integrated quality and information security management system later incorporating the environmental component. Hoy & Foley (2014) established a framework for the integration of quality and information audits based on the PAS 99 (BSI, 2012). Rebelo, Santos & Silva (2014) composed a model in order to integrate multiple management systems and recognized the information security along with the social accountability management as the two fundamental components of a sustainable integrated management system. In the same vein, Jørgensen (2008) suggests knowledge management and a basic standard to be used as the basis for integrated management and sustainability reporting.

Integration Motives

It is emphasized that an IMS implementation "stimulus" may be derived from various sources including regulatory, financial, marketing, social, and operational (Asif, de Bruijn, Fisscher, Searcy & Steenhuis, 2009). Oskarsson & von Malmorg (2005) identified two major driving forces for management systems integration, i.e. the anticipation of a more effective and simpler management structure as well as a tighter connection between specific-discipline management aspects and the core values of a company, while Salomone (2008) stressed that management systems integration is driven by the markets, human resources and continual improvement. Specifically for the certification of the IT-related activities customer orientation is found to be the higher ranked motive (Disterer, 2012; Hoy & Foley, 2013). Further external motives, such as seeking competitive advantage and improving company's image, and internal motives aiming to optimize internal procedures and functions were found to motivate ISO 22000 certification as well (Disterer, 2012). As regards the information security management standard's (ISO/IEC 27001) adoption, it is mostly driven by either government regulation or supplier/buyer demands or the necessity of outsourcing. Lower insurance premiums and participation in international tenders are driving ISMS implementation as well (Fomin, de Vries & Barlette, 2008).

Integration Constraints

Among the drawbacks to implementing integration are: incompatible concepts between systems, complex organizational systems, initial higher organizational problems, the dissemination risk of a single component problem across the overall management system, the need for updated documentation at the expense of other management activities, and the initial cost increase associated with an increase in non-conformities (Santos et al., 2011).

Narrowing research down to information management, one of the identified barriers to the adoption of information security standards is that they insufficiently address human and organizational aspects (Barlette & Fomin, 2010). Human resources aspects were also highlighted, in a public sector-oriented survey, where shortage of information security expertise, lack of awareness programs, insufficient understanding of the standard's requirements, and resistance to the introduction of the standard, were found to be the most significant barriers to the successful implementation of the ISO 27001 standard (Alshitri & Abanumy, 2014). Furthermore, 56 per cent of the organizations certified to the ISO 27001 standard that participated in an international survey identified cultural change as the main challenge (Gillies, 2011). In a qualitative study of 6 public sector and 3 non-public sector cases in Malaysia, Othman & Chan (2013) identified the lack of resources, lack of knowledge and skills and lack of awareness as the most highly rated barriers to information management, with the lack of knowledge and skills being more apparent in public sector organizations.

Integration Benefits

Integration benefits among others the internal cohesion, the use and performance of the systems, the corporate culture, the image and strategy and the stakeholders' implication (Khanna, 2010; Simon, Karapetrovic & Casadesús, 2012). Furthermore, process improvement through a common documentation system, the creation of a system adequately defined, ensuring the commitment and meeting the needs of the stakeholders, the increase of business performance, and the improved allocation of resources are highlighted as the major advantages of the integrated quality and information service management systems (Mesquida & Mas, 2014). Management of IT service quality brought about improved customer satisfaction, enhanced stability and quality of services and reduction in the number of incidents, facilitation of growth and better alignment of people and information (Mesquida & Mas, 2014). The benefits of managing information security are found similar to those accrued when managing quality, i.e. awareness increase and continuous improvement (Fomin, de Vries & Barlette, 2008).

Integration of Audits

Audits have two objectives: first, to detect and 'cure' non-conformities to the management systems standards' requirements and second, to highlight opportunities for improvement of the implemented management systems. However, the audits performance is questioned from many academics and practitioners over the years (Kaziliūnas, 2008). As far as the integrated management systems are concerned, the level of audits' integration can be assessed via a four-level scale: sequential, overlapping, simultaneous and fully integrated (Kraus & Grosskopf, 2008). Bernardo, Casadesús, Karapetrovic and Heras (2010; 2011) evaluated empirically the achieved level of audits' integration by identifying the integration level of the human resources, the planning, the methodology and the reporting of both the internal and the external audits of multiple management systems. The inadequacy of audit methodologies is mentioned in the literature as one of the common barriers to integration (Searcy et al., 2012).

Particularly, regarding information, Ferreira, Machado and Paulk (2011) introduce a conceptual framework with the intent to support management of quality goals information when conducting of multi-model audits and assessments. The incorporation of principles of quality management and informatics following the guidelines of ISO 9001, ISO/IEC 15504-2 (information technology - process assessment) and ISO/IEC 12207 (systems and software engineering - software life cycle processes) into an improvement and capability assessment scheme show how the exploitation of interdependencies and trade-offs may enhance the audit outcome. Crowder (2013) contends that the scope of the information security management standard (ISO 27001) should extend beyond the information and communication technology (ICT) domain and highlights the lack of the auditors' readiness in auditing the compliance of an information security management system within a non-IT organization. In a similar vein, the auditors' reluctance to include the IT operations within the scope of management systems' audits is emphasized by Hoy and Foley (2014).

Information, Energy, and Environmental Management

As discussed at the beginning of this section the research on integrated management and information-related systems refers mainly to the integration of information with quality management. However, there are certain authors that discuss the integration of the environmental and the energy management systems with the information systems. It should be clarified, that in this part of the literature there is no specific reference to the information service and/or the information security management standards. Nevertheless, the findings link the integrated adoption of the environmental and energy management systems with an information system or structure of some kind. This linkage directs to the potential implication of the integrated adoption of an information management system. The motivation for the formalization and certification of the information-related activities to a widely recognized and accepted standard and their integration within a broader web of management sub-systems may be a by-product of this discussion yet a desired one.

In this context, Watson, Boudreau and Chen (2010) raise the issue of energy management through an information system when they propose an energy informatics model embedding corporate sustainability criteria, i.e. eco-efficiency, eco-effectiveness and eco-equity, policies, regulations, social and corporate norms. In a similar vein, Elliot (2011) focuses on the environmental sustainability when discussing the transdisciplinary perspectives of environmental management and information technology and introduces the "green IT". It is projected that information technology shall intervene in the process coordination, management, monitoring, modeling, evaluation and reporting of measures to mitigate environmental impacts and allocate resources more efficiently. The proposed conceptual model for the environmental sustainability advances the role of technology- primarily information technology/information systems- as both a mediator in the communications among stakeholders, facilitating integrated activities and as a moderator of stakeholder actions, such as capital management capabilities and other resource-based capabilities. In a municipality case, the use of ICT and knowledge management are incorporated in a model to support an integrated environmental and energy management system (Kostevšek, Petek, Čuček & Pivec 2013).

A different perspective to the integration of information is given by Parker (2013) who studied a case where automated energy measurements carried out by "integrated information systems" and "technical

Figure 1. Information processing flow

diagnostics" outperformed both the environmental management system and the energy management system that were in place. The information systems outputs were directly used by the assigned employees at the operational level with no apparent need for further and more advanced handling of the data. Moreover, the documenting, formalizing and certifying of both management systems did not contribute to the overall performance. Thus, the integration of the management systems seemed less important or even non value adding than the integration of the systems for information and control.

INFORMATION AND MANAGEMENT: CURRENT SITUATION AND TRENDS

Issues, Controversies, Problems

Information and Management Systems Standards

ISO standards facilitate international trade and improve international communication and collaboration (Hudson & Orviska, 2013). Moreover, by formalizing processes and procedures, information costs are reduced. Most of all, the mitigation of information asymmetries is highlighted as the ultimate goal of management systems standards establishment (Heras-Saizarbitoria & Boiral, 2013). In simple words, information technology through the produced information systems receives data in oral or written form, introduces it into a codifying and storing bank and distributes it to the assigned points of delivery. However, information can only then be of use when it is transformed into knowledge, meaning when it is understood, given a context and assimilated within the body of tacit knowledge of employees. At this point a "language" is needed to accomplish the transformation both efficiently and effectively. Standardization bodies intend to play this "translating" role through dedicated standards and norms, such as the information security management and the information technology - service management standards, and eliminate any information asymmetries (Heras-Saizarbitoria & Boiral, 2013). To the other end of the line (see Fig. 1) managers have to acquire the processed and formalized information and use it to establish and maintain the management systems.

Information Standards Uptake

The International Organization for Standardization (ISO) conducts an annual survey on the number of certified organizations to certain management standards. According to the ISO survey data (ISO, 2013) it is evident that the number of ISO 27001 certified organizations is constantly rising (fig. 2). However, the adoption rate of the ISO 27001 and ISO 20000 standards is found significantly lower than the respective uptake of the ISO 9001 and ISO 14001 standards (Cots & Casadesús, 2014). Based on the latest ISO survey data in Table 2 the ISO 27001 standard's certification rate is compared to the corresponding

Figure 2. ISO 27001 certifications (source: ISO, 2013)

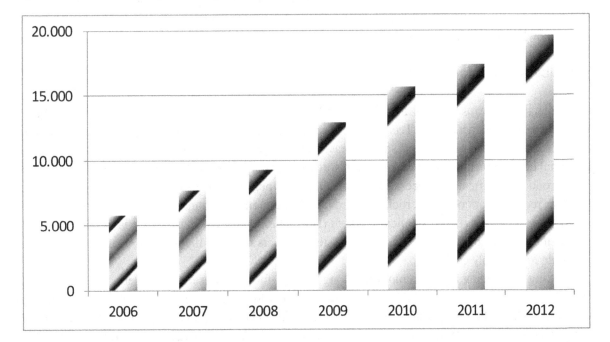

certification rates against the ISO 9001 and the ISO 14001 standards reaching at 1,8% (ISO 27001:ISO 9001) and 6,8% (ISO 27001:ISO 14001) respectively in 2012. Moreover, Cots and Casadesús (2014) emphasize a correlation of the ISO 20000 standard's adoption rate to the technological development in services by identifying small yet technically advanced and service-oriented countries to be ranked among the top fifteen countries adopting the standard.

To better understand the figures, it has to be emphasized, that the information-related standards were first released about two decades later than the quality and a decade later than the environmental standard and their scope have only recently been widened. Unfortunately there is a paucity of data on multiple management systems implementation. To acquire a hint of the proportion of organizations that adopt more than one system standard, with at least one being information-related, Gillies (2011) reports that in a worldwide survey, where 10% of the ISO 27001 certified companies have participated,

Table 3. ISO 9001, ISO 14001 and ISO 27001 certifications and rates (source: own elaboration of ISO survey data)

Year	2006	2007	2008	2009	2010	2011	2012
ISO 9001 certified	896.905	951.486	980.322	1.063.751	1.118.510	1.079.647	1.101.272
increase / decrease rate		6,09	3,03	8,51	5,15	-3,47	2,00
ISO 14001 certified	128.211	154.572	188.574	222.974	251.548	261.957	285.844
increase / decrease rate		20,56	22,00	18,24	12,81	4,14	9,12
ISO 27001 certified	5.797	7.732	9.246	12.935	15.626	17.355	19.577
increase / decrease rate		33,38	19,58	39,90	20,80	11,06	12,80

it was found that around 80% were prior certified to the quality management standard (ISO 9001). This implies that quality management culture fosters information management, since organizations become more "knowledgeable and amenable" (Gillies, 2011).

Traceability and Information

In manufacturing firms, mainly in the food industry, there is a high demand on information-based platforms to ensure traceability. Technologies for managing traceability data are mainly employed for product identification, quality and safety measurements, genetic analysis, environmental monitoring, geospatial data capturing, data exchange, and software development for integrated traceability analysis. In the product identification process, the most common types of capturing data in the food supply chain are paper records, bar codes, microcircuit cards, radio frequency tags and transponders, voice recognition systems, biocoding, and chemical markers (Bosona & Gebresenbet, 2013). It is important to note that the information quality of a traceability system impacts not only the focal company yet spreads to the whole food supply chain.

Tracking and tracing food commodities along the agri-food chain is a requirement of the food safety management standard (ISO 22000), which was launched long after the establishment of the Hazard Analysis of Critical Control Points (HACCP) principles. The ISO 22000 standard complements the HACCP by adding requirements for traceability, communication and emergency preparedness and, thus, assures compatibility of the food safety management standard with the ISO family standards. Moreover, food safety requirements rely on identifying and recording detailed data on microbiological and other potential sources of food contamination hazards. Hence, information systems are needed to provide both the dedicated software solutions, such as predictive microbiology application software, risk assessment software and decision support systems, and the adequately structured approach to facilitate traceability, e.g. "systems that communicate with finance software, business systems and work as an integrated part of production management" (McMeekin et al., 2006).

Integration, Information Management, and Performance

Research on the performance of the integrated management systems and the performance of the integrated audits has progressed. Karapetrovic and Willborn (1998) introduce the concept of an "integrated performance management system". Karapetrovic and Jonker (2003) recommend the establishment of a performance measurement system in parallel with the integration of management systems. Tarí and Molina-Azorin (2010) propose an integration approach of the quality and environmental management systems based on the excellence model of the European Foundation for Quality Management (EFQM), with the four 'results' components may be used as outcome measures of the integrated management system. Garengo and Biazzo (2013) present a performance measurement system based on the Balanced Scorecard.

The Balanced Scorecard is identified by Kumbakara (2008), as well, as the means to align business strategy with IT strategy and highlights the use of information management standards to provide the common "language" for the efficient and effective communication on his quest for monitoring the performance of "managed" (outsourced) information technology services. In a similar vein, Peppard and Ward (2004) contend that information technology has no inherent value by itself and cannot constitute an independent source of sustainable competitive advantage. Thus, they propose the alignment of information systems capability with the organizational performance by interlinking business strategy and operations along with information technology strategy and operations. Furthermore, the relationship between firms' information management practices and their business performance is recognized by both academics and practitioners (Mithas, Ramasubbu & Sambamurthy, 2011). In the framework of an empirical study, Disterer (2012) argues that the ISO 20000 international standard for IT service management offers a normative concept for aligning the performance provided by IT services.

SOLUTIONS AND RECOMMENDATIONS

On the one side, integrated management systems unlike information systems lack so far an internationally established standard against which they could be audited and certified. Instead, they are empirically evaluated according to the integration level of their goals, processes and resources (Karapetrovic, 2002). Information systems, on the other side, lag as regards the holistic managerial perspective which an integrated management system is able to provide for the organization's decision-making process. To address both shortcomings in a balanced and consolidated mode, an integrative framework is composed that incorporates all aspects related to information, both managerial and technological (fig. 2). Within this framework, all standardized management sub-systems including the information security and the information service management modules are fused into a homogenized texture. Apart from the quality and the environmental, other components, such as the occupational health and safety[2] and the energy (according to the ISO 50001:2011 standard) management sub-systems are included. Moreover, the integrated adoption of sector-specific standards, such as the ISO 22000:2005 for food safety and the ISO/TS 16949:2009 specification for the automotive industry, and corporate sustainability standards, such as the social responsibility (ISO 26000:2010) guidance, is compatible to the proposed framework, as well. The assimilation of all interrelated functions is improved by the information systems that are designed to support the mechanisms of recording, coding, processing and auditing the continuous flow of information related to the management modules.

Information systems are used to facilitate performance measurement, as well. Thus, information is leveraged to a management moderator and acts as a catalyst to the integration of all management modules in the same logic that different types and sources of information are integrated within the operations structure of an organization. In the proposed framework, the information service management sub-system (according to the ISO 20000-1:2011 standard) is embedded to address the particular needs of service firms and of those manufacturing firms that provide services of some kind, as well. Hence, it is not included, when solely manufacturing companies are integrating their management sub-systems.

Services and Information Management

At the time the ISO 9000 series was published in the 90's there were certain guidelines accompanying the flagship standard ISO 9001:9004 with the aim to assist organizations operating in specific sectors to adopt and comply with the generic requirements. As such, the ISO 9004-2:1991 guidelines were focused on services. The guidelines' structure was based on a key concept, i.e. the service quality loop, which included the service brief, the design process, service and delivery specification, the quality control, the service delivery, the service result (supplier's/customer's assessment), the service performance analysis and improvement. Standards and management systems have come a long way since then, along with the

Figure 3. The role of information in the integration of management systems

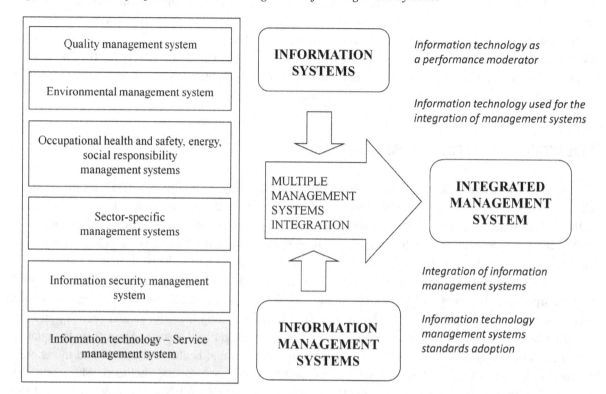

four generic product categories that were then identified, i.e. software, hardware, processed material and service. However, it seems that even nowadays organizations, particularly in non-manufacturing activities, encounter impediments when adopting the generic requirements of the ISO 9001 (Hudson & Orviska, 2013). Moreover, service provision industries, such as the education and health-care, look for a service-dedicated approach to manage their quality, environmental, health and safety and sustainability aspects (Lezcano, Adachihara & Prunie, 2010). To address this need, the scope of the ISO 20000 standard is gradually extended to other types of services different than information technology. Moreover, certain trade-offs take place between a service management standard initially IT-oriented, i.e. the ISO/IEC 20000, and the generic quality management standard (ISO 9001). As such, the integrated adoption of both standards is highlighted as a recommended practice within the service sector (Cots & Casadesús, 2014).

Knowledge Management and Management Systems Performance

As shown above, there is a growing interest in combining the formalized management of information and its related risks (information security management) with the management of sector-generic, such as quality, environment, health and safety and sector-specific disciplines, such as food safety, education, health-care, and hospitality. As regards the distinct management domains, there is an ongoing criticism over the motives and the benefits of standards adoption and management systems implementation and certification, otherwise emphasized as "impression management" (Disterer, 2012). Often organizations adopt standards and undergo certification audits just to signal their quality awareness to their current and potential customers. Within this line of reasoning, many auditors oversee certain indications of low performance level of the management systems, carry out mere conformity audits and keep their customers, namely the auditees, satisfied. However, the auditing of compliance against certain requirements of the reference standards does not guarantee the actual implementation of the management systems' principles, moreover the deepening and spreading of the scope towards the enhancement of the performance of the systems and the organization, in turn.

The internal motivation is claimed to be the critical factor for the meaningful adoption of the management systems standards (Gotzamani & Tsiotras, 2002). Top management has to be really committed and allocate the necessary resources. The employees need to actively participate in the continuous improvement process. In other words, this is defined as internalization, i.e. the in depth penetration and adoption of the standards' requirements into the daily operations by "consciously" using management practices to modify behavior and decision making (Nair & Prajogo, 2009). In a similar vein, Gotzamani & Tsiotras (2002) stress that the "long-term effectiveness and real value of the quality assurance standards is not based on their content and requirements but on the way that companies adopt and implement these requirements. The key for their success is the depth to which a company desires to proceed satisfying their requirements". The internalization concept is by its definition related to both the knowledge and the management systems implementation, since it refers to the "process of absorbing both tacit and explicit information into the organisation and translating it into knowledge, which is then applied to purpose" (Nair & Prajogo, 2009). Knowledge can be either explicit or tacit. Explicit knowledge is the codified information that can be stored and transmitted using formal and systematic means, whilst tacit knowledge is embedded among a system's users through underlying practices in a management system (Nair & Prajogo, 2009). Hence, information is being transformed into knowledge which is then assimilated into the management system. Knowledge management systems use information technology systems to manage organizational knowledge, namely to support and enhance the processes of knowledge creation, storage/retrieval, transfer, and application (Alavi & Leidner, 2001) yet keeping in mind that information technology alone cannot leverage knowledge (McDermott, 1999).

It is claimed that, knowledge management and quality management are considered interdependent, and the absence or insufficiency of one of them may cause the other one to fail (Akdere, 2009). Business excellence frameworks, like the Baldrige Award, increasingly recognize the importance of knowledge, e.g. the MBNQA category "Information and Analysis" was changed to "Measurement, Analysis, and Knowledge Management" (Linderman, Schroeder, Zaheer, Liedtke & Choo, 2004). This category of the Baldrige Award examines how an organization selects, gathers, analyzes, manages and improves its data, information, and knowledge assets and how it manages its information technology. The same category examines how the organization uses review findings to improve its performance (Akdere, 2009). Through this lens, organizations are seen as learning organisms that accumulate information, transform it into knowledge and make decisions. Therefore, "the semiotic link between knowledge and performance is crucial in the success and well-being of the organization" (Akdere, 2009). In the same vein, it is stressed that within normalized management systems information and data transformed into knowledge are used for performance evaluation and improvement and, thus, condition the sustainability of corporate entities (Ejdys & Matuszak-Flejszman, 2010).

FUTURE RESEARCH DIRECTIONS

The purpose of the preceding discussion is to illustrate that integration requires the intertwining of management principles and practices across the organization in an internalized mode. Therefore, a more sophisticated way is needed to manage information and documentation and meet standards' requirements and audits' specifications. However, there is a link missing from the chain connecting the incoming data to the manageable information resources. Data needs to be transferred into a more meaningful and adaptable form. In this context, the concept of knowledge is more comprehensible than ever. The necessity for this concept to be formalized and introduced to the management world is realized by the standardization bodies. So far, two relevant guidance standards have been released, one by the Australian standardization body (AS 5037:2005 – "Knowledge management - a guide") and one by the British Standards Institution (BS PAS 2001:2001 – "Knowledge management - Guide to good practice").

Moreover, both the integration and the internalization of management systems rely on the internally driven commitment of the organization, since there is no "signaling" effect expected. In other words, the lack of an auditable standard not only detaches both processes from the mere objective of certification and external recognition but also demands for a knowledge-based approach to adequately address the extent and the impact of an integrated-internalized management system. To this end, researchers and practitioners in the IT and management fields need to collaborate in order to develop a common "interface". Thus, exchange of knowledge will facilitate organizational learning through more efficient and effective combination of resources, such as standards, guidelines and software. Furthermore, it is anticipated that embedding knowledge in the form of a knowledge management system will enhance the decision making capacity of integrated management systems.

CONCLUSION

This chapter discusses the introduction of information management into a wide spectrum of management disciplines aiming at identifying the possible synergies. Literature on the topic is extremely recent, since the field is in its infancy. How far and at which rate the evolution will take place remains to be seen. Meanwhile, research may lead towards a lean path. From a wider perspective, combining knowledge and expertise may support learning organizations to adopt the best-fit approach to their needs following a general framework identified by the available standards. Thus, the information management standards' uptake will grow in analogy to the adoption rates of the older standards along with the increased awareness of the integrated management's potential. Particularly with regard to the information service management standard, service companies may profit from the advantages that a sector-specific standard has to offer to their advanced management within an integrated framework of quality and other management disciplines. Following this line of reasoning, this chapter introduces a framework to illustrate the integrated management system's synergies with the information management standards' adoption. Furthermore, it is suggested that the subsequent adoption of a knowledge management sub-system into an integrated platform already encompassing information management may multiply the integrated management systems synergistic effect on business performance.

REFERENCES

Abad, J., Lafuente, E., & Vilajosana, J. (2013). An assessment of the OHSAS 18001 certification process: Objective drivers and consequences on safety performance and labour productivity. *Safety Science, 60*, 47–56. doi:10.1016/j.ssci.2013.06.011

Akdere, M. (2009). The role of knowledge management in quality management practices: Achieving performance excellence in organizations. *Advances in Developing Human Resources, 11*(3), 349–361. doi:10.1177/1523422309338575

Alavi, M., & Leidner, D. E. (2001). Review: knowledge management and knowledge management systems: conceptual foundations and research issues. *Management Information Systems Quarterly, 25*(1), 107–136. doi:10.2307/3250961

Alshitri, K. I., & Abanumy, A. N. (2014). Exploring the reasons behind the low ISO 27001 adoption in public organizations in Saudi Arabia. In *Information Science and Applications (ICISA), 2014 International Conference on*. Seoul, Korea: ICISA.

Asif, M., de Bruijn, E. J., Fisscher, O. A. M., Searcy, C., & Steenhuis, H.-J. (2009). Process embedded design of integrated management systems. *International Journal of Quality & Reliability Management, 26*(3), 261–282. doi:10.1108/02656710910936735

Barlette, Y., & Fomin, V. V. (2010). The adoption of information security management standards: A literature review. In I. G. I. Global (Ed.), *Information Resources Management: Concepts* (pp. 69–90). Methodologies, Tools and Applications. doi:10.4018/978-1-61520-965-1.ch104

Beckmerhagen, I. A., Berg, H. P., Karapetrovic, S. V., & Willborn, W. O. (2003). Auditing in support of the integration of management systems: A case from the nuclear industry. *Managerial Auditing Journal, 18*(6/7), 560–568. doi:10.1108/02686900310482696

Bernardo, M., Casadesús, M., Karapetrovic, S., & Heras, I. (2009). How integrated are environmental, quality and other standardized management systems? An empirical study. *Journal of Cleaner Production, 17*(8), 742–750. doi:10.1016/j.jclepro.2008.11.003

Bernardo, M., Casadesús, M., Karapetrovic, S., & Heras, I. (2010). An empirical study on the integration of management system audits. *Journal of Cleaner Production, 18*(5), 486–495. doi:10.1016/j.jclepro.2009.12.001

Bernardo, M., Casadesús, M., Karapetrovic, S., & Heras, I. (2011). Relationships between the integration of audits and management systems - An empirical study. *The TQM Journal, 23*(6), 659–672. doi:10.1108/17542731111175266

Bosona, T., & Gebresenbet, G. (2013). Food traceability as an integral part of logistics management in food and agricultural supply chain. *Food Control, 33*(1), 32–48. doi:10.1016/j.foodcont.2013.02.004

BSI. (2012). Specification of common management system requirements as a framework for integration. *PAS, 99*, 2012.

Cots, S., & Casadesús, M. (2014). *Exploring the Service Management Standard ISO 22000*. Total Quality Management & Business Excellence; doi:10.1080/14783363.2013.856544

Crowder, M. (2013). Quality standards: Integration within a bereavement environment. *The TQM Journal*, *25*(1), 18–28. doi:10.1108/17542731311286405

Disterer, G. (2012). Why firms seek ISO 20000 certification – A study for ISO 20000 adoption. In *Proceedings of the 20th European Conference on Information Systems*. Barcelona, Spain: Academic Press.

Dyllick, T., & Hockerts, K. (2002). Beyond the Business Case for Corporate Sustainability. *Business Strategy and the Environment*, *11*(2), 130–141. doi:10.1002/bse.323

Ejdys, J., & Matuszak-Flejszman, A. (2010). New management systems as an instrument of implementation sustainable development concept at organizational level. *Technological and Economic Development of Economy*, *16*(2), 202–218. doi:10.3846/tede.2010.13

Elliot, S. (2011). Transdisciplinary perspectives on environmental sustainability: A resource base and framework for IT-enabled business transformation. *Management Information Systems Quarterly*, *35*(1), 197–236.

Ferreira, A. L., Machado, R. J., & Paulk, M. C. (2011). Supporting Audits and Assessments in Multimodel Environments: Product-Focused Software Process Improvement. In *Proceedings of the 12th International Conference, PROFES 2011* (LNCS), (*Vol. 6759*, pp. 73-87). Berlin, Germany: Springer doi:10.1007/978-3-642-21843-9_8

Ferreira, A. L., Machado, R. J., & Paulk, M. C. (2011). Supporting Audits and Assessments in Multimodel Environments: Product-Focused Software Process Improvement. In *Proceedings of the 12th International Conference, PROFES 2011* (LNCS) (*Vol. 6759*, pp. 73-87). Berlin, Germany: Springer. doi:10.1007/978-3-642-21843-9_8

Fomin, V. V., de Vries, H. J., & Barlette, Y. (2008). ISO/IEC 27001 information systems security management standard: Exploring the reasons of low adoption. In *Proceedings of the third European Conference on Management of Technology (EuroMOT)*. Nice, France: Academic Press.

Garengo, P., & Biazzo, S. (2013). From ISO quality standards to an integrated management system: An implementation process in SME. *Total Quality Management and Business Excellence*, *24*(3-4), 310–335. doi:10.1080/14783363.2012.704282

Gillies, A. (2011). Improving the quality of information security management systems with ISO27000. *The TQM Journal*, *23*(4), 367–376. doi:10.1108/17542731111139455

Gotzamani, K. D., & Tsiotras, G. D. (2002). The true motives behind ISO 9000 certification: Their effect on the overall certification benefits and long term contribution towards TQM. *International Journal of Quality & Reliability Management*, *19*(2), 151–169. doi:10.1108/02656710210413499

Griffith, A., & Bhutto, K. (2008). Improving environmental performance through integrated management systems (IMS) in the UK. *Management of Environment Quality*, *19*(5), 565–578. doi:10.1108/14777830810894247

Griffith, A., & Bhutto, K. (2009). Better environmental performance: A framework for integrated management systems (IMS). *Management of Environment Quality: An International Journal, 20*(5), 566–580. doi:10.1108/14777830910981230

Heras-Saizarbitoria, I. (2011). Internalization of ISO 9000: An exploratory study. *Industrial Management & Data Systems, 111*(8), 1214–1237. doi:10.1108/02635571111170776

Heras-Saizarbitoria, I., & Boiral, O. (2013). ISO 9001 and ISO 14001: Towards a research agenda on management system standards. *International Journal of Management Reviews, 15*(1), 47–65. doi:10.1111/j.1468-2370.2012.00334.x

Hoy, Z., & Foley, A. (2014). *A structured approach to integrating audits to create organisational efficiencies: ISO 9001 and ISO 27001 audits.* Total Quality Management & Business Excellence; doi:10.1080/14783363.2013.876181

Hudson, J., & Orviska, M. (2013). Firms' adoption of international standards: One size fits all? *Journal of Policy Modeling, 35*(2), 289–306. doi:10.1016/j.jpolmod.2012.04.001

ISO. (2013). *The ISO Survey of Management System Standards Certifications-2012.* Geneva: International Organization for Standardization.

Jonker, J., & Karapetrovic, S. (2004). Systems thinking for the integration of management systems. *Business Process Management Journal, 10*(6), 608–615. doi:10.1108/14637150410567839

Jørgensen, T. H. (2008). Towards more sustainable management systems: Through life-cycle management and integration. *Journal of Cleaner Production, 16*(10), 1071–1080. doi:10.1016/j.jclepro.2007.06.006

Karapetrovic, S. (2002). Strategies for the integration of management systems and standards. *The TQM Magazine, 14*(1), 61–67. doi:10.1108/09544780210414254

Karapetrovic, S. (2003). Musings on integrated management systems. *Measuring Business Excellence, 7*(1), 4–13. doi:10.1108/13683040310466681

Kaziliūnas, A. (2008). Problems of auditing using quality management systems for sustainable development of organizations. *Technological and Economic Development of Economy, 14*(1), 64–75. doi:10.3846/2029-0187.2008.14.64-75

Khanna, H. K., Laroiya, S. C., & Sharma, D. D. (2010). Integrated management systems in Indian manufacturing organizations: Some key findings from an empirical study. *The TQM Journal, 22*(6), 670–686. doi:10.1108/17542731011085339

Kostevšek, A., Petek, J., Čuček, L., & Pivec, A. (2013). Conceptual design of a municipal energy and environmental system as an efficient basis for advanced energy planning. *Energy, 60,* 148–158. doi:10.1016/j.energy.2013.07.044

Kraus, J. L., & Grosskopf, J. (2008). Auditing integrated management systems: Considerations and practice tips. *Environmental Quality Management, 18*(2), 7–16. doi:10.1002/tqem.20202

Kumbakara, N. (2008). Managed IT services: The role of IT standards. *Information Management & Computer Security, 16*(4), 336–359. doi:10.1108/09685220810908778

Lezcano, J.-M., Adachihara, H., & Prunier, M. (2010). Experimenting design and implementation of an educational services management system based on ISO/IEC 20000 standard. In M. Lytras, P. Ordonez De Pablos, D. Avison, J. Sipior, Q. Jin, W. Leal, & D. Horner et al. (Eds.), *Technology enhanced learning. Quality of teaching and educational reform (CCIS 73)* (pp. 55–60). Berlin: Springer. doi:10.1007/978-3-642-13166-0_8

López-Fresno, P. (2010). Implementation of an integrated management system in an airline: A case study. *The TQM Journal*, *22*(6), 629–647. doi:10.1108/17542731011085311

McDermott, R. (1999). Why information systems inspired but cannot deliver knowledge management. *California Management Review*, *41*(4), 103–117. doi:10.2307/41166012

McMeekin, T. A., Baranyi, J., Bowman, J., Dalgaard, P., Kirk, M., Ross, T., & Zwietering, M. H. et al. (2006). Information systems in food safety management. *International Journal of Food Microbiology*, *112*(3), 181–194. doi:10.1016/j.ijfoodmicro.2006.04.048 PMID:16934895

Mesquida, A.-L., & Mas, A. (2015). Integrating IT service management requirements into the organizational management system. *Computer Standards & Interfaces*, *37*, 80–91. doi:10.1016/j.csi.2014.06.005

Mithas, S., Ramasubbu, N., & Sambamurthy, V. (2011). How information management capability influences firm performance. *Management Information Systems Quarterly*, *35*, 237–256.

Nair, A., & Prajogo, D. (2009). Internalisation of ISO 9000 standards: The antecedent role of functionalist and institutionalist drivers and performance implications. *International Journal of Production Research*, *47*(16), 4545–4568. doi:10.1080/00207540701871069

Oskarsson, K., & von Malmborg, F. (2005). Integrated management systems as a corporate response to sustainable development. *Corporate Social Responsibility and Environmental Management*, *12*(3), 121–128. doi:10.1002/csr.78

Othman, M. F. I., & Chan, T. (2013). Barriers to Formal IT Governance Practice - Insights from a Qualitative Study. In *System Sciences (HICSS), 2013 46th Hawaii International Conference on*, (pp.4415-4424). Wailea, HI: IEEE.

Parker, T. (2013). The view from below – a management system case study from a meaning-based view of organization. *Journal of Cleaner Production*, *53*, 81–90. doi:10.1016/j.jclepro.2013.04.002

Peppard, J., & Ward, J. (2004). Beyond strategic information systems: Towards an IS capability. *The Journal of Strategic Information Systems*, *13*(2), 167–194. doi:10.1016/j.jsis.2004.02.002

Rebelo, M., Santos, G., & Silva, R. (2014). Conception of a flexible integrator and lean model for integrated management systems. *Total Quality Management & Business Excellence*, *25*(5-6), 683–701. doi:10.1080/14783363.2013.835616

Rocha, M., Searcy, C., & Karapetrovic, S. (2007). Integrating sustainable development into existing management systems. *Total Quality Management and Business Excellence*, *18*(1-2), 83–92. doi:10.1080/14783360601051594

Salomone, R. (2008). Integrated management systems: Experiences in Italian organizations. *Journal of Cleaner Production*, *16*(16), 1786–1806. doi:10.1016/j.jclepro.2007.12.003

Santos, G., Mendes, F., & Barbosa, J. (2011). Certification and integration of management systems: The experience of Portuguese small and medium enterprises. *Journal of Cleaner Production, 19*(17-18), 1965–1974. doi:10.1016/j.jclepro.2011.06.017

Satolo, E. G., Calarge, F. A., & Cauchick Miguel, P. A. (2013). Experience with an integrated management system in a sugar and ethanol manufacturing unit: Possibilities and limitations. *Management of Environmental Quality: An International Journal, 24*(6), 710–725. doi:10.1108/MEQ-10-2012-0068

Searcy, C., Morali, O., Karapetrovic, S., Wichuk, K., McCartney, D., McLeod, S., & Fraser, D. (2012). Challenges in implementing a functional ISO 14001 environmental management system. *International Journal of Quality & Reliability Management, 29*(7), 779–796. doi:10.1108/02656711211258526

Simon, A., Karapetrovic, S., & Casadesús, M. (2012). Difficulties and benefits of Integrated Management Systems. *Industrial Management & Data Systems, 112*(5), 828–846. doi:10.1108/02635571211232406

Tarí, J. J., & Molina-Azorín, J. F. (2010). Integration of quality management and environmental management systems. *The TQM Journal, 22*(6), 687–701. doi:10.1108/17542731011085348

von Ahsen, A. (2014). The integration of quality, environmental and health and safety management by car manufacturers – a long-term empirical study. *Business Strategy and the Environment, 23*(6), 395–416. doi:10.1002/bse.1791

Watson, R. T., Boudreau, M.-C., & Chen, A. J. (2010). Information systems and environmentally sustainable development: Energy informatics and new directions for the IS community. *Management Information Systems Quarterly, 34*(1), 23–38.

Zeng, S. X., Shi, J. J., & Lou, G. X. (2007). A synergetic model for implementing an integrated management system: An empirical study in China. *Journal of Cleaner Production, 15*(18), 1760–1767. doi:10.1016/j.jclepro.2006.03.007

KEY TERMS AND DEFINITIONS

Corporate Sustainability: A firm's ability to meet the needs of its direct and indirect stakeholders, such as shareholders, employees, clients, pressure groups, communities etc., without compromising its ability to meet the needs of future stakeholders as well (Dyllick & Hockerts, 2002).

Environmental Sustainability: Stakeholder behavior impacting on the natural environment that meets the needs of the present without compromising the ability of future stakeholders to meet their own needs (Elliot, 2011).

Food Traceability: A part of logistics management that captures, stores, and transmits adequate information about a food, feed, food-producing animal or substance at all stages in the food supply chain so that the product can be checked for safety and quality control, traced upward, and tracked downward at any time required (Bosona & Gebresenbet, 2013).

Information System: An integrated and cooperating set of people, processes, software, and information technologies to support individual, organizational, or societal goals (Watson, Boudreau & Chen, 2010)

Integrated Management System: A single set of interconnected processes that share a unique pool of human, information, material, infrastructure and financial resources in order to achieve a composite of goals related to the satisfaction of a variety of stakeholders (Karapetrovic, 2003).

Standard: Within the scope of this chapter a standard or a norm is a composite of requirements that incorporate changes and trends, filter and diffuse the state of the art and guide organizations to adapt to the environmental conditions by adopting the specified requirements.

ENDNOTES

[1]   ISO stands for the International Organization for Standardization and IEC stands for the International Electrotechnical Commission.

[2]   The occupational health and safety management systems are currently audited and certified to a non-ISO standard (OHSAS 18001:2007), which is going to be replaced by the under development ISO 45001:2016 standard.

Chapter 12
Managing Enterprise IT Risks through Automated Security Metrics

Aristeidis Chatzipoulidis
University of Macedonia, Greece

Dimitrios Michalopoulos
University of Macedonia, Greece

Ioannis Mavridis
University of Macedonia, Greece

ABSTRACT

Information systems of modern enterprises are quite complex entities. This fact has influenced the overall information technology (IT) risk profile of the enterprise and it has become all the more critical now to have sound information systems that can maximize business performance of an enterprise. At this point, the practical challenge for enterprises is how to manage enterprise IT risks for persistent protection of business and security goals. This chapter covers different aspects of managing enterprise IT risks, providing solutions in terms of risk management methods, automated security metrics and vulnerability scoring methods. The purpose is to introduce an in-depth study on enterprise IT risks and add value to enterprise sustainability through an extensive analysis of methods and automated security specifications.

INTRODUCTION

Information Technology (IT) risk is ambiguous and modern enterprise environments are no exception. Historically, the field of IT risk management has been dominated by theoretical discussions, practical misfits and indecipherable algorithms all of them adding to complexity and little in essence. Recent corporate failures, such as the collapse of Lehman Brothers which caused severe consequences including economic turndown and an extended systemic risk in every sector or industry, reveal the failure to identify and manage risk at an enterprise level.

DOI: 10.4018/978-1-4666-8841-4.ch012

Figure 1. Evolution of IT risk management

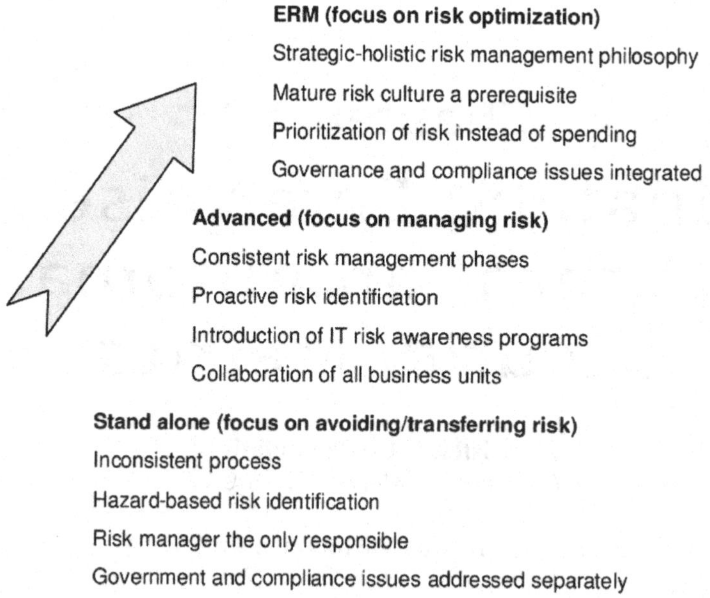

ERM (focus on risk optimization)

Strategic-holistic risk management philosophy

Mature risk culture a prerequisite

Prioritization of risk instead of spending

Governance and compliance issues integrated

Advanced (focus on managing risk)

Consistent risk management phases

Proactive risk identification

Introduction of IT risk awareness programs

Collaboration of all business units

Stand alone (focus on avoiding/transferring risk)

Inconsistent process

Hazard-based risk identification

Risk manager the only responsible

Government and compliance issues addressed separately

Fact is that enterprise IT risk management has evolved but to what extent? Evolution reveals that first attempts on managing risks on enterprises started as isolated and stand-alone process before becoming fully integrated with the business processes. Figure 1 demonstrates the evolution of risk management.

First, there was the philosophy that risk should be avoided at all costs. This notion was supported by the fact that the majority of enterprises transferred business and IT risk to third party insurance companies. This notion became quickly outdated since business community started to realize that managing IT enterprise risk is not an individual responsibility and transferring risk is not a viable option. Therefore, enterprises started to align IT risk management as part of business activities with sight of managing risk rather than avoiding it. This brought up the need for IT security awareness programs and training as well as involvement of all business units. However, there were missing parts, such as governance and compliance issues. Towards this perspective, the term Enterprise Risk Management (ERM) emerged to address the limitations of previous notions, such as static risk management procedures and the need to include governance and compliance issues into a unified approach (Hampton, 2015).

Developing effective risk management strategies requires the collection of data from various stakeholders from the enterprise's environment. In turn, stakeholders started to communicate an enterprise IT risk management philosophy as means to nurture a risk-oriented culture capable to add value to the enterprise and become a proactive solution to IT risks. Towards this perspective, stakeholders should develop a high level of competence reflecting the skills and know-how to perform assigned tasks (Hoyt & Liebenberg, 2011).

Delegation is vital for a more organized and decentralized decision-making however, at the same time, this may increase the number of undesired events and affect the internal environment if individuals are not accountable for their actions. In this regard, segregation of duties (SoD) is considered a key component to maintain a strong internal control environment because it delegates responsibility to those individuals capable to accomplish a task and avoid a fraudulent activity (Taylor, 2014).

As a result, Enterprise IT risk management principal aim is to focus on enterprise objectives, resources optimization and manage IT-related risks. Following the evolution of IT risk management in an enterprise environment, the main objectives of this chapter are as follows:

1. Decompose enterprise IT risk into areas of attention.
2. Describe enterprise IT risk management essentials.
3. Review and compare IT risk management approaches tailored to suit modern enterprise environments.
4. Present and classify automated security specifications, in terms of Security Content Automation Protocol (SCAP) and similar, as means to manage the security content of enterprise information systems.
5. Develop a state of the art research review on reputed vulnerability scoring methods as means to aid in vulnerability management for enterprise information systems.

DECOMPOSING ENTERPRISE IT RISK

Successful ERM requires a solid grasp of what is happening within and outside the enterprise. COSO defines ERM (COSO, 2004) as "a process, affected by an entity's board of directors, management and other personnel, applied in a strategy setting and across the enterprise, designed to identify potential events that may affect the entity, and manage risk to be within its risk appetite, to provide reasonable assurance regarding the achievement of entity goals".

ERM objectives are as follows: a) satisfy various stakeholders' values, b) surpass static risk methodologies, c) increase transparency of operations and d) add value and communicate decision making across the organization. Sound examples, such as General Motors, Lewis and Wal-Mart, use ERM initiatives to strengthen governance processes via the internal audit function. Organizations have the opportunity to gain a competitive advantage by using compliance efforts to build balance controls that are sustainable and add long term value to the organizational structure (Grace et al., 2014; Lam, 2014).

Addressing enterprise risk holistically is not trivial. Consequently, this raises major questions such as *what risks need to be controlled and how can enterprise sustainability be achieved*? The first part of the question lies on decomposing the nature of enterprise risk into other types of risks that are all considered as IT-related risks. Figure 2 illustrates how enterprise risk is decomposed into other types of risk and a brief description follows in bullets.

- *Strategic* risks are mainly associated with the board of directors and management decisions. Factors affecting strategic risks are summarized as follows: a) planning and investment decisions, b) design, delivery and pricing of services and products, c) competition issues, d) third party/outsourcing agreements and d) customer support services.
- *Credit* risks derive from the inability of counterparties to meet financial obligations. Factors usually affecting credit risks are summarized as follows: a) changes in interest rates, b) political instability, c) economic environment, d) liquidity issues and financial institutions ability to provide loans at low interest rates.
- *Reputational* risks involve issues related to public opinion and to actions that create and promote negative public relationships. Increased reputational risks impair customer relationships and also damage profits and competitive position. Factors affecting reputational risk are summarized as

Figure 2. Decomposition of enterprise risk

follows: a) loss of trust due to unauthorized activity on customer accounts, b) failure to deliver marketing plans, c) increased customer complaints and d) hacking on an enterprise website.

- *Market* risks derive from the industry and competition within which the enterprise operates. Factors affecting market risks are summarized as follows: a) market recessions, b) terrorist attacks, c) political instability, d) mergers and acquisitions, e) changes in demographic and customer profile and f) currency changes.

- *Outsourcing* risks derives from third party dependencies and services agreements. While enterprise outsourcing may provide a number of advantages such as cost benefits and optimization of in-house activities, this also becomes a great source of other risks including strategic, reputation, compliance, operational, exit strategy and systemic risk. Factors affecting market risks are summarized as follows: a) incomplete third party contracts, b) inability to comply with third party regulatory environment and c) reputation of the partner.

- *Compliance* risk emerges from violations or non-conformity with laws, regulations, practices or ethical standards. Non-compliance has serious consequences including financial penalties, damage to reputation, rating downgrades and removal of authority to operate. Factors affecting compliance risk are summarized as follows: a) staff expertise in following specific policies, b) regulatory requirement within the industry the enterprise operates, c) internal and external audit results and d) third party dependencies.

- *Operational* risk derives from inadequate or failed processes, people, or systems affecting the enterprises' ability to deliver products and services. This type of risk has a direct impact on customer

Table 1. High level risk management phases

Phase	Brief Description
Identification	Requires collecting data from decomposing enterprise risk based on risk scenario analysis
Assessment	Requires analyzing risk, taking into consideration the business relevance of risk factors
Monitoring	Requires maintaining a risk profile as an inventory of threats, vulnerabilities and their attributes, as well as monitoring their status over time

services. Factors affecting operational risk are summarized as follows: a) internal and external fraud, b) lack of training and misuse of confidential information, c) business disruption and damage to physical assets.

- *Information Security (IS)* risk derives from threats exploiting vulnerabilities that reside in an information infrastructure of an enterprise. Every information infrastructure is composed from enterprise information systems, such as hardware, software and applications. Factors affecting IS risk are summarized as follows: a) human participation, b) evolution of technology, c) misconfigurations of settings, d) adequacy of controls and e) Loss in security properties, namely confidentiality, integrity and availability (CIA).

ENTERPRISE IT RISK MANAGEMENT ESSENTIALS

All aforementioned IT-related risks require proper management in order to be controlled and minimized. For the process of enterprise IT risk management to be effective, requires the cohesion of three high level phases namely identification, assessment and monitoring. Table 1 describes the phases.

The *first phase* is to identify IT-related risks. A core approach to risk identification is the use of risk scenarios as means to decompose the complex nature of enterprise IT risk. A risk scenario can be described as the happening of an event that can lead to a business impact, if and when it occurs. In practice, the combination of generic and customized risk scenarios is the preferable solution to identifying risk. Figure 3 illustrates an indicative list of components that synthesize risk scenarios.

Ideally, risk scenarios should include threats and vulnerabilities of current and future conditions including trends in technology, compliance and governance requirements as well as changes in the business environment. The realism of risk scenarios depend heavily on the recognition and importance of risk factors. Risk factors are the conditions that shape the likelihood and impact of risk scenarios. Table 2 depicts indicative risk factors that affect risk scenarios.

After building a list of risk scenarios, the *second* phase is the assessment of risk scenarios. This means that analysis should be conducted in terms of likelihood and impact each scenario might have on enterprise goals. Towards this endeavour, risk practitioners use either qualitative or quantitative risk analysis.

Qualitative risk analysis is based on a scale of comparative values, such as low, medium, high or on numeric scale such as 1 to 10, to reveal the criticality of risk. This kind of analysis is based on subjective judgment and personal experience rather than on monetary values or statistical data. The aim is to provide an easy-to-understand result and is basically used to evaluate intangible assets such as reputation or image recognition. Typical qualitative methods include scorecards, likelihood - impact matrix,

Figure 3. Factors affecting risk scenarios

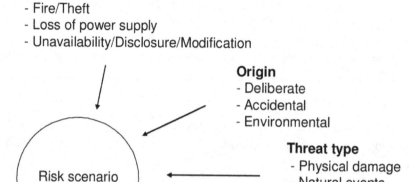

Threat event
- Fire/Theft
- Loss of power supply
- Unavailability/Disclosure/Modification

Origin
- Deliberate
- Accidental
- Environmental

Risk scenario

Threat type
- Physical damage
- Natural events
- Compromise of information

Actor
- Internal (staff)
- External (business partner, competitor)

Asset
- People
- Process
- Information
- Hardware/Software
- Network

Time
- Duration
- Time of occurrence (critical/non critical)
- Time to respond (lag)

Delphi forecasting and failure modes and effects analysis (FMEA). Table 3 demonstrates the pros and cons of using qualitative analysis.

On the other hand, quantitative risk analysis is based on numerical and statistical techniques to calculate risk. This measure produces more precise results in financial terms and is highly recommended when a cost-benefit analysis of controls is required. However, challenges such as the desired data format or standardized historical data are not always available for analysis. Typical quantitative methods are the internal loss data, business process modelling (BPM) and statistical analysis methods. Table 4 demonstrates the pros and cons of using quantitative risk analysis.

Table 2. Risk factors

External	Internal
Market/economic status	Organizational structure
Rate of change	Complexity of information infrastructure
Industry/competition	Maturity of organizational culture towards risk
Geopolitical situation	Risk management philosophy
Regulatory environment	Business model
Technology trends	Change management capability

Table 3. Pros and Cons of qualitative analysis

Pros	Cons
Low cost	Subjectivity/Bias
Easy to understand	Unsuitable for cost-benefit analysis
Consensus-based	Fuzzy ranking
Suitable for intangible assets	Low validity

Recently, there is an increased interest on hybrid methods that combine both quantitative and qualitative analysis. Therefore, semi-quantitative/qualitative methods classify risk using a combination of numerical values (Nikolic & Ruzic-Dimitrijevic, 2009). Usually, this type of analysis starts with qualitative measurement based on opinions and follows with quantitative analysis of data.

The *third* phase includes risk monitoring as means to control and maintain the performance of enterprise IT systems. This phase requires risk indicators to monitor business activities. This implies that risk thresholds should be clearly defined to address the acceptable levels of risk the enterprise is willing to accept and manage. Each enterprise varies in risk appetite and tolerance hence; risk thresholds should be based on strategic orientation, on the size and complexity of information infrastructure and the type of market in which the enterprise operates. Risk thresholds are supported by risk indicators that act as warnings to exceeding risks. Factors influencing the selection of risk indicators are depicted in Table 5.

When risk exceeds pre-defined thresholds, a risk indicator triggers a warning that enables stakeholders to take appropriate actions. In this respect, stakeholders should decide what controls should put in place

Table 4. Pros and Cons of quantitative analysis

Pros	Cons
Precision of results	Time-consuming
Statistically reliable results (objectivity)	Data collection in the desired format is a challenge
Allows for cost-benefit analysis	Increased cost
Provides anonymity of results	Requires higher staff expertise

Table 5. Factors influencing the selection of risk indicators

Factors	Brief Description
Stakeholders	Risk indicators are selected from stakeholders to ensure that satisfy business goals and security requirements
Balance	A balance of indicators include: - Lag indicators (post-indication of risk) - Lead indicators (preventive indicators) - Trend indicators (analyzing trends and insights)
Root cause	The effectiveness of indicators depend on the capability to trace the root cause of events, not just the consequences
Cost-benefit	Indicators should be based on a cost benefit analysis in order to optimize security spending and maximize business performance

Table 6. Enterprise controls

Control Category	Brief Description
Compensating	Controls designed to make up for the weakness in an existing control structure of the enterprise Example: Adding an additional verification procedure in an existing weak access control mechanism
Corrective	Controls designed to remediate errors after detection Example: Back up and restore procedures
Detective	Controls designed to provide warnings of attempted violations Example: Intrusion detection methods
Deterrent	Controls designed to deter a potential compromise Example: Login screens
Directive	Controls designed to direct the behaviour within the enterprise operates Example: Policies
Preventive	Controls designed to inhibit violation of a security policy Example: Access control methods

in order to remediate risks. The term "enterprise control" describes the set of policies, procedures and behaviour designed to mandate the operation of an enterprise by specifying what actions are, or are not, permitted (Lam, 2014). Table 6 describes the most common enterprise control categories.

Controls' effectiveness significantly influences the enterprises' risk profile. Therefore, the mix and importance of controls will be unique for each enterprise. In order to maximize the operability of controls, the risk practitioner must ensure that controls are properly managed throughout the various phases in the control life cycle. Figure 4 shows the phases of the control life cycle and each phase is briefly described.

- **Select:** The selection of enterprise controls depend on factors such as a) total cost of ownership (TCO), b) time constraints, c) personnel expertise, d) business priorities and e) security requirements.
- **Design and Develop:** This phase has to consider the "breadth" and "depth" of controls. The term "breadth" corresponds to the flow of information across multiple applications and "depth" corresponds to the different layers on which controls apply, as well as the dependence of a control to the operation of other controls.
- **Testing and Implementation:** Control effectiveness can be assessed by quantitative and qualitative testing to determine how well the control objectives are satisfied. Criteria that can be used to test and implement enterprise controls are, but not limited to, control sustainability, scalability, customizability, performance measures, interaction with other controls, complexity and return on investment.

Figure 4. Control life cycle phases

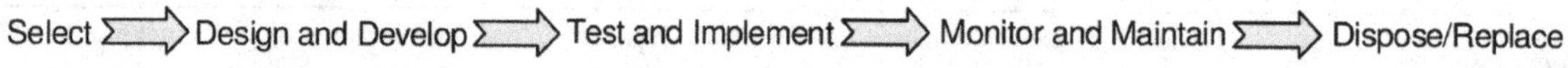

Select $\Longrightarrow$ Design and Develop $\Longrightarrow$ Test and Implement $\Longrightarrow$ Monitor and Maintain $\Longrightarrow$ Dispose/Replace

- **Monitor and Maintain:** This phase includes monitoring the performance of an enterprise through control and reporting on the effectiveness of controls as individual enterprise units. Controls should be updated regularly to maintain secure operation according to vendors' configuration.
- **Dispose/Replace:** The enterprise is responsible for ensuring that only the necessary controls are in place to monitor the status of an enterprise. In this respect, control effectiveness and cost benefit analysis should be conducted regularly to ensure whether a particular control is operational and sustainable at the time of the analysis. Optimization of resources requires that an enterprise utilizes controls that are perceived justifiable in monetary terms and satisfy business and security goals.

ERM LITERATURE REVIEW

Mathrani & Mathrani (2013), examined enterprise risk management (ERM) from the perspective of enterprise IT systems, such as software applications from Oracle and SAS. Authors concluded that such systems improve organizational efficacy and manage risks through analysis and reporting. Authors, based on a qualitative research methodology concluded that enterprise IT systems functionalities extend from an ordinary activity to decision making.

Tekathen & Dechow (2013), studied how ERM can lead to accountability. The study, based on COSO principles about ERM, observes that implementation of an ERM practice does not necessarily ensure organizational risk management. Authors argue that ERM does not minimize uncertainty but sometimes creates more. In terms of personal responsibility to risk management, authors suggest that there should be a clear distinction between local and global processes.

In addition, Caron et al., (2013) examined ERM from a process mining perspective. This study explores on the applicability of process mining techniques, such as fuzzy and heuristics miner, as means to support the activities related to the different phases of risk management such as identification, assessment and monitoring. Authors demonstrate the process of data mining based on Belgian practices from the insurance industry and conclude that analysis of internal data over external data can offer more reliable and less biased information for the ERM functions.

Research from Quon et al., (2012), focused on whether enterprise risk management affects enterprise performance. Authors claim that ERM has been examined in the context of governance and internal control but the relationship to enterprises' performance has yet to be established. Taking into consideration the current financial crisis, the study concludes that an ERM concept did not predict or affect significantly business performance.

Arnold et al., (2011) focused on the role of strategic ERM towards easing regulatory compliance. The study examines whether ERM processes can react to regulatory mandates, under the SOX 404 internal control reporting requirements. Research findings, based on 113 executive responses, reveal that strong ERM processes can smooth the implementation of SOX mandates, increase organizational flexibility and IT integration.

Moreover, Saleh & Alfantookh (2011) proposed an information security (IS), risk management framework as means to offer a holistic approach to enterprise security. This framework consists of two structural and two procedural dimensions which include the scope, assessment criteria, process and assessment tools. The highlights of the framework include the STOPE (strategy, technology, organization, people, and environment) approach and the six-sigma DMAIC (define, measure, analyze, improve, and control) cycle.

Gordon et al., (2009) suggested that for a holistic approach towards managing risk in an enterprise, the concept of ERM is required. The study is based on a sample of more than 100 US organizations and concludes that ERM should work in conjunction with the variables that affect enterprises' performance. This performance is comprised of five factors namely environmental uncertainty, industry competition, firm size, firm complexity, and board of directors' monitoring.

Arena et al., (2010) focused on the organizational dynamics of ERM. Authors suggest that ERM is capable to organize uncertainty taking into consideration organizational dynamics in the form of control, accountability and decision making. Based on a 7 year period study, authors conclude that the rise of ERM has led to the emergence of a) Chief Risk Officer (CRO), b) internal audit function, c) different actors that induce uncertainty and d) governance and compliance issues.

IT RISK MANAGEMENT METHODS

This section aim is to assist the implementation of a proper method within the context of enterprise environment. Generally, an effective IT risk management process should be based on well-defined steps, from identification to mitigation, underpin all enterprise activities and follow a formal governance process. According to literature (Koons & Minoli, 2010; Landoll, 2006; Strecker et al., 2011; Wheeler, 2011), most common challenges existing risk management methods share are summarized in the following bullets.

- **Disparity of risk terminology.** It is common that every method, technique, standard or other tend to differentiate. This differentiation includes inventories of assets, vulnerabilities, threats and controls.
- **Complex (inter)operability.** The majority of methods are deemed too complex to be deployed in real terms. Moreover, the lack of interoperability usually derives from qualitative risk analysis methods that lack the accuracy to compare results with other methods due to ambiguous risk scales.
- **Lack of a holistic approach.** Most methods focus on the technical side of risk, such as risk analysis, leaving aside governance and compliance issues which imply that risk methods lack of unified approach to enterprise risk management.

To confront the challenges, eleven risk management approaches, in terms of eight evaluation criteria, are compared. Key requirements for each criterion are presented in the following bullets. A short description of the IT risk management methods is provided after the criteria analysis.

- **Risk identification.** The key requirements are as follows:
  ○ Identify and anticipate assets, threats and vulnerabilities
  ○ Set the risk appetite and determine the level of acceptable risk
  ○ Adopt a common risk language as means to nurture an enterprise risk culture and foster communication
  ○ Identify compliance requirements
- **Risk assessment.** The key requirements are as follows:
  ○ Analyze and prioritize risks
  ○ Indicate the relationship among risks (dependencies)

- ○ Incorporate opinions from various stakeholders
- ○ Evaluate past data incidents
- **Risk monitoring.** The key requirements are as follows:
- ○ Implement risk indicators
- ○ Tracking the source of risk
- ○ Engage key stakeholders
- ○ Reporting
- **Risk mitigation.** The key requirements are as follows:
- ○ Induce risk responses
  - ▪ Avoid
  - ▪ Reduce
  - ▪ Share/transfer
  - ▪ Accept
- ○ Justification of controls (cost-benefit)
- ○ Accountability of controls
- **Compliance.** The key requirements are as follows:
- ○ Provide evidence of compliance
- ○ Justify compliance financially
- ○ Enable measurement of compliance
- ○ Integrate compliance with business and security goals
- ○ Educate personnel/allocate responsibilities
- **Complexity.** The key requirements are as follows:
- ○ Usable and repeatable results
- ○ Time to learn and adapt to the method
- ○ Easy to use
- ○ Add practical value to the enterprise operation
- **Interoperability.** The key requirements are as follows:
- ○ Allow synergy with other methods
- ○ Consider PEST factors
- ○ Support a common risk terminology
- **Governance.** The key requirements are as follows:
- ○ Align accountability to different stakeholders
- ○ Specify roles and individual responsibilities
- ○ Provide strategic direction through decision-making
- ○ Enable protection and enlargement of stakeholder value
- ○ Focus on resource management

OCTAVE (Operationally Critical Threat, Asset, and Vulnerability Evaluation)

OCTAVE (OCTAVE, 2003) is an engineering-oriented, risk management technique which aims to support business goals and security priorities by a) identifying critical assets, b) assessing risks to critical assets and based on the assessment it c) provides adequate reasoning about decision making. The approach is context-driven and self-directed requiring a small interdisciplinary team to perform the gathering, analysis of results and recommendations on risk management strategies. OCTAVE uses for analysis catalogs of information known as OCTAVE criteria. The catalogs are an inventory of best security practices, threat profiles and vulnerabilities. OCTAVE provides spreadsheets to support its process through a three-phase approach. Particularly, phase 1 includes asset-based threat profiles development (organizational evaluation), phase 2 includes identification of infrastructure vulnerabilities (information infrastructure evaluation) and phase 3 the development of security strategy and plans (risk prioritization). The next generation is the OCTAVE Allegro (Caralli et al., 2007), a method suitable for enterprises with a limited investment in terms of time, human resources, and other resources.

COBIT (Control Objectives for Information and Related Technology)

COBIT 4.1 (IT Governance Institute, 2007) and recently announced fifth version, is a process reference model for business and IT – related goals. Based on clear metrics, the model allows data collection based on the risk appetite and tolerance of an enterprise. The fifth version is composed from distinct processes that are split into two dimensions: a) enabler dimension and b) enabler performance management. The first dimension involves issues and processes about a) stakeholders, b) achievement of goals, c) control life cycle and d) recommended security practices. The second dimension involves the metrics and processes that allow the measuring of the first dimension. COBIT 5 provides a complete basis for an audit, compliance, and governance mindset such as that found in the financial services sector. COBIT allows interoperability with COSO, an internal control framework for enterprises.

CRAMM (CCTA Risk Assessment and Management Methodology)

CRAMM version 5 (British CCTA, 2003) is an advanced risk analysis method which is supported by the Central Communication and Telecommunication Agency (CCTA). The method is composed of a tool (aka CRAMM tool) which performs the risk assessment. The risk assessment based on input of data, such as asset identification, analyzes the security infrastructure with asset dependency modelling and business impact analysis. The assessment of risk leads to a recommendation of controls. CRAMM is compliant with ISO 27001:2005 a standard that defines requirements for an Information Security Management System (ISMS). CRAMM also provides a cost-benefit analysis based on estimated cost of controls.

ISO/IEC 27005

ISO 27005 (ISO/IEC 27005:2008) is a risk management standard, revised as ISO/IEC 27005:2011, which provides guidelines about the risk management phases. The standard has normative references the ISO/IEC 27001:2005 and ISO/IEC 27002:2005, referring to security requirements and codes of practice respectively. ISO 27005 offers advice on risk identification, analysis and assessment, and remediation in terms of risk treatment to all kinds of enterprises. It recommends qualitative risk analysis in terms of risk matrices as well as inventories for asset, vulnerability and threat.

ISAMM (Information Security Assessment and Monitoring Method)

ISAMM (ISAMM, 2002) is a quantitative method for identifying, assessing and supporting decision making about controls and risks. ISAMM consists of four phases namely: a) the scope of the assessment which includes identification of assets, threats and controls, b) assessment of compliance (vulnerability) and threats, c) validation of compliance and threats and d) analysis and reporting. The method provides realistic improvement simulation and residual risk evaluation. Moreover, it allows compliance with ISO 27001 and the analysis is based on monetary metrics such as annual loss expectancy (ALE) and return on investment (ROI).

FRAP (Facilitated Risk Assessment Process)

FRAP (Petlier, 2000) is a business-led, qualitative risk assessment process. The method allows for a) threat identification, b) likelihood of threat and impact evaluation, c) risk level determination and d) controls' recommendation. FRAP does not identify assets in terms of asset inventory but on threats' materialization. However, this implies that the risk assessment of a threat is calculated based on a defined asset. The process itself uses concepts derived from ISO/IEC Technical Report 13335-3:1998 which is a standard referring to techniques for the management of IT security. The process is established via a framework which shows how to prepare the risk assessment approach.

ETSI TVRA (European Telecommunication Standardization Institute Threat Vulnerability and Risk Analysis)

This method (European Telecommunications Standards Institute, 2006) uses qualitative analysis in the form of risk matrices to determine the risk. TVRA consists of 7 distinct phases: a, b) identification of security properties and requirements, c) identification of assets through an asset inventory, d-e) classification of vulnerabilities and threats and evaluation of likelihood and impact, f) determination of risks and g) countermeasures guidance. In 2010, an advance method consisting of 10 phases is introduced. TVRA allows interaction with ISO 15408, a standard also known as Common Criteria, an IT security evaluation methodology for systems and products.

NIST SP 800-39

This is special publication from the National Institute of Standards and Technology (NIST, 2011) which outlines the need for integrated, organization-wide risk management. It describes risk as a strategic capability that entails compliance and governance to fulfil the risk management process. This publication allows interoperability with other NIST and ISO publication such as NIST SP 800-37, a guide for applying the risk management framework to Federal information systems and ISO/IEC 27005 a risk management standard. The publication highlights include a) stakeholder accountability b) a proposed Risk Management Framework (RMF) and c) outsourcing relationships.

MAGERIT (Methodology for Information Systems Risk Analysis and Management)

MAGERIT (2006) is a Spanish standard, structured based on ISO 31000 and recommended for use by government agencies. MAGERIT v2, published in 2005, consists of three books a) the methodology itself, b) an inventory of criteria and risk modelling, c) risk analysis techniques. The method proposes a holistic approach to risk management along with awareness and training, operation and change management, incidents reporting and audit certification. There is no specified compliance with a certain standard however; the method is recognized from the Organization for Economic Cooperation and Development (OECD) which includes good practices for internal controls, ethics and compliance. Recently, MAGERIT updated in its version 3 in 2012 (in Spanish) to manage e-government principles.

PTA (Practical Threat Analysis)

PTA technologies (2005), build a threat modelling methodology which enables users to find the most cost-effective countermeasures to secure critical assets. The key point is the PTA libraries which are inventories consisting of pre-defined assets, threats, vulnerabilities and controls. PTA libraries allow compliance with standards such as ISO 27001 and 27002 and PCI Data Security Standard 1.1 (2010). The PTA threat model consists of four distinct phases namely a, b) identifying assets and vulnerabilities, c) countermeasure cost-benefit analysis and d) building threat scenarios and mitigation plans. The highlight of the methodology the cost-benefit analysis of controls which implies that the purpose is to ensure the information infrastructure has the most sustainable combination of controls.

ISO 31000

ISO 31000 (ISO 31000:2009) belongs to the ISO family and is dedicated to generic risk management. It defines risk management as an architecture that is used to handle risk. It proposes a risk management framework that comprises of foundations and organizational arrangements. The former include policy, objectives mandates and commitment and the latter includes relationships and accountabilities towards risk management. The standard outlines the need for a risk-based attitude and provides guidelines on monitoring risks however; the theoretical and generic base of this standard does not allow for a detailed guide in an IT domain and lacks the notion of monitoring risks. The interoperability of this standard is limited to the ISO/IEC Guide 73, which a risk management vocabulary. Another issue is governance which is partially analyzed only from the perspective of stakeholder commitment and generic policies.

Interpreting Table 7, FRAP scores partial in the identification criterion because it does not contain a stand alone asset inventory. However, the threat evaluation is conducted with an asset under consid-

Table 7. Risk management methods comparison (✓ = yes, / = partial, x = no)

Approaches	OCTAVE	COBIT	CRAMM	ISO 27005	ISAMM	FRAP	TVRA	NIST 800-39	MAGERIT	PTA	ISO 31000
Criteria											
Identification	✓	✓	✓	✓	✓	/	✓	✓	✓	✓	✓
Assessment	✓	✓	✓	✓	✓	✓	✓	✓	✓	✓	✓
Monitoring	x	✓	/	/	✓	x	/	✓	✓	✓	x
Mitigation	/	✓	✓	✓	✓	✓	/	✓	✓	✓	/
Compliance	✓	✓	✓	✓	✓	✓	✓	✓	✓	✓	x
Complexity	x	/	x	x	/	x	x	x	x	x	x
Interoperability	/	✓	/	x	✓	/	✓	✓	/	✓	/
Governance	x	✓	/	x	x	x	x	✓	✓	/	/

eration. In addition, OCTAVE entails a risk assessment process which allows cause and effect relationships, however; does not include stand-alone governance initiatives. Moreover, COBIT appears to offer a more holistic approach to ERM in terms of audit and governance initiatives however, due to the degree of customization required, the complexity to deploy COBIT may be overwhelming for small to medium enterprises (SMEs).

Without doubt, there is no such thing as a perfect risk management method. Each one is recognized for a particular domain, e.g. ISAMM for the quantitative analysis. Therefore, each enterprise, based on business and security requirements, should adapt a risk approach tailored to satisfy such requirements.

SCAP SPECIFICATIONS

This section emphasizes on automated security specifications from the Security Content Automation Protocol (SCAP) 1.2 version (Waltermire et al., 2011). The aim is to increase interoperability among enterprise information systems and manage security content homogeneously. Roussey et al., (2010), defines interoperability as the information systems' ability to share information and other applications. On this basis, SCAP allows information exchange, from asset identification to policy checking, in a uniform and automated process. Using SCAP, an enterprise is liable to relate data on a one-to-one relationship among enterprise IT systems and thereby, accelerate data analysis. In the following bullets, specifications from SCAP 1.2v are briefly described.

- **CVE (Common Vulnerabilities and Exposures):** Information security is often seen as a fast-pace race between hackers, that try to exploit vulnerability in an information system, and vendors that try to correct such vulnerabilities through the use of patches and updates. The CVE specification, supported by MITRE, contains for each vulnerability a) an identity (e.g. CVE-2003-0818), b) a standard description for a vulnerability (e.g. default password enables remote command execution) or an exposure (e.g. improper settings in an operating system), and c) references to other standards (e.g. OVAL - ID).
- **CCE (Common Configuration Enumeration):** An effort similar to the CVE is the CCE specification. This assigns a unique identifier for a security configuration that conforms to NIST policies. Currently, the focus of CCE is on software platform configuration. Each configuration issue gets an identity consisting of a) a number (e.g. CCE-1234-123), b) a description (e.g. operating system) c) conceptual parameters (e.g. specifications and settings), d) technical mechanisms for a given configuration issue (e.g. availability and download of an update), e) references to reports, tools or documents that support in more detail the configuration issue under consideration (e.g. OVAL - ID).
- **CPE (Common Platform Enumeration):** This specification describes the characteristics of a platform (hardware, system software and applications) into a unique collection of components (e.g. cpe://microsoft:windows:2000). The aim is to foster automation towards platform identification for vulnerability or configuration issues. CPE uniform naming specification encourages community members to generate names for existing and emerging information infrastructure platforms in a consistent and formal manner.
- **CVSS (Common Vulnerability Scoring System):** The CVSS is a standardized scoring method for software vulnerabilities. It features three measurement groups: a) Base (obligatory), describes

the fundamental characteristics of vulnerability that are constant over time, b) Temporal (optional), describes characteristics that vary in time and c) Environmental (optional), describes characteristics that relate to the user interface. The CVSS Severity Score formula produces a score as a decimal number ranging from 0 to 10 where the value 0 means vulnerability is impossible to exploit and value 10.0 means vulnerability easy to exploit. The National Vulnerability Database (NVD) supports CVSS scoring under each CVE identifier.

- **XCCDF (Extensible Configuration Checklist Description Format):** An XCCDF document is a structured collection of rules for system configuration in the form of security checklists. The aim is to support automated policy compliance. Each list is described in a XML format and is used to examine whether or not a system is vulnerable to a particular type of attack. The primary audience of the XCCDF specification is government, industry security analysts and product developers. XCCDF goals are to a) generate documentation and reporting, b) express policy-aware configuration rules, c) compliance checking, d) enable content customization, and e) perform as a vulnerability scanner.

- **OVAL (Open Vulnerability and Assessment Language):** OVAL is a method for performing structured tests for reporting purposes. The aim is to conduct tests to check if the values of a system (e.g. registry key) satisfy the security policies of XCCDF. OVAL uses XML format for storing system configuration information in local systems. The actual use is similar to a common risk assessment process namely a) identify and collect configuration data of the system under test (OVAL System Characteristics), b) analyze the system security incidents (OVAL Definition schema) and c) document and report the final results about the state of a system (OVAL Results schema). OVAL definitions are posted under a unique identifier (OVAL-ID).

- **CCSS (Common Configuration Scoring System):** A similar scoring system to CVSS is the CCSS which is a set of metrics related to software configuration issues. The CCSS supports an organization in making justifiable decisions as to how security configuration issues are to be treated, providing quantitative estimates regarding the overall security of a configuration issue. CCSS uses the same scoring as CVSS in the range of 0 (lowest severity) to 10 (highest severity) as means to prioritize the most critical configuration settings.

- **OCIL (Open Checklist Interactive Language):** Compliance checking may be quite complex to be automated in certain occasions. In this effort, OCIL based on an XML language, supports manual compliance checking. The difference from XCCDF lies in the fact that XCCDF supports the automated control compliance whereas OCIL the manual. OCIL describes in the form of questions to the user whether a particular process is in compliance with a set of regulations or policies. OCIL and XCCDF documents are easily communicated via the XML language and OCIL results are usually combined into a single XCCDF report.

- **ARF (Asset Reporting Format):** The ARF is a data model for the transport format of information about assets and the relationships between assets and reports. Due to the fact that data exist in various forms (e.g. reports, formats) and across different locations (e.g. database, sensors), ARF correlates different assets from different sources in a unified manner. ARF works in synergy with Asset Identification (AI) to enable the correlation and fusing of information from disparate data sources into a standardized format.

- **AI (Asset Identification):** The AI specification provides a unified approach to asset identification allowing for data correlation from multiple sources. AI defines eleven asset types which are expressed through an XML format. The proposed identifiers are as follows: a) literal (e.g. MAC address), b) relationship (under dependency), c) synthetic (during a process) and d) extension (outside AI vocabulary).

- **TMSAD (Trust Model for Security Automation Data):** TMSAD is a trust model and was developed to provide content integrity and authentication by ensuring that the content has not been altered since it was created. Conformity with this specification adds value to the security status of an information infrastructure.

SCAP-LIKE SPECIFICATIONS

This section examines specifications that either perform a similar role or can work in conjunction with SCAP specifications. In Table 8, SCAP-like specifications are presented with their primarily scope.

- **SWIDs (Software Identification Tags):** SWIDs have been primarily developed as means to identify and classify software applications specified with name, version and edition. SWIDs monitor the software status to verify whether the installed software is updated and not compromised. SWIDs are in accordance with ISO/IEC 19770-2:2009, a standard which refers to software asset management. SWIDs include Software Entitlement Tags (SWEN) that automatically measure whether license software has been expired.
- **CWE (Common Weakness Enumeration):** A similar specification to CVE is the CWE, which represents a set of documents that describe the weaknesses of software in the source code. CWE interacts with security taxonomies such as Gramma Tech and research centres as means to provide updated software weakness information. Moreover, CWE works in conjunction with CWSS, CWRAF and CAPEC as means to provide a complete picture of measuring software weaknesses.
- **CAPEC (Common Attack Pattern Enumeration and Classification):** This is an inventory of common attack patterns. Supported by MITRE, this specification describes attack methods and is designed to categorize the mechanism of attack into categories such as Spoofing, Data Leakage attacks, Injection and others. Each attack pattern is identified with a unique identification number and is briefly described. CAPEC allows interoperability with the Common Weakness enumeration (CWE) (Software Assurance, 2012). CAPEC also provides information about attack prerequisites and resources required in order an attack to succeed.
- **CWSS (Common Weakness Scoring System):** This is a specification for scoring and prioritizing software weaknesses (CWEs). The total score is calculated based on 18 factors that combine three metric groups: a) Base, captures the inherent characteristics of a weakness, b) Attack Surface,

Table 8. SCAP-like specifications based on category

Scope	Identification	Vulnerability Scoring	Event Characterization	Reporting/ Data Transport
Specifications	SWIDs	CWSS	MAEC	ASR
	CWE	CWRAF	CybOX	CVRF
	CAPEC	CCSS	STIX	xNAL
		CMSS		

refers to the attack nature of exploiting a weakness and c) Environmental, refer to factors that apply for an operational environment. Unlike CVSS, CWSS scoring range from 0 to 100 and is calculated by multiplying the subscores from each metric group.

- **CWRAF (Common Weakness Risk Analysis Framework):** This is a framework for scoring software weaknesses. It works in conjunction with CWE and CWSS and supports the automatic prioritization of weaknesses according to an organizations' business profile. With the use of vignettes, CWRAF provides short and formal descriptions about the operational environment, the security requirements and the role that software plays within a particular information infrastructure.

- **MAEC (Malware Attribute Enumeration and Characterization):** MAEC represents a standardized language for encoding and communicating malicious software (malware). By supporting a formal language on malware descriptions such as attack patterns and artifacts, it helps avoid data duplication. Adoption of MAEC can provide less ambiguity in malware description by using a) a common method of characterizing malware, b) improving organizational awareness related to malware handling and c) greater efficiency of controls related to malware management.

- **CybOX (Cyber Observable eXpression):** This specification represents a standardized language for events characterization. It includes the description and communication of a wide variety of events such as malware analysis, threats characterization and intrusion detection mechanisms. CybOX allows interoperability with STIX, CAPEC, and MAEC as means to communicate cyber observables across the entire operational environment in a consistent way. Cyber observables are descriptions of characteristics for an entity or event in a cyber environment such as a Windows registry key. Overall, CybOX offers a unified platform and related schemas for facilitating data automation of security events.

- **STIX (Structured Threat Information eXpression):** This is a standardized language which aims to capture and communicate cyber threat events. STIX uses a detailed representation of a cyber attack, such as indicators (e.g. IP address), specific threat data (e.g. attacker tactics), and exploitation targets (e.g. computer system). The principal aim of STIX is to offer a complete picture of the cyber adversary activities as means to provide a more defence in depth regarding the threat actor. STIX allows interoperability with CybOX.

- **ASR (Assessment Summary Results):** ASR is similar in scope with the ARF. As a result, it is an asset management tool that exchanges information from assessment tools related to assets, based on a structured language. This automation in data exchange further improves the process of collecting and analyzing data to create a unified asset database. The structured language ASR uses is based on the Policy Language for Assessment Results (PLARR).

- **CVRF (Common Vulnerability Reporting Framework):** CVRF is specified to standardize, the communication of vulnerability documentation. It allows interoperability with CPE, CVE and CWE by collecting and reporting product IDs, revision history, and document status. Its structure is based on a tree-based, mind-map diagram. CVRF aim to gather and structure data in the form of a report, without focusing on the appearance of data to the end user. In this regard, its potential is limited only to pure technical knowledge.

- **CMSS (Common Misuse Scoring System):** This specification is close in purpose with the CVSS, CCSS and CWSS. The noticeable difference is its scoring which focuses on what is called "software feature misuse vulnerability". This vulnerability derives from the software designers' trust assumptions about the use of a particular software product. For example, a designer who builds e-banking banners, made the trust assumption that the nature of the product could not be distorted by an attacker who can use such banners to attract the user into a malicious site. The scoring system is CVSS-alike with base, temporal and environmental metrics.

- **xNAL (eXtensible Name and Address Language):** This specification describes asset information and names of stakeholders within an organization. It has two sub-specifications, the extensible Address Language (xAL) and the extensible Name Language (xNL), both supported by the Organization for the Advancement of Structured Information Standards (OASIS). The principal aim of xNAL is to provide a common structure for representing open, vendor-neutral and application-independent information regardless of country or organizational culture.

VULNERABILITY SCORING METHODS

All enterprises rely on information infrastructures to perform business goals. Each information infrastructure relies on a variety of systems such as hardware, software and applications. Each system faces risks when a threat exploits vulnerability. According to Arbaugh et al., (2000) vulnerability is a "technological flaw in an information technology product that has security or survivability implications". De Ru & Eloff (1996), define software vulnerability as "a weakness in a system that can be exploited to violate the system's intended behavior". Schiffman (2007) describe vulnerability as a "bug, flaw, behavior, output, outcome or event within an application, system, device, or service that could lead to an implicit or explicit failure of confidentiality, integrity, or availability". The interest of this section lies on measuring the source of risk, the vulnerability. The reasons to research in vulnerability scoring methods are the following: a) accelerating rate of growth, b) increasing attack patterns and sophistication, c) multiple impacts on different enterprise IT systems, d) provide justification for existing risk. Vulnerability scoring methods are divided into three main types; qualitative, quantitative and hybrid. For each type, accompanied vulnerability scoring methods and characteristics are provided.

Qualitative Vulnerability Scoring

Symantec Security Response Threat Severity Assessment

Symantec (Symantec, 2002) focuses on software bugs (viruses, worms, Trojan horses and macros) which Symantec defines as threats. Based on identification, Symantec classifies such threats into "threat components" to determine the severity rating.

The threat components are: a) "in the wild", b) the damage occurred if exploited and c) the distribution of the damage. The first component measures the extent to which the threat is already spreading among computer users such as the number of affected computers and geographic distribution of infection. The second component measures the potential damage in terms of modified files, performance degradation and compromised security settings. The third component measures how rapidly it spreads such as large-scale email attack (worm), executable code attack (virus) and network drive infection capability. Each threat component is measured in a scale of High, Medium and Low.

When the threat analyst gathers all sub-component scorings then, categorizes each component within five (5) categories, category 5 being the most severe and category 1 the least.

Qualys Vulnerability Management

Qualys (Qualys, 1999) approach to scoring vulnerability comes with a range of activities such as a) identification of assets, vulnerabilities and threats, b) risk status reporting and c) compliance evaluation with the PCI standard.

Specifically, Qualys performs scanning for the network environment of an enterprise via a cloud premise (e.g. Amazon cloud) and identifies the most critical assets into business units and asset groups. The criticality is measured in a five tier scale from Low to Critical. Based on NVD, performs identification and correlation of vulnerabilities in terms of CVEs.

The highlights of Qualys include the iDefense Threat Intelligence module and the Zero-Day risk analyzer. Both enable to make predictions based on statistical data about zero-day vulnerabilities and allow interoperability with CVSS scoring.

Security Bulletin Severity Rating System of Microsoft

Microsoft (Microsoft, 2012) approach aims to score vulnerability in terms of exploitation. Microsoft associates the identification of a specific vulnerability with a CVE identifier and rates the exploitability on a three tier scale as follows: a) consistent exploit code likely, b) inconsistent code likely and c) functioning exploit code unlikely. Microsoft focus on the latest and older software releases in order to provide an aggregate exploitability assessment. This assessment is provided through an index (Microsoft's Exploitability Index) to customers. This index, compatible with CVSS since it uses CVE to identify vulnerability, is independent to other vulnerability scoring systems. Microsoft uses a four tier rating for vulnerability severity as follows: a) Low for a vulnerability whose exploitation or impact is low, b) moderate when vulnerability can be remediated via configuration or audit, c) important when it will have an impact on confidentiality, integrity and availability and d) critical when its exploitation could allow the distribution in the network of a Internet worm.

Secunia

Secunia (Secunia, 2002) is well known for the vulnerability advisories that contain vulnerability characteristics categorized by product and vendor. Secunia Advisory is dedicated to be a premier database of vulnerability knowledge which is updated on a daily basis and communicated via personalized e-mails to recipients who want to get acquainted with the latest information about the criticality, patch status and severity of vulnerabilities.

Secunia acknowledges three different types of vulnerabilities based on attack vector. These types are as follows: a) from local system, b) from local network and c) vulnerabilities that can be exploited remotely, without access to a system or local network. Secunia's severity rating is based on five tier scale, from "not critical", such as locally exploitable denial of service, to "extremely critical" such as vulnerabilities that are exploited remotely.

Red Hat Severity Classification Scheme

Red hat (Red Hat, 2005) has released the Red Hat Enterprise Linux 4 which is a vulnerability severity classification scheme. This scheme publicizes vulnerability ratings compared to the first version. Red

Hat uses CVEs as means to identify vulnerabilities and supports advisories that are updated regularly to provide users with a tool to assess vulnerabilities based on their network environment.

Red Hat's severity classification scheme has the following characteristics: a) it is based on a technical analysis of the type of vulnerability, b) helps users assess their network environment, c) provides automated update services, via the Red Hat network, as means to minimize the risk emerging from updates and d) it is independent from other vulnerability scoring systems. Red Hat uses a four tier scale from Critical to Low. For example, Red Hat considers as critical those flaws that can be exploited remotely and as low those flaws that will cause, if exploited, minimal consequences.

Mozilla's Vulnerability Rating System

Mozilla (Mozilla, 2005) supports security advisories for products such as Firefox, Thunderbird and Seamonkey. Each product advisory consists of vulnerabilities that are presented with: a) title, b) impact, c) discovery date, d) reporter and e) products affected. Vulnerabilities are rated in a four tier scale, from Low, which includes vulnerabilities that have minimal consequences, such as denial of service, to Critical, such as vulnerabilities that allow an attacker to exploit and distribute the damage into the whole system.

Google's Severity Rating System

Google (Google, 2007) supports guidelines for security issues regarding products based on Chromium browser to help vendors rate the severity of vulnerabilities. Google uses a four tier scale as follows: a) Low, rated as Pri-3, such as a bug that allows the attacker to hang the browser, b) Medium, rated as Pri-2, such a bug that allows an attacker to collect limited amount of information, c) High, rated as Pri-1, such as vulnerability exploitation modifies confidential data and d) Critical, rated as Pri-0, such as attackers' success to gain user's privileges during the normal operation of the browser.

Vupen Security

The principal aim of Vupen (Vupen, 2005) is to work in conjunction with government agencies and the community to combat 0-day and 1-day vulnerabilities and threats. Due to the increasing rising of most critical 1-day vulnerabilities in commercial programs, such as Adobe Acrobat or Microsoft Internet Explorer, Vupen, based on a series of sophisticated techniques, such as disassembly, reverse engineering, protocol analysis, and code auditing, aims to provide a proactive approach to risk. Vupen uses a four tier scale as follows: a) Low, for locally exploitable flaws which cannot put the system in danger c) Moderate, b) High and d) Critical, for remotely exploitable flaws, which could lead to system failure without user interaction.

Quantitative Vulnerability Scoring

Qualitative vulnerability scoring may have the advantage of interpreting vulnerability severity with a Likert type scale however, qualitative methods lack both the precision of results, due to the fuzziness of rating, and the interoperability with other methods, because the majority use own inventories or advisories.

In this respect, when a user requires increased accuracy of results, then, it becomes almost necessity, the need for a quantitative vulnerability scoring method. For this reasons, this sub-section describes the most reputed quantitative vulnerability scoring methods including formulas characteristics, terminology used and reporting aspects.

Common Vulnerability Scoring System

CVSS Version 1

This is, without doubt, one of the most reputed vulnerability scoring systems, which has inspired other researchers towards vulnerability scoring. Schiffman & CIAG, (2005) introduced CVSS v1 which consists of the base, temporal and environmental metric groups. Base metric group measures the inherent characteristics of vulnerability in order to capture the main profile and then based on temporal and environmental metrics detail the severity and overall status. The temporal group contains metrics that evaluate the vulnerability during its lifecycle and hence, are prone to change. The environmental group contains metrics that evaluate the surrounding attributes, such as stakeholder involvement, that affect the status of the vulnerability. The CVSS severity score takes values from 0 (vulnerability has no severity) to 10 (vulnerability has maximum severity).

CVSS Version 2

The updated CVSS v2 (Mell et al., 2007) relies on the foundations of v1. It is constructed to provide greater score diversity and better accuracy of vulnerability scoring in terms of prioritizing and reflecting the real impact of vulnerability. The difference between versions is that v2 offers a more balanced distribution scoring compared to v1. It consists of the same metric groups (base, temporal and environmental) and uses the same severity scoring from 0 to 10, but the highlights and main differences of CVSS v2 compared to v1 are as follows:

- The (B_IB) metric does not exist.
- Three additional metrics have been added in the environmental metric group and refer to security requirements, namely confidentiality, integrity and availability requirement.
- Metric values have become more granular
- Rating values also follow this notion.
- All group metric formulas have been updated.

WIVSS (Weighted Impact Vulnerability Scoring System)

WIVSS has roots in the CVSS and is proposed by Spanos et al., (2013) as means to improve even further the vulnerability scoring in terms of accuracy and balanced distribution. Authors claim that, based on statistical analysis in terms of median, mean, standard deviation and different scores, that WIVSS offer higher score diversity and spreading of scores, objectives required from the transition from CVSS v1 to v2. In the following bullets, the main characteristics that differentiate WIVSS from CVSS v2 are presented.

- Weight of Confidentiality Impact > Weight of Integrity Impact > Weight of Availability Impact.
- When "None" Confidentiality Impact then all other Impacts take value "None" = 0.
- Partial Impact = 0.5 * Complete Impact.

- The Impact Score ranges from 0 to 7.
- The 33 possible sums of the three Impact metrics must be different.
- Impact Score = Confidentiality Impact + Integrity Impact + Availability Impact.

PVL (Potential Value Loss)

Wang & Yang (2012) developed the PVL method for rating single vulnerabilities of computer networks. It uses seven indicators to describe vulnerability severity in terms of effectiveness, usability, accuracy and orderliness. The PVL metric offers higher vulnerability score diversity and vulnerability distribution evenness compared to CVSS v2. Authors demonstrate the practicality of PVL by using PVL to rate published vulnerabilities for IP Multimedia Subsystem.

Hybrid Vulnerability Scoring Systems

VRSS (Vulnerability Rating and Scoring System)

In order to bridge the gap between qualitative and quantitative vulnerability scoring methods, the VRSS hybrid scoring system is proposed (Liu & Zhang, 2011). This is basically a combination of qualitative methods such as ISS X-Force and Vupen Security and quantitative method such as CVSS. Based on normal distribution fitting analysis, the ISS X-Force and Vupen Security show greater consistency compared to the CVSS. VRSS prioritizes vulnerabilities into three parts: High, Medium and Low. The objective of VRSS is to replace different vendor-specific rating systems and offer a much more balanced distribution scoring compared to quantitative scoring methods.

VRSS Improvement

Liu et al., (2012) developed an updated version of VRSS as means to increase even further the diversity of scoring (in terms of separating vulnerabilities from each other as much as possible) and accuracy of results (in terms of prioritization). VRSS improvement is characterized, first, by enabling vulnerability type to prioritize vulnerabilities, in terms of Common Weakness Enumeration (CWE), and second, by an analytic hierarchy process (AHP) based on the VRSS. Again, authors use statistical analysis, in terms of standard deviation, mean, and distribution analysis, to support their results.

Vulnerability Prioritization via Fuzzy Logic Process

Huang et al., (2013) proposed fuzzy logic processes to prioritize vulnerabilities. Authors use a Fuzzy Delphi method which filters the subjectivity from stakeholders regarding the factors affecting security. Then, based on each factors' value, authors use a Fuzzy Analytical Hierarchy Process (AHP) to obtain the fuzzy membership values. The factor membership values are analyzed through a fuzzy synthetic decision making model in order to show the various degrees the vulnerability is affecting the security of a software system. This method highlights the fuzziness of stakeholder involvement and how different weights of evaluation criteria, which are based on CVSS v2 metrics, affect vulnerability prioritization.

CONCLUSION

Concerns about the possibility of compromise or business disruption, have reached critical levels in many enterprises. Therefore, the success of an enterprise is now determined by its ability to maximize business performance through the management of the diversity of enterprise IT risks. Automated security metrics, such as vulnerability scoring methods and standardized specifications, provide a new basis for enterprise IT risk management. At this point of time, the competitive advantage belongs to the enterprises which will use automated tools to maximize business performance, setting new boundaries for standardization and sustainability.

REFERENCES

Arbaugh, W. A., Fithen, W. L., & McHugh, J. (2000). *Windows of Vulnerability: A Case Study Analysis*. IEEE Computer.

Arena, M., Arnaboldi, M., & Azzone, G. (2010). The organizational dynamics of Enterprise Risk Management. *Accounting, Organizations and Society, 35*(7), 659–675. doi:10.1016/j.aos.2010.07.003

Arnold, V., Benford, T., Canada, J., & Sutton, S. G. (2011). The role of strategic enterprise risk management and organizational flexibility in easing new regulatory compliance. *International Journal of Accounting Information Systems, 12*(3), 171–188. doi:10.1016/j.accinf.2011.02.002

Assessment Summary Results (ASR). (n.d.). Retrieved December 2014 from http://measurablesecurity. mitre.org/incubator/asr/

Asset Identification (AI). (n.d.). Retrieved December 2014 from http://csrc.nist.gov/publications/nistir/ ir7693/NISTIR-7693.pdf

Asset Reporting Format (ARF). (n.d.). Retrieved December 2014 from http://csrc.nist.gov/publications/ nistir/ir7694/NISTIR-7694.pdf

British CCTA. (2003). *CRAMM (CCTA Risk Analysis and Management Method)*. Insight Consulting.

Caralli, R. A., Stevens, J. F., Young, L. R., & Wilson, W. R. (2007). *Introducing octave allegro: Improving the information security risk assessment process* (No. CMU/SEI-2007-TR-012). Carnegie Mellon University. Retrieved December 2014 from http://www.sei.cmu.edu/reports/07tr012.pdf

Caron, F., Vanthienen, J., & Baesens, B. (2013). A comprehensive investigation of the applicability of process mining techniques for enterprise risk management. *Computers in Industry, 64*(4), 464–475. doi:10.1016/j.compind.2013.02.001

Committee of Sponsoring Organizations of the Treadway Commission (COSO). (2004). *Enterprise Risk Management—Integrated Framework*. Retrieved December 2014 from http://www.coso.org/documents/ coso_erm_executivesummary.pdf

Common Attack Pattern Enumeration and Classification (CAPEC). (n.d.). Retrieved December 2014 from http://capec.mitre.org

Common Configuration Enumeration (CCE). (n.d.). Retrieved December 2014 from http://cce.mitre.org/

Common Configuration Scoring System (CCSS). (n.d.). Retrieved December 2014 from http://csrc.nist. gov/publications/nistir/ir7502/nistir-7502_CCSS.pdf

Common Misuse Scoring System (CMSS). (n.d.). Retrieved December 2014 from http://csrc.nist.gov/ publications/drafts/nistir-7517/Draft-NISTIR-7517.pdf

Common Platform Enumeration (CPE). (n.d.). Retrieved December 2014 from http://cpe.mitre.org/

Common Vulnerability and Exposures (CVE). (n.d.). Retrieved December 2014 from http://cve.mitre.org/

Common Vulnerability Reporting Framework (CVRF). (n.d.). Retrieved December 2014 from http:// www.icasi.org/cvrf

Common Vulnerability Scoring System (CVSS). (n.d.). Retrieved December 2014 from http://www.first. org/cvss/cvss-guide.pdf

Common Weakness Enumeration. (n.d.). Retrieved December 2014 from http://cwe.mitre.org/

Common Weakness Risk Analysis Framework (CWRAF). (n.d.). Retrieved December 2014 from https:// cwe.mitre.org/cwraf/

Common Weakness Scoring System (CWSS). (n.d.). Retrieved December 2014 from http://cwe.mitre. org/cwss/

Cyber Observable eXpression (CYBOX). (n.d.). Retrieved December 2014 from http://cybox.mitre.org/

De Ru, W. G., & Eloff, J. H. P. (1996). Risk analysis modelling with the use of fuzzy logic. *Computers & Security, 15*(3), 239–248. doi:10.1016/0167-4048(96)00008-9

European Telecommunications Standards Institute. (2006). *Telecommunications and Internet converged Services and Protocols for Advanced Networking (TISPAN); Methods and protocols; Part 1: Method and proforma for Threat, Risk, Vulnerability Analysis (ETSI TS 102 165-1 V4.2.1).* Retrieved December 2014 from http://portal.etsi.org/mbs/Referenced%20Documents/ts_10216501v040201p.pdf

Extensible Configuration Checklist Description Format (XCCDF). (n.d.). Retrieved December 2014 from http://nvd.nist.gov/scap/xccdf/docs/xccdf-spec-1.0.pdf

eXtensible Name and Address Language (xNAL). (n.d.). Retrieved December 2014 from http://www. immagic.com/eLibrary/TECH/OASIS/XAL_V2.PDF

Google. (2007). *Severity Guidelines for Security Issues.* Retrieved December 2014 from http://dev. chromium.org/developers/severity-guidelines

Gordon, L. A., Loeb, M., & Tseng, C.-Y. (2009). Enterprise risk management and firm performance: A contingency perspective. *Journal of Accounting and Public Policy, 28*(4), 301–327. doi:10.1016/j. jaccpubpol.2009.06.006

Grace, M. F., Leverty, J. T., Phillips, R. D., & Shimpi, P. (2014). The Value of Investing in Enterprise Risk Management. *The Journal of Risk and Insurance.*

Hampton, J. J. (2015). *Fundamentals of Enterprise risk management: How Top Companies assess risk, manage exposure, and seize opportunity* (2nd ed.). AMACOM Publication.

Hoyt, E. R., & Liebenberg, A. P. (2011). The Value of Enterprise Risk Management. *The Journal of Risk and Insurance, 78*(4), 795–822. doi:10.1111/j.1539-6975.2011.01413.x

Huang, C.-C., Lin, F.-Y., Lin, F., & Sun, Y. S. (2013). A novel approach to evaluate software vulnerability prioritization. *Journal of Systems and Software, 86*(11), 2822–2840. doi:10.1016/j.jss.2013.06.040

ISAMM. (2002). *Information Security Assessment and Monitoring Method*. Retrieved December 2014 from http://rm-inv.enisa.europa.eu/methods_tools/m_isamm.html

ISO/IEC 27005. (2008). *Information Technology -- Security techniques -- Information security risk management*. ISO.

IT Governance Institute. (2007). *COBIT 4.1 Excerpt: Executive Summary – Framework*. Retrieved December 2014 from http://www.isaca.org/KnowledgeCenter/cobit/Documents/COBIT4.pdf

Koons, J., & Minoli, D. (2010). *Information Technology Risk Management in Enterprise Environments, A Review of Industry Practices and a Practical Guide to Risk Management Teams*. John Wiley & Sons.

Lam, J. (2014). What is ERM? In *Enterprise Risk Management: From Incentives to Controls* (2nd ed.). Hoboken, NJ: John Wiley & Sons, Inc. doi:10.1002/9781118836477.ch4

Landoll, D. J. (2006). *The Security Risk Assessment Handbook: A Complete Guide for Performing Security Risk Assessments* (2nd ed.). Boca Raton, FL: Auerbach.

Liu, Q., & Zhang, Y. (2011). VRSS: A new system for rating and scoring vulnerabilities. *Computer Communications, 34*(3), 264–273. doi:10.1016/j.comcom.2010.04.006

Liu, Q., Zhang, Y., Kong, Y., & Wu, Q. (2012). Improving VRSS-based vulnerability prioritization using analytic hierarchy process. *Journal of Systems and Software, 85*(8), 1699–1708. doi:10.1016/j.jss.2012.03.057

MAGERIT. (2006). *Methodology for Information Systems Risk Analysis and Management – version 2*. Retrieved December 2014 from https://www.ccn-cert.cni.es/publico/herramientas/pilar44/en/magerit/index.html

Malware Attribute Enumeration and Characterization (MAEC). (n.d.). Retrieved December 2014 from http://maec.mitre.org/

Mathrani, S., & Mathrani, A. (2013). Utilizing enterprise systems for managing enterprise risks. *Computers in Industry, 64*(4), 476–483. doi:10.1016/j.compind.2013.02.002

Mell, P., Scarfone, K., & Romanosky, S. (2007). *A Complete Guide to the Common Vulnerability Scoring System Version 2*. Retrieved December 2014 from http://www.first.org/cvss/cvss-guide.pdf

Microsoft. (2012). *Security Bulletin Severity Rating System*. Retrieved December 2014 from http://technet.microsoft.com/en-us/security/gg309177.aspx

Mozilla. (2005). *Mozilla Foundation Security Advisories*. Retrieved December 2014 from http://www.mozilla.org/security/announce/

Nikolic, B., & Ruzic-Dimitrijevic, L. (2009). Risk assessment of information technology Systems. *Issues in Informing Science & Information Technology, 6*.

NIST. (2009). *Special Publication 800-117 (Draft), Guide to Adopting and Using the Security Content Automation Protocol (SCAP)*. Retrieved December 2014 from http://csrc.nist.gov/publications/nistpubs/800-117/sp800-117.pdf/

NIST. (2011). *Special Publication 800-39, Managing Information Security Risk, Organization, Mission, and Information System View*. Retrieved December 2014 from http://csrc.nist.gov/publications/nistpubs/800-39/SP800-39-final.pdf

OCTAVE. (2003). *Operationally Critical Threat, Asset, and Vulnerability Evaluation*. Retrieved December 2014 from http://www.cert.org/octave/approach_intro.pdf

Open Vulnerability Assessment Language (OVAL). (n.d.). Retrieved December 2014 from http://oval.mitre.org/language/version5.10/

Payment Card Industry (PCI). (2010). *Approved Scanning Vendors, Program Guide, Reference 1.0, PCI DSS 1.2*. Retrieved December 2014 from https://www.pcisecuritystandards.org/pdfs/asv_program_guide_v1.0.pdf

Peltier, T. R. (2000). *Facilated Risk Analysis Process (FRAP)*. Auerbach Publications.

Qualys. (1999). *Severities KnowledgeBase*. Retrieved December 2014 from http://www.qualys.com/research/knowledge/severity/

Quon, T. K., Zeghal, D., & Maingot, M. (2012). Enterprise Risk Management and Firm Performance. *Procedia: Social and Behavioral Sciences, 62*, 263–267. doi:10.1016/j.sbspro.2012.09.042

Redhat. (2005). *Classification of Security Issues*. Retrieved December 2014 from http://www.redhat.com/f/pdf/rhel4/SecurityClassification.pdf

Roussey, C., Pinet, F., Kang, M. A., & Corcho, O. (2011). An Introduction to Ontologies and Ontology Engineering. *Advanced Information and Knowledge Processing, 1*, 9-38.

Saleh, M. S., & Alfantook, A. (2011). A new comprehensive framework for enterprise information security risk management. *Applied Computing and Informatics, 9*(2), 107–118. doi:10.1016/j.aci.2011.05.002

Schiffman, M. (2007). *A Complete Guide to the Common Vulnerability Scoring System (CVSS)*. Retrieved December 2014 from http://www.first.org/cvss/cvss-guide.html

Schiffman, M., & Ciag, C. (2005). *CVSS: A Common Vulnerability Scoring System*. Retrieved December 2014 from http://www.first.org/cvss/v1/guide

Secunia. (2002). *Advisories*. Retrieved December 2014 from http://secunia.com/advisories/historic/

Software Assurance (SwA). (2012). Key practices for mitigating the most egregious exploitable software weaknesses, Software Assurance Pocket Guide Series: Development, Vol. II, Version 2.3. Author.

Software Identification Tags (SWIDs). (n.d.). Retrieved December 2014 from http://tagvault.org/swid-tags/

Spanos, G., Sioziou, A., & Angelis, L. (2013). WIVSS: a new methodology for scoring information systems vulnerabilities. In *Proceedings of the 17th Pan-Hellenic Conference on Informatics.* ACM. doi:10.1145/2491845.2491871

Strecker, S., Heise, D., & Frank, U. (2011). RiskM: A multi-perspective modelling method for IT risk assessment. *Information Systems Frontiers, 13*(4), 595-611.

Structured Threat Information, eXpression (STIX). (n.d.). Retrieved December 2014 from http://stix.mitre.org/

Symantec. (2000). *Symantec Security Response Glossary.* Retrieved December 2014 from http://www.symantec.com/security response/severityassessment.jsp

Taylor, L. (2014). *Practical enterprise risk management: How to optimize business strategies through managed risk taking.* Kogan Page Limited Publ.

PTA Technologies. (2005). *Practial Threat Analysis.* Retrieved December 2014 from http://www.ptat-echnologies.com/

Tekathen, M., & Dechow, N. (2013). Enterprise risk management and continuous re-alignment in the pursuit of accountability: A German case. *Management Accounting Research, 24*(2), 100–121. doi:10.1016/j.mar.2013.04.005

The Open Checklist Interactive Language (OCIL). (n.d.). Retrieved December 2014 from http://nvd.nist.gov/ocil/OCIL_language.pdf

Trust Model for Security Automation Data (TMSAD). (n.d.). Retrieved December 2014 from http://csrc.nist.gov/publications/nistir/ir7802/NISTIR-7802.pdf

VUPEN. (2005). *Vulnerability Research and Intelligence.* Retrieved December 2014 from http://www.vupen.com/

Waltermire, D., Quinn, S., Scarfone, K., & Halbardier, A. (2011). *The Technical Specification for the Security Content Automation Protocol (SCAP): SCAP Version 1.2.* Retrieved December 2014 from http://csrc.nist.gov/publications/nistpubs/800-126-rev2/SP800-126r2.pdf

Wang, Y., & Yang, Y. (2012). PVL: A Novel Metric for Single Vulnerability Rating and Its Application in IMS. *Journal of Computer Information Systems, 8*(2), 579–590.

Wheeler, E. (2011). *Security Risk Management: Building an Information Security Risk Management Program from the Ground Up* (1st ed.). Waltham: Syngress.

KEY TERMS AND DEFINITIONS

Enterprise IT Risk Management: A structured and unified enterprise risk management approach that takes into account strategic, credit, reputational, market, outsourcing, compliance, operational and information security risks. The purpose is to continually evaluate such risks with automated security metrics.

Information Security: The management of information systems (e.g. hardware, software, applications) against unauthorized access, unavailability or modification of data.

Information Technology (IT): A broad term which refers to the application of computing technology and telecommunications usually in favour of business purposes.

Risk Appetite: A broad-based amount of risk that an enterprise is willing to accept in quest for business goals.

Risk Management: A discipline used to identify, assess, prioritize and monitor risks that affect the ability of an enterprise to achieve strategic goals.

Risk Tolerance: The acceptable deviation from the level set by the risk appetite and business goals (e.g. The enterprise management requires business projects to be completed within a defined budget and time, however, overruns of 10 percent of budget and 20 percent of time are tolerated).

Security Content Automation Protocol: A suite of automated specification that aim to manage the security content of information systems, including compliance checking, homogeneously.

Systemic Risk: The risk that derives from a failure of one infrastructure or sector to meet its required obligations causes other infrastructures or sectors to be unable to meet their obligations.

Chapter 13

Information Security:
Application in Business to Maximize the Security and Protect Confidential and Private Data

Sofienne Srihi
University of Tunis, Tunisia

Ala Balti
University of Tunis, Tunisia

Farhat Fnaiech
University of Tunis, Tunisia

Habib Hamam
University of Moncton, Canada

ABSTRACT

In this chapter, we define Information Security (IS) and elaborate on the different methods and technology used. We proceed to explain some of the IS tools and risks found in private and confidential data. We detail the latest algorithms and systems of security and discuss how to implement those systems in business to upgrade performances and increase profits.

INTRODUCTION

The security of private and confidential data, and the security the transmission network handling these data are among the most prominent problems encountered in the field of data processing and communication. While data security is being developed and continuously improved, hackers are incessantly progressing in attacks by searching weak points and lacunas in the secure system.

Therefore the methodology of security varies depending on the situation and evolves in time with the attacks. In this chapter, we will focus on the encryption algorithms and the protection of data in the field of Automated Enterprise Systems.

DOI: 10.4018/978-1-4666-8841-4.ch013

1. THE GROWING INTEGRATION OF ENTERPRISE SYSTEMS

Employers within companies often complain that managers do not facilitate their work and continue to make their task heavy through bureaucracy, manual double checking, repetitive work, etc. Facilitating work is important and sometimes decisive for the success and development of businesses or companies.

Automated business enterprise systems are embedded in this spirit. While deployment of automated enterprise systems was once almost restricted to large companies and governmental agencies, today, the systems are largely deployed in medium and small businesses.

Marriage between BAS (Broadband Access Server: access equipment service IT) and enterprise systems is made possible by web technology (primarily extensible Mark-up language XML) enabling the treatment of data. Although some control softwares have been available for several years. Its use now allows the saving of space (land), which could be particularly advantageous for large companies based on integrated business infrastructure.

The advantages of this marriage include advanced network setting to optimize functions such as energy management, automated response on request, false detection, diagnosis and remote monitoring (Richard E, Daniel S, Robert J. 2005).

2. DATA MANAGEMENT

Data management is the implementation and development of policies, procedures, architectures, and practices in order to optimize the management and assessment of the information lifecycle requirements of the enterprise.

Compliance, biding, and restrictive regulations transformed corporate data and data management output to hold an extreme importance in shaping the strategic aspect of corporations, especially in a turbulent and highly competitive business environment. Thus, the ever growing volume of data that must be processed by organizations has increased remarkably and introduced the notion of "Big Data" (Margaret Rouse, 2003).

Generally, data management can be defined as a set of notions and processes to define, store, maintain, distribute and enforce a comprehensive view; reliably and timely reference data within information system, independent channels, and communication industries as well as occupations or geographical subdivisions.

2.1. Confidential Data

Much of collected or used data are classified as personal, confidential, sensitive or susceptible; these require data protection.

The procedure for handling such data is mastered through the combination of ethical and legal guidelines:

- Data Protection Act 1998;
- Freedom of Information Act 2000;
- Human Rights Act 1998;
- Statistics and Registration Services Act 2007;
- Environmental Information Regulations Act 2004.

Figure 1. Data management

Among the biggest obstacles in data protection is the defense of confidential data against espionage and piracy. This security issue has its origin in war and competition in the market. For example, methods of data protection were created to secure information and render it unreadable to intruders in times of multinational conflicts, when two competing companies seek to possess their competitor's data, and when there is a need to transmit confidential messages during war, such as military strategies. The fight against thieves and spies is another security reason. For example, concerning banking services where money is being dealt in large quantities, it is an obligation to secure banking and personal customer data. Data privacy touches almost all areas based on protection against thieves (hackers), enemies, and competitors. (Gartner I. 2011)

3. DATA TRANSMISSION

Nowadays, the transmission of data has become a common necessity in many fields. Facilitating the communication and the development of communication tools has required the use of data transmission. Yet the power of the internet, which has become necessary in several areas of the workforce, is a vital

Figure 2. Confidential data

element in every company and business which seek to be connected to the outside world, to stay updated, and to exchange data with customers and partners.

Data transmission, digital transmission, or digital communication is the transfer of data over a point-to-point or point-to-multipoint communication channel. It is the physical transmission of data. For data transmission we need channels, for example computer bases, wireless communication channels, storage media, copper wires, or optical fibers.

3.1. Transmission Methods

Data transmission is any process of several methods that realize transportation and transformation of any type of information. The different methods employed with its particular process make it possible to share

Figure 3. Transmission methods

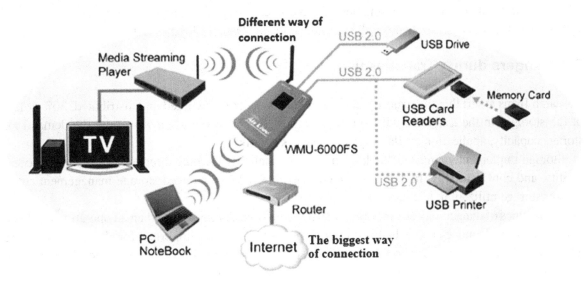

voice, video, and text easily using the strategies relevant to the particular kind of data of interest. The digital transmission of data occurs in a number of settings, including common patterns, such as email clients, audio, and web conferencing solutions and file sharing. While there are a number of different approaches to this type of information processing, they are ultimately grouped under three basic categories:

Audio data transmission: involves the conversion of audio to data streams that can be easily processed and successfully delivered to a point of reception. Signals of this type were once carried in analog signaling until advancements in technology and fiber optics made it possible to convert audio into digital formats. Transmission of this type occurs each time a telephone call is enabled using some type of Internet streaming to carry the signal. Since the latter part of the 20th century, the application of Voice over Internet Protocol (VoIP) has allowed communication with locations all over the world without incurring high cost.

Another example of data transmission is related to the processing of video data. Through this application, a video bit stream is established and used to direct the data from a point of origin to multiple destination points. This approach results in online video chats with distant locations, as well as allowing the use of video conferencing to conduct meetings involving members in multiple locations. Just as advancements in technology have greatly reduced the cost of long-distance audio solutions, the pricing associated with video conferencing is a fraction of what it was during the latter years of the 20th century.

A third classification of data transmission is the processing of text documents as part of a data stream. This application creates text using a word processing software, saves the information, and then transmits it to one or more recipients. One of the most common examples of this type of data transmission is email. Users can type in text and then send it to any number of recipients. Thanks to the protocols that help protecting the text from corruption, the recipients receive the document with the same basic formatting used by the originator.

The processing of texts is the most used method, because any information, message, service, or code can be transmitted by text. (In bank transactions, for example, the client is required to communicate with the bank by using some personal information with text transmission in order to carry out an operation.)

The creation and refinement of various options for data transmission continue to expand as newer forms of technology emerge and come into common use. Data transfer applications that were unheard-of a few years ago are now utilized by businesses and private users on a daily basis. As the public use of the Internet and personal computing devices continues to expand, the type, speed, and efficiency of various data transmission strategies will continue to grow. (Daniel Lloyd C. 2008)

3.2. Dangers during Transmission

Research firms assert that the majority of enterprise storage are networked and distributed. 30% or less of the storages in the last years will be directly attached. This evolution is driven by the demand for storage capacity, application availability and business continuity.

Storage implementers must tackle known security challenges, which threaten data integrity, accessibility, and confidentiality. In doing so, enterprises may achieve reduced storage-management costs, greater storage utilization, and increased data access.

Many types of danger may occur during data transmission. For instance, when an operation is related to a bank, people's money and valuable property are at risk; it is very important for all data to be secure and non-vulnerable to theft and hacking. However, most companies still do not report security incidents, and almost all companies that participated in the survey are using traditional network and Internet access

Figure 4. Dangers during transmission

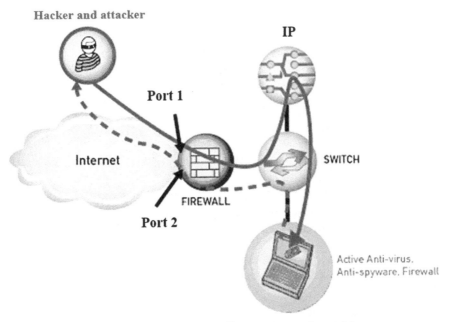

Computer vulnerable

controls and defenses. The costs may be even higher if the total downtime and response efforts associated with such breaches are figured into the equation. (Pistoia M, Chandra S, Fink S and Yahav E. 2007)

It is not hard to believe that networked storage resources represent prime targets given the importance and centralized nature of corporate data. In what concerns IP networks, they are susceptible to published security threats such as system breach, spoofing, denial of service, unauthorized access, internal attack, data theft, and corruption. Threat zones include systems connections, storage fabric and management services, subsystems media, and personnel with direct or indirect access to such storage components.

Since storage security often comes with costs and impacts, tradeoffs will be weighed against business requirements and desired profitability. Losses are associated with data corruption, suspension of operations, and theft. For example, corrupted data can seriously affect a company's ability to conduct business and can affect overall operations' output. Breached and/or abused storage resources can materially affect operations. Stolen data can compromise a company's intellectual property, strategies, and competitive advantage. In analyzing and establishing where and how to implement security practices, organizations must monitor, review and update their production and security policies – assuming they have any at all. Operational storage policies should be based on a risk assessment by storage function and business necessity.

Since no single security system is a silver bullet, a multi-tier defense strategy is a proven way to reduce risks (NeoScale Systems, 2002).

Countermeasures for storage would include system and device configuration, testing, auditing and monitoring, access authentication, logical unit number (LUN) masking, port zoning, and physical access controls. As companies embrace more complex storage models, such as remote backup, disaster recovery, peer production sites, resource pooling, and managed services, additional layers of data storage

Figure 5. Zones which affect networked storage

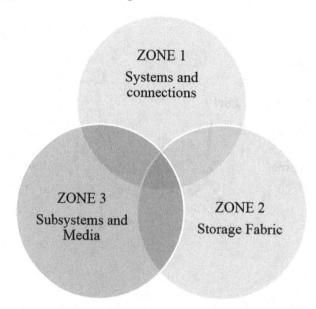

protection will be required to defend a more distributed infrastructure. This will require data storage protection during transport, on the storage subsystem, and on the media.

There are three threat zones that affect networked storage regardless of the network protocol employed. These threat zones are systems and connections, storage fabric and management services, and subsystems and media (NeoScale Systems, 2002).

3.2.1. System and Connection

The system and connection threat zone includes computer systems (such as application and management servers) and gateway devices that connect to storage infrastructures. Should administrative or application access to the system or device be compromised and abused, the storage network may be vulnerable to unauthorized data access, denial-of-service attack, and service loss.

Unauthorized systems access is often obtained through poorly managed configurations, unused services, or default settings. Once compromised, these systems can attempt to interfere with media servers or issue abusive requests to storage subsystems for the purposes of data theft, corruption, or service denial. IP and Fiber Channel (FC) defenses that thwart system breach include application and device access control, configuration policy assessment and system, as well as device monitoring. However, it is possible to introduce a new IP or FC attached system due to weak auditing or just newly emerging SAN protocols, which support authenticated storage access device provisions.

Fiber Channel storage area networks are associated with relatively short distances and restricted physical access. However, consideration should be made for protecting connected storage resources, shared storage, and data leaving the data center (this will be discussed in later sections). To extend the SAN, gateways provide remote backup, replication, and disaster recovery applications using dedicated, shared, or public connections.

The physical transport is also very significant; as it may be susceptible to wire-tapping (certainly difficult, but possible), traffic interception and re-direction, gateway attack, etc.

For example, without some degree of transport protection, frame or packet-based switching or routing networks can often be identified via ping sweeps and port scans. As such, enterprises are readopting company-leased or owned dark fiber 5 to gain greater physical protection of their data.

Almost all storage components support out-of-band management, thus adding a layer of access.

New IP and iSCSI devices also offer more ways to enter the storage network. Poorly configured access and management controls often allow the compromise of the devices' vulnerability. For example, default device settings or open management ports can be easy pickings for attackers.

Exploiting these vulnerabilities makes it possible to spoof FC or IP connections to capture, disrupt, or redirect stored data/processes. At present, pure FCP data transmission does not support native tunneling or virtual private network (VPN) services. Therefore, FC resident data and routing information are exposed. Until IP security (IPsec6) standards are adopted within FCP, the alternative method is to employ virtual private networking encryption services in conjunction with storage gateways that convert FC Protocols to IP. This protects data and routing information between IP-based SAN gateway connections. (Pistoia M, Chandra S, Fink S and Yahav E. 2007)

3.2.2. Storage Fabric

The second SAN threat zone is that of the storage fabric. It must be noted that in this discussion the fabric, while usually associated with Fiber Channel, will consist of the hubs, routers, switches, and applications that connect and manage data storage from data sources to disk/tape storage arrays regardless of transport protocol. As with most storage devices, vendors have implemented secure access capabilities to reduce the threat of device or management application hijacking – usually in the form of Telnet using SSH or Web using SSL for a secure connection. This is especially important for SAN applications such as port zoning, LUN masking, and virtualization. Since most of these devices and applications support remote management capabilities, physical security will not defend against remote, out-of-band attacks. Should the switch, management server, or management application be breached, the attack could result in material compromise of the storage network and pose a serious threat of data corruption. Even with strong access control policies, it is possible that a miss-configured or newly initialized storage device could lead to service interruption and data loss and/or corruption.

Today, the threat of unauthorized devices being attached to the fabric is relative to how closed the environment is to physical access and how often the fabric/network is audited. A common example revolves around a rogue storage network attached server – a system with a FC HBA (host bus adapter) connecting to the fabric using a hijacked WWN (worldwide name). Since there is no widely deployed authentication protocol between HBA, switch, and other devices on the FC network, this vulnerability is possible. A similar IP storage example occurs when a server with a network adapter attaches to a storage-segregated network by spoofing an authenticated IP address. In both cases, data being transported may be visible to the attached node within the storage fabric. This presents data theft, corruption, and denial of service vulnerabilities.

ESP (Encapsulating Security Payload) has been specified for secure transmissions between SAN devices. It is widely used in the IP world and is also proposed for iSCSI through the IETF (RFC 24067).

It provides message authentication and optional encryption using keys (as described further). Although vendors are just beginning to implement ESP, the future looks brighter for fabric entity authentication.

To minimize this risk, storage administrators can implement zoning measures, which would direct specific storage traffic through segregated switch ports – essentially configuring which storage sources and destinations can communicate. Soft zoning is accomplished through a switch's name server service by specifying nodes permitted to talk within a zone(s) by way of port number and/or World Wide Name. Inspecting the FC frame header, and allowing pass-through traffic within one or more permitted zones by way of the port number and World Wide Name enforce hard zoning. It is important to note that older switches, which are the installed majority, mainly supported hard zoning based on ports. Port-based zoning will rely on adequate physical security of the cabling. Soft zoning may allow a node to directly talk to a target thus bypassing the name server. This is similar to the approach to IP using router ACLs and stateful Firewalls.

Ultimately with zoning, only storage data and visible resources within the zone are susceptible to being captured, corrupted, and/or abused. Network system scanners can possibly identify rogue or mis-configured storage attached systems.

3.2.3. Subsystem and Media

The third SAN threat zone is subsystems, media, and storage devices. This threat to "data at rest" is often regarded as a more serious danger than access to data in transit – as the potential revelation is more perma-nent. Unless encrypted by an application, stockpiled data remains vulnerable. In many cases, applications are applied with a client-to-server data protection/encryption, but no server-to-backend storage. Beyond physical access controls and auditing, storage subsystem LUN's (Logical Unit Number) addresses can be masked to further limit storage data discernibility. The masking process is used to plan LUNs that can be retrieved only by specific hosts—essentially, a host founded view of the storage resources. Hosts will not be apt to request resources, which they cannot "realize". This can be implemented via LUN covering services available on array routers, controllers, device drivers, switches, and HBAs through specific vendor or universal purpose storage managing software.

Unauthorized users can readily read tape data, analyze confidential information, and in some cases re-build entire systems. Given that the data is removable, the perpetrators have more time and resources for tape inspection. In addition, failed disks with recoverable data may be sent to outside repair facilities where data may easily be copied or misplaced and scratch tapes can be accessed. This requires secure media handling, disposal and auditing.

Virtualized tape systems are visibly ahead due to the advantages of reinstatement speed and the sim-plicity of management. Here too, securing data protection and access to the abovementioned virtualized systems needs to be addressed.

3.3. Solution

Today, wireless data transmission holds a crucial importance in certain fields, notably banking, the management of confidential and classified information such as military secrets, private information for businesses or companies, police information, and state secrets.

Due to the importance of the information, they require secured instant access; also, the speed of which the information is sent is equally important. In these cases, many applications could suggest solutions to safety issues of this type of information and could allow users to safely and quickly connect to private networks, wherever they are located.

Today's defensive process is trying to explore new systems and methods to secure, transmit, extract, transform, and integrate data in the way required to harness its value across multiple usage patterns.

As mentioned above, routers, switches, and hubs have previously supported authentic access and the ability to apply port separation and zoning.

Most storage subsystems and storage-management applications support LUN masking. IP storage can support VPNs for data transport protection. In addition, vendors within the FC community are advancing their FC switch-to-switch authentication methods.

Storage fabric entity authentication will play a critical part in reducing unauthorized access risks, further enhancing availability, integrity, and confidentiality. As mentioned above, the T11 committee has proposed that storage devices employ ESP for authenticated communications. This will require key management, which includes session key lifetime (how much data and packets transfers are allowed before a new key is required). Again, these advances cover how devices will be allowed to attach and communicate in the fabric.

Tunneling protects data only while it is in transit between two tunneling devices. Encrypting stored data extends protection all the way to the physical media. A user or system can read encrypted data only if decrypted by the originating application's authentication method by using encryption/decryption key(s). Storage vendors are looking at cost effective means to deliver data privacy within a distributed storage infrastructure without impacting performance or increasing complexity.

Considerations for implementing data storage encryption include media type, strength, key manage-ability, performance, reliability, cost, and application.

Data encryption on storage media requires special consideration of compression, key management, data recovery, and strength. Writing data to tape does not impose fixed block sizes and is, thus, readily compatible with data compression, authentication, and encryption techniques. For recovery purposes, encrypted tapes may need to contain metadata that securely references the encryption system used to protect the tape. This security metadata is especially important if stored data is maintained for a long time, such as when data archives are mandated (e.g., by HIPAA). However, writing encrypted data to disk media may have additional restrictions which are imposed due to fixed block size. For disks, au-tomated key management and authentication may need to be addressed outside the disk media. In most cases, authentication can be handled directly or by encrypting the application-provided checksums that accompany the stored data. This approach complements and does not duplicate the authentication and integrity checks already supplied by most applications.

In terms of encryption, one should also consider the algorithm employed in terms of strength. For example, Data Encryption Standard's (DES) key length of 56 bits is now considered weak because brute-force testing of the entire key space is relatively quick and inexpensive using easily available processing capacity. 3DES is considered more credible because it's effective key length is 112 bits, therefore, requiring much more time and processing power to crack a key (3DES requires 2^{56} or $> 10^{16}$ more effort to break than DES). More recently, the U.S. government supported the AES (Advanced Encryption Standard) algorithm which employs 128-bit/256-bit block data encryption. Another outcome of encryption may include data integrity and authentication – preventing tampering or repudiation. They will also define how keys are selected or qualified, implemented, and maintained.

4. CRYPTOGRAPHY AND NETWORK SECURITY

Today's cryptography is vastly more complex than its former versions. Unlike the original use of cryptography in its classical roots where it was implemented to conceal both diplomatic and military secrets from the enemy, the cryptography of today, even though it continues to have far-reaching military implications, has expanded its domain and has been designed to provide a cost-effective mean of securing and, in the process, protecting large amounts of electronic data that is stored and communicated across corporate networks worldwide. Cryptography offers the means for protecting this data all while preserving the privacy of critical personal, financial, medical, and E-commerce data that may find itself in the hands of those who should not have access to it.

There have been many developments in the space of modern cryptography that have emerged in the commencement of the 1970s as the development of big encryption protocols and newly advanced cryptographic uses began to appear on the scene. In January 1977, the National Bureau of Standards:(NBS) approved a Data Encryption Standard (DES), which was a revolutionary in launching cryptography research and progress into the modern age of computer technology. Furthermore, cryptography found its mode into the commercial arena when, in December 1980, the same DES algorithm, was adopted by an American institute National Standards Institute (ANSI). Behind this milestone was yet one more when a new concept was planned to develop Public Key Cryptography (PKC), which is still experiencing research development today (Levy S, 2001).

When we talk about modern cryptography, we mean generally cryptosystems since the cryptography of today contains the study and practice of hiding information through using the principle of keys.

Cryptography is measured not only part of a part of mathematics, but also a part of computer science. There are two strong classification of cryptosystems: symmetric and asymmetric.

Figure 6. Network security

Figure 7. Symmetric cryptosystem

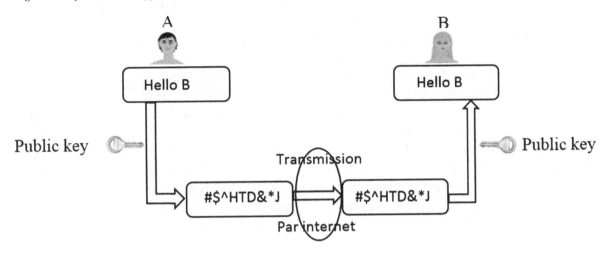

Symmetric cryptosystems include the use of a single key known as the secret key to encrypt and decrypt text, data or messages.

Asymmetric cryptosystems, on the other hand, make use of one key (the public key) to encrypt messages or data, and a second key (the secret key, private key) to decipher or decrypt these messages or data. For this reason, asymmetric cryptosystems are also known as public key cryptosystems.

The problem that symmetric cryptosystems have always confronted is the lack of a secure means for the distribution of the secret key by the individuals who wish to protect their data or communications. Public key cryptosystems explain this problem through the use of cryptographic algorithms used to create the public key and the secret key, such as DES, which has already been declared, and a much stronger algorithm– RSA. The RSA algorithm is the most popular form of public key cryptography, which was developed by Ron Rivest, Adi Shamir, and Leonard Adleman at the Massachusetts Institute of Technology in 1977 (Laurent B and Renata T. 2007).

Figure 8. Asymmetric cryptosystem

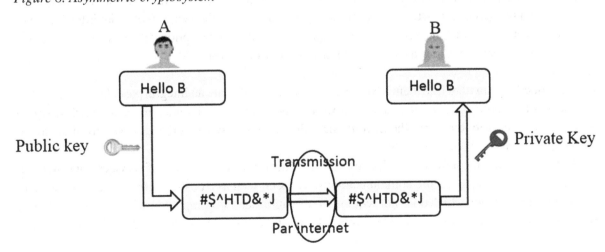

The RSA algorithm contains the process of generating the public key by multiplying two very large (>=100 digits) randomly chosen prime numbers, and then, by randomly choosing another very large number, called the encryption key. The public key would then contain of both the encryption key and the product of those two primes. Ron Rivest then developed a simple formula by which someone who wanted to scramble a message could use that public key to do so. The plaintext would then be converted to cipher text, which was transformed by a mathematic equation that included that large creation. Lastly, using an algorithm developed through the work of the great mathematician, Euclid, Ron Rivest provided a decryption key one that could only be calculated by the use of the original two prime numbers. Using this encryption key would unravel the cipher text and transform it once more into its original plaintext. What makes the RSA algorithm strong is the mathematics that it involves. Ascertaining the original randomly chosen prime numbers and the large randomly chosen number (encryption key) that was used to form the product that encrypted the data in the first place, becomes nearly impossible (Levy S, 2001).

Next, let's address the overall trends identified in the research that has been showed in the field of cryptography and network security.

In reviewing the research that has already been published with regard to cryptography and network security since the 1970s, some notable trends have emerged.

There is a prevailing myth that secrecy is beneficial for security, and since cryptography is based on secrets, it may not be of particular interest for security in a practical sense (Schneier B. 2005).

The mathematics involved in good cryptography are very complex and often difficult to understand, but many software applications tend to hide the details from the user, making cryptography a useful tool in providing network and data security (Fagin B, Baird L, 2008).

Many companies are incorporating data encryption and data loss prevention plans based on strong cryptographic techniques, into their network security strategic planning programs. Cryptographic long-term security is needed but is often difficult to achieve.

Cryptography attends as the groundwork for most IT security solutions, which include:

1. Personal banking, Ecommerce, and other Web-based applications that rely heavily on Secure Sockets Layer (SSL) and Transport Layer Security (TLS) for authentication and data security;
2. Digital signatures that are used to verify the authenticity of updates for computer operating systems, such as Windows XP;
3. The introduction of health cards that allow access to medical history, prescription history, and medical records in countries such as Germany, which contain the electronic health information of its citizens and which depend on digital signature and other encryption schemes for security and privacy of dangerous, private or personal data (Perspectives for, 2006).

Embedded systems that find themselves installed in devices that are an integral part of the manufacturing, health, transportation, finance sectors, as well as the military, without having near-flawless strong cryptographic security built into them would be vulnerable to hackers, terrorists, organized crime, or enemy governments (Webb W, 2006).

The concept of data protection technologies whose aim is to solve quality of services control, modern network security, and secure communications, has been seen as a cost-effective alternative to other means of data security, which does not require modifications and is compatible with existing standards of multimedia compression and communications (Lovoshynovskiy, Deguillaume, Koval, & Pun, 2005).

Figure 9. Example of data modification

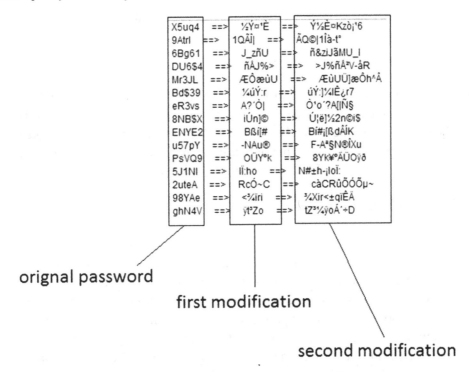

orignal password

first modification

second modification

Security is an important aspect of any network, but in particular to wireless ad-hoc networks where mobile applications are deployed to perform specific tasks. Since these networks are wireless, the potential for hacking into them using mobile devices is greater as there is no clear line of defense for protecting them. The development of the Mobile Application Security System (MASS) utilizing a layered security approach and strong cryptographic techniques is seen as a practical low-cost solution to protecting these application-based wireless networks (Floyd D, 2006).

Finally, a new concept in cryptographic security known as Quantum Encryption, which uses quantum fluctuations of laser light introduced into existing network transmission lines is seen as a means of allowing ultra-secure communications and near perfect security (Hughes D, 2007).

5. ENCRYPTION ALGORITHMS

5.1. Presentation

Many type of encryption like (FDE) Full Disk Encryption offers some of the best protection available. This new technology cut your way to encrypt every part of data on a hard disk drive or a disk. Full disk encryption is even more secure and powerful when hardware solutions are used in combination with software components. This combination is known as end-based or end-point full disk encryption (Laurent B and Renata T. 2007).

Conditional on the storage function, data encryption can be implemented at several levels which include:

- As part of the fabric switches,
- As a component of a storage application (e.g. backup or replication),
- At the application level,
- And now as an in-line storage security appliance.

Employing encryption at the application level introduces the challenge of coordinating different protection schemes which can complicate data recovery and restoration. Application data protection is usually applied between the client and the server but does not often range to the storage subsystem. Additional application-level encryption to the storage array may require modifying the database system, file system, or the application itself (Enterprise Storage Security, 2002).

5.2. Benefits of Data Encryption

For many commercial organizations, data security is not only a corporation option, it is lawfully biding; Losing sensitive data by way of natural disasters or physical theft can have deep impact on a company, possibly crippling the entire organization. While there are many different security mechanisms, data encryption is perhaps the most effective in regard to protecting confidential information.

Internal confidentiality such as your employee and client information, and intellectual property such as product descriptions and business outline all qualify as invaluable information. These critical details should be secured at all times to ensure the integrity and confidentiality of your organization. This information is the core of your business and without it, you can't sustain. If a criminal is able to access this data, there is no limit to the damage they can cause (David E. Sorkin, 1997).

6. SYMMETRIC CRYPTOGRAPHY

Symmetric cryptography, commonly known as secret key cryptography, has been long since been used and has an extensive variety of different implementations reaching from simple substitution ciphers such

Figure 10. Symmetric encryption

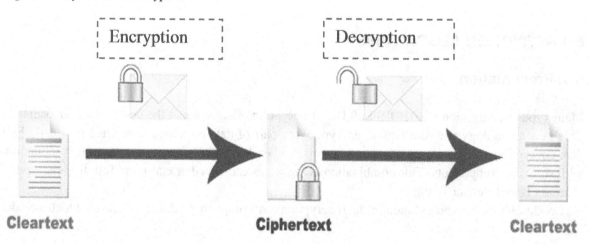

as Caesars Cipher to compound and supposedly "mathematically unbreakable" algorithms such as AES. Symmetric key cryptography makes use of one key that must be kept secret, this key is used for both the encryption and decryption of messages or password or text to be stored or sent.

We will outline some of these functions, how they work, and the relative amount of work required to perform each.

6.1. The Data Encryption Standard (DES)

DES: Data Encryption Standard was the first encryption technique based on the algorithm proposed by IBM Lucifer. This was the first encryption standard, it had many defects and several dangerous vulnerabilities have been discovered (Mactaggart M, 2001).

6.2. Triple DES (3DES)

3DES: Triple DES is an improvement of DES, which ensured the triple safety compared to DES. The algorithm is the same but the encryption technique is applied three times to upgrade the level of security.

In 1999 NIST set 3DES as the interim encryption standard for 1999. While 3DES is considered to be more secure than DES, it is also far more computationally intense. We can describe the algorithm as follows (B. Schneier, 2003).

6.3. AES: Advanced Encryption Standard

AES: Advanced Encryption Standard was proposed by the National Standard Institute and Technology (NIST) to replace DES. The attack for AES is known only by the brute force attack that allows an attacker to test the combination of characters to break security. However, brute force is not an easy task, even for a supercomputer if the number of combination is arbitrarily high (Carlton R. Davis, 2001).

7. ASYMMETRIC CRYPTOGRAPHY

Encryption was first created for the transmission of secret military posts, and is mostly used today for the security of civil, and especially private, transactions, banking, as well as to be used by several companies along with other encryption methods.

The goal is always to find a solution that will maximize safety. Asymmetric encryption was created to provide a public key that can be transmitted via the Internet to encode the message to be transmitted and a private one to allow decoding and inverse return.

The role of this encryption method is to ensure that in the case of a hacker successfully accessing this key, the hacker will remain unable to proceed with his or her activities until obtaining the private key.

After using this key, the message is transmitted and encrypted (totally modified according to the method or algorithm chosen by the programmer). When the recipient receives the encrypted message, he or she will use the private key, which will then allow for the decoding.

This method is the safest and most reliable transmission pattern and procedure.

Figure 11. Asymmetric encryption

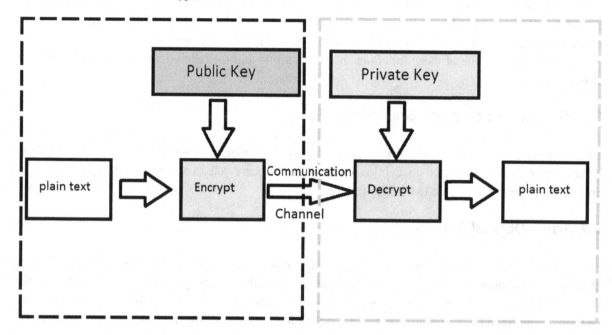

The manner in which we change messages or codes is always contingent to the choice of the programmer and based on mathematical formulas or algorithmic scheme, that specific change should be personal and private.

The key information held by concerned users is characterized with an asymmetry which explains the reason behind calling the setting of public-key cryptography "asymmetric". For further elaboration, one party has a secret key while another has the public key that matches this secret one. This is in contrast to the symmetry in the private key setting, where both parties are found to have the same key. Asymmetric encryption is, thus, another name for public-key encryption, the mechanism for achieving data privacy in the public key or asymmetric setting.

Our study of asymmetric encryption (following our study of other primitives) will begin by searching for appropriate notions of security, and models and formalizations via which they are captured. We then consider constructions, where we look at how to design and analyze various schemes.

In the matter of notions of security, we tend to believe on our ability to build considerably on our earlier study of symmetric encryption. Indeed, as this point of view may suggest, there is very little distinction between symmetric and asymmetric encryption; no more than the fact that in the latter the adversary gets the public key as input. This is important (and re-assuring) to remember. All the intuition and examples cited before remain relevant; how security is modeled, and what it means for a scheme to be secure. Accordingly, we will deal with the security issues quite briefly, just re-formulating the definitions we have seen before.

The second issue, constructions to be specific, is another story. Designs of asymmetric encryption schemes rely on tools and ideas different from those underlying the design of symmetric encryption schemes. Namely in the asymmetric case, the basis is, typically computationally intractable complications in number theory, while for the symmetric case we used block ciphers; Thus, the greater part of efforts in the context of this chapter will be on schemes and their security properties.

As symmetric key encryption introduced, it is challenging the distribution of symmetric keys due to the nature of symmetric key encryption i.e. if you poses the secret key you can encrypt/decrypt messages, so if the key is stolen through some means the encryption becomes with no utility. Further, for any couple of people who wish to communicate, a key is required to encrypt the communication, this creates a logistical challenges when attempting to manage all the keys that a system is set to need for communication (M. Bellare, P. Rogaway, 2005).

8. ASCII CODE

ASCII stands for American Standard Code for Information Interchange. It's a seven bit character code where every single bit signifies a unique character. On this table you will find 8 bits, 256 characters. Computers could only understand numbers, so an ASCII code is the numerical representation of a character such as 'b' or '&' or an action of some kind. ASCII was developed long time ago now and the non-printing characters are rarely used for their original purpose (Wikipedia Ascii code, 1977).

9. DATA MODIFICATION

As it is known, each message or password is a string of characters and each character is characterized by a different ASCII code; other encryption is indicated on the modification of the ASCII code. There are also several other methods of data modification, such as changing the way the data is encoded, changing the way the data is backed up, and changing the display of the data.

The technique to follow is to change the characters based on the modification of ASCII codes because it is the most used and controllable method and it provides a high level of accuracy (without loss of information or data).

According to the latest studies and search results, the most efficient algorithms for encryption are based on the modification of random data with the use of randomized modification.

Suppose one has created a password containing 4 characters and we wanted to secure it by changing all the elements. Each character will be modified in a different way from the others.

The ASCII code is an integer between 0 and 255. For example, changing this code can be done by following a mathematical algorithm that always produces results in a different and random order, as to avoid duplication and any pattern between the used integers. As an example we can use the four mathematical operation: subtraction "-", addition "+" multiplication "*" and "/" division for a different result. If the choice of one of these operators is randomly and the number with which these operations are applied are also randomly chosen so decryption and reverse return is impossible without knowing the operators and integers randomly selected to be stored in a very secure location outside.

Even if a hacker discovers or hacks the algorithm of public key encryption has the role it will never happen to decrypt the data because the results of this key are always different and no link between each other. Each character or element of this code is changed in a random process without following any procedure or deterministic manner.

10. AUTOMATING DATA PROTECTION

With the privileges of cloud-computing services, businesses are able now to show on market at lightning speed carrying on an enormously scalable infrastructure to address their just in time calculation needs. While the business benefits are indisputable, security worries remain the largest road-block to the wholesale to benefit those services (Arshad Noor, 2013).

Data lies as the nitty-gritty of every company and is the most precious asset of any strategic business decision and evolution. Companies need, and want, to know that they have a fully secured and protected data. "If a company cannot access its data, employees are left twiddling their thumbs, productivity declines and the business grinds to a halt until the data is brought back online". Protecting this data and assuring that it is accessible all day long, seven days a week, year-round is an exhausting task for IT and data center managers. However, companies have to be concerned about more than just the data. They need to look at the applications, systems and servers in which the data area cumulated. IT managers need to look at their data centers from the perspective of services. It is explained by the fact that companies must protect their entire infrastructure – not just the data that is associated with it.

Most people think of disasters as hurricanes, tsunamis or power grids failing. Yet the majority of data center disasters are not related to natural causes. It is smaller scope human mistakes and twisted acts that cause these incidents. Alternatively, disaster could affect an individual only ad not entire company.

IT faces an obstacles in providing these data protection and disaster recovery (DR) services for an entire infrastructure. The amount of data that needs safe-guarding is growing. The IT infrastructure is expanding in complexity with virtual and physical servers, cloud-based and hosted applications and network connectivity.

Every minute consumed trying to recuperate data or get service up and running again is time not spent on business processes. Most companies state-run that they can only have enough money downtime of four hours or less at one time and given the plan below on misplaced revenue based on publicly accessible data, it is understandable why this is the case. This data provides a sight into a baseline outage

Table 1. Data courtesy of Storage Area Network for Dummies by Chris Poelker and Alex Nikitin

Industry	Lost Revenue per Hour (U.S. dollars)
Energy	$ 2.8 million
Telecom	$ 2 million
Manufacturing	$ 1.6 million
Finance	$ 1.5 million
Information technology	$ 1.350 million
Insurance	$ 1.2 million
Retail	$ 1.1 million
Pharmaceutical	$ 1.1 million
Chemical	$ 700,000
Transport	$ 670,000
Utilities	$ 640,000
Healthcare	$ 640,000
Media	$ 340,000

charge. Protecting data is useless if it can't be recovered. One of the greatest data central tests today is ensuring a smooth recovery of processes after downtime. Downtime can be caused by data corruption or lost, equipment failure or a complete location outage after a loss of power or a natural disaster.

In fact, a recent IDG Research Services report, Disaster Recovery Trends and Metrics, demonstrates the result of data losses within a company, with damage of productivity being the biggest result shadowed closely by harm to an enterprise's reputation, loss of sensitive data financial losses, and procured costly technical assistance (Darrell Riddle, 2012).

CONCLUSION

With the increasing growth of the Internet, companies are being faced with the challenge to protect unprecedented amounts of data from targeted attacks and resolute. While security regulations instructing the protection of sensitive economic, health care or personally identifiable information (PII) serve as the primary motivation for data protection, breached enterprises have learned the hard way that brands can be injured, principal to significant financial costs when even unregulated data, such as e-mail and home-addresses, are breached1.

Although encryption technology has been existing for more than forty years two, its use was initially relegated to military and banking applications where any penetrated information has extremely high consequences. Twenty years ago, the world wide web (www) accompanied in the Secure Socket Layer (SSL) protocol with its use of encryption to protect information as it navigated the internet. However, it was professed as an enhancement to network protocols, and subsequently, encryption technology continued to persist outside the domain of commercial applications.

Figure 12. Data losses

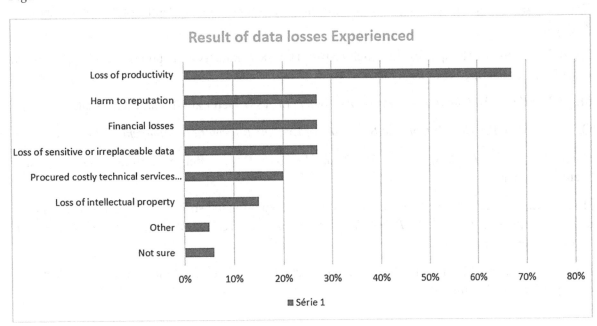

Security methods are constantly developing, but, on the other hand, there are always parties seeking to find flaws and vulnerabilities in each system; it is a never-ending technological race between the hacked and the hacker.

REFERENCES

Baker, M. (2005). *Keeping a Secret*. Technology Review. Retrieved, from Academic Search Premier Database.

Bhargav-Spantzel, A., Camenisch, J., Gross, T., & Sommer, D. (2007). User centricity: A taxonomy and open issues. *Journal of Computer Security*. Retrieved, from Academic Search Premier Database.

Bohli, J., González Vasco, M., & Steinwandt, R. (2007, July). Secure group key establishment revisited. *International Journal of Information Security*, *6*(4), 243–254. doi:10.1007/s10207-007-0018-x

Boneh, D., Canetti, R., Halevi, S., & Katz, J. (2006, December). Chosen-ciphertext security from identity-based encryption. *SIAM Journal on Computing*.

Callas, J. (2007). The Future of Cryptography. *Information Systems Security*.

Callas, J. (2007). The Future of Cryptography. *Information Systems Security*.

Carlton, R. (2001). *IPSec, Securing VPNs*. McGraw Hill Publishers.

Companies Integrate Encryption/Data Loss Prevention. (2008). Computer Security Update, from Academic Search Premier Database.

Daniel Lloyd, C. (2008). *Literature Review of Cryptography and its Role in Network Security Principles and Practice*. Capella University.

Dirk, R. (2000). *Framework design - a role modeling approach*. Wiss Federal Institute of Technology Zurich.

Fagin, B., Baird, L., Humphries, J., & Schweitzer, D. (2008, January). Skepticism and Cryptography. *Knowledge, Technology & Policy*.

Floyd, D. (2006). *Mobile application security system (MASS)*. Bell Labs Technical Journal.

Gartner. (2011). *Big Data is Only the Beginning of Extreme Information Management*. Gartner.

Harris, D. (2007). *Has Anyone Seen My Data. Electronic Design*. Retrieved from Academic Search Premier Database.

Homin, K., Lee, G., Malkin, T., & Erich, N. (2007). Cryptographic strength of ssl/tls servers: current and recent practices. In *IMC '07: Proceedings of the 7th ACM SIGCOMM conference on Internet measurement*. New York: ACM.

Hoque, S., Fairhurst, M., Howells, G., & Deravi, F. (2007, April 27). Feasibility of generating biometric encryption keys. *Electronics Letters*.

Hughes, D. (2007). Cyberspace Security via Quantum Encryption. *Military Technology*. Retrieved from Academic Search Premier Database.

Karl, D. (2009). *Modular mathematics, primitive root*. Academic Press..

Katz, J., & Yung, M. (2003). Scalable protocols for authenticated group key exchange. In D. Boneh (Ed.), *Advances in Cryptology—CRYPTO* (LNCS). Berlin: Springer. doi:10.1007/978-3-540-45146-4_7

Kim, H., Lee, S., & Lee, D. (2004). Constant-round authenticated group key exchange for dynamic groups. In P. J. Lee (Ed.), *Advances in Cryptology—ASIACRYPT (LNCS)*. Berlin: Springer. doi:10.1007/978-3-540-30539-2_18

Klappenecker, A. (2004). Remark on a non-breakable data encryption scheme by Kish and Sethuraman. *Fluctuation & Noise Letters*. Retrieved from Academic Search Premier Database.

Kodaganallur, V. (2006). Secure E-Commerce: Understanding the Public Key Cryptography Jigsaw Puzzle. *Information Systems Security*. Retrieved from Academic Search Premier Database.

Laurent, B., & Renata, T. (2007). Early recognition of encrypted applications. Academic Press.

Levy, S. (2001). *Crypto: How the code rebels beat the Government - Saving privacy in the digital age*. New York: Viking Penguin Publishing.

Li, C., Li, S., Zhang, D., & Chen, G. (2006). Cryptanalysis of a data security protection scheme for VoIP. *IEE Proceedings -- Vision, Image & Signal Processing*.

Lovoshynovskiy, S., Deguillaume, F., Koval, O., & Pun, T. (2005). Information-theoretic data-hiding: recent achievements and open problems. *International Journal of Image & Graphics*. Retrieved from Academic Search Premier Database.

Mactaggart, M. (2001). *Introduction to cryptography*. Academic Press.

Malcolm, T., & Bronwyn, H. (2013, July 29). *Conjecture Corporation*.

Margaret, R. (2005). *TechTarget's IT encyclopedia and learning center*. WhatIs.com.

Marlink, S. (2009). *New tricks for defeating sslin practice*. Academic Press.

McKinsey J. (2011). *Big Data: The Next Frontier for Innovation, Competition and Productivity*. McKinsey.

NeoScale Systems, Inc. (2002). *Entreprise storage security*. Author.

NIST. (n.d.). *National vulnerability database*. NIST.

Noor, A. (2003). *Creator of the industry's first open-source symmetric key-management system and many cryptographic tools to simplify the use of this technology within business applications*. Academic Press.

Paller, A. (2008). *Top ten cyber security menaces*. Academic Press.

Perspectives for cryptographic long-term security. (2006). *Communications of the ACM*. Retrieved from Academic Search Premier Database.

Pistoia, M., Chandra, S., Fink, S., & Yahav, E. (2007). A survey of static analysis methods for identifying security vulnerabilities in software systems. *IBM Systems Journal*. Retrieved from Academic Search Premier Database.

Pratt, M. (2006). Moving Target. *Computerworld*. Retrieved from Academic Search Premier Database.

Prince, B. (2008). *Playing the waiting game*. Retrieved from Academic Search Premier Database.

Reesa, E., & Abrams, A. (1982). Checklist for developing software quality metrics. In *ACM 82: Proceedings of the ACM '82 conference*. New York: ACM.

Richard, E., Daniel, S., Robert, J., & Byrnes, G. (2005). *SSH, the secure shell* (2nd ed.). O'Reilly.

Schneier, B. (1996). *Applied Cryptography*. Wiley and Sons.

Schneier, B. (1999). Security in the real world: How to evaluate security. *Computer Security Journal, 15*, 1–14.

Schneier, B., & Ferguson, N. (2003). *Practical Cryptography*. Wiley Publishing.

The Ponemon Institute. (2011). *2010 Annual Study: U.S. Cost of a Data Breach*. Author.

Todd, R., & Eric, W. (2009). *Groups*. Mathsworld.

Webb, W. (2006). *Hack-Proof Design*. Retrieved from Academic Search Premier Database.

Young, A. (2006, March). Cryptoviral extortion using Microsoft's Crypto API. *International Journal of Information Security, 5*(2), 67–76. doi:10.1007/s10207-006-0082-7

Zanin, G., Di Pietro, R., & Mancini, L. (2007). Robust RSA distributed signatures for large-scale long-lived ad hoc networks. *Journal of Computer Security*.

Compilation of References

Abad, J., Lafuente, E., & Vilajosana, J. (2013). An assessment of the OHSAS 18001 certification process: Objective drivers and consequences on safety performance and labour productivity. *Safety Science*, *60*, 47–56. doi:10.1016/j. ssci.2013.06.011

Abate, A. F., Esposito, A., Grieco, N., & Nota, G. (2002). Workflow Performance Evaluation Through WPQL. In *Proceeding of the 14th International Conference on Software Engineering and Knowledge Engineering* (Vol. 27). ACM Press. doi:10.1145/568760.568846

Abello, A., Samos, J., & Saltor, F. (2006). YAM2: A Multidimensional Conceptual Model Extending UML. *Information Systems*, 31.

Abent, E. (2013, November 18). *Android Enterprise Adoption Set to Grow Significantly In Coming Years According to ABI Research.* [Blog post]. Retrieved from http://www.androidheadlines.com/2013/11/android-enterprise-adoption-set-grow-significantly-coming-years-according-abi-research.html

Agerfalk, P., Goldkuhl, G., & Cronholm, S. (1999). Information Systems Actability Engineering - Integrating Analysis of Business Process and Usability Requirements. In *Proceedings of the 4th International Workshop on the Language Action Perspective on Communication Modeling.* Copenhagen, Denmark: Academic Press.

Aguilar-Saven, R. S. (2004). Business Process Modelling: Review and Framework. *International Journal of Production Economics*, *90*, 129–149.

Ai, L. M., & Tang (2008). A penatly-based genetic algorithm for QoS-aware web service composition with inter-service-dependencies and conflicts. In *International Conference on Computational Intelligence for Modelling Control & Automation* (CIMCA). Academic Press.

Ai, L., & Tang, M. (2008). QoS-based web service composition accommodating interservice dependencies using minimal-conflict hill-climbing repair genetic algorithm. In *IEEE International Conference on eScience*. IEEE.

Akdere, M. (2009). The role of knowledge management in quality management practices: Achieving performance excellence in organizations. *Advances in Developing Human Resources*, *11*(3), 349–361. doi:10.1177/1523422309338575

Akyildiz, I. F., & Can Vuran, M. (2010). *Wireless Sensor Networks*. Academic Press.

Akyildiz, I. F., Melodia, T., & Chowdury, K. R. (2007). Wireless multimedia sensor networks: A survey. *IEEE Wireless Communications*, *14*(6), 32–39. doi:10.1109/MWC.2007.4407225

Alavi, M., & Leidner, D. E. (2001). Review: knowledge management and knowledge management systems: conceptual foundations and research issues. *Management Information Systems Quarterly*, *25*(1), 107–136. doi:10.2307/3250961

Albin, A. (2012, October 12). Musical abstractions in distributed multi-robot systems. *Presented at the Intelligent Robots and Systems (IROS), 2012 IEEE/RSJ International Conference on 2012*. doi:10.1109/IROS.2012.6385688

Aldowaisan, T. A., & Gaafar, L. K. (1999). Business Process Reengineering: An Approach for Process Mapping. *Omega:International Journal of Management Sciences, 27*, 515–524.

Alippi, C., Camplani, R., Galperti, C., & Roveri, M. (2011). A robust, adaptive, solar-powered WSN framework for aquatic environmental monitoring. *IEEE Sensors Journal, 11*(1), 45–55. doi:10.1109/JSEN.2010.2051539

Al-Karaki, J. N., & Kamal, A. E. (2004). Routing techniques in wireless sensor networks: A survey. *IEEE Wireless Communications, 11*(6), 6–27. doi:10.1109/MWC.2004.1368893

Alliance, O. H. (2007, November 5). *Industry Leaders Announce Open Platform for Mobile Device*. Open Handset Alliance, Press release. Retrieved from http://www.openhandsetalliance.com/press_110507.html

Alrifai, M., Skoutas, D., & Risse, T. (2010). Selecting skyline services for qos-based web service composition. In *Proceedings of the 19th International Conference on World Wide Web, WWW '10*. New York, NY: ACM. doi:10.1145/1772690.1772693

Al-Saa'da, R., Abu Taleb, Y., Al-Mahasneh, R., Nimer, N., & Al-Weshah, G. (2013). Supply Chain Management and Its Effect on Health Care Service Quality: Quantitative Evidence from Jordanian Private Hospitals. *Journal of Management and Strategy, 4*(2), 42–51.

Alshitri, K. I., & Abanumy, A. N. (2014). Exploring the reasons behind the low ISO 27001 adoption in public organizations in Saudi Arabia. In *Information Science and Applications (ICISA), 2014 International Conference on*. Seoul, Korea: ICISA.

Alter, S. (2003, October). 18 Reasons Why IT-Reliant Work Systems Should Replace 'The IT Artifact' as the Core Subject Matter of the IS Field. *Communications of the Association for Information Systems, 12*(23), 365–394.

Alter, S. (2006). *The Work System Method: Connecting People, Processes, and IT for Business Results*. Works System Press.

Alter, S. (2013). Work System Theory: Overview of Core Concepts, Extensions, and Challenges for the Future. *Journal of the Association for Information Systems, 14*(2), 72–121.

Anderson, M., Banker, R. D., Menon, N. M., & Romero, J. A. (2011). Implementing enterprise resource planning systems: Organizational performance and the duration of the implementation. *Information Technology Management, 12*(3), 197–212. doi:10.1007/s10799-011-0102-9

Andrici, M. (2014, February 3). 8 Best Android App options to launch your productivity. *Joy of Android News*. Retrieved from http://joyofandroid.com/best-android-email-app/

Android Developers. (2014). Security Tips. *Android Developers Training*. Retrieved from http://developer.android.com/training/articles/security-tips.html

Android Official Web Site. (2014). Android history. *Android official web site*. Retrieved from http://www.android.com/history/

Arbaugh, W. A., Fithen, W. L., & McHugh, J. (2000). *Windows of Vulnerability: A Case Study Analysis*. IEEE Computer.

Archibald, J. A. (1975). Computer Science education for majors of other disciplines. In *Proceedings of AFIPS Joint Computer Conferences* (pp. 903–906). doi:10.1145/1499949.1500154

Ardagna, D., & Pernici, B. (2007). Adaptative service composition in flexible processes. *IEEE Transactions on Software Engineering, 33*(6), 369–384.

Arena, M., Arnaboldi, M., & Azzone, G. (2010). The organizational dynamics of Enterprise Risk Management. *Accounting, Organizations and Society*, *35*(7), 659–675. doi:10.1016/j.aos.2010.07.003

Arnold, V., Benford, T., Canada, J., & Sutton, S. G. (2011). The role of strategic enterprise risk management and organizational flexibility in easing new regulatory compliance. *International Journal of Accounting Information Systems*, *12*(3), 171–188. doi:10.1016/j.accinf.2011.02.002

Asif, M., de Bruijn, E. J., Fisscher, O. A. M., Searcy, C., & Steenhuis, H.-J. (2009). Process embedded design of integrated management systems. *International Journal of Quality & Reliability Management*, *26*(3), 261–282. doi:10.1108/02656710910936735

Aslan, B., Stevenson, N., & Hendry, L. C. (2012). Enterprise Resource Planning systems: An assessment of applicability to Make-To-Order companies. *Computers in Industry*, *63*(7), 692–705. doi:10.1016/j.compind.2012.05.003

Aspinall, S., & Langer, A. J. (2005). Connected Workforce: Essays from innovators in business mobility. In Connected Workforce. Premium Publishing.

Assessment Summary Results (ASR). (n.d.). Retrieved December 2014 from http://measurablesecurity.mitre.org/incubator/asr/

Asset Identification (AI). (n.d.). Retrieved December 2014 from http://csrc.nist.gov/publications/nistir/ir7693/NISTIR-7693.pdf

Asset Reporting Format (ARF). (n.d.). Retrieved December 2014 from http://csrc.nist.gov/publications/nistir/ir7694/NISTIR-7694.pdf

Au, G., & Choi, I. (1999). Facilitating implementation of quality management through information technology. *Information & Management*, *36*(6), 287–299. doi:10.1016/S0378-7206(99)00030-0

Badica, C., Badica, A., & Litoiu, V. (2003b). Role Activity Diagrams As Finite State Processes. In *Proceedings of Second International Symposium on Parallel and Distributed Computing* (pp. 15-22). doi:10.1109/ISPDC.2003.1267638

Badica, C., Badica, A., & Litoiu, V. (2003a). A New Formal IDEF-Based Modelling of Business Processes. In *Proceedings of the First Balkan Conference in Informatics (BCI)*. BCI.

Baker, H., Cade, S., Oudijk, M., Ramachandran, C., Roth, J., Schwarting, D., & van Leeuwen, J. (2000). E-sourcing: 21st Century Purchasing. *Booz Allen & Hamilton*. Retrieved July 14, 2014, from http://www.boozallen.com/media/file/80568.pdf

Baker, M. (2005). *Keeping a Secret*. Technology Review. Retrieved, from Academic Search Premier Database.

Bakker, E., Zheng, J., Knight, L., & Harland, C. (2008). Putting e-commerce adoption in a supply chain context. *International Journal of Operations & Production Management*, *28*(4), 313–330. doi:10.1108/01443570810861543

Bal, J. (1998). Process Analysis Tools for Process Improvement. *The TQM Magazine*, *10*(5), 342–354. doi:10.1108/09544789810231225

Bansal, S. (2014 February 24). *First Tor-based Android malware spotted in the wild*. Retrieved from http://thehackernews.com/2014/02/first-tor-based-android-malware-spotted.html

Barbier, G., Cucchi, V., & Hill, D. R. C. (n.d.). Model-driven engineering applied to crop modeling. *Ecological Informatics*.

Barcelo-Ordinas, J. M., Chanet, J. P., Hou, K. M., & Garcia-Vidal, J. (2013). *A survey of wireless sensor technologies applied to precision agriculture*. Academic Press.

Barlette, Y., & Fomin, V. V. (2010). The adoption of information security management standards: A literature review. In I. G. I. Global (Ed.), *Information Resources Management: Concepts* (pp. 69–90). Methodologies, Tools and Applications. doi:10.4018/978-1-61520-965-1.ch104

Basta, A., & Zgola, M. (2011). *Database Security*. Delmar Cengage Learning.

Basten, T., & van der Aalst, W. M. P. (1999). *'Inheritance of Behaviour', Computing Science Report 99/17*. Eindhoven: Eindhoven University of Technology.

Basu, A., & Blanning, R. W. (2000). A Formal Approach to Workflow Analysis. *Information Systems Research, 11*(1), 17–36. doi:10.1287/isre.11.1.17.11787

Batenburg, R. (2007). E-procurement adoption by European firms: A quantitative analysis. *Journal of Purchasing and Supply Management, 13*(3), 182–192. doi:10.1016/j.pursup.2007.09.014

Bazan, J., Nguyen, H. S., Skowron, A., & Szczuka, M. (2003). A View on Rough Set Concept Approximations. In *Proceedings of R.S.F.D.G.r.C., China*. Springer. doi:10.1007/3-540-39205-X_23

Bazan, J. G., Nguyen, H. S., Nguyen, S. H., Synak, P., & Wróblewski, J. (2000). Rough set algorithms in classification problem. In L. Polkowski, S. Tsumoto, & T. Lin (Eds.), *Rough Set Methods and Applications* (pp. 49–88). Heidelberg, Germany: Physica-Verlag. doi:10.1007/978-3-7908-1840-6_3

Beal, V. (2014). *BYOD: Bring Your Owen Device*. [Blog post]. Retrieved from http://www.webopedia.com/TERM/B/BYOD.html

Beall, S., Carter, C., Carter, P., Germer, T., Hendrick, T., Jap, S., & Petersen, K. et al. (2003). *The Role of Reverse Auctions in Strategic Sourcing*. CAPS Research.

Beard, J. W., & Sumner, M. (2004). Seeking strategic advantage in the post-net era: Viewing ERP systems from the resource-based perspective. *The Journal of Strategic Information Systems, 13*(2), 129–150. doi:10.1016/j.jsis.2004.02.003

Beckmerhagen, I. A., Berg, H. P., Karapetrovic, S. V., & Willborn, W. O. (2003). Auditing in support of the integration of management systems: A case from the nuclear industry. *Managerial Auditing Journal, 18*(6/7), 560–568. doi:10.1108/02686900310482696

Bédard, Y., & Paquette, F. (1989). *Extending entity/relationship formalism for spatial information systems*. Paper presented at the AUTO-CARTO 9, Baltimore, MD.

Bédard, Y., Proulx, M. J., Larrivée, S., & Bernier, E. (2002). *Modeling multiple representations into spatial data warehouses: A UML-based approach*. Paper presented at the Joint Int. Symp. ISPRS Commission IV, Ottawa, Canada.

Bédard, Y., Rivest, S., & Proulx, M. J. (2006). *Spatial online analytical processing (SOLAP): Concepts, architectures, and solutions from a geomatics engineering perspective Data Warehouses and OLAP: Concepts* (pp. 298–319). Architectures and Solutions.

Bédard, Y., Rivest, S., & Proulx, M. J. (2006). *Spatial online analytical processing (SOLAP): Concepts, architectures, and solutions from a geomatics engineering perspective. In Data Warehouses and OLAP: Concepts* (pp. 298–319). Architectures and Solutions.

Beekman, J., & Thompson, C. (2013 March 19). *Man-in-the-Middle Attack on T-Mobile Wi-Fi Calling*. Technical Report No. UCB/EECS-2013-18.

Beeny, R. (2014). Supply Chain Visibility in Healthcare – Beyond the Dashboard. *Hospital & Healthcare Management*. Retrieved July 14, 2014, from http://www.tecsys.com/company/news/TECSYS-LifeScienceLogistics-HealthcareVisibility.pdf

Bendoly, E., Rosenzweig, E. D., & Stratman, J. K. (2009). The efficient use of enterprise information for strategic advantage: A data envelopment analysis. *Journal of Operations Management, 27*(4), 310–323. doi:10.1016/j.jom.2008.11.001

Bentley, P. J., & Wakefield, J. P. (1998). Finding acceptable solutions in the Paretooptimal range using multiobjective genetic algorithms. In *Soft Computing in Engineering Design and Manufacturing*. Springer-Verlag.

Berbner, R., Spahn, M., Repp, N., Heckmann, O., & Steinmetz, R. (2006). Heuristics for QoS-aware web service composition. In *IEEE International Conference on Web Services (ICWS)*. IEEE.

Bernardo, M., Casadesús, M., Karapetrovic, S., & Heras, I. (2009). How integrated are environmental, quality and other standardized management systems? An empirical study. *Journal of Cleaner Production, 17*(8), 742–750. doi:10.1016/j.jclepro.2008.11.003

Bernardo, M., Casadesús, M., Karapetrovic, S., & Heras, I. (2010). An empirical study on the integration of management system audits. *Journal of Cleaner Production, 18*(5), 486–495. doi:10.1016/j.jclepro.2009.12.001

Bernardo, M., Casadesús, M., Karapetrovic, S., & Heras, I. (2011). Relationships between the integration of audits and management systems - An empirical study. *The TQM Journal, 23*(6), 659–672. doi:10.1108/17542731111175266

Berson, A., & Smith, S. (1997). *Data Warehousing, Data Mining, and OLAP (Data Warehousing/Data Management)*. Computing Mcgraw-Hill.

Beynon-Davies. (2009). *Business information systems*. Basingstoke, UK: Palgrave.

Beynon-Davies, P. (2009). *Business Information Systems*. Basingstoke, UK: Palgrave.

Bhargav-Spantzel, A., Camenisch, J., Gross, T., & Sommer, D. (2007). User centricity: A taxonomy and open issues. *Journal of Computer Security*. Retrieved, from Academic Search Premier Database.

Biazzo, S. (2000). Approaches to Business Process Analysis: A Review. *Business Process Management Journal, 6*(2), 99–112. doi:10.1108/14637150010321277

Biazzo, S. (2002). Process Mapping Techniques and Organisational Analysis. *Business Process Management Journal, 8*(1), 42–52. doi:10.1108/14637150210418629

Bidgoli, H. (2004). *The Internet Encyclopedia* (Vol. 1). John Wiley & Sons, Inc. doi:10.1002/047148296X

BieMme Italia. (2014). Android Hmi Multi Touch Panels. *BieMme Italia WebSite*. Retrieved from http://www.biemmeitalia.net/android-hmi multi-touch/

Bimonte, S., & Kang, M. A. (2010). Towards a model for the multidimensional analysis of field data. Lecture Notes in Computer Science, 6295, 58-72.

Bimonte, S., Boulil, K., Pinet, F., & Kang, M. A. (2013). *Design of complex spatio-multidimensional models with the ICSOLAP UML profile: An implementation in magicdraw*. Paper presented at the ICEIS 2013.

Bimonte, S., Tchounikine, A., & Miquel, M. (2006).GeoCube, a multidimensional model and navigation operators handling complex measures: Application in spatial OLAP. Lecture Notes in Computer Science, 4243, 100-109.

Bimonte, S. (2010). A Web-Based Tool for Spatio-Multidimensional Analysis of Geographic and Complex Data. *International Journal of Agricultural and Environmental Information Systems, 1*(2), 42–67. doi:10.4018/jaeis.2010070103

271

Bimonte, S., Kang, M. A., Paolino, L., Sebillo, M., Zaamoune, M., & Vitiello, G. (2014). OLAPing field data: A theoretical and implementation framework. *Fundamenta Informaticae, 132*(2), 267–290.

Bimonte, S., Tchounikine, A., Miquel, M., & Pinet, F. (2010). When spatial analysis meets OLAP: Multidimensional model and operators. *International Journal of Data Warehousing and Mining, 6*(4), 33–60. doi:10.4018/jdwm.2010100103

Bizer, C., Heath, T., & Berners-Lee, T. (2009). Linked Data - The Story So Far. *International Journal on Semantic Web and Information Systems, 5*(3), 1–22. doi:10.4018/jswis.2009081901

Blue Android Developers. (2013). *Android a Mobile Operating System.* [Blog post]. Retrieved from http://myblueandroid.weebly.com/

Bof, F., & Previtali, P. (2007). Organisational Pre-Conditions for e-Procurement in Governments: The Italian Experience in the Public Health Care Sector. *The Electronic Journal of E-Government, 5*(1), 1–10.

Bohli, J., González Vasco, M., & Steinwandt, R. (2007, July). Secure group key establishment revisited. *International Journal of Information Security, 6*(4), 243–254. doi:10.1007/s10207-007-0018-x

Boneh, D., Canetti, R., Halevi, S., & Katz, J. (2006, December). Chosen-ciphertext security from identity-based encryption. *SIAM Journal on Computing.*

Booch, G. (1996). The unified modeling language. *Performance Computing/Unix Review, 14*(13), 41–48.

Booch, G. (1986). Object-oriented development. *IEEE Transactions on Software Engineering, SE-12*(2), 211–221. doi:10.1109/TSE.1986.6312937

Bose, I., & Mahapatra, K. R. (2001). Business data mining – A machine learning perspective. *Information & Management, 39*(3), 211–225. doi:10.1016/S0378-7206(01)00091-X

Bosilj-Vuksic, V., Giaglis, G. M., & Hlupic, V. (2000). IDEF Diagrams and Petri Nets for Business Process Modelling: Suitability, Efficacy and Complementary Use. In *Proceedings of International Conference on Enterprise Information Systems Stafford.* Academic Press.

Bosona, T., & Gebresenbet, G. (2013). Food traceability as an integral part of logistics management in food and agricultural supply chain. *Food Control, 33*(1), 32–48. doi:10.1016/j.foodcont.2013.02.004

Boudreau, M., & Robey, D. (2005). Enacting integrated information technology: A human agency perspective. *Organization Science, 16*(1), 3–18. doi:10.1287/orsc.1040.0103

Boulil, K., Bimonte, S., & Pinet, F. (2012). *A UML & spatial OCL based approach for handling quality issues in SOLAP systems.* Paper presented at the ICEIS 2012.

Boulil, K., Bimonte, S., Mahboubi, H., & Pinet, F. (2010). *Towards the definition of spatial data warehouses integrity constraints with spatial OCL.* Paper presented at the ACM 13th international workshop on Data warehousing and OLAP. doi:10.1145/1871940.1871948

Boulil, K., Bimonte, S., & Pinet, F. (2014). Spatial OLAP integrity constraints: From UML-based specification to automatic implementation: Application to energetic data in agriculture. *Journal of Decision Systems, 23*(4), 460–480. doi:10.1080/12460125.2014.934120

Boulil, K., Pinet, F., Bimonte, S., Carluer, N., Lauvernet, C., Cheviron, B., & Chanet, J.-P. et al. (2013). Guaranteeing the quality of multidimensional analysis in data warehouses of simulation results: Application to pesticide transfer data produced by the MACRO model. *Ecological Informatics, 16*, 41–52. doi:10.1016/j.ecoinf.2013.04.004

Brasen, S. (2011, October 17). *Enterprise Mobile Device Management: How Smartphones and Tablets are Changing Workforce IT Requirements*. Enterprise Management Associates, Inc. Research Report – End-user. Retrieved from http://www.enterprisemanagement.com/research/asset.php/2101/Enterprise-Mobile-Device-Management:-How-Smartphones-and-Tablets-are-Changing-Workforce-IT-Requirements

Breault, J., Goodall, C., & Fos, P. J. (2002). Data mining a diabetic data warehouse. *Artificial Intelligence in Medicine, 26*(1), 37–54. doi:10.1016/S0933-3657(02)00051-9 PMID:12234716

British CCTA. (2003). *CRAMM (CCTA Risk Analysis and Management Method)*. Insight Consulting.

Brynjolfsson, E. (1993). The Productivity Paradox of Information Technology. *Communications of the ACM, 36*(12), 67–77. doi:10.1145/163298.163309

BSI. (2012). Specification of common management system requirements as a framework for integration. *PAS, 99*, 2012.

Buratti, C., Conti, A., Dardari, D., & Verdone, R. (2009). An overview on wireless sensor networks technology and evolution. *Sensors (Basel, Switzerland), 9*(9), 6869–6896. doi:10.3390/s90906869 PMID:22423202

BuyIT Best Practice Network. (2004). *E-Sourcing: A BuyIT e-Procurement Best Practice Guideline*. Retrieved July 14, 2014, from https://www.cips.org/Documents/Knowledge/Procurement-Topics-and-Skills/12-E-commerce-Systems/E-Sourcing-E-Procurement-Systems/BuyIT_e-Sourcing.pdf

BVMed Survey. (2007). *Elektronisches Beschaffungswesen im Gesundheitsmarkt vor dem Durchbruch. Bundesverband Medizintechnologie*. Retrieved July 14, 2014, from http://www.bvmed.de/print/de/bvmed/presse/pressemeldungen/bvmed-umfrage-elektronisches-beschaffungswesen-im-gesundheitsmarkt-vor-dem-durchbruch

Calì, A., Lembo, D., Lenzerini, M., & Rosati, R. (2003). Source Integration for Data Warehousing. In Multidimensional Databases: Problems and Solutions (pp. 361-392). Academic Press.

Calipinar, H., & Soysal, M. (2012). E-Procurement: A Case Study about the Health Sector in Turkey. *International Journal of Business and Social Science, 3*(7), 232–244.

Callas, J. (2007). The Future of Cryptography. *Information Systems Security*.

Canfora, G., Penta, M. D., Esposito, R., & Villani, M. (2008). A framework for QoSaware binding and re-binding of composite web services. *Journal of Systems and Software, 81*(10), 1754–1769. doi:10.1016/j.jss.2007.12.792

Canfora, G., Penta, M. D., & Villan, M. (2005). Approach on QoS-aware compositions based on genetic algorithm. In *Genetic and Evolutionary Computing Conference (GECCO)*. doi:10.1145/1068009.1068189

Caniels, M., & van Raaij, E. (2009). Do all suppliers dislike electronic reverse auctions? *Journal of Purchasing and Supply Management, 15*(1), 12–23. doi:10.1016/j.pursup.2008.10.003

Capital Network Solution. (2013, January). *Bring Your Owen Device*. [Blog post]. Retrieved from http://www.capital-networks.co.uk/news/2013/01/14/bring-your-own-device/

Caralli, R. A., Stevens, J. F., Young, L. R., & Wilson, W. R. (2007). *Introducing octave allegro: Improving the information security risk assessment process* (No. CMU/SEI-2007-TR-012). Carnegie Mellon University. Retrieved December 2014 from http://www.sei.cmu.edu/reports/07tr012.pdf

Cardellini, E., & Casalichio, V., Grassi, and Presti, F. L. (2007). Flow-based service selection for web service composition supporting multiple QoS classes. In *IEEE International Conference on Web Services* (ICWS). doi:10.1109/ICWS.2007.91

Carlton, R. (2001). *IPSec, Securing VPNs*. McGraw Hill Publishers.

Caron, F., Vanthienen, J., & Baesens, B. (2013). A comprehensive investigation of the applicability of process mining techniques for enterprise risk management. *Computers in Industry, 64*(4), 464–475. doi:10.1016/j.compind.2013.02.001

Caruso, A., Chessa, S., De, S., & Urpi, A. (2005). *GPS free coordinate assignment and routing in wireless sensor networks*. Paper presented at the IEEE INFOCOM. doi:10.1109/INFCOM.2005.1497887

Castellanos, M., Casati, F., Umeshwar, D., & Ming-Chien, S. (2004). A Comprehensive and Automated Approach to Intelligent Business Processes Execution Analysis. *Distributed and Parallel Databases, 16*(3), 1–35. doi:10.1023/B:DAPD.0000031635.88567.65

Castillo, C. (2012 April 13). *Android malware promises video while stealing contacts*. [Web log post]. Retrieved from http://blogs.mcafee.com/mcafee-labs/android-malware-promises-video-while-stealing-contacts

Cendrowska, J. (1987). PRISM: An algorithm for inducing modular rules. *International Journal of Man-Machine Studies, 27*(4), 349–370. doi:10.1016/S0020-7373(87)80003-2

Chand, D., Hachey, G., Hunton, J., Owhoso, V., & Vasudevan, S. (2005). A balanced scorecard based framework for assessing the strategic impacts of ERP systems. *Computers in Industry, 56*(6), 558–572. doi:10.1016/j.compind.2005.02.011

Chang, I.-C., Hwang, H.-G., Liaw, H.-C., Hung, M.-C., Chen, S.-L., & Yen, D. C. (2008). A neural network evaluation model for ERP performance from SCM perspective to enhance enterprise competitive advantage. *Expert Systems with Applications, 35*(4), 1809–1816. doi:10.1016/j.eswa.2007.08.102

Chapin, N. (1971). *Flowcharts*. Princeton, NJ: Auerbach Publishers.

Chapin, N. (1974). New Format for Flowcharts. *Software, Practice & Experience, 4*(4), 341–357. doi:10.1002/spe.4380040404

Chapple. (2012). *Databases Expert "Two-Tier or n-Tier"*. Academic Press.

Chaudhuri, S., & Dayal, U. (1997). An Overview of Data Warehousing and OLAP Technology. *SIGMOD Record, 26*(1), 65–74. doi:10.1145/248603.248616

Chen, D., & Varshney, P. K. (2004). *QoS support in wireless sensor networks: A survey*. Paper presented at the International Conference on Wireless Networks, ICWN'04.

Chen, D., Preston, D., & Xia, W. (2013). Enhancing hospital supply chain performance: A relational view and empirical test. *Journal of Operations Management, 31*(6), 391–408. doi:10.1016/j.jom.2013.07.012

Chen, M., Gonzalez, S., & Leung, V. C. M. (2007). Applications and design issues for mobile agents in wireless sensor networks. *IEEE Wireless Communications, 14*(6), 20–26. doi:10.1109/MWC.2007.4407223

Chen, P. (1976). The Entity-Relationship Model: Toward a Unified View of Data. *ACM Transactions on Database Systems, 1*(1), 9–35. doi:10.1145/320434.320440

Chen, Y., Li, Q., & Zhang, F. (2001). *Business Process Re-Engineering and Systems Integration*. Beijing: Tsinghua University Press.

Choksi, Sarvan & Vashi. (2013, June). Implementation and Direct Accessing of Android Authority Application in Smart Phones. *International Journal of Application or Innovation in Engineering & Management, 2*(6).

Chopra, S., & Meindl, P. (2001). *E-business and the supply chain, Supply Chain Management*. Upper Saddle River, NJ: Prentice-Hall.

Claburn, T. (2007, September 19). Google's Secret Patent Portfolio Predicts gPhone. *Information Week News*. Retrieved from http://www.informationweek.com/googles-secret-patent-portfolio-predicts-gphone/d/d-id/1059389

Coello, C. A. C., Lamont, G. B., & Veldhuizen, D. A. V. (2006). *Evolutionary Algorithms for Solving Multi-Objective Problems (Genetic and Evolutionary Computation)*. Springer-Verlag New York, Inc.

Committee of Sponsoring Organizations of the Treadway Commission (COSO). (2004). *Enterprise Risk Management — Integrated Framework*. Retrieved December 2014 from http://www.coso.org/documents/coso_erm_executivesummary.pdf

Common Attack Pattern Enumeration and Classification (CAPEC). (n.d.). Retrieved December 2014 from http://capec.mitre.org

Common Configuration Enumeration (CCE). (n.d.). Retrieved December 2014 from http://cce.mitre.org/

Common Configuration Scoring System (CCSS). (n.d.). Retrieved December 2014 from http://csrc.nist.gov/publications/nistir/ir7502/nistir-7502_CCSS.pdf

Common Misuse Scoring System (CMSS). (n.d.). Retrieved December 2014 from http://csrc.nist.gov/publications/drafts/nistir-7517/Draft-NISTIR-7517.pdf

Common Platform Enumeration (CPE). (n.d.). Retrieved December 2014 from http://cpe.mitre.org/

Common Vulnerability and Exposures (CVE). (n.d.). Retrieved December 2014 from http://cve.mitre.org/

Common Vulnerability Reporting Framework (CVRF). (n.d.). Retrieved December 2014 from http://www.icasi.org/cvrf

Common Vulnerability Scoring System (CVSS). (n.d.). Retrieved December 2014 from http://www.first.org/cvss/cvss-guide.pdf

Common Weakness Enumeration. (n.d.). Retrieved December 2014 from http://cwe.mitre.org/

Common Weakness Risk Analysis Framework (CWRAF). (n.d.). Retrieved December 2014 from https://cwe.mitre.org/cwraf/

Common Weakness Scoring System (CWSS). (n.d.). Retrieved December 2014 from http://cwe.mitre.org/cwss/

Companies Integrate Encryption/Data Loss Prevention. (2008). Computer Security Update, from Academic Search Premier Database.

Consortium, W. W. W. (2007). *OWL-S: semantic markup for Web services*. Author.

Coogan, P. (2014 March 05). *Android RATs Branch out with Dendroid*. [Web log post]. Retrieved from http://www.symantec.com/connect/blogs/android-rats-branch-out-dendroid

CosmoSim. (2015). Retrieved from www.cosmosim.org

Cots, S., & Casadesús, M. (2014). *Exploring the Service Management Standard ISO 22000*. Total Quality Management & Business Excellence; doi:10.1080/14783363.2013.856544

Council of Supply Chain Management Professionals. (2013). *Bylaws of CSCMP*. Retrieved July 14, 2014, from http://cscmp.org/sites/default/files/user_uploads/footer/downloads/bylaws/cscmp-bylaws-i.pdf

Coy, W. (2004, June). Between the disciplines. *ACM SIGCSE Bulletin, 36*(2), 7–10. doi:10.1145/1024338.1024340

Crowder, M. (2013). Quality standards: Integration within a bereavement environment. *The TQM Journal, 25*(1), 18–28. doi:10.1108/17542731311286405

Cunha, C. D. A., Agard, E., & Kusiak, A. (2006). Data mining for improvement of product quality. *International Journal of Production Research*, *44*(18-19), 18–19. doi:10.1080/00207540600678904

Cyber Observable eXpression (CYBOX). (n.d.). Retrieved December 2014 from http://cybox.mitre.org/

Dahlgaard, J. J., Kristensen, K., & Kanji, K. (1998). *Fundamentals of total quality management*. London: Chapman & Hall. doi:10.1007/978-1-4899-7110-4

Dalberg Global Development Advisors and the MIT-Zaragoza International Logistics Program (2008). *The Private Sector's Role in Health Supply Chains: Review of the Role and Potential for Private Sector Engagement in Developing Country Health Supply Chains*. Author.

Dale, G. D. (1994). *Managing quality* (2nd ed.). London: Prentice Hall.

Daniel Lloyd, C. (2008). *Literature Review of Cryptography and its Role in Network Security Principles and Practice*. Capella University.

Dar & Parvez. (2014, April). A Novel Strategy to Enhance the Android Security Framework. *International Journal of Computer Applications, 91*(8).

Das, I. (1999). On characterizing the knee of the Pareto curve based on normalboundary intersection. *Structural Optimization*, *18*(2-3), 107–115. doi:10.1007/BF01195985

Davenport, T. H. (1993). *Process Innovation: Reengineering Work Through Information Technology*. Boston: Harvard Business School Press.

Davenport, T. H., & Short, J. E. (1990). The New Industrial Engineering: Information Technology and Business Process Redesign. *Sloan Management Review*, 11–27.

David, M. (2000). *Kroenke*. The Hierarchical and Network Data Models.

Davila, A., Gupta, M., & Palmer, R. (2003). Moving Procurement Systems to the Internet: The Adoption and Use of E-Procurement Technology Models. *European Management Journal, 21*(1), 11–23. doi:10.1016/S0263-2373(02)00155-X

Davis, T., Geist, R., Matzko, S., & Westall, J. (2004). A First Step. In *Proceedings of Technical Symposium on Computer Science Education* (pp. 125–129). Academic Press.

De Boer, L., Harink, J., & Heijboer, G. (2002). A conceptual model for assessing the impact of electronic procurement. *European Journal of Purchasing and Supply Management*, *8*(1), 25–33. doi:10.1016/S0969-7012(01)00015-6

De Ru, W. G., & Eloff, J. H. P. (1996). Risk analysis modelling with the use of fuzzy logic. *Computers & Security*, *15*(3), 239–248. doi:10.1016/0167-4048(96)00008-9

De Vries, J., & Huijsman, R. (2011). Supply chain management in health services: An overview, *Supply Chain Management. International Journal (Toronto, Ont.)*, *16*(3), 159–165.

Deb, K., Agrawal, S., Pratap, A., & Meyarivan, T. (2000). A fast elitist nondominated sorting genetic algorithm for multi-objective optimization: NSGA-II. *Lecture Notes in Computer Science*, 849–858.

Decker, A. (2012 October 29). *How Mobile Ads abuse permissions*. [Web log post]. Retrieved from http://blog.trendmicro.com/trendlabs-security-intelligence/how-mobile-ads-abuse-permissions/

Denning, P. (1999). Computer science: The discipline. In *Encyclopedia of Computer Science*. Academic Press.

Denning, P. (2007). *Ubiquity a new interview with Peter Denning on the great principles of computing*. Academic Press.

Developers, A. (n.d.). Android, the World's Most Popular Mobile Platform. *Android Developers*. Retrieved from http://developer.android.com/about/index.html

Devine, R. (2014, May 12). *The best travel apps for Android*. [Blog post]. Retrieved from http://www.androidcentral.com/best-android-travel-apps

Di Pietro, R., Mancini, L. V., & Mei, A. (2006). Energy efficient node-to-node authentication and communication confidentiality in wireless sensor networks. *Wireless Networks*, *12*(6), 709–721. doi:10.1007/s11276-006-6530-5

Díaz, S. E., Pérez, J. C., Mateos, A. C., Marinescu, M. C., & Guerra, B. B. (2011). A novel methodology for the monitoring of the agricultural production process based on wireless sensor networks. *Computers and Electronics in Agriculture*, *76*(2), 252–265. doi:10.1016/j.compag.2011.02.004

Dirk, R. (2000). *Framework design - a role modeling approach*. Wiss Federal Institute of Technology Zurich.

Disterer, G. (2012). Why firms seek ISO 20000 certification – A study for ISO 20000 adoption. In *Proceedings of the 20th European Conference on Information Systems*. Barcelona, Spain: Academic Press.

Dobing, B., & Parsons, J. (2006). How UML is used. *Communications of the ACM*, *49*(5), 109–113. doi:10.1145/1125944.1125949

Donatelli, S., Ribaudo, M., & Hillston, J. (1995). *A Comparison of Performance Evaluation Process Algebra and Generalised Stochastic Petri Nets*. Paper presented at Sixth International Workshop on Petri Nets and Performance Models.

Dr.Web Company. (2014 January 24). *First Android bootkit has infected 350,000 devices*. Retrieved from http://news.drweb.com/show/?i=4206

Duhamel, A., Picavet, M., Devos, P., & Beuscart, R. (2001). *From data collection to knowledge data discovery: A medical application of data mining*. Paper presented at the Studies in Health Technology and Informatics.

Durillo, J., Nebro, A., & Alba, E. (2010). The jMetal framework for multi-objective optimization: Design and architecture. In *IEEE Congress on Evolutionary Computation (CEC)*. doi:10.1109/CEC.2010.5586354

Dustdar, S. & Schreiner, W. (2005). A survey on web services composition. *Int. Journal of Web and Grid Services, 1*(1).

Dwyer, C. (2010). *Strategic Sourcing: The 2010 Guide to Driving Savings and Procurement Performance*. Aberdeen Group. Retrieved July 14, 2014, from http://www.aberdeen.com/research/6305/ra-strategic-sourcing-savings-procurement/content.aspx

Dyllick, T., & Hockerts, K. (2002). Beyond the Business Case for Corporate Sustainability. *Business Strategy and the Environment*, *11*(2), 130–141. doi:10.1002/bse.323

Eiferman, O. (2014, June 6). With BYOD, You Don't Have to Choose Between Productivity and Security. *IT Briefcase: IT News, Research & Events*. Retrieved from http://www.itbriefcase.net/byod-dont-choose-between-productivity-and-security

Ejdys, J., & Matuszak-Flejszman, A. (2010). New management systems as an instrument of implementation sustainable development concept at organizational level. *Technological and Economic Development of Economy*, *16*(2), 202–218. doi:10.3846/tede.2010.13

Elinux. (2011, July 7). Android Kernel Versions. *Elinux.org*. Retrieved from http://elinux.org/Android_Kernel_Versions

Elliot, S. (2011). Transdisciplinary perspectives on environmental sustainability: A resource base and framework for IT-enabled business transformation. *Management Information Systems Quarterly*, *35*(1), 197–236.

Ernst & Young. (2012, January). *Mobile device security, Understanding vulnerabilities and managing risk.* Insights on governance, risk and compliance. Retrieved from http://www.ey.com/Publication/vwLUAssets/EY_Mobile_security_devices/$FILE/EY_Mobile%20security%20devices.pdf

European Telecommunications Standards Institute. (2006). *Telecommunications and Internet converged Services and Protocols for Advanced Networking (TISPAN); Methods and protocols; Part 1: Method and proforma for Threat, Risk, Vulnerability Analysis (ETSI TS 102 165-1 V4.2.1).* Retrieved December 2014 from http://portal.etsi.org/mbs/Referenced%20Documents/ts_10216501v040201p.pdf

Extensible Configuration Checklist Description Format (XCCDF). (n.d.). Retrieved December 2014 from http://nvd.nist.gov/scap/xccdf/docs/xccdf-spec-1.0.pdf

eXtensible Name and Address Language (xNAL). (n.d.). Retrieved December 2014 from http://www.immagic.com/eLibrary/TECH/OASIS/XAL_V2.PDF

Eyholzer, K., & Hunziker, D. (1999). *Internet-Einsatz in der Beschaffung – Eine empirische Untersuchung in Schweizer Unternehmen, Arbeitsbericht Nr. 118.* Universitaet Bern, Schweiz: Institut fuer Wirtschaftsinformatik.

Fagin, B., Baird, L., Humphries, J., & Schweitzer, D. (2008, January). Skepticism and Cryptography. *Knowledge, Technology & Policy.*

Fan, Y. S. (2001). *Fundamental of Workflow Management Technology.* New York: Springer-Verlag.

Faye, F., & Sene, M. (2013). Datamining tool: Multiple regression and logistic regression in a web platform of a datawarehouse. In Advanced Materials Research (pp. 2299-2307). Academic Press.

Fayyad, U., Piatetsky-Shapiro, G., Smyth, P., & Ramasami, U. (1996). *Advances in Knowledge Discovery and Data Mining.* Cambridge, MA: MIT Press.

Feldman, C. G. (1998). *The Practical Guide to Business Process Reengineering Using IDEF0.* New York: Dorset House.

Fernández-Quiruelas, V., Fernández, J., Cofiño, A. S., Fita, L., & Gutiérrez, J. M. (2011). Benefits and requirements of grid computing for climate applications. An example with the community atmospheric model. *Environmental Modelling & Software, 26*(9), 1057-1069.

Ferreira, A. L., Machado, R. J., & Paulk, M. C. (2011). Supporting Audits and Assessments in Multi-model Environments: Product-Focused Software Process Improvement. In *Proceedings of the 12th International Conference, PROFES 2011* (LNCS), (Vol. 6759, pp. 73-87). Berlin, Germany: Springer doi:10.1007/978-3-642-21843-9_8

Flach, P. A., & Lachiche, N. (1999b). *The Tertius system.* Retrieved from http://www.cs.bris.ac.uk/Research/MachineLearning/Tertius/

Flach, P. A., & Lachiche, N. (1999a). Confirmation-Guided Discovery of first-order rules with Tertius. *Machine Learning, 42*(1-2), 61–95.

Florio, N. (2012, November 17). *Enterprise Android Adoption.* [Blog post]. Retrieved from http://techcrunch.com/2012/11/17/will-android-adoption-become-a-dream-or-nightmare-for-cios/

Floyd, D. (2006). *Mobile application security system (MASS).* Bell Labs Technical Journal.

Fomin, V. V., de Vries, H. J., & Barlette, Y. (2008). ISO/IEC 27001 information systems security management standard: Exploring the reasons of low adoption. In *Proceedings of the third European Conference on Management of Technology (EuroMOT).* Nice, France: Academic Press.

Fowler, G. (1994). Flat file database query language. In *WTEC'94: Proceedings of the USENIX Winter 1994 Technical Conference on USENIX Winter 1994 Technical Conference*. USENIX.

Fragkiadakis, G., Doumpos, M., Zopounidis, C., & Germain, C. (2014). Operational and economic efficiency analysis of public hospital in Greece. *Annals of Operations Research*, (September), 2014.

Friedmana, J. & Hoffmanba, D.V. (2008). Protecting data on mobile devices: A taxonomy of security threats to mobile computing and review of applicable defenses. *Journal of Information Knowledge Systems Management*, 159-168.

Gao, F., Yu, L., Zhang, W., & Xu, Q. (2009). Research and design of crop water status monitoring system based on wireless sensor networks. *Nongye Gongcheng Xuebao/Transactions of the Chinese Society of Agricultural Engineering*, *25*(2), 107-112.

Gao, Y., Zeng, B., Na, J., Yang, L., Dai, Y., & Gong, Q. (2005). Optimal selection of web services for composition based on interface-matching and weighted multistage graph. In *6th International Conference on Parallel and Distributed Computing Applications and Technologies* (PDCAT). Academic Press.

Gao, C., Cai, M., & Chen, H. (2007). QoS-aware service composition based on tree-coded genetic algorithm. In *31st Annual International Computer Software and Application Conference Application Conference (COMPSAC)*. doi:10.1109/COMPSAC.2007.174

Gao, Y., Na, J., Zeng, B., Yang, L., & Gong, Q. (2006). Optimal selection using dynamic programming. In *11th IEEE International Symposium on Computers and Communications (ISCC)*. IEEE.

Garage, E. (2012). *What is Android*. [Blog post]. Retrieved from http://www.engineersgarage.com/articles/what-is-android-introduction

Garcia-Sanchez, A. J., Garcia-Sanchez, F., & Garcia-Haro, J. (2011). Wireless sensor network deployment for integrating video-surveillance and data-monitoring in precision agriculture over distributed crops. *Computers and Electronics in Agriculture*, *75*(2), 288–303. doi:10.1016/j.compag.2010.12.005

Garengo, P., & Biazzo, S. (2013). From ISO quality standards to an integrated management system: An implementation process in SME. *Total Quality Management and Business Excellence*, *24*(3-4), 310–335. doi:10.1080/14783363.2012.704282

Gartner. (2011). *Big Data is Only the Beginning of Extreme Information Management*. Gartner.

Garvey, M., & Jackson, M. (1989). Introduction to object-oriented databases. *Information and Software Technology*, *31*(10), 521–528. doi:10.1016/0950-5849(89)90173-0

Genius, B. (2012, June 28). *Benefits of Android OS*. [Blog post]. Retrieved from http://boygenius.hubpages.com/hub/Benefits-of-Android-OS

Ghoshal, A. (2013, May 13). 10 Gorgeous Personal Finance Apps for Tablets. *AppStorm News*. Retrieved from http://android.appstorm.net/roundups/finance-roundups/10-gorgeous-personal-finance-apps-for-tablets/

Gianforte, G. (2012, February). *Seven Power Lessons for Customer Experience Leaders*. Oracle Customer Relationship Management.

Gillies, A. (2011). Improving the quality of information security management systems with ISO27000. *The TQM Journal*, *23*(4), 367–376. doi:10.1108/17542731111139455

Goebel, S. (2012). Using the Android Platform to control Robots. In *Proceedings of 2nd International Conference on Robotics in Education* (RiE 2011). Austrian Society for Innovative Computer Sciences.

Goel. (2010). *Computer Fundamentals*. Pearson Education India.

Goel, A. (2010). *Computer Fundamentals*. Pearson Education India, User-Computer Interface.

Gómez, L. I., Gómez, S. A., & Vaisman, A. A. (2011). *Analyzing continuous fields with OLAP cubes*. Paper presented at the International Conference on Information and Knowledge Management.

Gómez, L. I., Gómez, S. A., & Vaisman, A. A. (2012). *A generic data model and query language for spatiotemporal OLAP cube analysis*. Paper presented at the ACM International Conference Proceeding Series. doi:10.1145/2247596.2247632

Gomez, L., Vaisman, A., & Zimanyi, E. (2010). *Physical design and implementation of spatial data warehouses supporting continuous fields*. Paper presented at the 12th international conference on Data warehousing and knowledge discovery. doi:10.1007/978-3-642-15105-7_3

Gómez, L. I., Gómez, S. A., & Vaisman, A. (2013). Modeling and querying continuous fields with OLAP cubes. *International Journal of Data Warehousing and Mining, 9*(3), 22–45.

Gómez, L., Kuijpers, B., Moelans, B., & Vaisman, A. (2009). A survey of spatio-temporal data warehousing. *International Journal of Data Warehousing and Mining, 5*(3), 28–55. doi:10.4018/jdwm.2009070102

Google I/O. (2008, May 28). Android Anatomy and Physiology. *Google I/O*. Retrieved from http://androidteam.googlecode.com/files/Anatomy-Physiology-of-an-Android.pdf

Google. (2007). *Severity Guidelines for Security Issues*. Retrieved December 2014 from http://dev.chromium.org/developers/severity-guidelines

Google. (2011, July 14). *Google Announces Second Quarter 2011 Financial Results*. Google Inc. Retrieved from http://investor.google.com/earnings/2011/Q2_google_earnings.html

Google. (2013, September 18). *Android KitKat*. Google Inc. Retrieved from http://www.android.com/versions/kit-kat-4-4/

Google. (2014). *Google I/O developer's conference in San Francisco*. Retrieved from https://www.google.com/events/io

Gordon, L. A., Loeb, M., & Tseng, C.-Y. (2009). Enterprise risk management and firm performance: A contingency perspective. *Journal of Accounting and Public Policy, 28*(4), 301–327. doi:10.1016/j.jaccpubpol.2009.06.006

Gotzamani, K. D., & Tsiotras, G. D. (2002). The true motives behind ISO 9000 certification: Their effect on the overall certification benefits and long term contribution towards TQM. *International Journal of Quality & Reliability Management, 19*(2), 151–169. doi:10.1108/02656710210413499

Grace, M. F., Leverty, J. T., Phillips, R. D., & Shimpi, P. (2014). The Value of Investing in Enterprise Risk Management. *The Journal of Risk and Insurance*.

Graham. (2006). *Market share: Relational database management systems by operating system, worldwide*. Gartner Report No: G00141017.

Griffith, A., & Bhutto, K. (2008). Improving environmental performance through integrated management systems (IMS) in the UK. *Management of Environment Quality, 19*(5), 565–578. doi:10.1108/14777830810894247

Griffith, A., & Bhutto, K. (2009). Better environmental performance: A framework for integrated management systems (IMS). *Management of Environment Quality: An International Journal, 20*(5), 566–580. doi:10.1108/14777830910981230

Grigori, D., Casati, F., Castellanos, M., Dayal, U., Sayal, M., & Shan, M.-C. (2004). Business Process Intelligence. *Computers in Industry, 53*(3), 321–343. doi:10.1016/j.compind.2003.10.007

Grispos, G., Glisson, W. B., & Storer, T. (2013). Using Smartphones as a Proxy for Forensic Evidence contained in Cloud Storage Services. In *Proceedings of 46th Hawaii International Conference on System Sciences*. IEEE. doi:10.1109/HICSS.2013.592

Grover. (2013, January 31). *Android forensics: Automated data collection and reporting from a mobile device.* Rochester Institute of Technology.

Guha, S., Kettinger, W. J., & Teng, J. T. C. (1993). Business Process Reengineering: Building a Comprehensive Methodology. *Information Systems Management, 10*(3), 13–22. doi:10.1080/10580539308906939

Gunasekaran, A., & Kobu, B. (2002). Modelling and Analysis of Business Process Reengineering. *International Journal of Production Research, 40*(11), 2521–2546. doi:10.1080/00207540210132733

Gunasekaran, A., & Ngai, E. (2008). Adoption of e-procurement in Hong Kong: An empirical research. *International Journal of Production Economics, 113*(1), 159–175. doi:10.1016/j.ijpe.2007.04.012

Gunther, C. (2011, September 9). *Android Jelly Bean up next after IceCream Sandwich.* [Blog post]. Retrieved from http://androidcommunity.com/android-jelly-bean-up-next-after-ice-cream-sandwich-20110909/

Hammer, M., & Champy, J. (1993). *Reengineering the Corporation: a Manifesto for Business Revolution, N.* London: Brealey.

Hampton, J. J. (2015). *Fundamentals of Enterprise risk management: How Top Companies assess risk, manage exposure, and seize opportunity* (2nd ed.). AMACOM Publication.

Harman, M. & Jones, B. (2001). Search based software engineering. *Journal of Information and Software Technology,* (14), 833–839.

Harman, M., Mansouri, S. A., & Zhang, Y. (2009). *Search based software engineering: A comprehensive analysis and review of trends techniques and applications.* Technical Report TR-09-03.

Harris, D. (2007). *Has Anyone Seen My Data. Electronic Design.* Retrieved from Academic Search Premier Database.

Havey, M. (2005). *Essential Business Process Modelling.* O'Reilly.

Hay, R. & Saltzman, R. (2012). *Weak randomness in Android's DNS resolver.* IBM Application Security Research Group, CVE-2012-2808.

Health Industry Distributors Association (H.I.D.A.) Educational Foundation. (2012). *Hospital Procurement Study: Quantifying Supply Chain Costs for Distributor and Direct Orders.* Retrieved July 14, 2014, from http://www.hida.org/App_Themes/Member/docs/Hospital_Procurement.pdf

Hendricks, K. B., Singhal, V. R., & Stratman, J. K. (2007). The Impact of Enterprise Systems on Corporate Performance: A Study of ERP, SCM, CRM System Implementations. *Journal of Operations Management, 25*(1), 65–82. doi:10.1016/j.jom.2006.02.002

Heras-Saizarbitoria, I. (2011). Internalization of ISO 9000: An exploratory study. *Industrial Management & Data Systems, 111*(8), 1214–1237. doi:10.1108/02635571111170776

Heras-Saizarbitoria, I., & Boiral, O. (2013). ISO 9001 and ISO 14001: Towards a research agenda on management system standards. *International Journal of Management Reviews, 15*(1), 47–65. doi:10.1111/j.1468-2370.2012.00334.x

Herden, O. (2000). A Design Methodology for Data Warehouses. *Paper presented at the CAISE Doctoral Consortium,* Stockholm.

Herrmann, J., & Hodgson, B. (2001). SRM: Leveraging the Supply Base for Competitive Advantage.*Proceedings of the SMTA International Conference*. Chicago, IL: SMTA.

Hickson, S. (2014 January 22). *Hacking Snapchat's people verification in less than 100 lines*. [Web log post]. Retrieved from http://stevenhickson.blogspot.in/2014/01/hacking-snapchats-people-verification.html

Hildenbrand, J. (2014). *Android Device Manager Other Devices*. [Blog post]. Retrieved from http://www.androidcentral.com/app/android-device-manager

Hirabayashi, S., Kroll, C. N., & Nowak, D. J. (2011). Component-based development and sensitivity analyses of an air pollutant dry deposition model. *Environmental Modelling & Software, 26*(6), 804-816.

Ho, T., Dean, D., Gu, X., & Enck, W. (2014). PREC: Practical Root Exploit Containment for Android Devices. San Antonio, TX: Academic Press.

Hodson-Gibbons, R. (2009). The NHS Procurement eEnablement Programme – Using information to deliver better healthcare. GS1 Healthcare Reference Book 2009/10 (pp. 22-25). GS1.

Hofacker, I., & Vetschera, R. (2001). Algorithmical Approaches to Business Process Design. *Computers & Operations Research, 28*(13), 1253–1275. doi:10.1016/S0305-0548(00)00038-1

Hoganson, K. (2001, December). Alternative curriculum models for integrating computer science and information systems analysis, recommendations, pitfalls, opportunities, accreditations, and trends. *Journal of Computing Sciences in Colleges, 17*(2), 313–325.

Holt, A. P. (2000). Management-Oriented Models of Business Processes. *Lecture Notes in Computer Science, 1806*, 99–109. doi:10.1007/3-540-45594-9_7

Holte, R. C. (1993). Very Simple Classification Rules Perform Well on Most Commonly Used Datasets. *Machine Learning, 11*(1), 63–90. doi:10.1023/A:1022631118932

Homin, K., Lee, G., Malkin, T., & Erich, N. (2007). Cryptographic strength of ssl/tls servers: current and recent practices. In *IMC '07: Proceedings of the 7th ACM SIGCOMM conference on Internet measurement*. New York: ACM.

Hoque, S., Fairhurst, M., Howells, G., & Deravi, F. (2007, April27). Feasibility of generating biometric encryption keys. *Electronics Letters*.

Hou, K. M., De Sousa, G., Zhou, H. Y., Chanet, J. P., Kara, M., Amamra, A., et al. (2007). LiveNode: LIMOS versatile embedded wireless sensor node. *Journal of Harbin Institute of Technology*, 140-144.

Hoyt, E. R., & Liebenberg, A. P. (2011). The Value of Enterprise Risk Management. *The Journal of Risk and Insurance, 78*(4), 795–822. doi:10.1111/j.1539-6975.2011.01413.x

Hoy, Z., & Foley, A. (2014). *A structured approach to integrating audits to create organisational efficiencies: ISO 9001 and ISO 27001 audits*. Total Quality Management & Business Excellence; doi:10.1080/14783363.2013.876181

Huang, Z., Jiang, W., Hu, S., & Liu, Z. (2009). Effective pruning algorithm for QoS-aware service composition. In *IEEE Conference on Commerce and Enterprise Computing*. IEEE. doi:10.1109/CEC.2009.41

Huang, C.-C., Lin, F.-Y., Lin, F., & Sun, Y. S. (2013). A novel approach to evaluate software vulnerability prioritization. *Journal of Systems and Software, 86*(11), 2822–2840. doi:10.1016/j.jss.2013.06.040

Hudson, J., & Orviska, M. (2013). Firms' adoption of international standards: One size fits all? *Journal of Policy Modeling, 35*(2), 289–306. doi:10.1016/j.jpolmod.2012.04.001

Hughes, D. (2007). Cyberspace Security via Quantum Encryption. *Military Technology*. Retrieved from Academic Search Premier Database.

Hunton, E. J., Lippincott, B., & Reck, L. J. (2003). Enterprise resource planning systems: Comparing firm performance of adopters and non-adopters. *International Journal of Accounting Information Systems*, *4*(3), 165–184. doi:10.1016/S1467-0895(03)00008-3

Hwang, J., Shin, C., & Yoe, H. (2010). Study on an agricultural environment monitoring server system using wireless sensor networks. *Sensors (Basel, Switzerland)*, *10*(12), 11189–11211. doi:10.3390/s101211189 PMID:22163520

Ignatiadis, I., & Nandhakumar, J. (2007). The impact of enterprise systems on organizational resilience. *Journal of Information Technology*, *22*(1), 36–43. doi:10.1057/palgrave.jit.2000087

Intelli3. (2014). Retrieved from http://www.intelli3.com/

IQMS. (2014). *Mobile ERP Apps for Manufacturing Companies*. IQMS Products. Retrieved from http://www.iqms.com/products/mobile-erp-software.html

Irani, Z., Hlupic, V., & Giaglis, G. M. (2002). Business Process Reengineering: An Analysis Perspective. *International Journal of Flexible Manufacturing Systems*, *14*(1), 5–10. doi:10.1023/A:1013868430717

ISAMM. (2002). *Information Security Assessment and Monitoring Method*. Retrieved December 2014 from http://rm-inv.enisa.europa.eu/methods_tools/m_isamm.html

Ishibuchi, H., Sakane, Y., Tsukamoto, N., & Nojima, Y. (2009). Evolutionary manyobjective optimization by NSGA-II and MOEA/D with large populations. In *IEEE International Conference on Systems, Man, and Cybernetics*. IEEE Computer Society.

Ishibuchi, H., Tsukamoto, N., & Nojima, Y. (2008). Evolutionary many-objective optimization: A short review. In *IEEE World Congress on Computational Intelligence*. IEEE.

ISO. (2013). *The ISO Survey of Management System Standards Certifications-2012*. Geneva: International Organization for Standardization.

ISO/IEC 27005. (2008). *Information Technology -- Security techniques -- Information security risk management*. ISO.

IT Governance Institute. (2007). *COBIT 4.1 Excerpt: Executive Summary – Framework*. Retrieved December 2014 from http://www.isaca.org/KnowledgeCenter/cobit/Documents/COBIT4.pdf

ITK. (2014). Retrieved from itkweb.com

Ivang, R., & Sorensen, O. (2005). E-markets in the Battle Zone between Relationship and Transaction Marketing. *Electronic Markets*, *15*(4), 393–404. doi:10.1080/10196780500303086

Jacobson, I., Booch, G., & Rumbaugh, J. (1999). Unified process. *IEEE Software*, *16*(3), 96–102.

Jacquot, A., Chanet, J. P., Hou, K. M., De Sousa, G., & Monier, A. (2010). *A new management method for Wireless Sensor Networks*. Paper presented at the 9th IFIP Annual Mediterranean Ad Hoc Networking Workshop, MED-HOC-NET 2010. doi:10.1109/MEDHOCNET.2010.5546866

Jacquot, A., De Sousa, G., Chanet, J. P., & Pinet, F. (2011). *Réseau de capteurs sans fil pour le suivi de l'humidité du sol des vignes*. Paper presented at the Symposium Ecotech'11.

Jain, P., Hitzler, P., Sheth, A. P., Verma, K., & Yeh, P. Z. (2010) Ontology alignment for linked open data. Lecture Notes in Computer Science, 6496, 402-417.

Jain, P., Hitzler, P., Yeh, P. Z., Verma, K., & Sheth, A. P. (2010). *Linked data is merely more data.* Paper presented at the AAAI Spring Symposium.

Jessup, L. M., & Valacich, J. S. (2008). Information Systems Today Aidan Earl created the first Information System in Dublin, Ireland (3rd Ed.). Pearson Publishing.

Jian-Hua, L., Song-Qiao, S., Yong-Jun, L., & Gui-Lin, L. (2008). Application of genetic algorithm to QoS-aware web service composition. In *3rd IEEE Conference on Industrial Electronics and Applications (ICIEA).* IEEE. doi:10.1109/ICIEA.2008.4582569

Ji-Dong, Y. (2010). Development of Communication Model for Social Robots Based on Mobile Service in Social Computing (SocialCom).*IEEE Second International Conference on 2010.* doi:10.1109/SocialCom.2010.18

Johanson, H. J., McHugh, P., Pendlebury, A. J., & Wheeler, W. A. I. (1993). *Business Process Reengineering - Breakpoint Strategies for Market Dominance.* Chichester, UK: Wiley.

Jonker, J., & Karapetrovic, S. (2004). Systems thinking for the integration of management systems. *Business Process Management Journal, 10*(6), 608–615. doi:10.1108/14637150410567839

Jørgensen, T. H. (2008). Towards more sustainable management systems: Through life-cycle management and integration. *Journal of Cleaner Production, 16*(10), 1071–1080. doi:10.1016/j.jclepro.2007.06.006

Joshi, G. (2013). *Management Information Systems.* New Delhi: Oxford University Press.

Kanellou, A., & Spathis, C. (2011). *Accounting benefits and satisfaction in an ERP environment.* Paper presented at International Conference on Enterprise Systems, Accounting and Logistics, Thassos Island, Greece. doi:10.1016/j.acinf.2012.12.002

Kang, M. A., Pinet, F., Schneider, M., Chanet, J. P., & Vigier, F. (2004). *How to design geographic database? Specific UML profile and spatial OCL applied to wireless Ad Hoc networks.* Paper presented at the 7th Conference on Geographic Information Science (AGILE'2004).

Kanji, K. G., & Asher, M. (1996). *100 methods for total quality management.* London: Sage Publications. doi:10.4135/9781446280164

Kanyoma, K., Khomba, J., Sankhulani, E., & Hanif, R. (2013). Sourcing Strategy and Supply Chain Risk Management in the Healthcare Sector: A Case Study of Malawi's Public Healthcare Delivery Supply Chain. *Journal of Management and Strategy, 4*(3), 16–26. doi:10.5430/jms.v4n3p16

Kara Page. (2014). *Mobile Technology in Business.* [Blog post]. Retrieved from http://www.ehow.com/about_6391136_mobile-technology-business.html

Karapetrovic, S. (2002). Strategies for the integration of management systems and standards. *The TQM Magazine, 14*(1), 61–67. doi:10.1108/09544780210414254

Karapetrovic, S. (2003). Musings on integrated management systems. *Measuring Business Excellence, 7*(1), 4–13. doi:10.1108/13683040310466681

Karch. (2010, September 1). *Android for Work, Productivity for Professionals.* Amazon.

Karl, D. (2009). *Modular mathematics, primitive root.* Academic Press..

Karl, H., & Willig, A. (2006). *Protocols and Architectures for Wireless Sensor Networks.* Academic Press.

Katz, J., & Yung, M. (2003). Scalable protocols for authenticated group key exchange. In D. Boneh (Ed.), *Advances in Cryptology—CRYPTO* (LNCS). Berlin: Springer. doi:10.1007/978-3-540-45146-4_7

Kaziliūnas, A. (2008). Problems of auditing using quality management systems for sustainable development of organizations. *Technological and Economic Development of Economy, 14*(1), 64–75. doi:10.3846/2029-0187.2008.14.64-75

Keen, P. (1981). Information systems and organizational change. *Communications of the ACM, 24*(1), 24–33. doi:10.1145/358527.358543

Keizer, G. (2012 May 04). *Android Malware used to mask online frauds, says expert.* Retrieved from http://www.computerworld.com/article/2503771/malware-vulnerabilities/android-malware-used-to-mask-online-fraud--says-expert.html

Ketikidis, P., Kontogeorgis, A., Stalidis, G., & Kaggelides, K. (2010). Applying e- procurement system in the healthcare: The EPOS paradigm. *International Journal of Systems Science, 41*(3), 281–299. doi:10.1080/00207720903326878

Kettinger, W. J., Teng, J. T. C., & Guha, S. (1997). Business Process Change: A Study of Methodologies, Techniques and Tools. *Management Information Systems Quarterly, 21*(1), 55–80. doi:10.2307/249742

Khanna, H. K., Laroiya, S. C., & Sharma, D. D. (2010). Integrated management systems in Indian manufacturing organizations: Some key findings from an empirical study. *The TQM Journal, 22*(6), 670–686. doi:10.1108/17542731011085339

Khazanchi, D., & Munkvold, B. E. (2000, Summer). Is information system a science an inquiry into the nature of the information systems discipline. *ACM SIGMIS Database, 31*(3), 24–42. doi:10.1145/381823.381834

Kiepuszewski, B., ter Hofstede, A. H. M., & van der Aalst, W. M. P. (2003). Fundamentals of Control Flow in Workflows. *Acta Informatica, 39*(3), 143–209. doi:10.1007/s00236-002-0105-4

Kimball, R. (2008). *The Data Warehouse Toolkit: The Complete Guide to Dimensional Modeling.* John Wiley & Sons.

Kim, C. H., Weston, R. H., Hodgson, A., & Lee, K. H. (2003). The Complementary Use of IDEF and UML Modelling Approaches. *Computers in Industry, 50*(1), 35–56. doi:10.1016/S0166-3615(02)00145-8

Kim, H., Lee, S., & Lee, D. (2004). Constant-round authenticated group key exchange for dynamic groups. In P. J. Lee (Ed.), *Advances in Cryptology—ASIACRYPT (LNCS).* Berlin: Springer. doi:10.1007/978-3-540-30539-2_18

Kincaid, J. (2011, January 12). *The Future Version Of Android Isn't Called IceCream. It's IceCream SANDWICH.* [Blog post]. Retrieved from http://techcrunch.com/2011/01/11/android-ice-cream-sandwich/

Klappenecker, A. (2004). Remark on a non-breakable data encryption scheme by Kish and Sethuraman. *Fluctuation & Noise Letters.* Retrieved from Academic Search Premier Database.

Kleidermacher. (2013, January). BYOD Industrial Control and Automation. *RTC Magazine.* Retrieved from http://www.rtcmagazine.com/articles/view/102915

Knowles, J., Thiele, L., & Zitzler, E. (2006). *A Tutorial on the Performance Assessment of Stochastic Mult iobjective Optimizers.* Technical Report. Computer Engineering and Networks Laboratory (TIK), ETH Zurich.

Knuth, D. E. (1963). Computer-Drawn Flowcharts. *ACM Communications, 6*(9), 555–563. doi:10.1145/367593.367620

Kodaganallur, V. (2006). Secure E-Commerce: Understanding the Public Key Cryptography Jigsaw Puzzle. *Information Systems Security.* Retrieved from Academic Search Premier Database.

Koenig, J. (2004). *JBoss JBPM White Paper, Version 2004.* Available at: http://www.jboss.com/pdf/jbpm_whitepaper.pdf

Koh, S. C. L., Gunasekaran, A., & Goodman, T. (2008). ERP II: The involvement, benefits and impediments of collaborative information sharing. *International Journal of Production Economics, 113*(1), 245–268. doi:10.1016/j.ijpe.2007.04.013

Kolarik, J. W. (1995). *Creating Quality: Concepts, Systems, Strategies and Tools.* New York: McGraw-Hill.

Koons, J., & Minoli, D. (2010). *Information Technology Risk Management in Enterprise Environments, A Review of Industry Practices and a Practical Guide to Risk Management Teams.* John Wiley & Sons.

Kostevšek, A., Petek, J., Čuček, L., & Pivec, A. (2013). Conceptual design of a municipal energy and environmental system as an efficient basis for advanced energy planning. *Energy, 60,* 148–158. doi:10.1016/j.energy.2013.07.044

Koubarakis, M., & Plexousakis, D. (2002). A Formal Framework for Business Process Modelling and Design. *Information Systems, 27*(5), 299–319. doi:10.1016/S0306-4379(01)00055-2

Krankenhaus IT-Journal. (2007). *Online-Beschaffung hilft den Krankenhäusern zu überleben. Bundesverband Medizintechnologie. Ausgabe 2/2007.* Retrieved July 14, 2014, from http://www.medizin-edv.de/ARCHIV/Online-Beschaffung_hilft_den_Krankenhaeusern....pdf

Kraus, J. L., & Grosskopf, J. (2008). Auditing integrated management systems: Considerations and practice tips. *Environmental Quality Management, 18*(2), 7–16. doi:10.1002/tqem.20202

Krestyaninova, M., Neogi, S. G., Viksna J., Celms E., Rucevskis P., Opmanis M., et al. (2007). *Building a data warehouse for the diabetes data.* Academic Press.

Kristian, Y., Armanto, H., & Frans, M. (2012, October9). Utilizing GPS and SMS for Tracking and Security Lock Application on Android Based Phone.*International Conference on Asia Pacific Business Innovation and Technology Management.* doi:10.1016/j.sbspro.2012.09.1189

Kritchanchai, D. (2012). A Framework for Healthcare Supply Chain Improvement in Thailand. *Operations and Supply Chain Management, 5*(2), 103–113.

Kulkarni, R. V., Förster, A., & Venayagamoorthy, G. K. (2011). Computational intelligence in wireless sensor networks: A survey. *IEEE Communications Surveys and Tutorials, 13*(1), 68–96. doi:10.1109/SURV.2011.040310.00002

Kumar, M. (2012 April 01). *Android malware as beware of Chinese called "The Roar of Pharaoh".* Retrieved from http://thehackernews.com/2012/04/android-malware-as-beware-of-chinese.html

Kumar, M. (2012 April 01). *POC android botnet-command and control channel over SMS".* Retrieved from http://thehackernews.com/2012/04/poc-android-botnet-command-and-control.html

Kumar, M. (2012 November 02). *Android 4.2 Jelly Bean Security Improvements Overview.* Retrieved from http://thehackernews.com/2012/11/android-42-jelly-bean-security.html

Kumar, M. (2012). *The hacker news: Malware June 2012.* Retrieved from http://news.thehackernews.com/THN-June2012.pdf

Kumar, M. (2014 April 01). *Researchers explained how Angry Birds sharing your personal data.* Retrieved from http://thehackernews.com/2014/04/researchers-explained-how-angry-birds.html

Kumar, A., Ozdamar, L., & Zhang, C. (2008). Supply chain redesign in the healthcare industry of Singapore. *International Journal of Supply Chain Management, 13*(2), 95–103. doi:10.1108/13598540810860930

Kumbakara, N. (2008). Managed IT services: The role of IT standards. *Information Management & Computer Security, 16*(4), 336–359. doi:10.1108/09685220810908778

Kuorilehto, M., Hännikäinen, M., & Hämäläinen, T. D. (2005). A survey of application distribution in wireless sensor networks. *EURASIP Journal on Wireless Communications and Networking,* (5): 774–788.

Kusiak, A., Larson, N. T., & Wang, J. (1994). Reengineering of Design and Manufacturing Processes. *Computers & Industrial Engineering, 26*(3), 521–536. doi:10.1016/0360-8352(94)90048-5

Kusiak, A., & Zakarian, A. (1996a). Reliability Evaluation of Process Models. *IEEE Transactions on Components Packaging & Manufacturing Technology Part A, 19*(2), 268–275. doi:10.1109/95.506113

Kusiak, A., & Zakarian, A. (1996b). Risk Assessment of Process Models. *Computers & Industrial Engineering, 30*(4), 599–610. doi:10.1016/0360-8352(95)00178-6

Lakin, R., Capon, N., & Botten, N. (1996). BPR Enabling Software for the Financial Services Industry. *Management Services, 40*, 18–20.

Lam, J. (2014). What is ERM? In *Enterprise Risk Management: From Incentives to Controls* (2nd ed.). Hoboken, NJ: John Wiley & Sons, Inc. doi:10.1002/9781118836477.ch4

Landoll, D. J. (2006). *The Security Risk Assessment Handbook: A Complete Guide for Performing Security Risk Assessments* (2nd ed.). Boca Raton, FL: Auerbach.

Larsbo, M., & Jarvis, N. J. (2003). *MACRO 5.0. A model of water flow and solute transport in macroporous soil. Technical description*. Studies in the Biogeophysical Environment.

Laudon, K. C., & Laudon, J. P. (2009). Management Information Systems: Managing the Digital Firm (11th ed.). Prentice Hall/CourseSmart.

Laudon, K., & Laudon, J. (2010). *Management information systems: Managing the digital firm* (11th ed.). Upper Saddle River, NJ: Pearson Prentice Hall.

Laurent, B., & Renata, T. (2007). Early recognition of encrypted applications. Academic Press.

Leal, P. (2010). *Evolution in public procurement and the impact of e-procurement platforms: a case study. Unpublished work project*. Portugal: University Nova de Lisboa.

Lecue, F., & L'eger, A. (2006). A formal model for semantic web composition. In *5th International Semantic Web Conference*. Academic Press.

Lee, J. (2013, February 8). *5 Excellent Email apps for android compared*. [Blog post]. Retrieved from http://www.makeuseof.com/tag/5-excellent-email-apps-for-android-compared/

Lee, D.-H., Kiritsis, D., & Xirouchakis, P. (2001). Branch and Fathoming Algorithms for Operation Sequencing in Process Planning. *International Journal of Production Research, 39*(8), 1649–1669. doi:10.1080/00207540010028100

Lee, S., Lee, D., & Schniederjans, M. (2011). Supply chain innovation and organizational performance in the healthcare industry. *International Journal of Operations & Production Management, 31*(11), 1193–1214. doi:10.1108/01443571111178493

Lega, F., Marsilio, M., & Villa, S. (2013). An evaluation framework for measuring supply chain performance in the public healthcare sector: Evidence from the Italian NHS. *Production Planning & Control: The Management of Operations, 24*(10-11), 931–947. doi:10.1080/09537287.2012.666906

Levy, S. (2001). *Crypto: How the code rebels beat the Government - Saving privacy in the digital age*. New York: Viking Penguin Publishing.

Lezcano, J.-M., Adachihara, H., & Prunier, M. (2010). Experimenting design and implementation of an educational services management system based on ISO/IEC 20000 standard. In M. Lytras, P. Ordonez De Pablos, D. Avison, J. Sipior, Q. Jin, W. Leal, & D. Horner et al. (Eds.), *Technology enhanced learning. Quality of teaching and educational reform (CCIS 73)* (pp. 55–60). Berlin: Springer. doi:10.1007/978-3-642-13166-0_8

Li, C., Li, S., Zhang, D., & Chen, G. (2006). Cryptanalysis of a data security protection scheme for VoIP. *IEE Proceedings -- Vision, Image & Signal Processing.*

Li, W., & Yan-xiang, H. (2010). A web service composition algorithm based on global QoS optimizing with MOCACO. In Algorithms and Architectures for Parallel Processing (LNCS), (vol. 6082, pp. 218 –224). Springer. doi:10.1007/978-3-642-13136-3_22

Li, Z., & Mao, X.-z. (2011). Global multiquadric collocation method for groundwater contaminant source identification. *Environmental Modelling & Software, 26*(12), 1611-1621.

Li, G., He, J., & Fu, Y. (2008). Group-based intrusion detection system in wireless sensor networks. *Computer Communications, 31*(18), 4324–4332. doi:10.1016/j.comcom.2008.06.020

Li, H., Yang, Y., & Chen, T. Y. (2004a). Resource Constraints Analysis of Workflow Specifications. *Systems and Software, 73*(2), 271–285. doi:10.1016/S0164-1212(03)00250-4

Li, J., Fan, Y., & Zhou, M. (2004b). Performance Modelling and Analysis of Workflow. *IEEE Transactions on Systems, Man, and Cybernetics. Part A, Systems and Humans, 34*(2), 229–242. doi:10.1109/TSMCA.2003.819490

Li, J., Maguire, B., & Yao, Y. (2003). A Business Process Centered Software Analysis Method. *International Journal of Software Engineering, 13*(2), 153–168.

Limberakis, C. (2012). *Advanced Sourcing: Maximizing Savings Identification.* Aberdeen Group. Retrieved July 14, 2014, from http://www.aberdeen.com/research/7398/ra-strategic-sourcing-management/content.aspx

Lindsay, A., Downs, D., & Lunn, K. (2003). Business Processes - Attempts to Find a Definition. *Information and Software Technology, 45*(15), 1015–1019. doi:10.1016/S0950-5849(03)00129-0

Lindsay, M. W., & Petrick, A. J. (1997). *Total quality and organization development.* Florida: St. Lucie Press.

List, B., Bruckner, R. M., Machaczek, K., & Schiefer, J. (2002). A Comparison of Data Warehouse Development Methodologies Case Study of the Process Warehouse. *Lecture Notes in Computer Science, 2453*, 203–215. doi:10.1007/3-540-46146-9_21

Liu, F. (2014 January 23). *Windows Malware Attempts to Infect Android Devices.* [Web log post]. Retrieved from http://www.symantec.com/connect/blogs/windows-malware-attempts-infect-android-devices

Liu, L., Miao, R., & Li, C. (2008). The Impacts of Enterprise Resource Planning Systems on Firm Performance: An Empirical Analysis of Chinese Chemical Firms. *IFIP, 252*, 579–587.

Liu, Q., & Zhang, Y. (2011). VRSS: A new system for rating and scoring vulnerabilities. *Computer Communications, 34*(3), 264–273. doi:10.1016/j.comcom.2010.04.006

Liu, Q., Zhang, Y., Kong, Y., & Wu, Q. (2012). Improving VRSS-based vulnerability prioritization using analytic hierarchy process. *Journal of Systems and Software, 85*(8), 1699–1708. doi:10.1016/j.jss.2012.03.057

Loo, I., Bots, J., Louwvrink, E., Meeuwsen, D., van Moorsel, P., & Rozel, C. (2013). The effects of ERP-implementations on the non-financial performance of small and medium-sized enterprises in the Netherlands. *The Electronic Journal Information Systems Evaluation, 16*(2), 103–116.

Lopez Jaimes, A., & Coello, C. A. C. (2009). Study of preference relations in many-objective optimization.*Genetic and Evolutionary Computation Conference (GECCO).* doi:10.1145/1569901.1569986

López Riquelme, J. A., Soto, F., Suardíaz, J., Sánchez, P., Iborra, A., & Vera, J. A. (2009). Wireless Sensor Networks for precision horticulture in Southern Spain. *Computers and Electronics in Agriculture, 68*(1), 25–35. doi:10.1016/j.compag.2009.04.006

López-Fresno, P. (2010). Implementation of an integrated management system in an airline: A case study. *The TQM Journal, 22*(6), 629–647. doi:10.1108/17542731011085311

Lovoshynovskiy, S., Deguillaume, F., Koval, O., & Pun, T. (2005). Information-theoretic data-hiding: recent achievements and open problems. *International Journal of Image & Graphics.* Retrieved from Academic Search Premier Database.

Lujan-Mora, S., Trujillo, J., & Song, I.-Y. (2006). A UML profile for multidimensional modeling in data warehouses. *Data & Knowledge Engineering, 59*(3), 725–769. doi:10.1016/j.datak.2005.11.004

Lynn, J. (2014, March 11). Android App automation. *Droid Report News.* Retrieved from http://www.droidreport.com/android-app-automation-7241

Lynn, S. (2014). *What is CRM.* PC Mag.

MaaS360 by Fiberlink, an IBM Company. (2012, August 15). *Does Android Dream of enterprise adoption.* White Paper published by Health IT Outcomes. Retrieved from http://www.healthitoutcomes.com/doc/does-android-dream-of-enterprise-adoption-0001

Mactaggart, M. (2001). *Introduction to cryptography.* Academic Press.

Madapusi, A., & D'Souza, D. (2012). The influence of ERP system implementation on the operational performance of an organization. *International Journal of Information Management, 32*(1), 24–34. doi:10.1016/j.ijinfomgt.2011.06.004

MAGERIT. (2006). *Methodology for Information Systems Risk Analysis and Management – version 2.* Retrieved December 2014 from https://www.ccn-cert.cni.es/publico/herramientas/pilar44/en/magerit/index.html

Mahapatra, L. (2013, November 11). Android Vs. iOS: What's The Most Popular Mobile Operating System In Your Country. *International Business Times.* Retrieved from http://www.ibtimes.com/android-vs-ios-whats-most-popular-mobile-operating-system-your-country-1464892

Mahboubi, H., Bimonte, S., & Deffuant, G. (2011) Analyzing demographic and economic simulation model results: A semi-automatic spatial OLAP approach. Lecture Notes in Computer Science, 6782, 17-31.

Mahboubi, H., Bimonte, S., Deffuant, G., Chanet, J. P., & Pinet, F. (2013). Semi-automatic Design of Spatial Data Cubes from Structurally Generic Simulation Model Results. *International Journal of Data Warehousing and Mining, 9*(1), 70–95. doi:10.4018/jdwm.2013010104

Mahboubi, H., Bimonte, S., Faure, T., & Pinet, F. (2010). Data warehouse and OLAP for Environmental Simulation Data. *International Journal of Agricultural and Environmental Systems, 1*(2).

Malcolm, T., & Bronwyn, H. (2013, July 29). *Conjecture Corporation.*

Malinowski, E., & Zimányi, E. (2008). A conceptual model for temporal data warehouses and its transformation to the ER and the object-relational models. *Data & Knowledge Engineering, 64*(1), 101–133. doi:10.1016/j.datak.2007.06.020

Malinowski, E., & Zimanyi, E. (2008). *Advanced Data Warehouse Design: From Conventional to Spatial and Temporal Applications.* Springer.

Malinowski, P., & Suchy, J. S. (2010). Database for foundry engineers "simulationDB" a modern database storing simulation results. *Journal of Achievements in Materials and Manufacturing Engineering, 43*(1).

Malware Attribute Enumeration and Characterization (MAEC). (n.d.). Retrieved December 2014 from http://maec.mitre.org/

Mancuso, M., & Bustaffa, F. (2006). *A Wireless Sensors Network for monitoring environmental variables in a tomato greenhouse.* Paper presented at the IEEE International Workshop on Factory Communication Systems. doi:10.1109/WFCS.2006.1704135

Manuel Di, C. & Andreas, R. (2010, January 29). *Using Android in Industrial Automation.* Technical Report, University of Applied Sciences North western Switzerland for the Institute of Automation. FHNW/IA, 29.01.2010.

Margaret, R. (2005). *TechTarget's IT encyclopedia and learning center.* WhatIs.com.

Marlink, S. (2009). *New tricks for defeating sslin practice.* Academic Press.

Martin, C. (2014, July 28). *New Android L release date and new features: Chrome hints at version 4.5.* [Blog post]. Retrieved from http://drippler.com/drip/new-android-l-release-date-and-new-features-chrome-hints-version-45

Martin, R. (2008). *Data Warehouse 100 Success Secrets - 100 most Asked questions on Data Warehouse Design, Projects, Business Intelligence, Architecture, Software and Models.* Emereo Pty Ltd.

Maslennikov, D. (2012 August 7). *New ZitMo for Android and Blackberry.* Retrieved from http://securelist.com/blog/virus-watch/57860/new-zitmo-for-android-and-blackberry/

Mathrani, S., & Mathrani, A. (2013). Utilizing enterprise systems for managing enterprise risks. *Computers in Industry, 64*(4), 476–483. doi:10.1016/j.compind.2013.02.002

Matunga, D., Nyanamba, S., & Okibo, W. (2013). The Effect of E-Procurement Practices on Effective Procurement in Public Hospitals: A Case of KISII Level 5 Hospital. *American International Journal of Contemporary Research, 3*(8), 103–111.

Ma, Y., & Zhang, C. (2008). Quick convergence of genetic algorithm for QoS-driven web service selection. *International Journal of Computer and Telecommunications Networking, 52,* 1093–1104.

Mayer, R. J., Paintec, M. K., & Dewitte, P. S. (1994). *IDEF Family of Methods for Concurrent Engineering and Business Reengineering Applications.* Technical Report. Knowledge Based Systems Inc.

Mazon, J. N., & Trujillo, J. (2008). An MDA Approach for the Development of Data Warehouses. *Decision Support Systems, 45*(1), 41–55. doi:10.1016/j.dss.2006.12.003

McDermott, R. (1999). Why information systems inspired but cannot deliver knowledge management. *California Management Review, 41*(4), 103–117. doi:10.2307/41166012

McHugh, R. (2008). *Intégration de la structure matricielle dans les cubes spatiaux.* Université Laval.

McHugh, R., Roche, S., & Bedard, Y. (2008). Towards a SOLAP-based public participation GIS. *Journal of Environmental Management, 14.* PMID:18562083

McKinsey J. (2011). *Big Data: The Next Frontier for Innovation, Competition and Productivity.* McKinsey.

McMeekin, T. A., Baranyi, J., Bowman, J., Dalgaard, P., Kirk, M., Ross, T., & Zwietering, M. H. et al. (2006). Information systems in food safety management. *International Journal of Food Microbiology, 112*(3), 181–194. doi:10.1016/j.ijfoodmicro.2006.04.048 PMID:16934895

Meier, R. (2010). *Professional Android 2 Application Development.* Indianapolis, IN: Wiley Publishing, Inc.

Meijboom, B., Schmidt-Bakx, S., & Westert, G. (2011). Supply chain management practices for improving patient-oriented care. *Supply Chain Management: An International Journal, 16*(3), 166–175. doi:10.1108/13598541111127155

Melao, N., & Pidd, M. (2000). A Conceptual Framework for Understanding Business Process Modelling. *Information Systems*, *10*, 105–129.

Mell, P., Scarfone, K., & Romanosky, S. (2007). *A Complete Guide to the Common Vulnerability Scoring System Version 2*. Retrieved December 2014 from http://www.first.org/cvss/cvss-guide.pdf

Menzel, C., & Mayer, R. (1998). The IDEF Family of Languages. In P. Bernus, K. Mertins, & G. Schmidt (Eds.), *Handbook on Architectures for Information Systems*. New York: Springer-Verlag. doi:10.1007/3-540-26661-5_10

Mesquida, A.-L., & Mas, A. (2015). Integrating IT service management requirements into the organizational management system. *Computer Standards & Interfaces*, *37*, 80–91. doi:10.1016/j.csi.2014.06.005

Mettler, T., & Rohner, P. (2009). Supplier Relationship Management: A Case Study in the Context of Health Care. *Journal of Theoretical and Applied Electronic Commerce Research*, *4*(3), 58–71. doi:10.4067/S0718-18762009000300006

Mhay, S., & Coburn, C. (n.d.). *Request for Procurement Processes (RFT RFQ RFP RFI)*. The Negotiation Experts. Retrieved July 14, 2014, from http://www.negotiations.com/articles/procurement-terms

Microsoft S. Q. L. Server. (2014). Hierarchies (Master Data Services). Author.

Microsoft. (2012). *Security Bulletin Severity Rating System*. Retrieved December 2014 from http://technet.microsoft.com/en-us/security/gg309177.aspx

MicroTronics Technologies. (2014). *Projects of 8051*. Micro Tronics Technologies Projects. Retrieved from http://www.projectsof8051.com/

Ming, C., & Zhen-wu, W. (2007). An approach for web services composition based on QoS and discrete particle swarm optimization. In *8th ACIS International Conference on Software Engineering, Artificial Intelligence, Networking, and Parallel/Distributed Computing*. ACIS.

Min, H., & Galle, W. (2003). E-purchasing: Profiles of adopters and nonadopters. *Industrial Marketing Management*, *32*(3), 227–233. doi:10.1016/S0019-8501(02)00266-3

Mithas, S., Ramasubbu, N., & Sambamurthy, V. (2011). How information management capability influences firm performance. *Management Information Systems Quarterly*, *35*, 237–256.

Mizuno, S. (1988). *Management for quality improvement: The seven new QC tools*. Cambridge, MA: Productivity Press.

Mozilla. (2005). *Mozilla Foundation Security Advisories*. Retrieved December 2014 from http://www.mozilla.org/security/announce/

Muñoz, L., Mazón, J.-N., Pardillo, J., & Trujillo, J. (2009). Modelling ETL Processes of Data Warehouses with UML Activity Diagrams. In Proceedings of On the Move to Meaningful Internet Systems: OTM 2008 Workshops (pp. 44-53). OTM.

Mustaffa, N., & Potter, A. (2009). Healthcare supply chain management in Malaysia: A case study. *Supply Chain Management: An International Journal*, *14*(3), 234–243. doi:10.1108/13598540910954575

MWR InfoSecurity. (2012, September 12). *Mobile Pwn2Own at EuSecWest2012*. Retrieved from https://labs.mwrinfosecurity.com/blog/2012/09/19/mobile-pwn2own-at-eusecwest-2012/

Nachtmann, H., & Pohl, E. (2009). *The State of Healthcare Logistics: Cost and Quality Improvement Opportunities*. Center for Innovation in Healthcare Logistics, University of Arkansas.

Nair, A., & Prajogo, D. (2009). Internalisation of ISO 9000 standards: The antecedent role of functionalist and institutionalist drivers and performance implications. *International Journal of Production Research, 47*(16), 4545–4568. doi:10.1080/00207540701871069

Nakano, S., & Higuchi, T. (2014). Simulation and big data in geosciences: Data assimilation and emulation. *Journal of the Institute of Electronics, Information, and Communication Engineers, 97*(10), 869–875.

Narang, J. (2013, May 10). 5 advantages of Android OS for developing scalable Apps. *The Mobile App Development Experts.* Retrieved from http://www.techaheadcorp.com/android/5-advantages-developing-scalable/

Nasser, N., & Chen, Y. (2007). SEEM: Secure and energy-efficient multipath routing protocol for wireless sensor networks. *Computer Communications, 30*(11-12), 2401–2412. doi:10.1016/j.comcom.2007.04.014

Nazemi, E., Tarokh, M. J., & Djavanshir, G. R. (2012). ERP: A literature survey. *International Journal of Advanced Manufacturing Technology, 61*(9-12), 999–1018. doi:10.1007/s00170-011-3756-x

Nel, J., & Badenhorst-Weiss, J. (2010). Supply chain design: Some critical questions. *Journal of Transport and Supply Chain Management, 4*(1), 198–223.

NeoScale Systems, Inc. (2002). *Entreprise storage security.* Author.

News from the lab. (2013 July 1). *Android Hack-Tool Steals PC Info.* Retrieved from https://www.fsecure.com/weblog/archives/00002573.html

Nicolaou, A., & Bhattacharya, S. (2008). Sustainability of ERPS Performance Outcomes: The Role of Post-Implementation Review Quality. *International Journal of Accounting Information Systems, 9*(1), 43–60. doi:10.1016/j.accinf.2007.07.003

Nikolic, B., & Ruzic-Dimitrijevic, L. (2009). Risk assessment of information technology Systems. *Issues in Informing Science & Information Technology, 6.*

Nilakanta, S., Scheibe, K., & Rai, A. (2008). Dimensional issues in agricultural data warehouse designs. *Computers and Electronics in Agriculture, 60*(2), 263–278. doi:10.1016/j.compag.2007.09.009

NIST. (2009). *Special Publication 800-117 (Draft), Guide to Adopting and Using the Security Content Automation Protocol (SCAP).* Retrieved December 2014 from http://csrc.nist.gov/publications/nistpubs/800-117/sp800-117.pdf/

NIST. (2011). *Special Publication 800-39, Managing Information Security Risk, Organization, Mission, and Information System View.* Retrieved December 2014 from http://csrc.nist.gov/publications/nistpubs/800-39/SP800-39-final.pdf

NIST. (n.d.). *National vulnerability database.* NIST.

Noor, A. (2003). *Creator of the industry's first open-source symmetric key-management system and many cryptographic tools to simplify the use of this technology within business applications.* Academic Press.

NQ Mobile Security Research Center. (2012 March 29). *Security Alert: New AndroiMalware — DKFBootKit — Moves Towards the First Android BootKit.* [Web log post]. Retrieved from http://research.nq.com/?p=391

Nzuve, M. (2013). *Implementation of e-Procurement Practices among Private Hospitals in Nairobi, Kenya. Unpublished research project.* Kenya: University of Nairobi.

O'Brien, J. (1999). *Management Information Systems – Managing Information Technology in the Internetworked Enterprise.* Boston: Irwin McGraw-Hill.

OCTAVE. (2003). *Operationally Critical Threat, Asset, and Vulnerability Evaluation.* Retrieved December 2014 from http://www.cert.org/octave/approach_intro.pdf

Omogiade, S. N. (2014, March 3). *Google Android OS: World leading Mobile Operating System.* Hub Pages Inc. Retrieved from http://infotechnology.hubpages.com/hub/What-is-Google-Android-OS

Open Handset Alliance. (2009). Android overview. *Open handset alliance.* Retrieved from http://www.openhandsetalliance.com/android_overview.html

Open Vulnerability Assessment Language (OVAL). (n.d.). Retrieved December 2014 from http://oval.mitre.org/language/version5.10/

Orman, L. V. (1995). A Model Management Approach to Business Process Reengineering. In *Proceeding of the 1995 American Conference on Information Systems.* Pittsburgh, PA: Academic Press.

Oros, N., & Krichmar, J. L. (2013, November 26). *Android Based Robotics: Powerful, Flexible and Inexpensive Ronots for Hobbyists, Educators, Students and Researchers.* CECS Technical Report 13-16. Center for Embedded Computer Systems, University of California, Irvine. Retrieved from http://www.socsci.uci.edu/~jkrichma/ABR/

Orozco, A. (2013 October 23). *Trojan looks to "Wrob" Android users.* [Web log post]. Retrieved from https://blog.malwarebytes.org/mobile-2/2013/10/trojan-looks-to-wrob-android-users/

Oskarsson, K., & von Malmborg, F. (2005). Integrated management systems as a corporate response to sustainable development. *Corporate Social Responsibility and Environmental Management, 12*(3), 121–128. doi:10.1002/csr.78

Othman, M. F. I., & Chan, T. (2013). Barriers to Formal IT Governance Practice - Insights from a Qualitative Study. In *System Sciences (HICSS), 2013 46th Hawaii International Conference on,* (pp.4415-4424). Wailea, HI: IEEE.

Ould, M. A. (1995). *Business Processes: Modelling and Analysis for Re-Engineering and Improvement.* John Wiley & Sons.

Paganini, P. (2013 December 07). *Rogue Android Gaming app that steals WhatsApp conversations.* Retrieved from http://thehackernews.com/2013/12/hacking-whatsapp-chat-apps-malware_7.html

Pakzad, S. N., Fenves, G. L., Kim, S., & Culler, D. E. (2008). Design and implementation of scalable wireless sensor network for structural monitoring. *Journal of Infrastructure Systems, 14*(1), 89–101. doi:10.1061/(ASCE)1076-0342(2008)14:1(89)

Paller, A. (2008). *Top ten cyber security menaces.* Academic Press.

Pall, G. A. (1987). *Quality Process Management.* Englewood Cliffs, NJ: Prentice-Hall.

Pan, J., Hou, Y. T., Cai, L., Shi, Y., & Shen, S. X. (2003). *Topology Control for Wireless Sensor Networks.* Paper presented at the Annual International Conference on Mobile Computing and Networking. doi:10.1145/938985.939015

Panayiotou, N., Gayialis, S., & Tatsiopoulos, P. (2004). AN e-procurement system for governmental purchasing. *International Journal of Production Economics, 90*(1), 79–102. doi:10.1016/S0925-5273(03)00103-8

Pant, S., & Hsu, C. (1995). *Strategic Information Systems Planning: A Review.* Paper presented at Information Resources Management Association International Conference, Atlanta, GA.

Paolo, O. (2012). *Database schema.* Moodle Database Schema.

Parker, T. (2013). The view from below – a management system case study from a meaning-based view of organization. *Journal of Cleaner Production, 53,* 81–90. doi:10.1016/j.jclepro.2013.04.002

Payment Card Industry (PCI). (2010). *Approved Scanning Vendors, Program Guide, Reference 1.0, PCI DSS 1.2.* Retrieved December 2014 from https://www.pcisecuritystandards.org/pdfs/asv_program_guide_v1.0.pdf

Pearce & Quintana. (2007, September 20). *Google's Strong Mobile-Related Patent Portfolio.* [Blog post]. Retrieved from https://gigaom.com/2007/09/20/419-googles-strong-mobile-related-patent-portfolio/

Peltier, T. R. (2000). *Facilated Risk Analysis Process (FRAP).* Auerbach Publications.

Peppard, J., & Ward, J. (2004). Beyond strategic information systems: Towards an IS capability. *The Journal of Strategic Information Systems, 13*(2), 167–194. doi:10.1016/j.jsis.2004.02.002

Perry, D. (2011, July 16). *Google Android Now on 135 Million Devices.* [Blog post]. Retrieved from http://www.toms-guide.com/us/google-android-installations-app-downloads,news-11861.html

Perspectives for cryptographic long-term security. (2006). *Communications of the ACM.* Retrieved from Academic Search Premier Database.

Pestana, G., da Silva, M. M., & Bedard, Y. (2005). *Spatial OLAP modeling: an overview base on spatial objects changing over time.* Paper presented at the Computational Cybernetics. doi:10.1109/ICCCYB.2005.1511565

Peters, L., & Peters, J. (1997). Using IDEF0 for Dynamic Process Analysis. In *Proceedings of the 1997 IEEE International Conference on Robotics and Automation.* IEEE.

Petrovan, B. (2012, February 26). *Android Everywhere: 10 Types of Devices That Android Is Making Better.* [Blog post]. Retrieved from http://www.androidauthority.com/android-everywhere-10-types-of-devices-that-android-is-making-better-57012/

Pfaltz, J. L., & Orlandic, R. (1999). *A scalable DBMS for large scientific simulations.* Paper presented at the Database Applications in Non-Traditional Environments. doi:10.1109/DANTE.1999.844970

Phalp, K., & Shepperd, M. (2000). Quantitative Analysis of Static Models of Processes. *Systems and Software, 52*(2-3), 105–112. doi:10.1016/S0164-1212(99)00136-3

Piatetsky-Shapiro, G., Frawley, W. J., & Matheus, C. (1991). *Knowledge Discovery in Databases.* A.A.A.I./MIT Press.

Pierce, F. J., & Elliott, T. V. (2008). Regional and on-farm wireless sensor networks for agricultural systems in Eastern Washington. *Computers and Electronics in Agriculture, 61*(1), 32–43. doi:10.1016/j.compag.2007.05.007

Pijanowski, B. C., Tayyebi, A., Doucette, J., Pekin, B. K., Braun, D., & Plourde, J. (2014). A big data urban growth simulation at a national scale: Configuring the GIS and neural network based Land Transformation Model to run in a High Performance Computing (HPC) environment. *Environmental Modelling & Software, 51*, 250–268. doi:10.1016/j.envsoft.2013.09.015

Pinet, F., & Schneider, M. (2009). Precise Design of Environmental Data Warehouses. Operational Research, 9.

Pinet, F. (2012). Entity-relationship and object-oriented formalisms for modeling spatial environmental data. *Environmental Modelling & Software, 30*, 80–91. doi:10.1016/j.envsoft.2012.01.008

Pinet, F., & Schneider, M. (2010). Precise design of environmental data warehouses. *Operations Research, 10*(3), 349–369. doi:10.1007/s12351-009-0069-z

Pistoia, M., Chandra, S., Fink, S., & Yahav, E. (2007). A survey of static analysis methods for identifying security vulnerabilities in software systems. *IBM Systems Journal.* Retrieved from Academic Search Premier Database.

Pleasant, J. (2009). Change has finally come: U.S. Healthcare industry to implement common data standards to improve safety, reduce costs. GS1 Healthcare Reference Book 2009/10 (pp. 6-9). GS1.

Pogson, M., Hastings, A., & Smith, P. (2012). Sensitivity of crop model predictions to entire meteorological and soil input datasets highlights vulnerability to drought. *Environmental Modelling & Software, 29*(1), 37-43.

Pokorný, J. (2006). Database architectures: Current trends and their relationships to environmental data management. *Environmental Modelling & Software, 21*(11), 1579-1586.

Pop, C., Chifu, V., Salomie, I., Dinsoreanu, M., David, T., & Acretoaie, V. (2011). Ant-inspired technique for automatic web service composition. In *International Symposium Selection Symbolic and Numeric Algorithms for Scientific Computing* (SYNASC). SYNASC.

Poston, R., & Grabski, S. (2001). Financial impacts of enterprise resource planning implementations. *International Journal of Accounting Information Systems, 2*(4), 271–294. doi:10.1016/S1467-0895(01)00024-0

Powell, D., Riezebos, J., & Strandhagen, J. O. (2013). Lean production and ERP systems in small- and medium-sized enterprises: ERP support for pull production. *International Journal of Production Research, 51*(2), 395–409. doi:10.1080/00207543.2011.645954

Powell, O., Leone, P., & Rolim, J. (2007). Energy optimal data propagation in wireless sensor networks. *Journal of Parallel and Distributed Computing, 67*(3), 302–317. doi:10.1016/j.jpdc.2006.10.007

Powell, S. G., Schwaninger, M., & Trimble, C. (2001). Measurement and Control of Business Processes. *System Dynamics Review, 17*(1), 63–91. doi:10.1002/sdr.206

Pratt, M. (2006). Moving Target. *Computerworld*. Retrieved from Academic Search Premier Database.

Prescott, R. (2014, January 29). Reality Check: Virtualization can be a safe alternative for BYOD adoption. *RCR Wireless News: Intelligence on all things wireless*. Retrieved from http://www.rcrwireless.com/20130129/opinion/reality-check-virtualization-can-safe-alternative-byod-adoption

Presutti, W. Jr. (2003). Supply management and e-procurement: Creating value added in the supply chain. *Industrial Marketing Management, 32*(3), 219–226. doi:10.1016/S0019-8501(02)00265-1

Prince, B. (2008). *Playing the waiting game*. Retrieved from Academic Search Premier Database.

Principia, The National Computing Centre. (2006, March). *Inventing the future with mobile technologies*. Principia, National Computing Centre Oxford House.

PTA Technologies. (2005). *Practial Threat Analysis*. Retrieved December 2014 from http://www.ptatechnologies.com/

Puschmann, T., & Alt, R. (2005). Successful use of e-procurement in supply chains. *Supply Chain Management: An International Journal, 10*(2), 122–135. doi:10.1108/13598540510589197

Qualys. (1999). *Severities KnowledgeBase*. Retrieved December 2014 from http://www.qualys.com/research/knowledge/severity/

Quatrani, T. (2001). *Introduction to Unified Modelling Language (UML)*. Rational Developer Network.

Quek, T. Q. S., Dardari, D., & Win, M. Z. (2007). Energy efficiency of dense wireless sensor networks: To cooperate or not to cooperate. *IEEE Journal on Selected Areas in Communications, 25*(2), 459–469. doi:10.1109/JSAC.2007.070220

Quinlan, R. (1986). Induction of decision trees. *Machine Learning, 1*(1), 81–106. doi:10.1007/BF00116251

Quon, T. K., Zeghal, D., & Maingot, M. (2012). Enterprise Risk Management and Firm Performance. *Procedia: Social and Behavioral Sciences, 62*, 263–267. doi:10.1016/j.sbspro.2012.09.042

Raposo, A. B., Magalhaes, L. P., & Ricarte, I. L. M. (2000). Petri Nets Based Coordination Mechanisms for Multi-Flow Environments. *International Journal of Computer Systems Science and Engineering, 15*(5), 315–326.

Rebelo, M., Santos, G., & Silva, R. (2014). Conception of a flexible integrator and lean model for integrated management systems. *Total Quality Management & Business Excellence, 25*(5-6), 683–701. doi:10.1080/14783363.2013.835616

Redhat. (2005). *Classification of Security Issues.* Retrieved December 2014 from http://www.redhat.com/f/pdf/rhel4/SecurityClassification.pdf

Reesa, E., & Abrams, A. (1982). Checklist for developing software quality metrics. In *ACM 82: Proceedings of the ACM '82 conference.* New York: ACM.

Reimer, U., Margelisch, A., & Staudt, M. (2000). EULE: A Knowledge-Based System to Support Business Processes. *Knowledge-Based Systems, 13*(5), 261–269. doi:10.1016/S0950-7051(00)00086-1

Richard, E., Daniel, S., Robert, J., & Byrnes, G. (2005). *SSH, the secure shell* (2nd ed.). O'Reilly.

Richards, L. A. (1931). Capillary conduction of liquids through porous mediums. *Journal of Applied Physics, 1,* 318–333.

Richter, F. (2014, March 4). Android to Retain Big Lead in Maturing Smartphone Market. *Statista: The Statistics Portal, Statistics and Studies.* Retrieved from http://www.statista.com/chart/1961/smartphone-market-share-2014/

Riebe, K. (2014). *Introduction to simulation databases using CosmoSim* (Technical Report). Leibniz-Insitute for Astrophysics Potsdam.

Riehle, D., & Zullinghoven, H. (1996). Understanding and Using Patterns in Software Development. *Theory and Practice of Object Systems, 2*(1), 3–13. doi:10.1002/(SICI)1096-9942(1996)2:1<3::AID-TAPO1>3.0.CO;2-#

Rizzi, S., Abello, A., Lechtenborger, J., & Trujillo, J. *Research in data warehouse modeling and design: dead or alive?* Paper presented at the 9th ACM international workshop on Data warehousing and OLAP. doi:10.1145/1183512.1183515

Rocha, M., Searcy, C., & Karapetrovic, S. (2007). Integrating sustainable development into existing management systems. *Total Quality Management and Business Excellence, 18*(1-2), 83–92. doi:10.1080/14783360601051594

Roussey, C., Pinet, F., Kang, M. A., & Corcho, O. (2011). An Introduction to Ontologies and Ontology Engineering. Advanced Information and Knowledge Processing, 1, 9-38.

Rudy, M. E., & Suryani, E. (2014). Implementation of datawarehouse, datamining and dashboard for higher education. *Journal of Theoretical and Applied Information Technology, 64*(3), 710–717.

Ruiz-Garcia, L., Lunadei, L., Barreiro, P., & Robla, J. I. (2009). A review of wireless sensor technologies and applications in agriculture and food industry: State of the art and current trends. *Sensors (Switzerland), 9*(6), 4728–4750. doi:10.3390/s90604728 PMID:22408551

Sadiq, W., & Orlowska, M. (2000). Analyzing Process Models Using Graph Reduction Techniques. *Information Systems, 25*(2), 117–134. doi:10.1016/S0306-4379(00)00012-0

Saleh, M. S., & Alfantook, A. (2011). A new comprehensive framework for enterprise information security risk management. *Applied Computing and Informatics, 9*(2), 107–118. doi:10.1016/j.aci.2011.05.002

Salomone, R. (2008). Integrated management systems: Experiences in Italian organizations. *Journal of Cleaner Production, 16*(16), 1786–1806. doi:10.1016/j.jclepro.2007.12.003

Santos, G., Mendes, F., & Barbosa, J. (2011). Certification and integration of management systems: The experience of Portuguese small and medium enterprises. *Journal of Cleaner Production, 19*(17-18), 1965–1974. doi:10.1016/j.jclepro.2011.06.017

Sato, H., Aguirre, H. E., & Tanaka, K. (2007). *Controlling Dominance Area of Solutions and Its Impact on the Performance of MOEAs*. Lecture Notes in Computer Science, 4403, 5–20. doi:10.1007/978-3-540-70928-2_5

Satolo, E. G., Calarge, F. A., & Cauchick Miguel, P. A. (2013). Experience with an integrated management system in a sugar and ethanol manufacturing unit: Possibilities and limitations. *Management of Environmental Quality: An International Journal, 24*(6), 710–725. doi:10.1108/MEQ-10-2012-0068

Scheer, A. W. (1994). *Business Process Reengineering, Reference Models for Industrial Enterprises*. Berlin: Springer.

Schiffman, M. (2007). *A Complete Guide to the Common Vulnerability Scoring System (CVSS)*. Retrieved December 2014 from http://www.first.org/cvss/cvss-guide.html

Schiffman, M., & Ciag, C. (2005). *CVSS: A Common Vulnerability Scoring System*. Retrieved December 2014 from http://www.first.org/cvss/v1/guide

Schneider, M. (2008). A general model for the design of data warehouses. *International Journal of Production Economics, 112*(1), 309–325. doi:10.1016/j.ijpe.2006.11.027

Schneier, B. (1996). *Applied Cryptography*. Wiley and Sons.

Schneier, B. (1999). Security in the real world: How to evaluate security. *Computer Security Journal, 15*, 1–14.

Schneier, B., & Ferguson, N. (2003). *Practical Cryptography*. Wiley Publishing.

Schulze, C., Spilke, J., & Lehner, W. (2007). Data modeling for Precision Dairy Farming within the competitive field of operational and analytical tasks. *Computers and Electronics in Agriculture, 59*(1), 39–55. doi:10.1016/j.compag.2007.05.001

Schweiger, J., Ortner, W., Tschandl, M., & Busse, K. (2009). *Supplier Relationship Management: Bewertung und Auswahl von SRM-Portallösungen*. Unpublished work project, FH Joanneum, Kapfenberg, Austria.

Searcy, C., Morali, O., Karapetrovic, S., Wichuk, K., McCartney, D., McLeod, S., & Fraser, D. (2012). Challenges in implementing a functional ISO 14001 environmental management system. *International Journal of Quality & Reliability Management, 29*(7), 779–796. doi:10.1108/02656711211258526

Secunia. (2002). *Advisories*. Retrieved December 2014 from http://secunia.com/advisories/historic/

Shen, H., Wall, B., Zaremba, M., Chen, Y., & Browne, J. (2004). Integration of Business Modelling Methods for Enterprise Information System Analysis and User Requirements Gathering. *Computers in Industry, 54*(3), 307–323. doi:10.1016/j.compind.2003.07.009

Shih, D., Lin, B., Chiang, H., & Shih, M. (2008). Security aspects of mobile phone virus: A critical survey. *Industrial Management & Data Systems, 108*(4), 478–494. doi:10.1108/02635570810868344

Shimizu, Y., & Sahara, Y. (2000). A Supporting System for Evaluation and Review of Business Process through Activity-Based Approach. *Computers & Chemical Engineering, 24*(2-7), 997–1003. doi:10.1016/S0098-1354(00)00536-6

Sila, I., Ebrahimpour, M., & Birkholz, C. (2006). Quality in supply chains: An empirical analysis. *Supply Chain Management: An International Journal, 11*(6), 491–502. doi:10.1108/13598540610703882

Silva, J. D., Times, V. C., & Salgado, A. C. (2008). *A set of aggregation functions for spatial measures*. Paper presented at the DOLAP. doi:10.1145/1458432.1458438

Simon, A., Karapetrovic, S., & Casadesús, M. (2012). Difficulties and benefits of Integrated Management Systems. *Industrial Management & Data Systems, 112*(5), 828–846. doi:10.1108/02635571211232406

Skutt, T., & River, W. (2012, October 20). *Securing Android for warfare.* UBM Canon Electronics Engineering Communities. Retrieved from http://www.embedded.com/design/safety-and-security/4398993/Securing-Android-for-warfare

Smith, A., & Flanegin, F. (2004). E-procurement and automatic identification: Enhancing supply chain management in the healthcare industry. *International Journal of Electronic Healthcare, 1*(2), 176–198. doi:10.1504/IJEH.2004.005866 PMID:18048219

Smith, H. (2003). Business Process Management - the Third Wave: Business Process Modelling Language and Its Pi-Calculus Format. *Information and Software Technology, 45*(15), 1065–1069. doi:10.1016/S0950-5849(03)00135-6

Software Assurance (SwA). (2012). Key practices for mitigating the most egregious exploitable software weaknesses, Software Assurance Pocket Guide Series: Development, Vol. II, Version 2.3. Author.

Software Identification Tags (SWIDs). (n.d.). Retrieved December 2014 from http://tagvault.org/swid-tags/

Soliman, F. (1998). Optimum Level of Process Mapping and Least Cost Business Process Re-Engineering. *International Journal of Operations & Production Management, 18*(9/10), 810–816. doi:10.1108/01443579810225469

Solomon, S. (2014, June 25). *Android for the enterprise: Google debuts enterprise security and productivity features.* [Blog post]. Retrieved from http://blogs.air-watch.com/2014/06/android-enterprise-google-debuts-enterprise-security-productivity-features/#.U9qfZah5N54

Solution, O. M. (2013, June 21). *7 Must have mobile applications for 2013.* Opti Matrix Solution. Retrieved from https://optiinfo.wordpress.com/category/mobile-application-development/

Spanos, G., Sioziou, A., & Angelis, L. (2013). WIVSS: a new methodology for scoring information systems vulnerabilities. In *Proceedings of the 17th Pan-Hellenic Conference on Informatics.* ACM. doi:10.1145/2491845.2491871

Spathis, C., & Ananiadis, J. (2005). Assessing the benefits of using an enterprise system in accounting information and management. *Journal of Enterprise Information Management, 18*(2), 195–210. doi:10.1108/17410390510579918

Spatialytics. (2014). Retrieved from http://www.spatialytics.org/

SQL Server Architecture. (2000). *Relational Database Components.* Author.

Steed, C. A., Ricciuto, D. M., Shipman, G., Smith, B., Thornton, P. E., & Wang, D. et al.. (2013). Big data visual analytics for exploratory earth system simulation analysis. *Computers & Geosciences, 61,* 71–82.

Stefanou, C., Manthou, V., & Tigka, K. (2014). The ERP Systems Impact on Business Performance. In *Proceedings: European, Mediterranean & Middle Eastern Conference on Information Systems 2014 (EMCIS2014).* Doha, Qatar: EMCIS.

Stefanou, C.J. and Revanoglou, A. (2006). ERP integration in a health care environment: A case study. *Journal of Enterprise Information Management, 19*(1).

Stefanou, C. J. (2001). A Framework for the ex-ante Evaluation of ERP Software. *European Journal of Information Systems. Special Issue on IT Evaluation, 10,* 204–215.

Stefanou, C., & Revanoglou, A. (2006). ERP integration in a healthcare environment: A case study. *Journal of Enterprise Information Management, 19*(1), 115–130. doi:10.1108/17410390610636913

Stock, J. R., & Lambert, D. M. (2001). *Strategic Logics Management.* McGraw-Hill, Irwin.

Stohr, E. A., & Zhao, J. L. (2001). Workflow Automation: Overview and Research Issues. *Information Systems Frontiers*, *3*(3), 281–296. doi:10.1023/A:1011457324641

Strategic Growth Concepts. (2014). *Mobile Technology for Increased Productivity & Profitability*. [Blog post]. Retrieved from http://www.strategicgrowthconcepts.com/growth/increase-productivity--profitability.html

Strecker, S., Heise, D., & Frank, U. (2011). RiskM: A multi-perspective modelling method for IT risk assessment. *Information Systems Frontiers, 13*(4), 595-611.

Structured Threat Information, eXpression (STIX). (n.d.). Retrieved December 2014 from http://stix.mitre.org/

Strunk, A. (2010). QoS-aware service composition: a survey. In *IEEE European Conference on Web Services*. IEEE.

Sudzina, F., Pucihar, A., & Lenart, G. (2011). A comparative study of the impact of ERP systems implementation on large companies in Slovakia and Slovenia. In Proceedings: CONFENIS 2011. doi:10.1007/978-3-642-24358-5_32

Sung, H. H., & Sang, C. P. (2006). Service quality improvement through business process management based on data mining. *ACM SIGKDD Explorations Newsletter*, *8*(1), 49–56. doi:10.1145/1147234.1147242

Sutton, S. G. (2006). Enterprise systems and the reshaping of accounting systems: A call for research. *International Journal of Accounting Information Systems*, *7*, 1–6. doi:10.1016/j.accinf.2006.02.002

Symantec Security Response. (2013 June 13). *Linux Kernel Exploit Ported to Android*. [Web log post]. Retrieved from http://www.symantec.com/connect/blogs/linux-kernel-exploit-ported-android

Symantec. (2000). *Symantec Security Response Glossary*. Retrieved December 2014 from http://www.symantec.com/security response/severityassessment.jsp

SYSPRO Products. (2014). *What is ERP – Enterprise Resource Planning*. SYSPRO Impact Software, Inc. Retrieved from http://www.syspro.com/product/what-is-erp

Tarí, J. J., & Molina-Azorín, J. F. (2010). Integration of quality management and environmental management systems. *The TQM Journal*, *22*(6), 687–701. doi:10.1108/17542731011085348

Tatsis, V., Mena, C., Van Wassenhove, L., & Whicker, L. (2006). E-procurement in the Greek food and drink industry: Drivers and impediments. *Journal of Purchasing and Supply Management*, *12*(2), 63–74. doi:10.1016/j.pursup.2006.04.003

Taylor, V. (2011, September 12). Supply Chain Management: The Next Big Thing. *Business Week*.

Taylor, L. (2014). *Practical enterprise risk management: How to optimize business strategies through managed risk taking*. Kogan Page Limited Publ.

Technology Coast Consulting and Galvin Consulting Mobile Report. (2010, December). *Smartphones in the US enterprise*. A report published in December 2010. Technology Coast Consulting and Galvin Consulting Mobile.

Techopedia. (2014, July 3). *An Overview of the Android Architecture*. [Blog post]. Retrieved from http://www.techotopia.com/index.php/An_Overview_of_the_Android_Architecture

Tekathen, M., & Dechow, N. (2013). Enterprise risk management and continuous re-alignment in the pursuit of accountability: A German case. *Management Accounting Research*, *24*(2), 100–121. doi:10.1016/j.mar.2013.04.005

Templeman, R., Rahman, Z., Crandall, D., & Kapadia, A. (2012). *PlaceRaider: Virtual Theft in Physical Spaces with Smartphones*. arXiv:1209.5982v1

The Open Checklist Interactive Language (OCIL). (n.d.). Retrieved December 2014 from http://nvd.nist.gov/ocil/OCIL_language.pdf

The Ponemon Institute. (2011). *2010 Annual Study: U.S. Cost of a Data Breach*. Author.

Themistocleous, M., Irani, Z., & O'Keefe, R. (2001). ERP and Application Integration: Exploratory Survey. *Business Process Management Journal, 7*(3), 195–204. doi:10.1108/14637150110392656

Thomas, T. (2012). Visual Obstacle Avoidance using Optical Flow on the Android-powered HTC EVO for Safe Navigation of the iRobot Create. *Aspiring Robotics Projects*. Retrieved from http://teyvoniathomas.com/index.php/projects/55-opticalflow.html

Tinnila, M. (1995). Strategic Perspective to Business Process Redesign. *Business Process Re-Engineering and Management Journal, 1*(1), 44–59. doi:10.1108/14637159510798202

Tiwari, A. (2001). *Evolutionary computing techniques for handling variables interaction in engineering desing optimisation*. (Ph.D. Thesis). Cranfield University.

Toba, S., Tomasini, M., & Yang, H. (2008). Supply Chain Management in Hospital: A Case Study. *California Journal of Operations Management, 6*(1), 49–55.

Todd, A. (2014, October 23). What is Android and what is Android phone. *Recombo editorial team*. Retrieved from http://recombu.com/mobile/news/what-is-android-and-what-is-an-android-phone_M12615.html

Todd, R., & Eric, W. (2009). *Groups*. Mathsworld.

Trolle, D., Hamilton, D. P., Pilditch, C. A., Duggan, I. C., & Jeppesen, E. (2011). Predicting the effects of climate change on trophic status of three morphologically varying lakes: Implications for lake restoration and management. *Environmental Modelling & Software, 26*(4), 354-370.

Trujillo, J., Palomar, M., Gomez, J., & Song, I. Y. (2001). Designing Data Warehouses with OO Conceptual Models. *IEEE Computer, 34*(12), 66–75. doi:10.1109/2.970579

Truong, T. M., Amblard, F., Gaudou, B., Sibertin-Blanc, C., Truong, V. X., Drogoul, A., ... (2013). *An implementation of framework of business intelligence for agent-based simulation*. Paper presented at the Fourth Symposium on Information and Communication Technology.

Trust Model for Security Automation Data (TMSAD). (n.d.). Retrieved December 2014 from http://csrc.nist.gov/publications/nistir/ir7802/NISTIR-7802.pdf

TrustGo Security Labs. (2012 August 15). *New Virus SMSZombie.A Discovered by TrustGo Security Labs*. [Web log post]. Retrieved from http://blog.trustgo.com/SMSZombie/

Tsironis, L., Bilalis, N., & Moustakis, V. (2005). Using machine learning to support quality management: Framework and experimental investigation. *The TQM Magazine, 17*(3), 237–248. doi:10.1108/09544780510594207

Tsitchizris, D. C., & Lochovsky. (1982). Data Models. Englewood-Cliffs, NJ: Prentice–Hall.

Uncheck, R. (2013 June 06). *The most sophisticated Android Trojan*. Retrieved from https://securelist.com/blog/research/35929/the-most-sophisticated-android-trojan/

United Nations Commission on Life-Saving Commodities. (2014). *Private Sector Engagement A Guidance Document for Supply Chains in the Modern Context*. UN CoLSC Technical Reference Team. Retrieved July 14, 2014, from http://unfpa.org/webdav/site/global/shared/procurement/10_supply_chain/UNCoLSC%20Private%20Sector%20Engagement%20Guidance%20Document_FINAL.pdf

UPS Pain in the Supply Chain Survey. (2013). Retrieved July 14, 2014, from http://pressroom.ups.com/pressroom/staticfiles/pdf/fact_sheets/2013_UPS_Pain_in_the_Supply_Chain_Exec_Summary.pdf

Vakalfotis, N., Ballantine, J., & Wall, A. (2011). A Literature Review on the Impact of Enterprise Systems on Management Accounting. In *Proceedings of International Conference on Enterprise Systems, Accounting and Logistics*. ICESAL. Retrieved from www.icesal.org

Valiris, G., & Glykas, M. (1999). Critical Review of Existing BPR Methodologies, The Need for a Holistic Approach. *Business Process Management Journal*, *5*(1), 65–86. doi:10.1108/14637159910249117

van der Aalst, W. M. P. (1995). *A Class of Petri Nets for Modelling and Analyzing Business Processes, Computing Science Reports 95/26*. Eindhoven: Eindhoven University of Technology.

van der Aalst, W. M. P. (1998a). The Application of Petri-Nets to Workflow Management. *Journal of Circuits, Systems, and Computers*, *8*(1), 21–66. doi:10.1142/S0218126698000043

van der Aalst, W. M. P. (1998b). *Formalisation and Verification of Event-Driven Process Chains, Computing Science Reports 98/01*. Eindhoven: Eindhoven University of Technology.

van der Aalst, W. M. P., & ter Hofstede, A. H. M. (2002). Workflow Patterns: On the Expressive Power of (Petri-Net-Based) Workflow Languages. In *Proceedings of the Fourth Workshop on the Practical Use of Coloured Petri Nets and CPN Tools (CPN 2002)*. University of Aarhus.

van der Aalst, W. M. P., & ter Hofstede, A. H. M. (2003). *YAWL: Yet Another Workflow Language (Revised Version), QUT Technical Report, FIT-TR-2003-04*. Brisbane: Qeensland University of Technology.

van der Aalst, W. M. P., ter Hofstede, A. H. M., & Weske, M. (2003). Business Process Management: A Survey. *Lecture Notes in Computer Science*, *2678*, 1–12. doi:10.1007/3-540-44895-0_1

van der Aalst, W. M. P., & van Hee, K. M. (1996). Business Process Redesign: A Petri-Net-Based Approach. *Computers in Industry*, *29*(1-2), 15–26. doi:10.1016/0166-3615(95)00051-8

van der Aalst, W., & ter Hofstede, A. (2005). YAWL: Yet another workflow language. *Information Systems*, *30*(4), 245–275.

Van Hoesel, L., Nieberg, T., Wu, J., & Havinga, P. J. M. (2004). Prolonging the lifetime of wireless sensor networks by cross-layer interaction. *IEEE Wireless Communications*, *11*(6), 78–86. doi:10.1109/MWC.2004.1368900

Vanrompay, Y., Rigole, P., & Berbers, Y. (2008). Genetic algorithm-based optimization of service composition and deployment. In *International Workshop on Services Integration in Pervasive Eenvironments* (SIPE). Academic Press.

Vasilakis, C., El-Darzi, E., & Chountas, P. (2004). *A data warehouse environment for storing and analyzing simulation output data*. Paper presented at the 36th conference on Winter simulation. doi:10.1109/WSC.2004.1371379

Velcu, O. (2005). Impact of the Quality of ERP Implementations on Business Value. *The Electronic Journal Information Systems Evaluation*, *8*(3), 229–238.

Veldhuizen, D. A. V., & Lamont, G. (2000). On measuring multiobjective evolutionary algorithm performance. In Congress on Evolutionary Computation. doi:10.1109/CEC.2000.870296

Volkner, P., & Werners, B. (2000). A Decision Support System for Business Process Planning. *European Journal of Operational Research*, *125*(3), 633–647. doi:10.1016/S0377-2217(99)00273-8

von Ahsen, A. (2014). The integration of quality, environmental and health and safety management by car manufacturers – a long-term empirical study. *Business Strategy and the Environment*, *23*(6), 395–416. doi:10.1002/bse.1791

Vulnerability Notes Database. (2013 September 03). *AirDroid web interface XSS vulnerability*. Retrieved from http://www.kb.cert.org/vuls/id/557252

VUPEN. (2005). *Vulnerability Research and Intelligence*. Retrieved December 2014 from http://www.vupen.com/

Wada, H., Champrasert, P., & Suzuki, J. (2008). Multiobjective optimization of SLAaware service compositions. In *IEEE Congress on Services*. IEEE.

Waltermire, D., Quinn, S., Scarfone, K., & Halbardier, A. (2011). *The Technical Specification for the Security Content Automation Protocol (SCAP): SCAP Version 1.2*. Retrieved December 2014 from http://csrc.nist.gov/publications/nistpubs/800-126-rev2/SP800-126r2.pdf

Wamelink, J. W. F., Stoffele, M., & van der Aalst, W. M. P. (2002). Workflow Management in Construction: Opportunities for the Future. In *Proceedings of CIB W78 Conference: Distributing Knowledge in Building*. CIB.

Wang, J., & Hou, Y. (2008). Optimal web service selection based on multi-objective genetic algorithm. In *International Symposium on Computational Intelligence and Design (ISCID)*. doi:10.1109/ISCID.2008.197

Wang, M., & Wang, H. (2005). Intelligent Agent Supported Business Process Management. In *Proceedings of the 38th Hawaii International Conference on System Sciences*. doi:10.1109/HICSS.2005.332

Wang, Y., Attebury, G., & Ramamurthy, B. (2006). A survey of security issues in wireless sensor networks. *IEEE Communications Surveys and Tutorials*, *8*(2), 2–22. doi:10.1109/COMST.2006.315852

Wang, Y., & Yang, Y. (2012). PVL: A Novel Metric for Single Vulnerability Rating and Its Application in IMS. *Journal of Computer Information Systems*, *8*(2), 579–590.

Waqas, A. (2011, September 28). *Android 2.3.6 Gingerbread Update for Nexus S Available*. [Blog post]. Retrieved from http://www.addictivetips.com/mobile/android-2-3-6-gingerbread-update-for-nexus-s-available-wi-fi-and-tethering-fix/

Watson, R. T., Boudreau, M.-C., & Chen, A. J. (2010). Information systems and environmentally sustainable development: Energy informatics and new directions for the IS community. *Management Information Systems Quarterly*, *34*(1), 23–38.

Webb, W. (2006). *Hack-Proof Design*. Retrieved from Academic Search Premier Database.

Welch, C. (2013, April 16). *Before it took over smartphones, Android was originally destined for cameras*. [Blog post]. Retrieved from http://www.theverge.com/2013/4/16/4230468/android-originally-designed-for-cameras-before-smartphones

WfMC. (1995). *The Workflow Reference Model, WFMC-TC-1003, 19-Jan-95, 1.1*. Available at: http://www.wfmc.org

Wheeler, E. (2011). *Security Risk Management: Building an Information Security Risk Management Program from the Ground Up* (1st ed.). Waltham: Syngress.

While, L., Hingston, P., Barone, L., & Huband, S. (2006). A faster algorithm for calculating hypervolume. *IEEE Transactions on Evolutionary Computation*, *10*(1), 29–38. doi:10.1109/TEVC.2005.851275

White, A., & Daniel, E. (2004). The impact of e-marketplaces on dyadic buyer-supplier relationships: Evidence from the healthcare sector. *Journal of Enterprise Information Management*, *17*(6), 441–453. doi:10.1108/17410390410566733

Wieder, B., Both, P., Matolcsy, Z. P., & Osimitz, M.-L. (2006). The impact of ERP systems on firm and business process performance. *Journal of Enterprise Information Management*, 13-29

Wier, B., Hunton, J., & HassabElnaby, H. R. (2007). Enterprise resource planning systems and non-financial performance incentives: The joint impact on corporate performance. *International Journal of Accounting Information Systems*, *8*(3), 165–190. doi:10.1016/j.accinf.2007.05.001

Wikipedia Encyclopedia. (2011, 3 September). Android (Operating System). *Wikipedia*. Retrieved from http://en.wikipedia.org/wiki/Android_%28operating_system%29

Wikipedia Encyclopedia. (2014). Opto 22. *Wikipedia*. Retrieved from http://en.wikipedia.org/wiki/Opto_22

Wikipedia Encyclopedia. (2014, December 4). Material Requirement Planning. *Wikipedia Encyclopaedia*. Retrieved from http://en.wikipedia.org/wiki/Material_requirements_planning

Witten, I. H., & Frank, E. (2005). *Data Mining: Practical Machine Learning Tools and Techniques*. Morgan Kaufmann.

Wohed, P., van der Aalst, W. M. P., Dumas, M., ter Hofstede, A. H. M., & Russell, N. (2004). *Pattern-Based Analysis of UML Activity Diagrams, BETA Working Paper Series, WP 129*. Eindhoven University of Technology.

Wohed, P., van der Aalst, W. M. P., Dumas, M., & ter Hofstede, A. H. M. (2002). *Pattern-Based Analysis of BPEL4WS, QUT Technical Report, FIT-TR-2002-04*. Brisbane: Queensland University of Technology.

Wu, Y., Li, X. Y., Liu, Y., & Lou, W. (2010). Energy-efficient wake-up scheduling for data collection and aggregation. *IEEE Transactions on Parallel and Distributed Systems, 21*(2), 275–287. doi:10.1109/TPDS.2009.45

Wyatt, T. (2012 April 03). *Security Alert: New Variants of Legacy Native (LeNa) Identified*. [Web log post]. Retrieved from https://blog.lookout.com/blog/2012/04/03/security-alert-new-variants-of-legacy-native-lena-identified

Xu, Z., Ba, K., & Zhu, S. (2012 April 16). *TapLogger: Inferring User Inputs On Smartphone Touchscreens Using Onboard Motion Sensors*. ACM.

Xu, J., & Reiff-Marganiec, S. (2008). Towards heuristic web services composition using immune algorithm. In *IEEE International Conference on Web Services*. IEEE. doi:10.1109/ICWS.2008.16

Yibo, C., Jean-Pierre, C., Kun Mean, H., & Hong Ling, S. (2013). Extending the RPL Routing Protocol to Agricultural Low Power and Lossy Networks (A-LLNs). *International Journal of Agricultural and Environmental Information Systems, 4*(4), 25–47. doi:10.4018/ijaeis.2013100102

Yick, J., Mukherjee, B., & Ghosal, D. (2008). Wireless sensor network survey. *Computer Networks, 52*(12), 2292–2330. doi:10.1016/j.comnet.2008.04.002

Young, A. (2006, March). Cryptoviral extortion using Microsoft's Crypto API. *International Journal of Information Security, 5*(2), 67–76. doi:10.1007/s10207-006-0082-7

Yu, T. & Lin, K.-J. (2007). Efficient algorithms for web services selection with endto-end QoS constraints. *ACM Transactions on Web, 1*.

Zaamoune, M., Bimonte, S., Pinet, F., & Beaune, P. (2013). *A new relational spatial OLAP approach for multi-resolution and spatio-multidimensional analysis of incomplete field data*. Paper presented at the 15th International Conference on Enterprise Information Systems.

Zaamoune, M., Bimonte, S., Pinet, F., & Beaune, P. (2013). *A new relational spatial OLAP approach for multi-resolution and spatio-multidimensional analysis of incomplete field data*. Paper presented at the ICEIS 2013.

Zakarian, A. (2001). Analysis of Process Models: A Fuzzy Logic Approach. *International Journal of Advanced Manufacturing Technology, 17*(6), 444–452. doi:10.1007/s001700170162

Zakarian, A., & Kusiak, A. (2000). Analysis of Process Models. *IEEE Transactions on Electronics Packaging Manufacturing, 23*(2), 137–147. doi:10.1109/6104.846937

Zakarian, A., & Kusiak, A. (2001). Process Analysis and Reengineering. *Computers & Industrial Engineering, 41*(2), 135–150. doi:10.1016/S0360-8352(01)00048-1

Zanin, G., Di Pietro, R., & Mancini, L. (2007). Robust RSA distributed signatures for large-scale long-lived ad hoc networks. *Journal of Computer Security*.

Zapf, M., & Heinzl, A. (2000). Evaluation of Generic Process Design Patterns: An Experimental Study. *Lecture Notes in Computer Science, 1806*, 83–88. doi:10.1007/3-540-45594-9_6

Zeng, L., Benatallah, B., Dumas, M., Kalagnanam, J., & Sheng, Q. Z. (2003). Quality driven web services composition. In *International Conference on World Wide Web* (WWW). Academic Press.

Zeng, L., Benatallah, B., Ngu, A., Dumas, M., & Kalagnanam, J. (2004). QoSaware middleware for web services composition. *IEEE Transactions on Software Engineering, 30*(5), 311327.

Zeng, S. X., Shi, J. J., & Lou, G. X. (2007). A synergetic model for implementing an integrated management system: An empirical study in China. *Journal of Cleaner Production, 15*(18), 1760–1767. doi:10.1016/j.jclepro.2006.03.007

Zhang, C. (2012, June15). A Simple Platform of Brain-Controlled Mobile Robot and Its Implementation by SSVEP. *International Joint Conference on Neural Networks (Ijcnn)*. doi:10.1109/IJCNN.2012.6252579

Zhang, W., Chang, C. K., Feng, T., & Jiang, H. (2010). QoS-based dynamic web service composition with ant colony optimization. In *34th Annual IEEE Computer Software and Applications Conference*. doi:10.1109/COMPSAC.2010.76

Zhanh, C.-W., Su, S., & Chen, J.-L. (2006). Efficient population diversity handling genetic algorithm for QoS-aware web service selection. In *International Conference on Computational Science* (ICCS). Academic Press.

Zheng, J., Bakker, E., Knight, L., Gilhespy, H., Harland, C., & Walker, H. (2006). A strategic case for e-adoption in healthcare supply chains. *International Journal of Information Management, 26*(4), 290–301. doi:10.1016/j.ijinfomgt.2006.03.010

Zhou, J., & Ross, K. A. (2003). A multi-resolution block storage model for database design. In *Database Engineering and Applications SymposiumProceedings* (pp. 22-31). IEEE. doi:10.1109/IDEAS.2003.1214908

Zhou, Y., & Chen, Y. (2002). Business Process Assignment Optimisation. In *Proceedings of the IEEE International Conference on Systems, Man and Cybernetics* (vol. 3, pp. 540-545). IEEE.

Zhu, F., Turner, M., Kotsiopoulos, I., Bennett, K., Russell, M., Budgen, D., ... (2004). *Dynamic data integration using web services*. Paper presented at the IEEE International Conference on Web Services.

Zitzler, E. (1999). *Evolutionary algorithms for multiobjective optimization: Methods and applications*. Shaker, Diss. Technische Wissenschaften ETH Zrich.

Zitzler, E., Deb, K., & Thiele, L. (2000). Comparison of multiobjective evolutionary algorithms: Empirical results. *Evolutionary Comput Computation, 8*(2), 173–195. doi:10.1162/106365600568202 PMID:10843520

Zunk, B., Marchner, M., Uitz, I., Lerch, C., & Schiele, H. (2014). The Role of E-Procurement in the Austrian Construction Industry: Adoption Rate, Benefits and Barriers. *International Journal of Industrial Engineering and Management, 5*(1), 13–21.

About the Contributors

Petraq Papajorgji is dean of Engineering Canadian Institute of Technology, Tirana, Albania. His area of expertise is modelling methodologies with a strong focus on model driven development. He is one of Editor in Chief: International Journal of Agricultural and Environmental Information Systems (IJAEIS), Associate Editor of Journal of Biomedical Data Mining, Associate Editor of Iberoamerican Journal of Applied Computing, Advisory Board Member of Caspian Journal of Mathematics. Prof. Papajorgji is Courtesy Faculty at University of Ponta Grossa, Ponta Grossa, Parana, Brazil and together with a group of French scientists organize the annual course on "Modeling agricultural and environmental information systems using Object-Oriented and UML" at the premises of Maison de la Teledetection, Montpelier, France. Prof. Papajorgji is author and co-author of a number of books published by Springer and IGI Global. He is member of HIPEAC, a well-known European project.

François Pinet (http://www.irstea.fr/pinet) received his M.Sc. in Computer Science in 1997 (ENS Lyon) and his PhD in Computer Science in 2002 (INSA Lyon). He is currently a research director at the French Institute for Agricultural and Environmental Engineering (Irstea—Clermont-Ferrand). His field of research is in data warehouse, environmental information systems and geomatics. He is member of several scientific committees of different international conferences and journals in the fields of geomatics. Dr. Pinet has coauthored over 100 papers (Geoinformatica, IJGIS, Sigmod Record, Environmental Modelling & Software, ER, ACM GIS, ISSDQ, etc.) and has been involved in numerous national and international IT projects. He has been a co-organizer for several conferences and workshops on information systems. In France, he also teaches graduate courses (M.Sc and PhD degrees) on computer science and GIS (Blaise Pascal University). Petraq Papajorgji and François Pinet are the editors-in-chief of the International Journal of Agricultural and Environmental Information Systems.

Alaine Guimarães is a professor at Department of Computer Science, State University of Ponta Grossa (UEPG) and Vice Coordinator of the Master Program in Applied Computing at UEPG. She is a member of the Managing Board of the Brazilian Association of Computing Applied to Agriculture (SBIAgro). Dr. Guimarães Graduated in Bachelor of Computing (1989) from State University of Ponta Grossa. Master in Computer Science (2000) from Federal University of Paraná (UFPR) and Ph.D. in Agronomy (2005) by the State Univeristy Paulista Júlio de Mesquita Filho (UNESP). She conducted part of her doctoral thesis at the University of Florida, USA (2005). Dr. Guimarães participates in the scientific and execution team of projects in which more than U$ 2,000,000.00 was raised on resources for research development, equipment acquirement, and buildings construction for the University in which she works. That resources were obtained from agencies fostering (FINEP, CNPq, Araucaria Foundation,

CAPES). She served as Director of Research and Program Coordinator of Scientific Initiation UEPG from 2010-2013. Conducts research in the areas of Computing Applied to Agriculture, Machine Learning, and Data Mining.

Jason Papathanasiou is an Assistant Professor at the Department of Business Administration, University of Macedonia, Greece. He holds a PhD in Operational Research and Informatics and a degree in Physics from the Aristotle University of Thessaloniki. He has worked for a number of years at various institutes and has organized and participated in a number of international scientific conferences and workshops. He has published papers in international scientific peer referred journals like the Environmental Monitoring and Assessment, Regional Studies, European Journal of Operational Research, PNAS and has participated in many research projects in FP6, FP7, Interreg and COST; he served also as a member of the TDP Panel of COST and currently serves at the coordination board of the EURO Working Group of Decision Support Systems. His research interests include Decision Support Systems, Operational Research and Multicriteria Decision Making.

* * *

Ezzedine Ben Braiek obtained his HDR in 2008 in Electrical engineering from ENSET Tunisia. He is presently a professor in the department of electrical engineering at the technical university ES-STT and manager of the research group on vision and image processing at the CEREP. His fields of interest include automatics, electronics, control, computer vision, image processing and its application in handwritten data recognition.

Christos Bialas is a Lecturer at the Department of Accounting and Finance of the Alexander TEI of Thessaloniki, Greece and a SAP Project Manager specializing in Supply Chain Management. He has a diploma in Electrical and Computer Engineering from the Aristotle University of Thessaloniki, Greece and a postgraduate diploma in Business and Financial Engineering from the RWTH Aachen, Germany. He has 20 years of experience in implementing ERP Systems in multinational companies in Germany, Switzerland, USA and Greece and is currently a doctoral candidate in the field of Supply chain Management.

Sandro Bimonte, Born in 1978, is a researcher at Irstea (TSCF lab). He obtained his PhD at INSA-Lyon, France (2004-2007). He carried out researches at IMAG (2007-2008), France. He is editorial board member of International Journal of Decision Support System Technology, and International Journal of Data Mining, Modelling and Management and member of the Commission on GeoVisualization of the International Cartographic Association. His research activities is in Spatial Data Warehouses and Spatial OLAP, Visual Languages, Geographic Information Systems, Spatio-temporal Databases and GeoVisualization.

Nadia Carluer works in the non-point pollution team, in the Freshwater Systems, Ecology and Pollution research unit of Irstea, in Lyon. The team is interested in the fate of pesticides from the cultivated field to water resources, and focuses its researches and studies on the role of buffer zones, in the form of ditches, vegetated filter strips or constructed wetland. Nadia Carluer works mainly in the field of numerical modelling, from the vegetative buffer strip scale to the catchment scale. She supervised the Miriphyque project.

Jean-Pierre Chanet, 48 years old, is an electronic engineer from the Polytech Clermont school (1990). He obtained his Master in robotic in 1992 and his PhD in computer science in 2007 from the University Blaise Pascal (Clermont-Fd). He is at the head of the "Technologies and information systems for agrosystems" research unit of Irstea since 2014. He contributes to several European projects (TWISTER, NetAdded, OTAG, Eranet ICT-Agri). He works on data integration from wireless sensor networks in information systems and information management in agriculture. He is a member of different review comities for conferences and revues on wireless sensor networks and information systems for agriculture and environment. He is the president of the French Association of Computer Science in Agriculture (AFIA).

Aristeidis Chatzipoulidis holds a PhD in Enterprise Management and Software Risk Prediction Based on Security Metrics from the department of Applied Informatics, University of Macedonia, Greece. He received his bachelor degree in Marketing from the Alexander Technological Educational Institute of Thessaloniki and his Master in International Marketing from the University of Strathclyde, Scotland. His main research interests include the holistic enterprise management, risk analysis and information security.

Bruno Cheviron graduated in Physics and Geophysics and received his PhD in 2004 from the University Paris VI-Pierre and Marie Curie, on the subject of determining vertical water fluxes from soil temperature measurements. His past research activities cover pesticide leaching in groundwater contamination, free-surface flow and erosion modeling, sediment transport and model analysis. He has joined Irstea, the French National Research Institute of Science and Technology for Environment and Agriculture, in Montpellier in 2012. He works on the development and automation of the PILOTE crop model, for scenarios of agricultural yield, and on the automation of the hydrological MACRO model, for pesticide fate scenarios. Renewed collaborations target the use of high-precision temperature sensors to follow shallow water and vapor movements in soils.

Arion de Campos Jr. is an Adjunct Professor at State University of Ponta Grossa, Brazil, since 2002. He received his M. Sc. degree from University of São Paulo, Brazil (2001) and D. Sc. degree from Federal University of Paraná, Brazil (2014).

Gil De-Sousa is a research engineer at Irstea (National Research Institute of Science and Technology for Environment and Agriculture). His research interest deals with agricultural and environmental data collection and management using Wireless Sensor Networks (WSN). He received a PhD degree in Computer Science from the Blaise Pascal University, Clermont-Ferrand (France), in 2008.

Maria Gianni is a Ph.D. student in the Department of Business Administration at the University of Macedonia, Greece. She holds an M.Sc. in Management of Production Systems from the Aristotle University of Thessaloniki, Greece. Her first degree is B.Sc. in Chemical Engineering from the Aristotle University of Thessaloniki, Greece.

Katerina D. Gotzamani is an Associate Professor in the Department of Business Administration at the University of Macedonia, Greece. She holds a Ph.D. in Quality Management from the University of Macedonia, Greece. Her previous degrees are M.Sc. in Operations Research & Information Systems from the London School of Economics and B.Sc. in Mathematics from the Aristotle University of Thessaloniki, Greece. She is teaching courses in Total Quality Management and Operations Management. Her research interests include total quality management, quality management in the public sector, quality management in e-commerce, quality management standards ISO 9000, OR methodologies integrated in service quality management, logistics and supply chain management. She has participated in a number of conferences and seminars and she has published more than 40 articles.

Habib Hamam obtained the B.Eng. and M.Sc. degrees in information processing from the Technical University of Munich, Germany 1988 and 1992, and the PhD degree in Physics and applications in telecommunications from Université de Rennes I conjointly with France Telecom Graduate School, France 1995. He also obtained a postdoctoral diploma, "Accreditation to Supervise Research in Signal Processing and Telecommunications", from Université de Rennes I in 2004. He is currently a full Professor in the Department of Electrical Engineering at the Université de Moncton and a Canada Research Chair holder in "Optics in Information and Communication Technologies". He is an IEEE senior member and a registered professional engineer in New-Brunswick. He is among others associate editor of the IEEE Canadian Review, member of the editorial boards of Wireless Communications and Mobile Computing - John Wiley & Sons - and of Journal of Computer Systems, Networking, and Communications - Hindawi Publishing Corporation. His research interests are in optical telecommunications, Wireless Communications, diffraction, fiber components, optics of the eye, RFID and E-Learning.

Nazih Heni obtained the BS in Computer and Multimedia degrees from the University of Mannouba, Tunisia 2008 to 2011, and the engineering degree in Computer and Multimedia from University of Mannouba, Tunisia 2011 to 2014. Heni is now a Masters student in the Faculty of Engineering/University of Moncton and is a Google developer.

Myoung-Ah Kang is an associate professor at Blaise Pascal University (Clermont-Ferrand, France). She received her PhD in Computer Science in 2001 (INSA Lyon). Her field of research is in geographical information systems. She teaches graduate courses on computer science, software engineering and information systems.

Claire Lauvernet is a junior research scientist in mathematics applied to environment. She received her PhD in Applied Mathematics in 2005 from the University Grenoble-Alpes, on the subject of Variational assimilation of remote sensing data into canopy functioning models, using temporal and spatial constraints. She then worked as a research associate in INRA (French National Institute for Agricultural Research) to work on radiative transfer model inversion, and then in CNRS (French National Center for Scientific Research) to improve ocean modeling using Reduced Rank Kalman Filtering on non-gaussian variables. She works now in Irstea, the French National Research Institute of Science and Technology for Environment and Agriculture, that she joined in Lyon in 2008. Her work consists in modeling water and pesticides transfer at different scales, from the plot to the hillslope, taking into account some landscape elements (buffer zones, vegetative filter strips). Part of her work aims at turning models into operationnal tools, using mathematical methods such as global sensitivity analysis, metamodeling, optimization.

Vicky Manthou is a Professor of Information Systems & Logistics of the University of Macedonia, School of Information, Department of Applied Informatics, Thessaloniki, Greece. Dr. Manthou received her bachelor's degree from Louisiana State University, in Baton Rouge, La, U.S.A. (1976) and her PhD from the University of Macedonia, Department of Applied Informatics (1991). She was a visiting research professor at Loyola University, New Orleans, U.S.A. Her teaching, research and consulting interests include analysis and design of management information systems, Supply Chain Management, Logistics, ERP, e- commerce, health information systems. She has, and still is participating in European Projects in the above fields and has published papers and reports in Greek and International Journals, and books. She acts as a reviewer for many scientific journals, such as the International Journal of Production Economics, Supply Chain Management an International Journal, the TQM magazine, the International Journal of Enterprise Information Systems, and for IST projects for the European Commission. She has been chairman in many scientific conferences, and member of organizing and scientific committees. She is a member of Hellenic and International Associations.

Ioannis Mavridis is an Associate Professor of Information Systems Security at the Department of Applied Informatics of University of Macedonia, Greece. He holds a Diploma in Computer Engineering and Informatics from the University of Patras, Greece and a Doctor's degree (PhD) in Mobile Computing Security from the Aristotle University of Thessaloniki, Greece. He has published over 100 articles in international and national scientific journals and conferences, mainly on applied informatics and information security related topics. His research interests include the areas of computer and network security, cyber-crime, access control in collaborative, mobile, pervasive and cloud systems, and critical infrastructure protection.

Dimitrios Michalopoulos was born in Thessaloniki. He completed his postgraduate studies in 2004 at the Department of Electrical Engineering and Computer Engineering, Aristotle University of Thessaloniki. He did his postgraduate studies at the University of Plymouth, U.K. and got specialized in system's security. In April 2014 he granted his PhD with his thesis subject on protecting children from cyberthreats. He has working experience as a software developer, as a teacher, and as a researcher.

André Miralles received his Mechanical Engineer degree in 1976 (INSA Toulouse). In 1978, he was employed as researcher at the French Institute for Agricultural and Environmental Engineering where he works since. He leads during 5 years hydraulic investigations on three-dimensional stream generating into the fishway devices equipping the dams to facilitate the upstream migration of the anadromous fishes (salmon, etc.). Then, he is in charge of the laboratory doing on one hand standardized tests of the sprayers applying pesticides on the cereals or on the orchards and, on the other hand, the researches to improve the spraying techniques and the application techniques of the products. It is involved in different European projects and leads some of them. He assumes also the charge of President of the CIETAP, French committee where the manufacturers of sprayers, the industrialists of chemistry, the representatives of the government and the scientists exchange ideas and organize conferences or the exposures. In 2000, he moves to a position of computing researcher and received his PhD in Computing Science in 2006 (University of Montpellier). Currently, he works in the Joint Research Unit named Territories, Environment, Remote Sensing & Spatial Information. His main interest is focused on the design of new methodologies for software development allowing a better flexibility and a better interactivity with the users. For that, he carries out researches on the Model Driven Architecture and on business design patterns of the agricultural and environmental domains. He applies his currently research in data processing in an important project involving many research teams working on pesticides in order to improve the data capitalisation but also the diffusion and the sharing of the knowledge. He is Associate Editor of the International Journal of Agricultural and Environmental Information Systems and Guest Editor of the Special issue on Environmental and agricultural data processing for water and territory management.

Fahmi Ncibi obtained his Master degree on 2014 in Electrical engineering from National High School of Engineering of Tunisia. He is presently a Master Student in Applied Sciences at the Faculty of Engineering Moncton University and researcher in a Research Chair "Optics in Information and Communication Technologies". His fields of interest include IT, electronics, control, computer vision, image processing and its applications, Wireless Communications, RFID.

Aurora T. R. Pozo, is an Associate Professor at Federal University of Paraná, Brazil, since 1997. She received her M. Sc. and Ph.D. in electrical engineering from Federal University of Santa Catarina, Brazil (1991 and 1996, respectively). Hers research interests include evolutionary computation, data mining and software engineering.

Constantinos J. Stefanou is Professor of Business Information Systems and the Director of the Laboratory of Enterprise Resources (ERP Lab), which he established in 2004, of the Department of Accounting and Finance, Alexander Technological Educational Institute (ATEI) of Thessaloniki, Greece. Prof. Stefanou holds an MSc degree in Economics from the University of London and a PhD in Accounting Information Systems from Brunel University, London. Currently, he is adjunct professor at the Hellenic Open University and teaches Enterprise Resource Planning at a postgraduate level. Prof. Stefanou has supervised a large number of students' theses at both undergraduate and postgraduate levels as well as several PhD dissertations. He publishes, speaks at conferences and seminars, and has authored four books on Business Software Applications, ERP (SAP) Systems, Enterprise Systems, and Financial Analysis using Excel. He has been on the editorial boards of international journals and currently joins the editorial board of the International Journal of Accounting Information Systems. He holds the foundation chair of the International Conference on Enterprise Systems, Accounting and Logistics (ICESAL).

Loukas K. Tsironis is a Lecturer of Operations Management and a member of the Business Excellence Laboratory (BEL) at the Department of Business Administration of the University of Macedonia. He received his B.Sc from Aristotelian University of Thessaloniki, Department of Forestry & Natural Environment (1993). His M.Sc. (1995) and Ph.D. (2001) from Technical University of Crete, Department of Production Engineering & Management. His research interests extended in the Operations and Supply Chain Management, Total Quality Management, Business Process Modelling and Management, on which he recently published several articles in journals and referred conferences.

Silvia Regina Vergilio, received her M. Sc. (1991) and D. Sc. (1997) degrees from University of Campinas, UNICAMP, Brazil. She is currently with the Computer Science Department at Federal University of Paraná, Brazil.

Index

Printed in the United States
By Bookmasters